THE LEGAL FRAMEWORK OF EU-CHINA INVESTMENT RELATIONS

China and International Economic Law Series

Editors-in-General: Wenhua Shan, Qing Zhang and Xin Zhang

The Legal Framework of EU-China Investment Relations: A Critical Appraisal *Wenhua Shan*

To Christy and Charlie

The Legal Framework of EU-China Investment Relations

A Critical Appraisal

WENHUA SHAN

•HART•
PUBLISHING

OXFORD AND PORTLAND, OREGON
2005

Published in North America (US and Canada) by

Hart Publishing
c/o International Specialized Book Services
920 NE 58th Avenue, Suite 300
Portland, OR 97213-3786
USA
Tel: +1 503 287 3093 or toll-free: (1) 800 944 6190
Fax: +1 503 280 8832
Email: orders@isbs.com
Website: www.isbs.com

Hart Publishing, Salter's Boatyard, Folly Bridge, Abingdon Rd, Oxford, OX1 4LB
Telephone: +44 (0)1865 245533 Fax: +44 (0)1865 794882
Email: mail@hartpub.co.uk
Website: http//:www.hartpub.co.uk

British Library Cataloguing in Publication Data
Data Available

ISBN-13: 978-1-84113-391-4 (hardback)
ISBN-10: 1-84113-391-4 (hardback)

Typeset by Forewords, Oxford
Printed and bound in Great Britain by
TJ International, Padstow, Cornwall

Foreword

By Professor Sir Elihu Lauterpacht CBE QC

This is a remarkable book on a subject of growing importance. It deals with the manner and extent to which those of the world's most traditional economies assembled in the European Union invest in the world's most rapidly expanding economy. China's success in attracting foreign direct investment (FDI) in the last decade is unprecedented. In 2003 it had become the largest FDI recipient in the world, outstripping even the United States. Three years earlier the EU had already become the largest foreign investor in China, its investment having increased more than twenty-five fold since 1986.

Previous major studies on economic relations between the EU and China have focused principally on trade, rather than investment. The present work fills a gap in research on the law of EU investment in China by comprehensively examining three relevant areas of law, namely, international investment law (including especially bilateral investment treaties), EU law and Chinese law itself.

The study is critical and constructive: critical, for example, of some aspects of the Chinese investment regime and the applicable international treaties; constructive, for example, in its suggestions for reform and the development of an improved legal framework for EU-China investment relations.

Dr Shan's scholarly work will be of great value as a guide to EU investors, as an aid to China in its relations with those investors and as an academic resource for all who are interested in this area of increasing significance. He is to be congratulated on his imagination and dedication in collecting so much material that is not easily gathered, on presenting it in such lucid form and on his perceptive and positive comments.

E Lauterpacht
Emeritus Director of the Lauterpacht Research Centre
for International Law
University of Cambridge
October 2004

Acknowledgements

This book is based on my second PhD dissertation, which has been submitted to and approved by the University of Cambridge. It is also the main outcome of my seven-year research life in England since September 1998 when I first set foot on this foreign land. As I have said elsewhere, when one arrives in a foreign country, it is rather like beginning a second life. In my brief 'second life', there have been many persons and many events that I will never forget. Yet it would not be possible, nor would it be appropriate, to list them all here. However, I must take this opportunity to acknowledge those who have had a significant impact on my dissertation and subsequently this book.

First and foremost, I would like to express my deepest appreciation to my supervisor and friend Mr. Daniel Bethlehem QC. Without his stimulating guidance and enduring support and encouragement, I would have never been able to start this research project, let alone complete it. Secondly, I would like to express my deep gratitude to my College Contact, Professor Sir Elihu Lauterpacht. As a leading international lawyer, Sir Eli has offered me not only insights into how to do research and how to write a dissertation, but also fatherly advice and care relating to both my career and my family. I will never forget that the first bouquet of flowers that my son Charles received was from Sir Eli and his wife Lady Lauterpacht, soon after Charlie was born in Cambridge. Sir Eli has also kindly written a Foreword for this book.

I would also like to thank Professor Alan Dashwood who supported my application for a PhD studentship and directed my studies, particularly in EU law, during my first year. I would also like to show my appreciation to Professor Michael Palmer, Professor Kevin Gray, Professor James Crawford, Mr. Nicholas Sinclair-Brown, Professor Vincent Johnson, Professor Simon Deakin, Professor HAN Depei and Professor LI Xueling, who have given me important and generous support in the PhD project and in my career. Special acknowledgement should also go to Miss Noelle L'Hommedieu. Her help with regard to both linguistic and academic matters relating to the dissertation was invaluable.

I want to express my appreciation to my lovely college, Trinity College, which has provided a comfortable home for me and my family, a home in both the physical and the spiritual sense. I thank her, in particular, for awarding me the External Research Studentship, without which I would have not been able to conduct this research. I would like especially to thank Professor Amartya Sen, Dr. Christopher Thomas Morley, Dr. Jean Khalfa, Mr. Alexander Paul Simm, Mr. David Coleman, Mrs. Hazel Felton, Mrs. Hélène Sutton and Ms. Sheila Roberts, for their care and support. I also acknowledge respectfully the Committee of Vice-Chancellors and Principals of the Universities of the United Kingdom (CVCP, now Universities UK) for awarding me an Overseas Research Studentship (ORS) and the Cambridge Overseas Trust (COT) for an Honorary COT Scholarship and a Fellowship of the Cambridge Overseas Society.

I would like to thank the Faculty of Law, the Lauterpacht Research Centre for International Law (LRCIL) and the Centre for European Legal Studies (CELS) for their world class scholarship environment (and free lunches!). I am particularly grateful to Miss Alison Hirst and Dr. Matt Kramer for handling various official matters in relation to the Degree Committee. I thank the Squire Law Library staff for being patient and considerate when I left the library late in the evening, which was not rare. I am also grateful for the friendship and help from staff of the LRCIL, particularly Mrs. Anne Skinner, Mrs. Glen Howard, Miss Cairo Robb, Mr. Edward Helgeson, Dr. Roger O'Keefe, Dr. John Barker, Dr. Sandra Bunn-Livingstone, Dr. Joanna Gomula, Ms. Karen Lee and Miss Shelly Brereton.

My research, particularly the field work, has received support from many people outside the University. I would like to thank Lord Brittan for kindly referring my queries to relevant officials of the European Commission. Dr. Amanda Joan Perry kindly helped in designing the Questionnaire. Although for reasons of confidentiality I cannot identify the interviewees and participants in the Questionnaire, I am most grateful for their cooperation and support. I also thank Oxford Brookes University, particularly Professor Susan McRae, Professor Derek Elsom, Professor Diana Woodhouse, Professor Peter Edge, Professor Meryll Dean and Dr. Lucy Vickers, and the East Asia Institute of the National University of Singapore, particularly Professor WANG Gungwu and Professor John WONG, for their support in the writing-up of this book.

I thank Mr. Richard Hart of Hart Publishing and his team for being very supportive during the production of this book, as well as this series. Portions of some chapters of this book have appeared in the *Journal of World Trade* (Vol. 34 No. 5), the *Chinese Journal of International Law* (Vol. 1, No. 2), the *Journal of World Investment* (Vol. 2 No. 3 and Vol. 3 No. 2), the *Manchester Journal of International Economic Law* (Vol. 2, No. 2) and the *Journal of World Investment and Trade* (Vol. 6, No. 2). I thank these journals for their kind permission.

Almost finally, I want to thank my mentors and friends in Cambridge and the UK, particularly for their support, help and understanding when I served as the President of both the Cambridge Chinese Students and Scholars Association (CSSA-CAM) and the United Kingdom Chinese Law Association

(UKCLA). I especially thank His Excellency Ambassador MA Zhengang, former Chinese Ambassador to the UK, and many other officials from the Chinese Embassy for their invaluable support. I also thank Lady Mirrlees, Dr. YUAN Boping, Mr. YE Liang, Mr. WANG Shiyun, Mr. LI Xihe, Mr. Albert Shuyuan LEE, Mr. JIANG Weibin, Mr. ZENG Jianqiu, Ms. JIN Limin, Ms. CAO Li, Mr. Mon-Han Tsai, Ms. Caroline Foster, Mr. Ralph Wilde, Ms. Rania Katsirea and Ms. Lucky Huang, for their friendship and care.

Last but not least, my biggest thank you must go to my family. I deeply appreciate the sacrifices my wife Christy Xin Wang has made in supporting my research. Although my son Charlie is too young to understand, he has been one of the most important sources of strength and happiness, particularly during difficult times. I would like to express my gratitude to my mother-in-law who has been a great help to me and my family, particularly in looking after Charlie. I must also thank my parents and grandparents, in particular, my grandfather, who first inspired me and led me into the wonderful intellectual world.

Wenhua Shan
Oxford, April 2005

Contents

List of Abbreviations

AAA	American Arbitration Association
ACP	African, Caribbean and Pacific (states)
AISCC	Arbitration Institute of the Stockholm Chamber of Commerce
AJIL	American Journal of International Law
AOA	Articles of Association
AOC	Amount of Compensation
APEC	Asian Pacific Economic Cooperation
ASEM	Asia-Europe Meeting
BCCC	British Chamber of Commerce in China
BECZs	Border Economic Cooperation Zones
BIT	Bilateral Investment Treaty
BLEU	Belgium-Luxemburg Economic Union
BOP	Balance of Payment
BOT	Built-Operate-Transfer
BYIL	British Yearbook of International Law
CAEFI	The China Association of Enterprises with Foreign Investment
CBBC	China-Britain Business Council
CCP	Common Commercial Policy
CCPIT	China Council for the Promotion of International Trade
Chinese JIEL	Journal of International Economic Law (Chinese)
CIP	Common Investment Policy
CJV	Contractual Joint Venture
CMIT	Committee of Capital Movement and Invisible Transactions (of the OECD)
CMLR	Common Market Law Review
COCs	Coastal Open Cities
COERs	Coastal Open Economic Regions
DTT	Double Taxation Treaty
EAD	Euro-Arab Dialogue
EAER	East Asia Executive Report
EC	European Community
ECIP	European Community Investment Partnership

ECJ	European Court of Justice
ECR	European Court Report
EEC	European Economic Community
EIU	European Investment Unit
EJV	Equity Joint Venture
EP	European Parliament
EPZs	Export Processing Zones
ETDZs	Economic and Technology Development Zones
EU	European Union
EUCCC	European Chamber of Commerce in China
F&E	Fair and Equitable
FDI	Foreign Direct Investment
FIEs	Foreign Invested Enterprises
FIPs	Foreign Investment Projects
FTA	Free Trade Agreement
GATS	General Agreement on Trade in Services
GSP	General System of Preferences Scheme
HCFI	Holding Companies with Foreign Investment
HCs	Horizontal Commitments
HNTIDZs	High and New Technology Industries Development Zones
ICC	International Chamber of Commerce
ICJ	International Court of Justice
ICLQ	International and Comparative Law Quartly
ICSID Review-FILJ	ICSID Review-Foreign Investment Law Journal
ICSID	International Centre for the Settlement of Investment Disputes
IGC	Intergovernmental Conference
Int'l Law.	The International Lawyer
Iran-US CTR	Iran-United States Claims Tribunal Reports
JV	Joint Venture
JWI	The Journal of World Investment
JWT	Journal of World Trade (formerly Journal of World Trade Law)
M&A	Merger and Acquisition
MAA	Minority Autonomous Areas
MFN	Most-Favoured-Nation
MIA	Multilateral Investment Agreement
MIGA	Multilateral Investment Guarantee Agency
MNEs	Multinational Enterprises
MOFCOM	The Ministry of Commerce (of the Chinese Government)
MOFTEC	The Ministry of Foreign Trade and Economic Cooperation (now replaced by MOFCOM)
MRIIs	Multilateral and Regional Investment Instruments
NAFTA	North America Free Trade Agreement

ND	Non-Discrimination
NIEO	New International Economic Order
NILF	New International Legal Framework
NPC	National People's Congress
NT	National Treatment
NTVZs	National Tourist and Vacation Zones
Nw J. Int'l L. & Bus.	New York Journal of International Law and Business
OECD	Organisation of Economic Cooperation and Development
PCIJ	Permanent Court of International Justice
PEFI	State Council Provisions for Encouraging Foreign Investment
PICC	People's Insurance Company of China
PRC	People's Republic of China
PRs	Perforce Requirements
PSNR	Permanent Sovereignty over Natural Resources
RFEA	Regulations on Foreign Exchange Administration
RMB	Renminbi (Chinese Currency)
SAA	State Asset Administration
SAIC	State Administration for Industry and Commerce
SARs	Special Administrative Areas
SCFI	Stock Companies with Foreign Investment
SCNPC	Standing Committee of the National People's Congress
SCs	Specific Commitments
SDRC	State Development Reform Commission
SETC	State Economic and Trade Commission (now the MOFCOM)
SEZs	Special Economic Zones
SMEs	Small and Medium Enterprises
SOEs	State-Owned Enterprises
SREs	State-Run Enterprises
TNC	Transnational Corporations
TRIMs	Trade-Related Investment Measures
TRIPs	Trade-Related Aspects of Intellectual Property Rights
UN	United Nations
UNCTAD	United Nations Conference on Trade and Development
UNGA	United Nations General Assembly
WFE	Wholly Foreign Owned Enterprises
WGTI	Working Group on Trade and Investment
WTO	World Trade Organisation

List of Tables

List of Charts

List of Cases

List of Treaties and other International Legal Instruments

List of Chinese and EC Legislation

Introduction

'The EU should aim at improving the investment environment for European companies in China. The construction of a sound and transparent regulatory framework for investment and a better enforcement of Chinese regulations on intellectual property rights are prime examples to achieve this objective.'

—COM (1998) 181 final: Building a Comprehensive Partnership with China.

'China is committed to developing dynamic, long-term and stable economic co-operation and trade with the EU and expects the latter to become China's largest trading and investment partner.'

—China's EU Policy Paper (Chinese Government, 13 October 2003).

As two of the largest, mutually complementary markets in the world, the European Union (the EU)[1] and the People's Republic of China[2] (China or PRC) have everything to gain by strengthening their trade and investment ties.[3] On the one hand, since 1986, EU investment in China has increased more than 25-fold (*Chart 1: EU Investment in China 1986–2000* and *Chart 2: Percentage of EU Investment in Total FDI[4] in China*)[5] and in 2000, the EU

1 On 1 May 2004, the European Union realised its fifth enlargement and became a union of 25 member states, including 10 new member states. However, since the research was mostly conducted before the enlargement, unless otherwise specified, the 'EU' referred to in this Chapters 1 through to Chapter 9 means the pre-enlargement EU comprising 15 member states. The legal framework governing investment relations between China and the 10 new members are, nevertheless, specifically dealt with in Chapter 10.

2 Unless otherwise stated, 'China' refers to Mainland China, which does not cover Hong Kong, Macau and Taiwan, where different economic and legal systems are in operation, despite the fact that they are legally recognised as indispensable parts of the State of China.

3 EU Directorate-General of Trade (DG Trade)'s Overview on its '*Bilateral Trade Relations*' with China (October 2002), posted at http://europa.eu.int/comm/trade/index_en.htm (visited on 1 June 2003).

4 Throughout this book, FDI stands for 'foreign direct investment' and 'FIEs' for 'foreign invested enterprises'.

5 During that period (1986–2000), both the contractual value and the realised value of EU investment in China increased by more than 25 times respectively from US$ 351.94 million to US$ 8.86 billion and from US$ 178.53 million to US$ 4.48 billion. At the same time, the portion that EU investment occupied in total foreign investment in China increased significantly and consistently since 1992, which demonstrates the growing interests of EU investors in the Chinese market. For details, see *Chart 1: EU Investment in China 1986–2000* and *Chart 2: Percentage of EU Investment in Total FDI in China.*

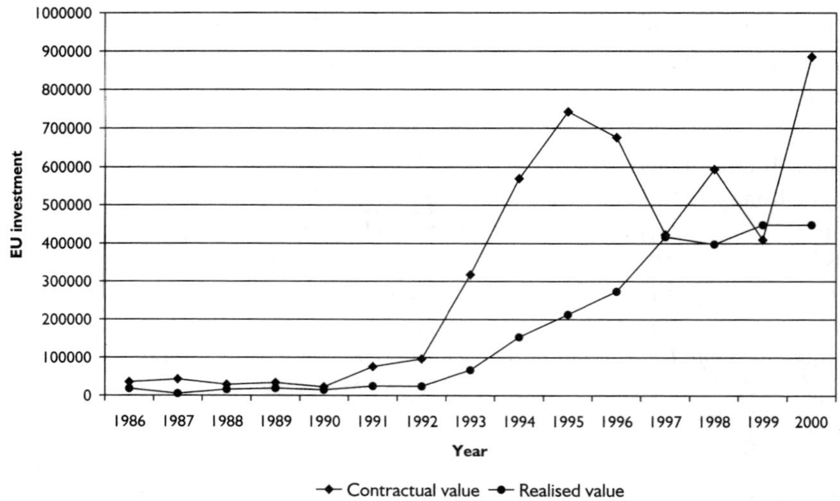

Chart 1: EU Investment in China 1986–2000 (unit: US$10,000)

Source: Compiled by the Author according to FDI Statistics from the Ministry of Commerce of the PRC (MOFCOM), posted at http://www.etisu.com/investment/ics/02020702.html (visited on 28 June 2003).

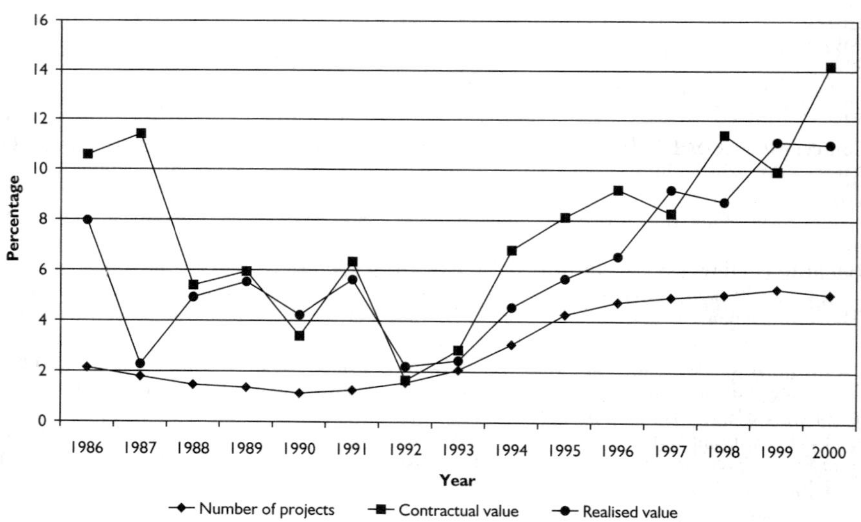

Chart 2: Percentage of EU Investment in Total FDI in China (1986–2000)

Source: FDI Statistics from the Ministry of Commerce of the PRC (MOFCOM), posted at http://www.etisu.com/investment/ics/02020702.html (visited on 28 June 2003).

Table 1: Foreign and EU Investment in China by 2002 (unit: US$ million)

Country/ region	Projects	%	Contractual amount	%	Actual amount	%
China Total	**424,196**	**100**	**828,060**	**100**	**447,966**	**100**
Hong Kong	210,876	49.71	373,806	45.14	204,875	45.73
Japan	25,147	5.93	49,532	5.98	36,340	8.11
US	37,280	8.79	76,282	9.21	39,889	8.90
EU	**14,084**	**3.32**	**60,088**	**7.26**	**33,943**	**7.58**
Germany	3,053	0.72	14,322	1.73	7,994	1.78
France	2,033	0.48	7,192	0.87	5,543	1.24
Italy	1,840	0.43	3,193	0.39	2,229	0.5
Netherlands	1,065	0.25	8,974	1.08	4,338	0.97
Belgium	403	0.10	907	0.11	561	0.13
Luxembourg	80	0.02	557	0.07	107	0.02
UK	3,418	0.81	19,633	2.37	10,696	2.39
Ireland	52	0.01	110	0.01	35	0.01
Denmark	225	0.05	1,331	0.16	477	0.11
Finland	155	0.04	544	0.07	353	0.08
Sweden	517	0.12	1,156	0.14	810	0.18
Austria	509	0.12	908	0.11	348	0.08
Greece	41	0.01	107	0.01	29	0.01
Spain	626	0.15	1,041	0.13	354	0.08
Portugal	67	0.02	113	0.01	69	0.02

Source: MOFCOM FDI Statistics: 'FDI from Some Countries and Regions by 2002', at MOFCOM website: http://www.fdi.gov.cn/common/ info.jsp?id=ABC00000000000014161 (visited on 12 May 2004).

became the largest foreign investor in China (*Table 1: Foreign and EU Investment in China by 2002* and *Chart 3: Major Investors in China in 2000*).[6] On

[6] In 2000, the EU became the largest *foreign* investor in China (following Hong Kong, which is a part of China but enjoys economic autonomy, in accordance with the *Basic Law of the Hong Kong Special Administrative Region*), overtaking both the United States and Japan that used to lead the FDI league table. For details, see *Chart 3: Major Investors in China in 2000*. See also *Table 1: Foreign and EU Investment in China by 2002* and *Chart 2: Percentage of EU Investment in Total FDI in China*. It is noted that the figures provided by the Chinese Customs and the Ministry of Commerce (MOFCOM) on EU investment in China in 1998 are slightly different, as shown in *Chart 1* and *Table 1*. Nevertheless, the EU seemed to rely on MOFCOM's statistics in its official document entitled *EU Strategy towards China: Implementation of the 1998 Communication and future steps for a more effective policy* (a Communication from the Commission to the Council and the European Parliament), which reported that, in 2000, EU became the largest foreign investor in China with contractual and realised investment amounted to US$ 8.8 and 4.5 billion respectively. See COM (2001) 265 final, at 12. See also EU Directorate-General of Trade (DG Trade)'s Overview on its '*Bilateral Trade Relations*' with China (October 2002), above note 3.

the other hand, recent years have witnessed a rapid increase of Chinese investment in the EU[7] (*Table 2: China's approved Overseas Investment Enterprises*). Needless to say, China's successful accession to the World Trade Organisation (WTO)[8] has significantly boosted, and will continue to catalyse foreign[9] and EU[10] investment in China.

As this book will demonstrate,[11] law plays a significant role in the development of Sino-EU investment relations. However, there is virtually no dedicated study on the law of EU investment in China. This research intends

[7] For instance, Eurostat figures indicate that although China accounted for only 1.3% of extra-EU FDI average over 1992–94, it was running at 2.4% or 507 million ECU by 1994—a five-fold increase in two years. Eurostat Press Releases No.7096 (21–10–1996): *EU Direct Investment in the Rest-of-world*, posted at http://europa.eu.int/en/comm/eurostat/compres/en/7096/6207096a.htm (visited on 11 November 1999). On China's outward investment in general, a recent survey by the United Nations Conference on Trade and Development (UNCTAD) shows that China is becoming one of the important foreign investors in the world. See Chen, Weihua, 'China is Becoming an Important Outward Investor', (2003) 22 May, *People's Daily* (overseas edition), at 3. For a statistics on Chinese outward investment, see *Table 2: China's approved Overseas Investment Enterprises.*

[8] China became a Member of the WTO on 11 December 2001. For more on China's participation with the WTO, see WTO: *China and the WTO*, posted at http://www.wto.org/english/thewto_e/countries_e/china_e.htm (visited on 29 June 2003).

[9] The tremendous impact of WTO admission on foreign investment in China is best proved by the fact that, in 2003, 2 years after WTO entry, China outstripped the US and become the world' largest FDI recipient. Its total FDI stock had reached US $ 501.4 by the end of 2003. It was widely reported that China had already achieved this in 2002. However, a revision of data revealed that China was actually still in the second place in the FDI recipient league table in 2002, next to the United States. In consequence, 2003 became the first year on record in which China surpassed the US as the world's largest FDI recipient. See OECD, *Trends and Recent Development in Foreign Direct Investment, June 2004*, at 3, 5, posted at http://www.oecd.org/dataoecd/52/11/2958722.pdf (visited on 10 July 2004). For previous reports about China's performance in attracting FDI in 2002, see OECD: *Trends and Recent Developments in Foreign Direct Investment*, June 2003, posted at http://www.oecd.org/pdf/M00042000/M00042212.pdf (visited on 1 July 2003); *UNCTAD Predicts 27% Drop in FDI Inflow this Year and China May Outstrip U.S. as World's Largest FDI Recipient*, UNCTAD Press Release TAD/INF/PR/63 (24/10/02). See also Qian, Weizeng, 'International Investors Favours China the Most', Ce, Yuming, 'China Received FDI 52.7 Billion Last Year', and Yang, Qing, 'Sharp Increase of Investment Opportunities in China for Multinationals', in (2003) 28 June, 15 Jan, 24 May *People's Daily* (overseas edition), at 5, at 1 and at 5 respectively. For a Chinese report on China's performance in attracting FDI in 2003, see (2004) 15 Jan *People's Daily* (overseas edition), at 1.

A number of recent surveys have confirmed the significant positive impact of China's WTO accession on FDI inflows into China. These surveys include surveys done by the American Chamber of Commerce in China, German Chamber of Commerce in China, Multilateral Investment Guarantee Agency and Goldman Sachs. For an overview of these surveys, see UNCTAD, *China: WTO Accession and Growing FDI Inflows*, 11 December 2002, at 5, posted at http://r0.unctad.org/en/subsites/dite/pdfs/PRChina.pdf (visited on 18 July 2003).

[10] It can be anticipated that WTO accession of China will significantly increase EU investment in China. Indeed, for instance, Mr. Perodi, the then President of the European Commission, said that China's accession to the WTO 'will provide substantial new market opportunities for European companies selling to China or investing there, and will create or secure many European jobs', posted at http://europa.eu.int/comm/trade/bilateral/china/prodi.htm (visited on 7 June 2001).

[11] See Section II in the Introduction for further discussion on the role of law in the development of EU investment in China.

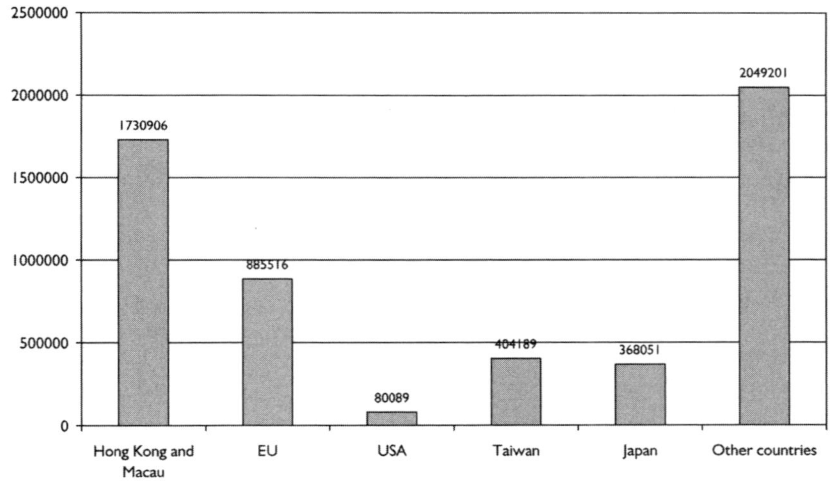

Chart 3: Major Investors in Mainland China in 2000 (unit: US$10,000)

Source: Compiled by the author according to data from China's semi-official China Association of Enterprises with Foreign Investment (CAEFI), posted at: http://www.etisu.com/investment/img/fis/fis.html (visited 28 June 2003).

to fill the gap by exploring and critically examining the existing legal framework governing EU-China investment relations, particularly EU investment in China, with a view towards identifying and analysing the direction of its future development. The Introduction will consider the history of EU investment in China, the role of law in the development of such investment, and the existing research thereon. It then proceeds to present the arrangement of this book: its objectives, its structure and scope, and the research methodologies employed.

I. EUROPEAN INVESTMENT IN CHINA: PAST HISTORY AND PRESENT SITUATION

A brief look at the history of EU investment in China helps one to understand the background against which the current legal framework evolved. It also helps one to analyse and predict how that framework might develop in the future. The following sections present such a history.

Since the People's Republic of China was established in 1949, European investment in China has undergone dramatic changes. European investment was in a dominant position in 1949, but totally disappeared in the 1950s. In the late 1970s, EU investment resumed and in the early 1990s it rapidly increased. Thus, five phases in the development of EU investment in China may be identified: nationalisation (1949–1957), exclusion (1958–1979),

Table 2: China's Approved Overseas Investment Enterprises by 1997 (unit: US $ 10000)

Country/ region	Until 1997				1997			
	No. of enterprises	Total investment	Chinese contribution	Chinese proportion	No. of enterprises	Total investment	Chinese contribution	Chinese proportion
Total	2143	484328.1	234861.4	48.5	158	32535.1	19630.2	60.3
Hong Kong	172	35786.2	21766.6	60.8	14	803.1	566.6	70.5
Macao	37	9319.2	4721.3	50.6	4	265.3	264.5	99.7
USA	257	56657.2	37541.0	66.3				
Japan	86	4447.2	1648.7	37.1	4	179.0	123.8	69.2
Russia	234	19417.0	9707.7	50.0	7	161.4	119.2	73.8
EU	109	10901.9	4652.3	47.6	5	391.8	165.3	54.5
Ger	30	1543.2	932.1	60.4	1	83.3	33.3	40.0
France	14	3059.8	947.7	31.0				
Neth	12	816.2	528.9	64.8	2	238.5	92.0	38.6
Belg	6	207.0	162.1	78.3	1	20.0	20.0	100
Italy	6	1568.5	298.6	19.0				
UK	10	1313.1	675.2	51.4	1	50.0	20.0	40.0
Lux	1	40.0	20.0	50.0				
Den	2	73.9	34.9	47.2				
Fin	1	120.0	23.6	19.7				
Swe	5	318.3	184.1	48.2				
Aus	7	369.8	203.9	55.0				
Spain	12	1047.1	411.7	39.3				
Port	3	425.0	229.5	54.0				
Ire								
Greece								

Source: Compiled by the author according to the *Chinese Foreign Economic and Trade Yearbook* (1998/1999), China Economy Press, pp. 739–44.

Table 3: European and Foreign Investments in China 1902–1936 (unit: US$ millions)

Country	1902	1914	1931	1936
Great Britain	260.3 (33.0)	607.5 (37.7)	1189.2 (36.7)	1220.8 (35.0)
France	91.1 (11.6)	171.4 (10.7)	192.4 (5.9)	234.1 (6.7)
Germany	164.3 (20.9)	263.6 (16.4)	87.0 (2.7)	148.5 (4.3)
Belgium	4.4 (0.6)	22.9 (1.4)	89.0 (2.7)	58.4 (1.7)
Netherlands	0.0	0.0	28.7 (0.9)	0.0
Italy	0.0	0.0	46.4 (1.4)	72.3 (2.1)
Scandinavia	0.0	0.0	2.9 (0.1)	0.0
European total	**520.1 (66.1)**	**1065.4 (66.2)**	**1635.6 (50.4)**	**1734.1 (49.8)**
Japan	1.0 (0.1)	219.6 (13.6)	1136.9 (35.1)	1394.0 (40.0)
Russia	246.5 (31.3)	269.3 (16.7)	273.2 (8.4)	0.0
United States	19.7 (2.5)	49.3 (3.1)	196.8 (6.1)	298.8 (8.6)
Others	0.6 (0.0)	6.7 (0.4)	0.0	56.3 (1.6)
Total	**787.9 (100)**	**1610.3 (100)**	**3242.5 (100)**	**3483.2 (100)**

Sources: Chi-Ming Hou, *Foreign Investment and Economic Development in China 1840–1937* (Harvard University Press, 1964), p. 17; for 1902–1931, see CF Remer, *Foreign Investment in China* (Macmillan Company, 1933), p. 76. See also Tomas N Thompson, *China's Nationalisation of Foreign Firms: The politics of hostage capitalism, 1949–1957*, University of Maryland Law School Occasional Papers/Reprints Series in Contemporary Asian Studies, No. 6–1979 (27), p. 5.

resumption (1980–1992), rapid increase (1993–1999) and further development in the new Millennium (2000–).

I.1 Nationalisation (1949–1957)

Until 1949, when the PRC was established, there had been foreign control of key sectors of the 'modern' economy,[12] in which the European enterprises played a dominant role. Statistics show that in 1936, European enterprises had an investment of US$1734.1 million in China, which accounted for about half of the total foreign investment. Moreover, before the Japanese invaded China in 1931, European investment had been in an even more dominant position, amounting to approximately two-thirds of total foreign investment in China (See *Table 3: European and Foreign Investments in China 1902–1936*). However, as a part of the foreign colonial establishment in China, the effect of European and foreign enterprises upon China had been

[12] They controlled certain north-eastern and south-western railways, the principal mine and heavy industries, a part of the textile industry, the principal urban services and the major share of steam navigation. Thompson, Tomas N, *China's Nationalisation of Foreign Firms: The politics of hostage capitalism, 1949–1957*, University of Maryland Law School Occasional Papers/Reprints Series in Contemporary Asian Studies, No. 6–1979 (27), at 3.

negative.[13] Thus, there was a vigorous rejection of the foreign presence and an upsurge in anti-imperialism sentiments throughout country in the 1940s.[14] As a result of such national sentiments, as well as Communist ideology and US-led diplomatic isolation and economic impediments, the new Communist government committed itself to eliminate western industrial and commercial enterprise in China when it came to power.[15] However, the Communists realised that this goal could not be achieved immediately, and consequently they took a progressive and balanced approach. The methods adopted by the new Chinese government were called 'socialist transformation of capitalist industry and commerce' or 'hostage capitalism' or 'creeping expropriation'.[16] Occasionally, the government engaged in outright nationalisation of foreign firms in retaliation for what they considered hostile or unlawful actions by the firms' home countries.[17] This alternative approach was sometimes called 'retaliatory requisition'.[18] Through these measures, the Chinese government effectively redefined and eliminated foreign investment in China (except for Sino-Soviet Union Joint Ventures) over a period of seven years, from 1949 to 1957[19] (See *Table 4: Change of Contribution of Ownership Sectors to National Income 1952–1978*).

[13] The vast majority of foreign investment was in Shanghai and Manchuria, which did little to stimulate new economic activities elsewhere. On the contrary, the Chinese state was weakened as a result of foreign establishments in China, which were, as a whole, 'an invasion of China's sovereignty, which derogated the autonomy not only of an abstract polity but also, more critically, the autonomy of particular and individual Chinese who apprehended and reacted to the intruding foreign presence'. Feuerwerker, Albert, *The Foreign Establishment in China in the Early Twentieth Century* (Ann Arbor, Centre for Chinese Studies, 1976), at 111. See also Thompson, above note 12, at 3–4; Murphy, Rhoads, *The Outsiders* (Ann Arbor, University of Michigan Press, 1977), at 126.

[14] Thompson, above note 12, at 4.

[15] Thompson, above note 12, at 4.

[16] It is observed that, through this approach, the government took numerous piecemeal actions over an extended period. Thus, it would intervene in foreign firms' business operations by, for example, prohibiting transfer of funds out of China or the cancellation of agreements, and at the same time imposing price controls, tax increases and wage increases. Eventually, foreign investors would lose control of their business and the investments would lose their value. Therefore, Thompson called it 'hostage capitalism' and Chew thought it constituted 'massive creeping expropriation', though the Chinese government had said nothing about its nationalisation programme for foreign enterprises, nor did it admit that nationalisation had actually happened. Chew, Pat K, 'Political Risks and US Investment in China: Chimera of Protection and Predictability?' (1994) *Virginia Journal of International Law*, at 4. See also Thompson, above note 12, at 67 and 68.

[17] Chew, above note 16, at 4.

[18] An example of such measures happened in May 1951 when China took over all of Shell Oil Co.'s installations in China, after the Hong Kong government took possession of an oil tanker, the ownership of which was disputed with China. Moreover, it has been noted that the break-out of the Korea War in 1950 in particular must have accelerated the nationalisation process, as the PRC Government took radical economic measures against major western powers, in retaliation for measures which the latter had previously taken against the PRC. Thompson, above note 12, at 68; Cohen, Jerome Alan and Chiu, Hungdah, *People's China and International Law* (Princeton University Press, 1974), at 682.

[19] Thompson, above note 12, at 6.

Table 4: Change of Contribution of Ownership Sectors to National Income 1952–1978 (% of total)

	1952	1956	1978
State owned	19.1	32.2	80.8
Collective	1.5	53.4	19.2
Individual	71.8	7.1	–
Other*	7.6	7.3	–
Total	100.0	100.0	100.0

*Private and joint state-private ownerships.
Source: The Economist Intelligence Unit (EIU), Investing in China: where, how and why, Special Report No. 1071 by Lynette Kemp, The Economist Publications, 1987, p. 13.

For the investors who suffered from the nationalisation process, these experiences were extremely bitter, as no compensation was made when such expropriations took place. However, compensation did come at later stage, in formal or informal ways. Since 1954, for instance, these firms have been employed as consultants in the interest of promoting Sino-Western trade, which was something they had hoped for in the years of 'hostage capitalism'.[20] All indications show that these firms have profited handsomely, especially after the late 1970s when China's reformist leaders greatly increased the purchase of foreign technology and attraction of foreign investment.[21] Indeed, since the 1970s, when China officially restored diplomatic relations with western countries and adopted the economic reform and 'opening-up' policy, it began to settle these historical property disputes. For instance, in 1987, the Chinese Government and the British Government entered into an agreement, as a 'final and comprehensive settlement of mutual historical property claims between the two countries arising before 1 January 1980'.[22] According to the agreement, China agreed to pay Britain US$ 23.5 million, while Britain agreed to pay China US$ 3.8 million.[23]

[20] Thompson, above note 12, at 69.

[21] Thompson, above note 12, at 69. In the author's Questionnaire, companies having long experience of investing in China indicated that their earlier experience in China had served as a source of confidence.

[22] 1987 Agreement between the Government of UK and the Government of PRC Concerning the Settlement of Mutual Historical Property Claims, United Nations Treaty Series (UNTS), Vol. 1656, I–28495 1991, at 1.

[23] In return, both governments undertook that each government should neither on its own behalf nor on behalf of its natural and judicial persons pursue or support any claims arising before 1980 with the other government. *Ibid.*, Articles 1–4. See also Campbell, Colin, 'China to pay Britons compensation', *Times*, 26 February 1988, at 4.

I.2 Exclusion (1958–1977)

The 20 years following the complete withdrawal of foreign enterprises from China in 1957 was a 'quiet' period in terms of foreign investment. During this period, the Chinese leadership employed harsh and radical economic measures that were intended to construct a pure, self-reliant, socialist country in a short period of time. Those measures resulted in huge social disorder and economic disruption.[24] As a result, the economy was on the brink of collapse by the late 1970s.

However, political relations between China and European countries had improved in the 1960s following China's split from the Soviet Union and still more during the early 1970s when China was accepted as a member of the United Nations.[25] Trade between China and European countries subsequently resumed.[26] This period also witnessed a turning-point in the political relationship between China and the European Union (then the European Economic Community, the EEC). In May 1975, Sir Christopher Soames, Vice-President of the European Commission, paid a historic visit to China,[27] after which formal diplomatic relations between the two sides were soon established.[28] This political event stimulated further development in the bilateral trade and economic relations in the years to come.

I.3 Resumption (1978–1992)

The return of European investment in China did not occur until 1980,[29] two years after China embarked on 'opening-up' and economic reform policy[30] and signed a trade agreement[31] with the EEC in 1978.

[24] These measures include the 'Great Leap Forward' in 1958 and the ten-year 'Cultural Revolution' between 1966 and 1976. The Great Leap Forward campaign was a militant Five-Year-Plan to promote technology and agricultural self-sufficiency which was held responsible for famine in 1960 and 1961 and resulted in Mao's temporary withdrawal from the public scene. The Cultural Revolution was a ten-year political experiment aimed at rekindling revolutionary fervour and purifying the party, which caused huge social disorder. For more information about these campaigns, see the British Broadcasting Corporation (BBC): *China's Communist Revolution*, posted at http://news.bbc.co.uk/hi/english/static/ special_report/1999/09/99/china_50/great.htm (visited on 29 June 2003).

[25] Hu, Yuangxiang, *Legal and Policy Issues of the Trade and Economic Relations between China and the EEC* (Kluwer, 1991), at 3–4.

[26] *Ibid.*

[27] EC Bull. 5–1975, points 1.2.01–1.2.05.

[28] EC Bull. 5–1975, point 1.2.04 and EC Bull. 9–1975, point 2.3.44.

[29] It is said that the first European-Chinese joint venture was the Sino-French Remy Martin Joint Venture Co. Ltd, which was approved in May 1980. See *The China Investment Guide 1984/1985* (Longman, 1984), at 348.

[30] The decision was made during the Third Plenary Session of the 11th Central Committee of the Communist Party of China in 1978. See WANG, Yongjun, *Investment in China: A question and answer guide on how to do business* (CITIC Publication House, 1997), at 1.

[31] For the text of the EEC-China Trade Agreement, see OJ L123 (11 May 1978).

Inside China, the new leadership headed by Deng Xiaoping took a pragmatic view toward the future of China and socialism, and decided to implement in China a 'socialist system with Chinese characteristics'.[32] In a famous quotation, he said, 'it does not matter whether a cat is black or white, as long as it catches mice'.[33] Attracting FDI was one of the 'black cats' that was ideologically inconsistent with accepted communist ideas but practically useful in solving compelling internal problems. In an effort to boost the confidence of foreign investors, China promulgated the Chinese-Foreign Equity Joint Venture Law (EJVL) in 1979, which aimed to protect and promote FDI in China. As the very first law on foreign-related economic activities of the PRC, this law legally signalled a new era in China, as well as in its relations with the western world. In a further move, in the following year, China decided to create several 'Special Economic Zones' (SEZs),[34] as 'experimental fields' and 'windows of opening-up policy' where 'special policies' and 'flexible measures'[35] could be adopted to attract foreign capital, technology and managerial skills. Accordingly, the Chinese Government promulgated numerous laws and regulations on FDI and foreign trade.[36]

At the same time, the bilateral China-EC relationship was becoming more favourable to EU investment in China. On 3rd April 1978, the EC and China signed a trade agreement[37] (hereinafter 'the EEC-China Trade Agreement') in Brussels, which was the first trade agreement that the EC concluded with a state-trading country and which marked a new phase of Sino-EC trade relations. A year later, an agreement on textiles[38] was concluded, and China became a beneficiary of the Community General System of Preferences Scheme (the GSP).[39] In 1985, the Trade Agreement was replaced by a new trade and economic co-operation agreement (the EC-China Co-operation

[32] The theory of 'Socialism with Chinese Characteristics' aims to integrate 'the universal truth of Marxism' with 'the concrete reality of China'. It was put forward by Deng Xiaoping in 1982 and has been established as the second historic leap in the process of combining Marxism with practice in China, following the realisation of the first one after China found its path in the New-Democratic Revolution. For further information about this theory, see Beijing Review, *The Theory of Building Socialism with Chinese Characteristics*, posted at http://www.bjreview.com.cn/2001/200126/CoverStory-200126(Background-3).htm (visited on 29 June 2003).

[33] See BBC, *China's Communist Revolution*, posted at http://news.bbc.co.uk/hi/english/static/special_report/1999/09/99/china_50/deng.htm (visited on 29 June 2003).

[34] The first four SEZs include Zhenzhen, Zhuhai, Shantou in Guangdong Province and Xiamen in Fujian Province. In the 1990s, Hainan Province as a whole and Pudong New District in Shanghai were granted the same status.

[35] The 'special policies' and 'flexible measures' can be interpreted as special privileges and treatments for foreigners investing in these zones where they could carry out investment and trading activities that were not allowed in the rest of the country, or were allowed but with less favourable conditions.

[36] For details of Chinese laws and regulations on FDI, see Section 1.2.

[37] Officially, the Trade Agreement between the European Economic Community and the People's Republic of China, OJ L123 (11 May 1978).

[38] EC Bull. 7/8–1979 point 2.2.16. This agreement was renegotiated in 1988 and has ever since been amended several times. For details of this agreement and EC-China trade in textile products, see Hu, Yuanxiang, above note 25, at 291–340.

[39] EC Bull. 5–1979.

Agreement),[40] which was also the first co-operation agreement that the EC signed with a state-trading country. It provided an ever wider and more comprehensive legal framework for trade and economic co-operation, including co-operation in the field of investment. Indeed, it enabled China to enjoy preferential treatment by the EC, as compared with other state-trading countries, such as the former USSR and Eastern European countries. The 'June 4th' event in 1989, however, had caused the EC to freeze its relations with China.[41] Nevertheless, relations were soon restored and China was reinstated on the list of countries eligible for co-operation commencing in 1992.[42] In 1992, most trading relations (except in the area of arms trading) between the China and the EC were normalised.[43]

At the EU member state level, the legal environment for mutual investment exchange was also improved. As early as 1982, China signed its first bilateral investment treaty (BIT) with Sweden, followed by treaties with Germany, France, the Belgium-Luxembourg Economic Union (hereinafter 'BLEU'), Finland, Italy, Denmark, UK, the Netherlands, Austria, Portugal, Spain and Greece. By 1992, China had concluded bilateral investment protection and promotion agreements with 14 of the 15 EU Member States, with Ireland being the only exception. This situation continues today, except that some EU member states, such as Netherlands and Germany, have managed to renegotiate new BITs with China (*Table 5: BITs between China and the EU member States*). In addition, during the resumption of investment period China and most EU member states became parties to two of the important investment conventions, namely the 1965 Convention Establishing the International Centre for the Settlement of Investment Disputes (the ICSID Convention) and the 1988 Convention Establishing the Multilateral Guarantee Agency (the MIGA Convention).[44] China had also concluded numerous agreements on economic and industrial co-operation with EU member states.[45]

These events, particularly the restoration of relations and the conclusion

[40] OJ L250/1 (19 September 1985).

[41] EC Bull. 6–1989 point 2.3.2.

[42] *Chronology of EU-China relations*, posted at http://www.delchn.cec.eu.int/en/eu_and_china/Milestones.htm (visited on 20 August 2003).

[43] *Ibid.* In the first EU policy of the Chinese government, China urged the EC to lift the arms trading ban. See China's Policy Document towards the European Union (published in October 2003), Part 5.

[44] The MIAG Convention aims to promote investment flow from developed countries to developing countries by providing investment insurance against political risks, whilst the ICSID Convention sets up a permanent arbitration mechanism to settle state-investor investment disputes. By now China and the 15 EU member states have all become contracting parties to the two conventions. See Section 3.2.2 for details.

[45] These agreements are related to investment as the forms of co-operation cover construction of new industrial plants or expansion of existing plants, as well as establishing joint projects in the respective countries, including joint production of goods and equipment and marketing co-operation. Since they only have very limited impact on investment protection and promotion, they are not discussed in this book. Details of these agreements can be seen in Hu, Yuanxiang, above note 25, at 79–85.

Table 5: BITs between China and the EU Member States

Parties from the EU	Signature	Entry into force
Austria	Sep. 12, 1985	Oct. 11, 1986
BLEU*	June 4, 1984	Oct. 5, 1986
Denmark	Apr. 29, 1985	Apr. 29, 1985
Finland	Sep. 4, 1984	Jan. 26, 1986
France	May 30, 1984	Mar. 19, 1985
Germany	Oct. 7, 1983	Mar. 18, 1985
Greece	June 25, 1992	Dec. 21, 1993
Italy	Jan. 28, 1985	Aug. 28, 1987
Netherlands	June 17, 1985	Feb. 1, 1987
Portugal	Feb. 3, 1992	Dec. 1, 1992
Spain	Feb. 6, 1992	May 1, 1993
Sweden	Mar. 29, 1982	Mar. 29, 1982
UK	May 15, 1986	May 15, 1986
Netherlands (new)	Nov. 26, 2001	–
Germany (new)	Dec. 1, 2003	–

*BLEU refers to the 'Belgium Luxembourg Economic Union'.
Source: Compiled by the author in accordance with ICSID and UNCTAD data. See ICSID, Bilateral Investment Treaties, posted at http://www.worldbank.org/icsid/treaties/china.htm (18/09/2004); UNCTAD, Total Number of Bilateral Investment Treaties Concluded, 1 January 2003 (by China), posted at http://stats.unctad.org/fdi/treaties/bits/China.htm (18/09/2004).

of BITs, paved the way for a rapid growth of EU investment in China after 1992. As *Chart 1* and *Chart 2* show, although EU investment in China resumed after 1980, its volume remained insignificant throughout that decade. However, this situation changed dramatically in the 1990s, particularly after 1992.

I.4 Rapid Increase (1993–1999)

The years following 1993 saw a dramatic surge of EU investment in China. As *Chart 1* shows, the contractual value of EU investment increased sevenfold within three years (1993 to 1995). In terms of realised value, EU investment also increased fourfold within a span of five years (1993–1997). The weight of EU investment in total investment inflows to China rose significantly. As *Chart 2* indicates, in 1992, contractual and realised values of EU investment accounted for approximately only two per cent of total FDI in China, while it reached near or beyond ten percent in 1999. Furthermore, this period also witnessed a rapid growth of Chinese direct investment in the EU[46] (*Table 2: China's Approved Overseas Investment Enterprise*).

[46] For example, Eurostat figures show that there was a five-fold increase of Chinese investment in the EU in two years (1992–1994). See above note 7.

Apart from the restoration of EU-China relations and the signing of BITs, the following events may have contributed to such a sudden growth. On China's side, in 1992, the investment environment further improved as China determined to establish a 'Socialist Market Economy'.[47] One of the major moves related to foreign investment was to gradually implement 'national treatment' to foreign invested enterprises (FIEs), which aimed to build a level playing-field for FDI in China.[48] On its part and for the first time in its history, in 1995, the EU adopted 'A Long Term Policy for China-EU Relations'.[49] This policy 'put forth a philosophy for dealing constructively with China by providing a framework for national and private initiatives by Europeans'.[50] In March 1998 the Commission adopted a Communication 'Building a Comprehensive Partnership with China'[51] (the 1998 Communication), which further upgraded and intensified the 'Long Term Policy' and stated that 'improving the climate for European investment in China should also be one of the EU's top objectives'.[52] In April of the same year, the first EU-China summit meeting took place in London.[53]

I.5 Further Development (2000–)

The year 2000 marked an impressive beginning for EU investment in China in the new millennium. In that year, the EU overtook Japan and the US, becoming the biggest foreign investor in China[54] (*Chart 3: Major Investors in China in 2002*). The coming years will see a further significant increase in EU direct investment in China because of three major factors.

Firstly, the EU and China are two of the biggest, mutually complementary markets in the world and there is huge potential for a significant further expansion of EU direct investment in China. China is indisputably one of the world's largest potential markets and fastest growing economies, and thus

[47] See *The Central Committee of the Chinese Communist Party (CCCPC) Decision on Some Issues Related to the Establishment of the Socialist Market Economy*, (1993) 7 Nov *People's Daily*.

[48] For further decisions on national treatment of FIEs in China, see Section 5.3.

[49] COM (95) 279 (5 July 1995). It is sometimes called the 'Brittan Report', as Lord Brittan (Sir Leon Brittan as he then was), the then Vice-President of European Commission, authored it.

[50] Menotti, Reberto, *European-Chinese Relations in the Nineties*, The International Spectator, Vol. XXX, No. 4, Oct.–Dec. 1995.

[51] Communication from the Commission, '*Building a Comprehensive Partnership with China*', COM (1998) 181 Final (25 March1998).

[52] *Ibid*, Section C.1.

[53] The Joint Press Statement can be found in the Chinese Embassy in the UK's website, posted at http://www.chinese-embassy.org.uk/eng/13917.html (visited on 30 June 2003).

[54] The contracted and utilised EU FDIs were respectively US$ 8.8 and US$ 4.5 billion. See Communication from the Commission to the Council and the European Parliament, *EU Strategy towards China: Implementation of the 1998 Communication and future steps for a more effective policy*, COM (2001) 265 final, at 12. As said, the EU seems to have adopted the statistics of the MOFCOM of the Chinese government, above note 6.

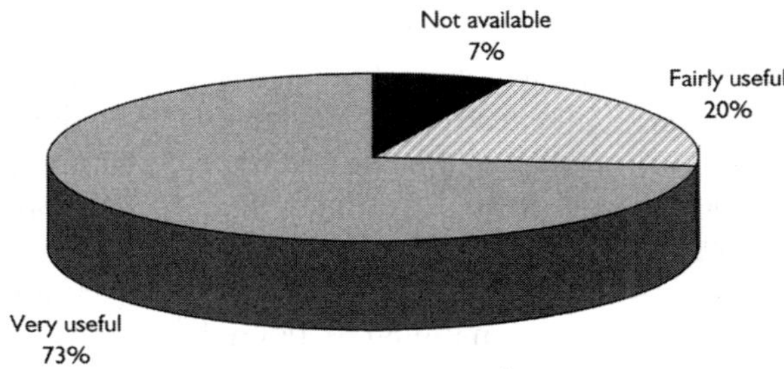

Chart 4: WTO to Improve Investment Climate

provides infinite investment opportunities. Indeed, a recent report from the Organisation of Economic Co-operation and Development (OECD) has confirmed the United Nations Conference on Trade and Development's (UNCTAD's) prediction that China would overtake the US and become the largest FDI recipient in the world in the year 2002.[55] At the same time, the EU as a whole is one of the biggest investor in the world, and so far its investment in China is relatively small. For example, in 1997, the EU invested US$ 4.2 billion in China, which accounted for only 2.44 per cent of its total outward investment (US$ 172 billion).[56] Thus, the potential for the growth of EU investment in China is tremendous.

Secondly, bilateral political relations between the two sides have never been so favourable for EU investment in China. Acknowledging China's growing political and economic weight in the world, the EU is further enhancing its engagement with China. In May 2001, the Commission produced a Communication to the Council and the European Parliament on the implementation of the 1998 Communication, which concluded that EU global and long term objectives in its relations with China as defined in 1998 remained largely valid.[57] It also pointed out that there had been significant developments in EU-China relations since 1998, including 'the growing importance of China as a trade and investment partner for the EU', and that 'all these developments point to the scope and need for further enhancement of our engagement with China'.[58] This strategy was taken further in the 2003

[55] See above note 9. See also Tian, Li, 'China will Become the Largest FDI Recipient in the World', Gong, Wen, 'A Year of Changes', and Gong, Wen, 'We Have Utilised More Than 48 Billion US$ of FDI in the First 11 Months', in (2002) 7 Dec, 10 Dec, 12 Dec *People's Daily* (overseas edition), at 2, at 1, at 1 respectively.

[56] Qiu, Yuanlun, 'The EU's China Policy and Sino-EU Trade and Economic Relations', (1999) 8 *World Economy* (Shijie Jingji), at 8.

[57] See Communication from the Commission to the Council and the European Parliament, *EU Strategy towards China: Implementation of the 1998 Communication and future steps for a more effective policy*, COM (2001) 265 final, at 4–5.

[58] *Ibid*, at 6.

Community policy paper on China.[59] Taking into account changes happened in the EU and China including the fact that a new generation of leadership has recently taken the reigns, this policy paper describes the EU-China relationship as a 'maturing partnership' and proposes to 'upgrade' the action plan put forward in the 2001 strategy.[60] Among other issues, the EU plan to strengthen dialogue with China on bilateral investment issues 'at all level'.[61] On the Chinese side, moreover, EU investment projects are favoured in China as they tend to be large projects[62] accompanied by the transfer of high technologies which are sought after by China.[63] Attracting EU investment is therefore an established policy in China. This has been particularly true since the Asian financial crisis of 1997, when FDI from China's major FDI sources, Hong Kong and other Asian countries and regions, dropped sharply.[64] In October 2003, China published its first EU policy, in which it echoed the EU's plan to strengthen investment dialogue and establish mutual investment promotion agencies.[65] This was further affirmed by the joint press communiqué published as a result of the Sixth EU-China Summit taking place also in October 2003.[66]

Finally, China's recent accession to the WTO will undoubtedly boost the growth of EU investment in China.[67] Although there has been no published assessment of the impact of the accession on EU investment in China such as that carried out by the US International Trade Commission,[68] it has been widely recognised that accession will greatly boost EU investment in China, as well as EU-China trade. For example, upon hearing that the EU-China bilateral negotiation had been concluded, the President of the European Commission, Romano Prodi said, '[T]his will provide substantial new market opportunities for European companies selling to China or investing there, and will create or secure many European jobs.'[69] The Questionnaire survey conducted by the author shows that EU investors also view China's WTO accession as very useful in improving its investment climate (*Chart 4: WTO to Improve Investment Climate*). In fact, a close look at the result of the

[59] See Commission Policy Paper for Transmission to the Council and the European Parliament: *A maturing partnership-shared interest and challenges in EU-China relations*, COM (2003), 533 fin.

[60] *Ibid*, at 5.

[61] *Ibid*, at 18.

[62] Qiu, above note 56, at 7.

[63] Qiu observed that the average project value of EU investment between 1979 and 1998 was US$ 3.9 million, much higher than the average project value (US$ 1.76 million) of FDI in China. *Ibid*.

[64] Qiu, *ibid*.

[65] *China Policy towards the European Union*, published in October 2003.

[66] Para. 18, Joint Press Communiqué of the Sixth EU-China Summit (03 October 2003).

[67] China's membership to the WTO was officially realised on 11 December 2001.

[68] For details, see US International Trade Commission (USITC), *Assessment of the Economic Effects on the United States of China's Accession to the WTO*, Investigation No. 332–403, publication 3229, September 1999.

[69] See above note 10.

EU-China Bilateral WTO negotiations confirms that, in particular, the access and operational conditions for EU investment in some of its strong sectors including services and agriculture will be significantly improved by the WTO accession.[70] A survey among EU small and medium-sized enterprises (SMEs) also shows that rapid increase of EU investment is most likely to occur in areas such as telecommunication, finance and insurance, wholesale and retail and power, gas and coal production.[71]

II. THE ROLE OF LAW IN THE DEVELOPMENT OF EU INVESTMENT IN CHINA

What is the role of law in the development of EU investment in China? This question is the fundamental query that underlies this research project. Outsiders tend to discount the importance of law in the light of East Asian history, particularly that of China after World War II.[72] However, law has been among the most important factors in the Pacific economic boom.[73] In China's case, the great effort that the Chinese government has made to establish a favourable foreign direct investment (FDI) regulatory system has been regarded as one of the most important factors[74] fuelled its success in attracting FDI.[75] The promulgation of the EJVL in 1979 signalled a new era of an

70 For details of the results of the bilateral EU-China talk, see http://europa.eu.int/comm/trade/bilateral/china/res.pdf (visited on 22 November 2001). For a general view of the conditions of China's accession to the WTO, see the World Trade Organisation Working Party on the Accession of China: *Report of the Working Party on the Accession of China* (hereinafter *'Working Party Report'*), WT/ACC/CHN/49 (1 October 2001). For a table on the schedule for liberalisation in the service sectors, see *Table 1: Schedule for Liberalisation in Services: Ownership Control,* in UNCTAD, *China: WTO Accession and Growing FDI Inflows*, 11 December 2002, at 7, posted at http://r0.unctad.org/en/subsites/dite/pdfs/PRChina.pdf (visited on 18 July 2003).

71 See ZHAO, Jingping, *Analysis and Prediction on the Trends of Foreign-Invested Industries*, posted at http://www.fdi.gov.cn/common/frnreport.jsp?id=CENSOFT0000000007250 (visited on 4 June 2003).

72 Emilou, Nicholas and O'Keeffe, David, *The European Union and the World Trade Law: after the Uruguay Round* (John Wiley & Sons Ltd, 1996), at 363.

73 *Ibid.*

74 Other factors include the country's large and continuously growing market; its export-oriented strategy and successful penetration of world markets; significant improvement of its macro-economic environment; the spill-over effects of industrial upgrading in neighbouring economies. See Ricupero, Rubens (Secretary General of UNCTAD), *Recent Development in FDI Trends and Policies and Their Implications for Developing Counties*, a paper submitted on the Forum on Direct Investment Strategies of the Multinational Corporations, Sept. 1998, Xiamen, at 7; OECD Press Release: *Reforms Could Boost China's Ability to Attract Foreign Investment*, posted at http://www.oecd.org/document/8/0,2340,en_2649_37467_3240968_1_1_1_37467,00.html (visited 10 July 2004).

75 The success of the People's Republic of China (hereinafter referred to as 'China') in attracting foreign direct investment (FDI) in the last decade is unprecedented. Since 1993, China has maintained its position as the second largest FDI recipient in the world for at least six years, and the single largest among developing countries for ten consecutive years. In 2003, China outstripped the United States and became the largest FDI recipient in the world. The growth rate of its FDI stock over the past decade has outpaced that of all other major economies in the world, with the total stock reaching $ 501 billion by the end of 2003. See Ricupero, Rubens (Secretary General of UNCTAD), *Recent Development in FDI Trends and Policies and Their Implications for*

'Open-door' and economic reform. Since then, continuous efforts have been made by the Chinese Government to improve the legal environment of foreign investment in China. Laws and regulations have been adopted and attractive incentives have been offered by local and central governments. In 1992, China embarked on the implementation of 'national treatment' for foreign invested enterprises (FIEs) with a view to building a level playing field for FDI in China.[76] Currently, the Chinese Government is sorting out and reshaping its FDI laws and regulations, to bring them into conformity with the requirements of the WTO.[77] The preceding survey on the history of EU investment in China also suggests a positive influence of the various international treaties, including BITs and MIGA and ICSID Conventions, on the flow of EU investment in China. A Questionnaire survey conducted by the author has confirmed that, law did have played a significant role when EU investors made their investment decisions, and that most of them had actually conducted an in-depth investigation of the domestic and international legal regimes before they decided to invest in China.[78]

It is therefore unsurprising that there are still deep concerns among EU investors about the FDI legal environment in China. Some potential investors previously suffered from 'retaliatory confiscation' or 'hostage capitalism' during an earlier era and have not forgot those bitter experiences. Other potential investors may be discouraged by more recent incidents such as the 'June 4th Event'[79] or the 'Beijing McDonald's' case,[80] both of which drew wide and continuous international attention. Indeed, as Chew observed, the

Developing Countries, a paper presented at the *Forum on Direct Investment Strategies of the Multinational Corporations*, Sept. 1998, Xiamen, at 7; Yu, Jijun, 'China Has Become One of the Top Destinations of Foreign Investments', (2002) 10 Sep *People's Daily* (overseas edition), at 1. See also OECD, *Trends and Recent Development in Foreign Direct Investment, June 2004*, at 3, 5, posted at http://www.oecd.org/dataoecd/52/11/2958722.pdf (visited on 10 July 2004); OECD: *Trends and Recent Developments in Foreign Direct Investment*, June 2003, posted at http://www.oecd.org/pdf/M00042000/M00042212.pdf (visited on 1 July 2003); *UNCTAD Predicts 27% Drop in FDI Inflow this Year and China May Outstrip U.S. as World's Largest FDI Recipient*, UNCTAD Press Release TAD/INF/PR/63 (24/10/02). See also Qian, Weizeng, 'International Investors Favours China the Most', Ce, Yuming, 'China Received FDI 52.7 Billion Last Year', Yang, Qing, 'Sharp Increase of Investment Opportunities in China for Multinationals', and Zhang, Yi, 'China attracted FDI 53.5 Billion in 2003', (2003/2004) 28 June, 15 Jan, 24 May and 15 Jan *People's Daily* (overseas edition), at 5, at 1, at 5, at 1, respectively.

[76] For details, see Section 5.3.

[77] See Li, Pengxiang, Yang, Xiwei, 'China Adopts Vigorous Measures to Improve Investment Climate', (2000) 21 June *People's Daily* (overseas edition), at 1. See also Lu, Bin, etc., 'American Asian Association Annual Enterprises Meeting Opened in Shanghai: Zhu Rongji Attended and Made Important Speech', (2000) 11 May *People's Daily* (overseas edition), at 1. For more on the amendment of major FDI laws and regulations, see Section 1.4.

[78] According to the author's Questionnaire, when deciding to invest in China, most EU investors (82%) consider law to be an element of substantial importance (top, high or medium) and most of them have made in-depth investigation of the legal regime. See Section 8.1 for details.

[79] In spring through summer 1989, thousands of university students demonstrated in the streets to protest against corruption, among other issues. Students took to Tiananmen Square, a symbol of the State, for months. On June 4th, the Chinese Government mobilised the army to expel the students from the Square and reportedly thousands of students were killed as a result.

facts that China is in transition and undergoing rapid changes imply huge potential political risks.[81] Among the uncertainties are the leadership succession, the nature of a 'socialist market economy', and the power of individuals under a Chinese rule of law.[82]

These concerns have been expressed by the EU institutions in their official documents and speeches. For instance, in the 1998 Communication the EU stated that improving the legal climate for European investment in China should be one of the EU's top objectives in building a comprehensive partnership with China.[83] Lord Brittan (Sir Leon Brittan as he then was), the EC's then Vice-President in charge of external trade issues further affirmed in a speech that 'the biggest contribution that Europe can make is to provide consistent and vigorous support, as China seeks to build the institutions, rules and policies that makes it the first place investors want to come and the last place that they wish to leave'.[84]

III. EXISTING RESEARCH ON THE LAW OF EU INVESTMENT IN CHINA

Unfortunately there has been so far no specific study of the legal aspects of EU-China investment relations, although there have been some studies of the laws and policies of EC-China trade and economic relations in general.[85] As a result, EU investors' knowledge of the legal environment of EU investment in

For more information on the event, see http://www.christusrex.org/www1/sdc/tiananmen.html (visited on 30 June 2003).

80 In 1994, McDonald's Corporation's land lease on its flagship restaurant near Tiananmen Square was reportedly cancelled following a decision by Beijing municipal authorities. The city's position was that the location was needed as part of a larger redevelopment project funded by a Hong Kong investor. A settlement of the dispute, providing compensation to McDonald's, was reportedly reached between the parties in mid-1996. McDonald's was also allowed to open at least two more outlets along an adjacent street. See US and Foreign Commercial Service (US&FCS) (Telegraphic Report from the American Embassy in Beijing): *China: Investment Climate Statement for 1997*. See also Friedman, Thomas L, 'Fed up', New York Times, 04-12-1996, at 29.

81 Chew, above note 16, particularly part I.B and II.C. On a global scale, a recent MIGA survey showed that, when evaluating foreign investment, investors were generally 'very concerned' with all the key political risks such as physical security of staff, war and civil disturbance, currency inconvertibility, expropriation and compensation, government refusal or inability to enforce laws and breach of contracts. See *Foreign Direct Investment Survey: A study conducted by the MIGA with the assistance of the Deloitte and Touche LLP.* January 2002, posted at http://www.ipanet.net/fdisurvey (visited on 16 July 2004), at 27.

82 Chew, *ibid.*

83 COM (1998) 181 Final, at Section C.1.

84 Lord Brittan (Sir Leon Brittan as he then was): *Opening Address at the EU-China Business Dialogue*, 1998, Beijing.

85 The most relevant books are the *Legal and Policy Issues of the Trade and Economic Relations between China and the EEC* by Hu and *The EC and China* by Xiao. As the titles suggest, both books were focused on general trade relations between China and the European Community and have only very limited discussions on investment matters. Also, both were published in early 1990s and have been largely outdated. See Hu, Yuanxiang, above note 25, particularly pp 131–184. See also Xiao, Zhiyue, *The EC and China* (Butterworths, 1993).

China has been modest. For instance according to the author's Questionnaire, although most EU investors investigated governing national and international laws before they invested in China, less than fifty per cent of them knew that there were bilateral investment treaties, and less than twenty per cent of them knew of the MIGA and ICSID Conventions.[86] Such a lack of legal knowledge has prevented EU investors from taking full advantage of the market opportunities provided by China[87] and probably has contributed to the relatively small size of total EU investment in China compared with EU investments elsewhere.

IV. THIS BOOK: PURPOSES, SCOPE AND RESEARCH METHODS

IV.1 Purposes

Against this background, this research aims to provide a comprehensive investigation of the existing legal regime governing EU-China investment relations focusing on the law of EU investment in China, with a view to exploring the direction of its future development. In particular, this work intends:

a To explore both the structure and the substance of the current legal framework governing EU investment in China;
b To investigate the effectiveness of the current legal framework as experienced by EU investors;
c To discuss the future agendas for improving the legal environment, with a view to proposing a new international legal framework for EU-China investment relations.

IV.2 Structure

The book is divided into five parts. Parts I to III discuss the current legal framework: its structure, substance and effectiveness. The essential questions to be answered in the three parts are: a) what the law governing EU investment in China is; b) whether this law is adequate in protecting and promoting EU investment in China; and c) whether this law is effective in protecting and

[86] See Section 8.1.2 for details.

[87] For example, EU investors have long been hesitant in taking the CJV form of investment, as a result of a lack of knowledge about this form and the Chinese legal and business cultures in general. See eg, Hu, Yuanxiang, above note 25, at 142–143.

promoting EU investment in China. Part IV discusses possible future agendas that might help to improve the legal environment of EU investment in China. Part V complements the preceding part by analysing the legal framework governing investment relations between China and the ten new EU member states, which joined the Union in May 2004.

IV.3 Definitions

It is necessary to define the phrase 'EU investment in China' in order to define the scope of the book. The first term to be clarified is the core concept 'investment', which primarily refers to 'foreign direct investment (FDI)', although it may also cover foreign 'indirect investment' or 'portfolio investment' depending on the context. The distinction between FDI and foreign 'portfolio investment' has been a controversial one.[88] However, it is generally accepted that the exercise of control or management over the investment is the critical factor distinguishing these two forms of investment. For example, Sornarajah maintains that FDI involves the transfer of tangible and intangible assets from one country to another for the purpose of generating wealth in that country 'under the total or partial control of the owner of the assets'.[89] By contrast, foreign portfolio investment is 'a movement of money for the purpose of buying shares in a company formed or functioning in another country' and therefore represents 'a divorce between management and control of the company and share ownership in it'.[90] However, the minimum 'control' required to be classified as FDI is a matter of domestic regulation. Under Chinese law, 'control' seems to be reflected by the investor's shares in the enterprise. For example, Chinese law requires that the foreign share of an Equity Joint Venture, a Stock Company with Foreign Investment, or a Contractual Joint Venture qualified as a legal person, shall be no less than twenty-five per cent.[91] In other words, the foreign investors must control at least a quarter of the whole enterprise in these types of FDI. Obviously if they

[88] Zeng, Huaqun, *International Investment Law* (*Guoji Touzi Faxue*) (Peking University Press, 1999), at 2–5.

[89] Sornarajah, M, *The International Law on Foreign Investment* (Cambridge University Press, 1994), at 4–5.

[90] *Ibid.*

[91] Xu, Congli and Lin, Zhong, *Chinese Foreign Investment Law* (*Zhongguo Waizi Fa*) (Law Publishing House, 1998), at 1. If they do not meet this requirement, they cannot enjoy any of the preferential tax treatment that a regular foreign invested enterprise may do. See Article 2 of the Circular on the Strengthening of the Administration of the Examination, Approval, Registration, Foreign Exchange Issues and Taxation of Foreign-invested Enterprises, jointly issued by the Ministry of Foreign Trade and Economic Co-operation (MOFTEC) (now the Ministry of Commerce, MOFCOM), the State Administration of Tax (SAT), the State Administration of Industry and Commerce (SAIC) and the State Administration of Foreign Exchange (SAFE) on December 30 2002. See also Han, Christopher & Qin, Sidney, 'FIE Status and the 25% Rule', (2001/2002) 15 *China Law & Practice*, at 106.

want to establish a wholly foreign owned enterprise, they take complete control.

Secondly, for the purpose of this book, 'investment in China' means investment in Mainland China, excluding Hong Kong, Macau and Taiwan where the trade and investment regimes are different from those of the mainland.[92] Accordingly, the 'Chinese' or 'China' used in phrases such as 'Chinese FDI law' or 'foreign investment law of China' refers to those of Mainland China unless otherwise indicated. Moreover, 'EU investment in China' refers to investment in China that has originated from the European Union or its member states.[93] However, should a subsidiary of a Chinese company incorporated in the EU be treated as an EU investment? There is no clear answer in Chinese law, though it happens very frequently in practice, as many flagship Chinese companies take this route to get the preferential treatment available only to 'foreign' invested enterprises. In theory, there are basically two tests to identify the nationality of an investor: the test of nationality and the test of 'effective control'.[94] If the former test is adopted, such 'round investment' can be accepted as EU investment. On the contrary, if the latter test is to be adopted, these investments will be excluded from 'EU investment in China'. It could be argued that the latter test might be preferred, as it would root out 'cheating' to obtain preferential treatment and would better satisfy China's intention of attracting 'foreign' investment and technology. In this book, therefore, such 'round investment' by Chinese subsidiaries in the EU is not viewed as EU investment.

Finally, but importantly, 'EU investment in China' refers only to private outward direct investment from the EU. According to Chinese FDI laws and regulations, foreign invested enterprises (FIEs) are enterprises either exclusively funded by foreign companies, enterprises and other 'economic' organisations or individuals, or jointly funded by them and Chinese companies, enterprises or other economic organisations. Hence, 'public' investment such as loans or financial aid from the European Community or its member state governments to China falls outside the scope of this book.

IV.4 Research Methods

This research will primarily employ traditional legal research methods such as review of literature, the examination of legislation and case studies. Questionnaires and interviews have been used to produce empirical evidence of the role and the effectiveness of the law governing EU investment in China.

[92] See above note 2.
[93] See above note 1.
[94] Xu and Lin, above note 91, at 3.

IV.4.1 The Questionnaire

IV.4.1.1 Purposes. The Chinese legal system, the primary legal source governing EU investment in China, is characterised by a significant gap between law and reality.[95] It is therefore of essential importance to ascertain the law as experienced by foreign investors, rather than the law as intended and designed by the government. Since there has been virtually no empirical evidence about the law governing EU investment in China,[96] the author designed a 'Questionnaire on Law and EU Investment in China' to solicit such evidence (See *Appendix I*).

IV.4.1.2 Structure. The Questionnaire[97] consists of three sections which contain twenty-seven questions, in addition to a section on the basic information about the investor being surveyed. The first part of the Questionnaire relates to the general role of law in investment decision-making. It aims to establish whether and to what extend the investors take into account governing domestic and international laws when they make investment decisions. Questions address the relative importance of law in investment decision- making, the investigation of the law before making investments, the specific laws investigated, including particularly the awareness of international agreements at the time of making investments, and the impact of investment incentives on investment decision-making.

The second part of the Questionnaire focuses on the experience of the Chinese legal system in relation to foreign investment, which covers both substantive investment issues and issues concerning the effectiveness of the general legal system. The substantive issues covered are the most important

[95] For an insightful discussion of the gap, see Corne, Peter Howard, *Foreign Investment in China: the Administrative Legal System* (Transnational Publishers, 1997), at 1–50.

[96] Despite the widely accepted importance, empirical evidence on the interrelationship between law and FDI and development remains rare. For instance, a recent report by the UNCTAD Secretariat addressing the issues of effectiveness of FDI laws and policies concluded that specialised studies are required to answer the question, among others, 'What are private sector views on effective FDI policy measures and the role of investment promotion institutions?' Perry also observed that there was 'little empirical evidence' to support that argument that the effectiveness of a legal system should be a determinant of FDI. On the lack of evidence in development studies, an area closely associated with international investment, Joseph Stiglitz, the former chief economist of the World Bank wrote, 'if we believe our policies were helping East Asia, where was the evidence? As a participant in these debates, I got to see the evidence. There was none.' See UNCTAD, *Effectiveness of Foreign Direct Investment Policy Measures* (Note by the UNCTAD Secretariat), TD/B/COM.2/EM.13/2 (22 April 2003). Perry, Amanda, 'Effective Legal System and Foreign Direct Investment: In Search of the Evidence', 49 *International and Comparative Law Quarterly* 779, at 779; J. Stiglitz, 'What I Learned at the World Economic Crisis', (2000) April *The New Republic*.

[97] In the designing of the Questionnaire, references have been made to Perry's questionnaire on laws and law enforcement in Sri Lanka and the '*Survey of the Attitudes of the European Business Community to International Investment Rules*' by TN SOFRES Consulting (hereinafter referred as the SOFRES Survey). See Perry, Amanda J, *Legal Systems as a Determinant of Foreign Direct Investment: The Case of Sri Lanka*, London School of Economics PhD Dissertation, 2000, Appendix 2: Questionnaire; TN SOFRES Consulting (on behalf of the European Commission DG Trade), *Survey of the Attitudes of the European Business Community to International Investment Rules: Final Report*, April 2000.

and controversial ones, such as safety of investment, expropriation and compensation, national treatment, monetary transfer, intellectual property rights protection, political risk insurance, disputes with Chinese governmental entities and performance requirements. The aim of these questions is to explore how frequently these problems have been encountered by EU investors in practice and how they feel about them. The other category of questions relates to effective enforcement of law, including accessibility, stability, consistency, administrative and judicial remedies, political interference with court decisions, and delay.

The third part is designed to determine investors' preferences in a possible investment agreement to which the EU and China would be parties. Specific questions in this category cover the impact of the WTO on the investment environment, the implications of a bilateral or multilateral investment treaty between the two sides and the provisions that the EU investors would prefer to have included.

IV.4.1.3 Feedback. Because contact information of EU investors in China is not publicly available, the survey was carried out among members of chambers of commerce connected with EU investment in China. From April to July 2001, 549 questionnaires were therefore sent to members of the China-Britain Business Council (CBBC), European Union Chamber of Commerce in China (EUCCC) and the British Chamber of Commerce in China (BCCC). Among those, 203 questionnaires were sent by post to CBBC members in Britain, 174 were sent via email to EUCCC members and 162 to BCCC members that are not CBBC members. The questionnaire was sent out in English, accompanied by introductions and a letter from the author explaining the objectives of the survey. Companies which did not respond were contacted either by telephone (for those in Britain and Europe) or by further email (for those in China).

Of the fifty-four responses received, twenty-two were usable.[98] The ten per cent response rate is not low compared with other similar postal questionnaire surveys.[99] The number of usable responses is admittedly rather small, mainly because many of these particular chamber members are not engaged in direct investment in China.[100] Such a low number of usable reponses suggests that one should treat the questionnaire results with caution.

[98] A Swiss response was discarded, as Switzerland is not an EU country even though it is in Europe.

[99] For instance, the mentioned TN SOFRES Consulting Survey, which was supported by the European Commission, had attained only 7% response rate. See TN SOFRES Consulting. See TN SOFRES Consulting, above, note 97, at 1.

[100] Most of the unusable responses stated that they would like to help but this questionnaire did not apply to them as they did not directly invest in China. Some of them are not precisely EU investment but investment from the US or other places like Switzerland. Some expressed that they were not in the best position to answer the questions and would pass the questionnaire to better-positioned persons, which resulted in no further communication. Few companies simply said that they were too busy to participate in this exercise.

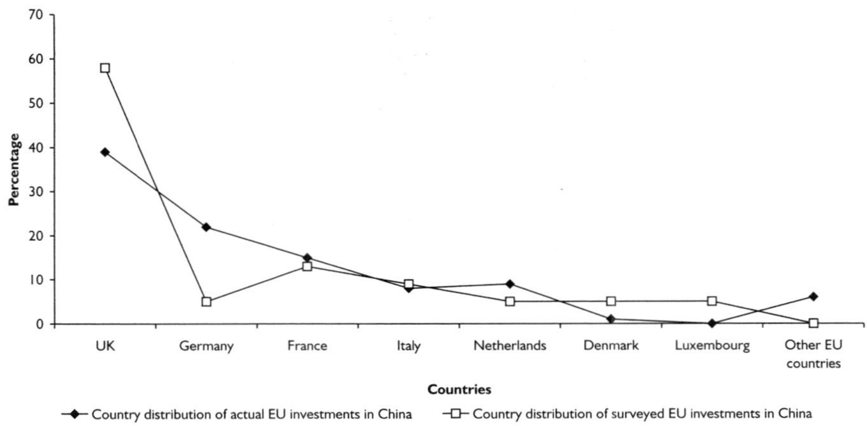

Chart 5: Country distribution between respondent EU investment and actual investment in China (Source: *Yearbook of China Customs Statistics*, 1980–1999)

However, a close look at the responses shows that the representative quality of the twenty-two usable responses should not be underestimated. Firstly, the responses cover seven major EU countries, which account for ninety-five per cent of total EU investment in China, including Britain, Germany, France, Italy, Netherlands, Denmark and Luxembourg.[101]

As *Chart 5* shows, the country distribution of respondent EU investments is generally consistent with that of actual EU investments in China. (*Chart 5: Country Distributions between Respondent EU Investments and Actual EU Investments in China*). Also, these responses include all the three major industries and many different sectors of the economy, including agriculture, manufacturing, infrastructure, energy and service sectors. From *Chart 6*, one can see that the industry distribution of the respondent EU investments actually coincides that of the general foreign investment in China.[102] (*Chart 6: Industry Distributions between Respondent EU Investments and Actual Foreign Investment in China*). Thirdly, investment sizes of the responding companies range from £100,000 to one billion Deutschmarks (approximately £ 357 million).[103] Fourthly, although most of the investment projects are situated in eastern China, some are located in western China (including central China). As can be seen from *Chart 7*, the location distribution of the respondent EU investments is also in conformity with that of actual foreign investment in China. (*Chart 7: Location Distributions between Respondent EU Investments and Actual Foreign Investment in China*). Moreover, while

101 Britain may be relatively 'over-represented' for obvious reasons. However, this is still justifiable as Britain is the top EU investor in China.

102 Unfortunately, the data on EU investment in these industries and sectors is not available.

103 This conversion is in accordance with the conversion rate published in the *Financial Times* on 1 July 2003. See http://mwprices.ft.com/custom/ft-com/currency.asp (visited 1 July 2003).

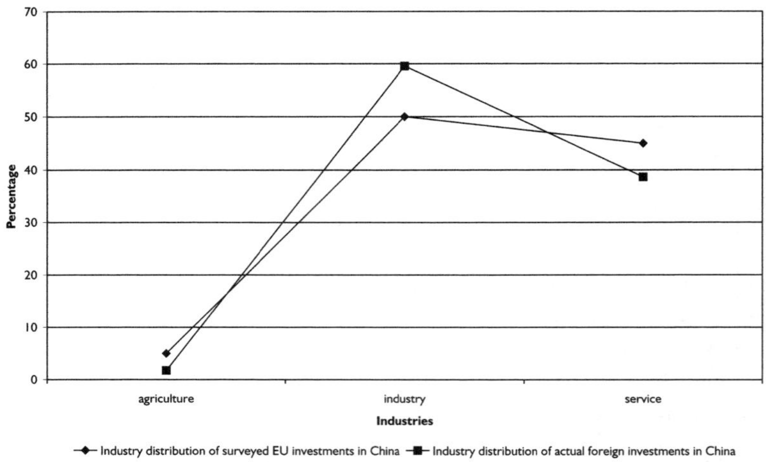

Chart 6: Industry distributions between respondent EU investments and actual foreign investments in China

Source: MOFTEC FDI Statistics: Industry Distribution of Foreign Direct Invesment by 1999, available at: http://www.moftec.gov.cn/moftec_cn/tjsj/wztj/2000)9-22-23.html (visited on 15 July 2002)

most of the EU investments were established in the 1990s, some were set up as early as the 1980s and some as late as 2001 (*Chart 8: Establishing Dates of Respondent Investors*). Finally, other elements, finally, such as investment duration, foreign equity and foreign participation in management, also demonstrate that these responses reflect the general picture of EU investment in China.

The results of the Questionnaire survey are presented mostly in Chapter 8, though some of them, particularly on the substantive aspects, are integrated into other chapters as well.

IV.4.2 The Interviews

The interviews conducted within this research fall into three categories: interviews with government officials, interviews with investment promotion agencies and interviews with private companies. In June 2001, the author went to Brussels and interviewed officials in charge of the Community's investment or China business issues, including two of the major negotiators from the EU in the EU-China WTO talks. Several officials from the Ministry of Foreign Trade and Economic Co-operation (MOFTEC, now the Ministry of Commerce (MOFCOM)) were also interviewed at about the same time by email and via telephone conversations.

Interviews with investment promotion agencies include those with the Chief Executive Officer (CEO) of China-Britain Business Council (CBBC),

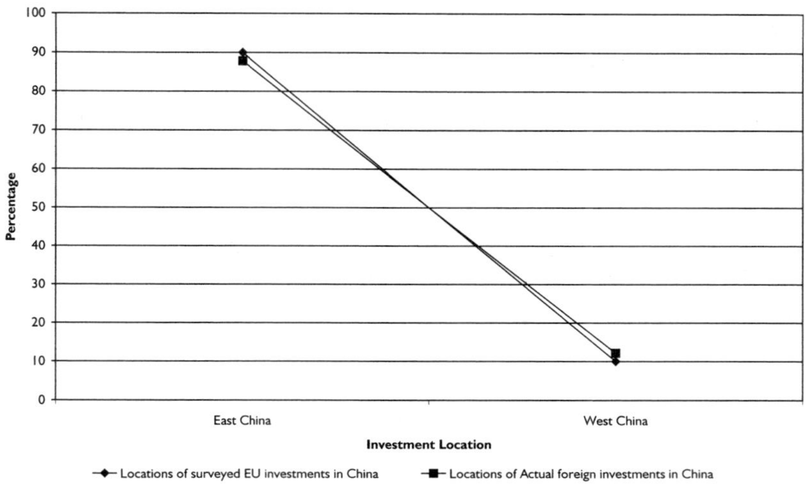

Chart 7: Location distributions between respondent EU investments and actual foreign investments in China

Source: MOFTEC FDI Statistics: Foreign Direct Investment in the East, West and Middle China by 1999, available at: http://www.moftec.gov.cn/moftec_cn/tjsj/wztj/2000_9-22–28.html> (visited on 15 July 2002). Here the FDI in the West and the Middle China are counted together as foreign investment in the Western China.

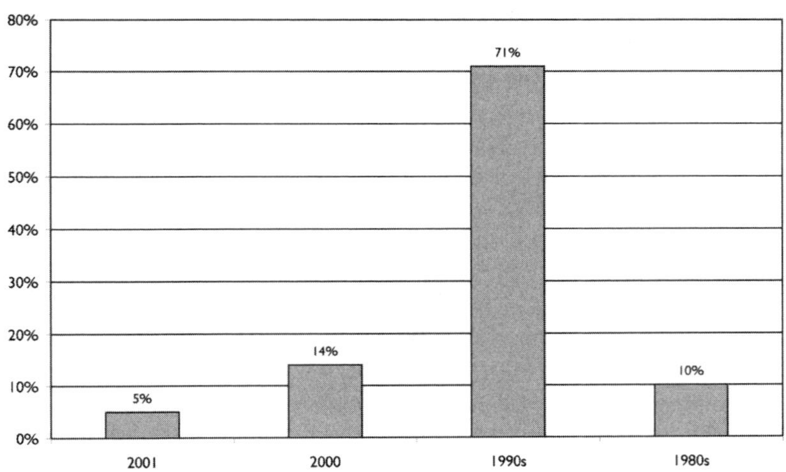

Chart 8: Establishing dates of respondent investors

the Chief Representative of the Representative Office of the China Commission for the Promotion of International Trade (CCPIT) in the EU, China's biggest trade and investment promotion agency, and the China Manager of the Asia Invest, a privately run European Union programme. The author has also followed up Questionnaire responses with interviews with London-based companies which have invested in China.

All interviews were based on semi-structured questions similar to those in the Questionnaire. The questions are slightly adapted to suit the special circumstances of interviewees. In general, the interviews have enabled the author to know the common attitudes of the business communities and government agencies towards the legal environment of EU investment in China, and their concerns and preferences on the subject of its direction in future development. The outcomes of these interviews are integrated into the following chapters, particularly in Chapters 8 and 9.

PART I

The Current Legal Framework of EU Investment in China: The Components

The legal framework governing EU investment in China is composed of EU law, Chinese law and international law as it is applicable to EU investment in China. More specifically, the components of the current legal framework governing EU investment in China include the law of China on inward investment (Chinese law on inward investment), the law of the EU and its member states on outward investment (EU law on outward investment), and international law as applicable to EU investment in China (applicable international law).

Further, it is worthwhile to note that, while all three categories of laws are relevant, the roles that they play are different. As *Chart 9* shows, the current legal framework for EU investment in China may be illustrated as a three-layer globe. The Chinese FDI law constitutes the innermost layer, or the core, as it looks after the whole lifecycle of foreign investments in China and prescribes detailed conditions for every aspect of these daily operations, such as taxation, labour, land use, foreign exchange, material supply and domestic or internationals sales. In contrast, the law of the EU and its member states on outward investment may be regarded as the outer layer as it

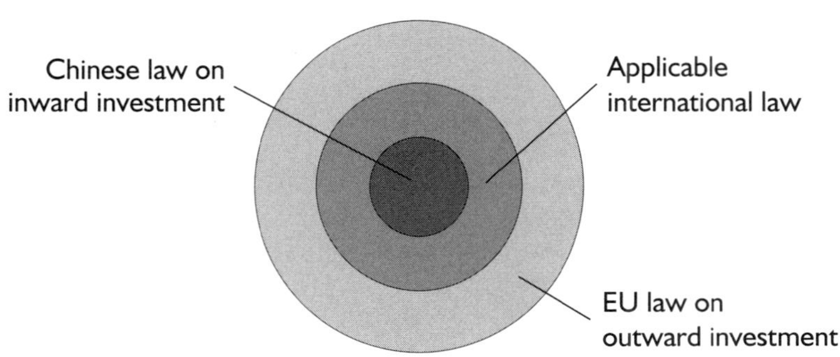

Chart 9: The Legal Framework Governing EU Investment in China

mostly relates to investment promotion. Its influence on EU investment in China is therefore indirect and less significant. In the middle, there are principles and rules of applicable international law, which concentrate on the protection of EU investment in China.

This Part, therefore, will identify these three categories of laws and analyse them from a structural point of view. It will thereby, provide not only an overview of the structure and components of the legal framework that governs EU investment in China, but will also try to discuss whether this legal framework is structurally complete and coherent and therefore sufficient to protect and promote EU investment in China.

1

Chinese Law on Inward Investment

To study the law of EU investment in China, one must first investigate the Chinese law on inward investment, or Chinese FDI law. In practice, it is Chinese law that lays down conditions for the entry and operation of EU investment in China. It therefore constitutes the most important source of law governing foreign and EU investment in China. This has been confirmed by the survey conducted by the author, which shows that approximately forty percent of EU investors have investigated the Chinese legal system only, without studying applicable international agreements. This Chapter thus intends to identify and analyse the structure and components of the Chinese FDI legal system. It first reviews the evolution of the law and policy on FDI in China, followed by an exploration of the structure and features of the Chinese FDI legal system. It then elaborates the major forms of FDI in China. Finally, it examines and assesses China's recent amendment to its major FDI laws and proposes that China should further reform its FDI legal system as a whole.

1.1 THE 'OPENING-UP' POLICY AND FOREIGN INVESTMENT LAW MAKING IN CHINA

As mentioned in the Introduction, the resumption of EU investment in China was the result of the 'Opening up' policy adopted by Deng Xiaoping in the late 1970s. However, China's opening-up to the world has been a gradual process, starting from certain eastern coastal cities and then moving to the inland areas and eventually the huge western areas. At the beginning, in the early 1980s, Special Economic Zones (SEZs)—Shenzhen, Zhuhai, Shantou in Guandong Province and Xiamen in Fujian Province—were created as 'experimental areas' and 'windows' for China's new economic reform and 'Opening up' policy, particularly aimed at attracting foreign investment. Later, in 1984, the Chinese Government decided to open 14 coastal cities (Coastal Open Cities—COCs) to foreign investment.[1] Since 1984, China has established numerous Economic and Technological Development Zones (ETDZs) to

[1] These cities include Dalian, Qingdao, Tianjing, Yantai, Qinghuadao, Lianyungang, Nantong, Shanghai, Ningbo, Wenzhou, Fuzhou, Guangzhou, Zhanjiang and Beihai.

foster foreign-oriented economy and technology development.[2] The open areas stretched further in 1985 with the opening of the three coastal open economic regions (COERs), namely the Yangtze River Delta, the Zhujiang River Delta and the South Fujian (Xiamen-Zhangzhou-Quanzhou) Delta[3] and the entirety of Hainan Island, the largest SEZ.[4] In early 1990, Shanghai Pudong New Area was opened to attract foreign capital and technology to revive the glory and prosperity of the city's past[5]. In 1992, approval was given to open five more cities along the Yangtze River, 18 provincial capital cities, and 13 border towns in China's northeast, northwest and southwest regions.[6] Moreover, in the 1990s, other special economic areas, such as High and New Technology Industries Development Zones (HNTIDZs), Bonded Areas (BAs), National Tourist and Vacation Zones (NTVZs), Border Economic Co-operation Zones (BECZs) and Export Processing Zones (EPZs) were also established.[7] Thus an all-round, multi-level opening up took shape in China, with SEZs, COCs and COERs in the east, Yangtze River-side open regions crossing the country from the east to the west headed by Shanghai Pudong New Area, BECZs along the north and western borders, and with inland regions centred around provincial capitals. At the turn of the century, China started to counterbalance the inequality of wealth and prosperity between the coastal East and the inland West of China and launched a 'Go West' campaign to encourage investment in western China.[8]

When foreign investors were first allowed to participate in the Chinese economy in the late 1970s, equity joint venture (EJV)[9] was the only form of investment available. In an attempt to attract foreign investment to the exploitation of petroleum resources, the Chinese government adopted the Regulations on the Exploitation of Offshore Petroleum Resources in Co-operation with Foreign Enterprises (REOFF) in 1982. Four years later, the Wholly Foreign Owned Enterprises Law (WFEL) was adopted to embrace wholly foreign-funded enterprises. In 1988, China promulgated the long-discussed Chinese-Foreign Contractual Joint Ventures Law (CJVL), an alternative to the EJV which allows more flexibility.[10] Exploitation of on-shore petroleum resources was also permitted in 1993, when the Regulations on Exploitation of Onshore Petroleum Resources in Co-operation with Foreign

[2] Wang, Yongjun, *Investment in China: a question and answer guide on how to do business* (CITIC Publication House, 1997), at 31.

[3] Hu, Yuanxiang, *Legal and Policy Issues of the Trade and Economic Relations between China and the EEC* (Kluwer, 1991), at 133.

[4] Wang, above note 2, at 18.

[5] *Ibid*, at 34.

[6] *Ibid*, at 18.

[7] For details of the establishment of these zones and regions, see Wang, above note 2, at 27–43.

[8] See Liu, Dongkai, 'China Encourages Foreign Investors to Participate in the Development of the West', (2001) 21 Dec *People's Daily* (overseas edition), at 1.

[9] For further information about EJV and other major forms of foreign investment in China, see Section 1.3.1.

[10] See Section 1.3.2 for further details.

Enterprises (REON) were adopted. By then, the core of the Chinese FDI legal system, including laws and regulations of all the major forms of FDI in China, had been formally established.

Apart from these basic laws and regulations, China has also adopted laws and regulations, from the revised Constitution, to local regulations and rules. In 1982, China modified the Constitution to 'permit foreign enterprises, other foreign economic organisations and individual foreigners to invest in China and enter into various forms of economic co-operation with Chinese economic organisations'.[11] Now there are thousands of laws and regulations relating to FDI or foreign invested enterprises (FIEs) passed by central and local governments.[12] These laws and regulations combined constitute the general FDI law system in China.[13]

1.2 THE CURRENT CHINESE FOREIGN INVESTMENT LAW SYSTEM

1.2.1 Composition of the Current Chinese Foreign Investment Law System

The Chinese foreign investment law system is normally divided into three levels of law: Constitutional provisions, national laws and regulations and sub-national regulations.[14]

1.2.1.1 Constitutional provisions

As mentioned above, foreign investment was not permitted in the Chinese Constitution until 1982, when it was amended.[15] In the 'Preamble', the

[11] Article 18, paragraph 1, the *Constitution of the People's Republic of China*.

[12] CCH's *China Law for Foreign Business* (loose-leaf, Vol. 1–9) contains several thousand central and local laws and regulations on foreign-related investment, taxation, customs, intellectual property rights, labour, banking, insurance, import and export, etc. See WANG, Kui Hua, *Chinese Commercial Law* (Oxford University Press, 2000), at 83 and note 2.

[13] Here, it means merely the law system for inward FDI. There are also some regulations on outward investment, which are not discussed here.

[14] Yao, Meizhen, *Textbook on Foreign Invested Enterprises Law* (in Chinese) (Law Press, 1989), at 26–34. See also Xu, Congli and Lin, Zhong, *Chinese Foreign Investment Law* (*Zhongguo Waizi Fa*) (Law Publishing House, 1998), at 4–7.

[15] In a 1981 publication, Wan had argued that China's foreign investment laws were in conflict with the public (state) ownership and the planned economy principles established in the then Constitution. Now the Constitution has allowed other forms of ownership to play significant roles in China's economy whilst maintaining the dominant position of public (state) ownership. Moreover, since 1993, the Constitution has established that 'a Socialist Market Economy' is the nature of China's economic system. See Wan, Timothy Haosen, 'A Comparative Study of Foreign Investment Laws in Taiwan and China', (1981) *Western California International Law Journal*, as cited in Zhang, Xiangyu, 'China's Foreign Investment Law System', (1985) *5 Social Sciences in China*, at 1.

amended Constitution announces that China will develop its economic, diplomatic and cultural exchanges with other countries. A specific provision on FIE is included in Article 18, which stipulates that the PRC permits foreign organisations and individuals to invest in China and enter into co-operation with Chinese economic organisations.[16] The rights and benefits of all foreign enterprises and Chinese-foreign joint ventures in the Chinese territory are protected by the law of China.[17] Obviously these constitutional provisions are fairly brief. Nevertheless they are an assurance for foreign investors, as the protection of FIEs has been specifically addressed in the basic law of the State.[18] Other constitutional laws also contain provisions related to FIEs. For instance, the Law of Legislation maintains that the expropriation of non-state-owned properties must be laid down in the form of 'Law' (*Falu*),[19] which means it must be formulated by the National People's Congress or its Standing Committee.[20]

1.2.1.2 National Laws and Regulations

National laws and regulations on FIEs come under the Constitution. These laws and regulations comprise a substantial part of the FIE law system and are in the form of Laws (*Falu*), Administrative Regulations (*Xingzhen Fagui*) or Departmental Rules (*Bumen Guizhang*). They may be classified into two general categories: FIE-specific laws and FIE-related laws.[21]

FIE-specific laws are laws specifically addressing FIE issues. There are two sub-categories within FIE-specific laws: basic FIE laws and supplementary FIE laws. To date, China has not had a unified law for all forms of foreign investment. Instead there are a few basic laws on different forms of FIEs, which may be called 'basic FIE laws'. The core of these laws and regulations is EJVL, CJVL and WFEL and their respective implementing regulations.[22] There are, in addition, regulations on the joint exploitation of onshore and offshore petroleum resources[23] and some other individual regulations on what the Chinese government calls 'new forms of foreign investment' including Build-Operate-Transfer (BOT) investment, holding companies with

[16] Article 18 paragraph 1, the *Constitution of the People's Republic of China*.

[17] At the same time, they are required to abide by the law of China. Article 18 paragraph 2, the *Constitution of the People's Republic of China*.

[18] Yao, Meizhen, *Textbook on Foreign Invested Enterprises Law* (in Chinese) (Law Press, 1989), at 27.

[19] Article 8, the *Law of Legislation*, passed on 15 March 2000 by the National People's Congress.

[20] Article 7, the *Law of Legislation*.

[21] Xu and Lin, above note 14, at 6–7.

[22] Indeed, since these laws deal with the most important aspects of the three basic forms of FIEs, they can be regarded as 'Chinese FDI laws' in a narrow sense.

[23] Including *Regulations on the Exploitation of Offshore Petroleum Resources in Co-operation with Foreign Enterprises* (REOFF), *Regulations on the Exploitation of Onshore Petroleum Resources in Co-operation with Foreign Enterprises* (REON).

foreign investment (HCFI), stock companies with foreign investment (SCFI) and merger and acquisition (M&A).[24]

There are many FIE-specific laws to supplement these basic FIE laws and regulations. These laws cover such aspects as the entry, registration, operation, employment, and tax of FIEs in China.[25] Among them, the 2002 Guidance on the Direction of Foreign Investment (the Investment Guidance) and its attached Guiding Catalogue of Industries for Foreign Investment (Guiding Catalogue), the 1991 Foreign Invested Enterprises and Foreign Enterprises Income Tax Law (FIEs and FEs Income Tax Law) and its Implementing Regulations, 1986 State Council Provisions for Encouraging Foreign Investment (hereinafter 'PEFI')[26] and the 1999 Opinions on Further Encouraging Foreign Investment are of the most importance.[27]

Apart from FIE-specific laws, national FDI law also includes many national laws and regulations that are not dedicated to, but rather related to, FIE matters. Some of them are foreign-specific ones, such as the 1995 Foreign Trade Law, 2001 Regulations on Technology Import and Export, 1996 Rules for the Administration of Employment of Foreigners in China, and 1996 Regulations on Foreign Exchange Administration (RFEA). The others are of general application (ie, not specially dealing with foreign relations), including the 1986 General Principles of Civil Law (GPCL), the 1993 Company Law, the 1999 Contract Law, the 1995 Insurance Law, the 1995 Guarantee Law, the 1995 Negotiable Instruments Law, the 1992 Maritime Law, the 1987 Customs Law, the 1989 Import and Export Commodities Inspection Law and its implementing regulations, the 1985 Regulations on Import and Export Duties, and intellectual property rights laws, such as the 2000 Patent Law, the 2001 Copyrights Law and the 2001 Trademark Law.[28]

1.2.1.3 Sub-National Regulations

In China, sub-national authorities, including People's Congresses and their Standing Committees of Provinces, Special Economic Zones (SEZ) and Minority Autonomous Areas (MAAs),[29] can promulgate Provincial Regula-

[24] For further information on these new forms of investment, see Section 1.3.5.

[25] Xu and Lin, above note 14, at 6–7.

[26] It is sometimes called the '21 Articles' as it has 21 articles.

[27] Most of them are reprinted in the *Handbook of Foreign Economic Law* (in both Chinese and English) (edited by the State council), Volumes 1 and 2 (Law Press, 1997). An updated publication is *The New Compilation of Laws, Regulations and Ministerial Rules on Foreign Trade and Economic Co-operation of the People's Republic of China* (hereinafter "*the New Compilation*"), edited by the Ministry of Foreign Trade and Economic Co-operation (now the Ministry of Commerce, the MOFCOM), in Chinese (Law Press, 2002). For a web-based source, see Invest in China (a MOFCOM website): *Laws and Regulations*, posted at http://www.fdi.gov.cn/ltlawpackage/index.jsp?app=1&language=en (visited on 15 July 2003).

[28] For a comprehensive list of these laws and regulations, see Yao, above note 18, at 27–33. For an updated web-based list of all these laws and regulations, see Invest in China (a MOFCOM website): Laws and Regulations, above note 26.

[29] MAAs exist at different levels, from provincial to township. As long as there is a substantial

tions (*Difangxing Fagui*), SEZ Regulations or MAA Regulations.[30] Provincial governments, in turn, can promulgate Provincial Governmental Rules (*Difangxing Xingzhen Guizhang*).[31] Since economic construction is the central function of local governments and attracting FDI is one of the most important components of that function, a large proportion of these regulations and rules apply to FIEs. They cover business registration, labour management, border management, land management, technology transfer, tax, foreign exchange, loan, banking, and so on.[32] Among them, a considerable number of regulations and rules target FIEs in special economic areas within their localities, including SEZs, MAAs, border economic co-operation regions, open coastal cities, economic and technical development zones and other areas where special regimes for tariff, taxes and regulations are established.[33]

In theory, these sub-national regulations and rules should be in conformity with national Laws and Administrative Regulations.[34] However, because sub-national governments compete to attract FDI to their localities, it is not unusual for them to lay down regulations or rules which in fact change the national laws and policies and offer further investment incentives, in the areas of fiscal, financial and budgetary activities.[35] This was a cause for concern in the course of China's WTO accession negotiations.[36] Some WTO members believed that the continued presence of multiple trade instruments by different levels of government in China resulted in a lessening of the security and predictability of access to the Chinese market.[37] In response, the Chinese Representative stated that sub-national governments had no autonomous authority over issues of trade policy in relation to the 1994 Agreement Establishing the World Trade Organisation (the WTO Agreement) and the Draft Protocol. He also confirmed that China would, in a timely manner, annul local regulations, government rules and other local measures inconsistent with China's obligations.[38] Accordingly, actions have been taken by

or dominant ethnic minority group(s) in a specific area there can be a MAA as approved by the central or local government. However, only Provincial MAAs' Peoples' Congresses and Governments have the authority to lay down MAA Regulations while other levels of MAAs may make rules of their MAAs according to the law. Article 66, the *Law of Legislation*.

[30] For details, see Chapter 4 of the *Law of Legislation*.

[31] *Ibid.*

[32] Yao, above note 18, at 34.

[33] For details of Chinese law on those special economic areas, see Li, Xueling (ed), *The Laws of Special Economic Areas* (in Chinese) (Law Press, 1996).

[34] For instance, Article 63 of the *Law of Legislation* stipulates that Provincial Regulations should not be in violation of the Constitution, Laws or Administrative Regulations. See Article 63, the *Law of Legislation*.

[35] See eg Zhang, Chongming, 'Do Not 'Scare off' Foreign Investors with Incentives', (2001) 20 Jan *People's Daily* (overseas edition), at 8. See also the World Trade Organisation Working Party on the Accession of China: *Report of the Working Party on the Accession of China* (hereinafter "*Working Party Report*"), WT/ACC/CHN/49 (1 October 2001), para. 66–70.

[36] See *Working Party Report*, above note 35, para. 66–70.

[37] *Ibid.*

[38] *Ibid.*

central and local government to review relevant local regulations and bring them into conformity with China's WTO commitments.[39]

1.2.2 The Features of the Current Chinese Foreign Investment Law System

The current Chinese FDI law system has three major features: 'foreign', 'enterprise'-oriented and unsystematic.

In the first place, the current Chinese FDI law system has a special set of norms for 'foreign' investment, which is, by and large, separated from the legal system governing 'domestic' investment. Even though there has been a trend to merge the two investment regimes, the differences between them are still significant. For example, the most important laws governing FIEs are EJVL, CJVL and WFEL, while the basic laws governing domestic funded enterprises are the 1988 Whole People-Owned Industrial Enterprises Law, the 1996 Township Enterprises Law and the 1999 Private Enterprises Law. In an effort to consolidate these laws and set up a uniform corporate system, China promulgated the Company Law in 1993, followed by the Partnership Law in 1996. The Company Law applies to all limited liability companies and stock companies incorporated in China, including foreign invested limited liability companies, so that it covers virtually all of the existing FIEs.[40] However, it follows that if the EJVL, CJVL or WFEL have different provisions, these provisions shall control.[41] The interpretations of this provision have been so controversial that in 1998 a special conference was held to discuss it in depth.[42] Some scholars argued that this provision had in fact enabled FIEs to choose the method of incorporation that suited them best, according to the EJVL, CJVL or WFEL, or with Company Law.[43] However, other scholars believed that FIE laws are '*lex speciali*', in relation to Company Law and accordingly that the principle of '*lex speciali derogate generalis*' shall apply.[44]

In practice, since FIE laws were published (with EJVL published as early as 1979) and implemented much earlier than Company Law, FIEs have nearly all followed the FIE laws when incorporating, rather than Company Law. In

[39] It is reported that, since 1999, MOFTEC (now MOFCOM) has set up a working group to sort out, amend and modify foreign related economic laws and regulations. So far, it has finished the sorting out of related national laws and regulations and has started to examine local regulations and measures. See Zhang, Xiangsong, and Liu, Shiping, 'Our Country is Urgently Sorting out Departmental Rules and Judicial Interpretations', (2001) 11 Dec *People's Daily* (overseas edition), at 1.

[40] Article 18, *Company Law*, promulgated on 29 December 1993 by the National People's Congress.

[41] *Ibid.*

[42] Yang, Zhongxiao, 'Report of the Conference on "How to Apply Company Law to Joint Ventures"', (1998) 8 *Legal Science* (Faxue).

[43] *Ibid*, at 63–64.

[44] See eg, Xu, Congli, 'From China-Foreign Joint Venture Enterprises to China-Foreign Joint Capital Companies: the multiplication of the internal organization structure system', (2000) 5 *Tribune of Political Science and Law* (Zhengfa Luntan), at 135.

1995, MOFTEC (now MOFCOM) published the Provisional Regulations on the Establishment of Stock Companies with Foreign Investment (PRSF), which made it possible for foreign investors to adopt the form of stock company, in accordance with Company Law. Nevertheless, under the current system, most FIEs are still incorporated according to their respective FIE Laws. In other words, in spite of the Company Law, the special 'foreign' law nature of FIE laws in China still remains unchanged.

Secondly, the current Chinese FDI legal system is a set of 'enterprise' or company-oriented laws and regulations. As mentioned above, there is no unified FDI law in China at the moment and all the basic FDI laws and regulations are laws of certain forms of FIEs.[45] As a result, most of these laws and regulations deal with issues of corporate governance, rather than with government management and supervision of foreign investment. In other words, they are more like FIE laws than FDI laws. The adoption of Company Law did not help in this sense, as it only applies to stock companies with foreign investment, while most FIEs are still being incorporated under their respective FIE laws and regulations even though they are in the form of 'Limited Liability Companies (LLCs)'. As a result, there are repetitions among these major laws and regulations on corporate governance, as shown below.

Finally, the current Chinese FDI legal system is unsystematic. Indeed, there are many repetitions, loopholes and contradictions. On the one hand, since the three basic laws and their implementing regulations are different rules governing, in parallel, more or less similar FIEs, they are bound to be similar in both structure and content. These similarities and repetitions are more common between the EJVL and CJVL, as they are closer in nature. For instance, the three basic laws have the same provisions on the purposes of the laws and the protection of FDI. In legal form they are all limited liability companies if they satisfy the basic legal requirements. In the approval mechanism, the approval authority, approval term, approval competence and procedure and the required documentation are all the same. In short, within the three laws and their implementing regulations, identical provisions far outnumber differing ones.[46] On aspects such as establishment, organisation and management, registered capital and enterprise conducts, there are numerous repeated provisions.[47] On the other hand, there are also many legal loopholes and contradictions in the current FDI legal system. For example, there is no provision in any of the three laws and their implementing regulations defining the general legal treatment which will be accorded to foreign investors and their investments. On investment protection, while there are provisions

[45] For a discussion of the relationship between a unified FDI law and a set of varied FIE laws, see Section 1.5.1.

[46] Zhang, Mei, 'The Unification of Foreign Invested Enterprises', in *Legal Aspects of Doing Business in China* (*zhongguo touzi falu zhinan*), Vol. 1 (Law Press, 1999), at 70–74.

[47] *Ibid.*

on nationalisation and compensation in the EJVL and WFEL, there is no such rule in the CJVL, or in its implementing regulations. Moreover, in practice, there are a number of legal problems with which the current laws have not effectively dealt.[48] For instance, in a Sino-foreign joint venture company, if the directors of one partner do not turn up to the Board of Directors meeting, the Board may not be able to make any effective decision as it could not meet the legally required number of attending directors,[49] which obviously significantly jeopardises the operation of the company.[50] These facts show that the Chinese FDI law system is still immature and needs to be consolidated and further reformed. This will be further discussed in Section 1.5.

1.3 THE PRINCIPAL FORMS OF INVESTMENT

Under such an 'enterprise'-oriented law system, foreign investors have many forms of investment from which to choose. They may choose traditional forms such as Equity Joint Venture (EJV), Contractual Joint Venture (CJV) or Wholly Foreign Owned Enterprise (WFE) and Joint Exploitation (JE). Alternatively, they may select a new form such as SCFI, HCFI, BOT and M&A. Other possible choices include foreign invested financial institutions, Transfer-Operate-Transfer (TOT) investment, international leasing, compensation trade and export processing and assembly.[51] In addition, foreign investors may purchase shares (B Share) of companies listed in China's stock exchanges.[52] Here, only the traditional and the major new forms of foreign investment are discussed.

1.3.1 Equity Joint Venture (EJV)

Equity Joint Venture (EJV) is a joint venture set up by foreign companies, enterprises, other economic organisations or individuals in conjunction with Chinese companies, enterprises and other economic organisations, within the territory of China. The joint venture agreement, a contract between the joint investors and the articles of association of the joint venture, which are subject to approval by the government, are the legal basis of the venture that stipulate

[48] *Ibid.*
[49] Sun, Zhangli, 'Several Legal Issues Concerning the Board of Directors of the Foreign Invested Enterprises', (2001) *Law Review* (Faxue Pinglum), at 123.
[50] Indeed, the fundamental differences in the perceptions entertained by Chinese and foreign parties to a joint venture have resulted in the general failure of some JV projects. Ye, Ariel L. and Valentine, Stuart, 'More Haste, Less Speed: The Secret to Investing in China', (2000) January *International Financial Law Review*, at 17–19.
[51] For further information, see China's semi-official China Association of Enterprise with Foreign Investment (CAEFI), *Forms of Foreign Investment*, posted at http://www.etisu.com.cn/invest/tzzn/tzbscx-touzifs.htm (visited on 28 June 2003).
[52] *Ibid.*

the rights and obligations of the parties. An EJV takes the legal form of Limited Liability Company (LLC). Each party can contribute capital in cash, in kind, industrial property rights, and so on. There is no upper ceiling on the proportion of foreign investment, but there is a minimum capital contribution requirement consisting of twenty five percent of the registered capital. Accordingly, the parties share the profits, risks and losses in proportion to their respective contributions to the registered capital. The Board of Directors, the Chairman of which may be Chinese or foreign, shall decide all the major policies in the venture, while day to day operations are under the charge of its general manager or the president. In short, the features of an EJV are joint contribution of investment, joint management, and sharing risks, profits and losses in proportion to capital contributions.

An EJV is probably the safest form for foreign investors because of its legal features such as the status of a legal person, limited liability, formal management structure and sharing of profits, risks and losses with a Chinese partner. Understandably, this form has been adopted by most EU investors who are not very familiar with the Chinese market[53] and who usually invest a large amount of money, as well as advanced technologies.[54]

1.3.2 Contractual Joint Venture (CJV)

Contractual Joint Venture (CJV), sometimes called Co-operative Joint Venture, is another form of joint venture in China which is much more flexible than an equity joint venture.[55] Its flexibility can be seen in the following aspects.[56] Firstly, although it is also established jointly by a Chinese partner and a foreign partner by contributing cash, materials, rights to use sites, industrial property, know-how or other kinds of investment, their contributions are not necessarily priced and calculated into shares.[57] Consequently, the partners do not have to share the profits, risks and losses in exact proportion to their contributions as in an equity joint venture, but must agree on a way of sharing in their joint venture contract.[58] Secondly, there is no minimum or maximum requirement of foreign investment proportion. Also, if it

[53] A survey of foreign investment contracts shows that most European companies invested as EJVs, more investors from Hong Kong and Macao took the CJV form, while only a small number of investors from the US, Hong Kong and Japan adopted the form of WFE. See Hu, Yuanxiang, note 4, at 142.

[54] Investment projects from the EU tend to be capital intensified projects and are often accompanied by the transfer of technologies. See Qiu, Yuanlun, 'The EU's China Policy and Sino-EU Trade and Economic Relations,' (1999) 8 *World Economy* (*Shijie Jingji*), at 7.

[55] See Mo, Lingxia, 'The Legal Nature and Features of the Chinese-Foreign CJVs', (2000) 3 *Tribune of Political Science and Law* (*Zhengfa Luntan*), at 36–38.

[56] Mo, Lingxia, *ibid*.

[57] Articles 2 & 8, the CJVL.

[58] *Ibid*, Art. 22.

is qualified to be a judicial person, it may take the form of a limited liability company. Otherwise it could carry out the co-operation on an individual basis, with unlimited liability.[59] Moreover, the decision-making body of the joint venture may be a joint management committee, or a Board of Directors with the Chairman being a Chinese or foreign partner.[60] Alternatively, the joint venturers might entrust the joint venture to be managed by a third party.[61] Finally, if the parties agree in their joint venture contract that upon the expiration of the venture's operation period all the fixed assets of the venture shall belong to the Chinese party, the foreign investor could recover their investment in advance, by means of increasing the foreign party's proportion of the distribution of earnings, or recovering investment prior to the payment of income tax, or by other means as approved by the financial and tax authorities.[62] In most CJV projects, the foreign investor contributes all or most of the capital whilst the Chinese counterpart provides land, factory, other equipment and facilities and, in some cases, certain quantities of capital.[63]

As explained above, European investors prefer EJVs to CJVs. Initially, the CJV form has been favoured by overseas Chinese investors from Hong Kong, Macao and other nearby regions, because they are familiar with the legal and business cultures of China and may therefore take full advantage of the flexibility available.[64] However, since the adoption of the Implementation Regulations of the CJVL, which tightened up the requirements, the proportion of CJVs in all FIEs in China has declined.[65]

1.3.3 Wholly Foreign Owned Enterprise (WFE)

A wholly foreign invested enterprise (WFE) is an enterprise established in China with capital solely invested by one or more foreigners, excluding branches or offices which foreign enterprises or other organisations have in

[59] *Ibid*, Art. 2.

[60] *Ibid*, Art. 12.

[61] *Ibid*.

[62] *Ibid*, Art 22. See also Art 44, the Chinese-Foreign Contractual Joint Ventures Law Implementation Regulations.

[63] Ministry of Foreign Trade and Economic Co-operation (MOFTEC) (now Ministry of Commerce, MOFCOM), *China's Attracting Foreign Investment Policy*, posted at http://www.moftec.gov.cn/moftec_en/zcjs/wzgl/wzgl_01_en.html (visited on 22 February 2002), at 1.

[64] CJVs first emerged in Fujian and Guangdong Provinces and then spread over the whole country. The two provinces are the home provinces of most overseas Chinese. See Yao, Meizhen, above note 18, at 55–6; Zeng, Huaqun, *International Investment Law* (*Guoji Touzi Faxue*) (Peking University Press, 1999), at 259.

[65] Xu and Lin, above note 14, at 78. It is notable that by the mid-1980s, CJVs had made near 59.5% of total FIEs in China and 71.9 % of FIEs in Guandong Province, the province where most FIEs were located. See Mo, Lingxia, above note 55, at 37. For details on CJVs, see Liu, Fengming etc, *Introduction to Chinese-Foreign Contractual Joint Ventures Law* (in Chinese) (Wuhan University Press, 1992); Chu Baotai and Dong Huiyuan, *Chinese-Foreign Contractual Joint Ventures Law* (in Chinese) (Zhongxin Press, 1992).

China.[66] A wholly foreign invested enterprise must be beneficial to the development of the Chinese Economy and be able to achieve remarkable economic results.[67] As a result of the recent amendment to the WFEL, WFEs are no longer required to adopt advanced technology and equipment[68] or market all or most of their products outside China,[69] although they are still encouraged to do so. Furthermore, WFEs are excluded or restricted in certain fields, as stipulated in the Investment Guidance[70] and the Guiding Catalogues.

As long as these sometimes stringent conditions are met, a WFE takes a shorter time to get approval.[71] Once a WFE is approved and established, it can enjoy the autonomy of management according to its approved Articles of Association, free from any intervention.[72] As foreign investors are becoming familiar with the Chinese investment environment, more and more of them adopt WFE as the vehicle to make investments.[73] For instance, in the first 8 months in 2002, there were 14,024 WFEs established in China, which accounted for sixty-five percent of total FIEs established in that period and which marked a six percent increase as compared with the same period of 2001.[74]

1.3.4 Joint Exploitation (JE)

Joint exploitation (JE) includes joint exploitations of either onshore or offshore petroleum resources. In order to accelerate the development of the petroleum industry, the Chinese government allows foreign companies to invest in the joint exploitation of both onshore and offshore petroleum resources. The Chinese partners that have the exclusive rights in this field are the state-owned China National Offshore Oil Company, China National Petroleum and Natural Gas Group Corporation and the China Petroleum Chemical Group Corporation[75] (hereinafter referred to collectively as Chi-

[66] Art 2, the *WFEL*.

[67] *Ibid*, Art 3.

[68] According to Article 3 of the previous *Wholly Foreign Owned Enterprises Law Implementing Regulations*, this means to 'conserve energy and raw materials, and realise the upgrading of products and the replacement of old products with new ones, or the replacement of similar imports'.

[69] It means that its annual output value of export products accounts for more than 50% of its annual output value of all products, and thereby realising the balance between revenues and expenditures in foreign exchange or with a surplus. *Ibid*.

[70] Art 8, *Investment Guidance*.

[71] It is reported that setting up a WFE will need 6–9 months only, while it will take at least 18–24 months to establish a JV. Xu and Lin, above note 14, at 81.

[72] Art 11, the *WFEL*.

[73] Xu and Lin, above note 14, at 81.

[74] Zhang, Yi, 'China Attracted 34.4 Billion US Dollars of Realised Foreign Investment in the First 8 Months', (2002) 14 Sept People's Daily (overseas edition), at 1.

[75] The former is in charge of the exploitation of offshore oil resources while the latter two are in charge of onshore oil resources. The last one was added to the list on 23 September 2001, when the REON was revised.

nese Oil and Petroleum Companies). A contract of joint exploitation may be signed if the Chinese Oil and Petroleum Companies accept the offer made by a foreign company. According to the two regulations, unless otherwise specified by the Chinese authority or in the contract, the foreign contractors are the sole investors and undertake all the commercial risks at the stage of exploration.[76] After a commercial oil or gas field is discovered, the Chinese Oil and Petroleum Companies and the foreign partner invest jointly for the operation development, and the foreign company shall be responsible for the development operation and production operation until the Chinese Oil and Petroleum Companies takes over the production operation.[77] The foreign company may recover its investment and expenses and attain profits from the petroleum produced.[78] Therefore, they do not form a new economic entity. Owing to the huge investment and risk, normally only large companies or company consortia have the ability to make this kind of investment. Hence, compared with the aforementioned three forms it makes up a rather small proportion of total FIEs in China.[79]

1.3.5 New Forms of Foreign Investment

1.3.5.1 Build-Operate-Transfer (BOT)

Build-Operate-Transfer (BOT)[80] is a new form of investment in China, which is used mostly in the infrastructure sectors, such as energy, transport, communication and environment. For example, it is reported that the first BOT water project has begun to provide water in Chengdu Municipality.[81] At present, the governing regulations on BOT investment in China are the 1995 MOFCOM (then MOFTEC) Notice on Some Issues about Utilising Foreign Investment in the Form of BOT (the MOFCOM BOT Notice) and the 1995 Notice on Issues about Approval Procedures of Foreign Invested Concession Projects jointly promulgated by the State Planning Commission, the Ministry of Electricity and the Ministry of Transportation (the Joint BOT Notice).

[76] See Art 7 of the *REOFF*, and Art 13 of the *REON*.

[77] *Ibid.*

[78] See Art 7 of the *REOFF*, and Art 14 of the *REON*.

[79] MOFTEC, *China's Attracting Foreign Investment Policy*, above note 63, at 1–2.

[80] For general discussions on BOT investment in China, see Yu, An, *Foreign Invested BOT Projects and Administrative Contract Law* (Law Press, 1998); Sun, Chao and Shen, Wei, 'BOT Investment: the Legal Conflicts and Analysis', (1997) 1 *Chinese Legal Science* (*Zhongguo Faxue*); Zhu, Shuibing and Lin, Weiming, 'The Legal Nature of BOT Concession Agreements', (1999) 4 *Chinese Legal Science* (*Zhongguo Faxue*); Beijing Engineering Consultancy, *Guidelines to BOT Projects* (Dizhen Press, 1995); Xie, Lan, 'Government Intervention and the Legislation on BOT Concession Agreements', (1999) 4 *Law Review* (*Faxue Pinglun*).

[81] See China Central Television (CCTV), *The First BOT Water Project has Started to Provide Water*, posted at http://www.cctv.com (visited 26 July 2001 at 18:21). Other well known projects include Guangdong Shajiao B Power Project, Guangxi Laibing B Power Project, etc. See Zhu and Lin, above note 79, at 115.

According to the Joint BOT Notice, a BOT investment in China is one in which a government authority enters into a concession agreement with a Project Company set up by foreign investors for the purpose of the BOT project.[82] Under the agreement, the government authority authorises the Project Company to be in charge of the investment and finance, engineering design, construction, equipment purchase, operation management and fees charged, and also designates it responsible for the maintenance of the project equipment and facilities.[83] The government authority supervises, examines and audits the BOT project. It may also penalise the Project Company if it is behaving inconsistently with the Concession Agreement.[84] The MOFCOM BOT Notice requires the Project Company to be established in the form of an EJV, CJV or a WFE.[85]

With regard to government guarantees, the two BOT Notices are somewhat inconsistent. The MOFCOM BOT Notice requires that government authorities normally shall not offer any guarantees or promises to the project (eg, guarantees on forex convertibility and loans).[86] By contrast, the Joint BOT Notice provides that the State will guarantee the conversion and repatriation of foreign exchange that the Project Company pays back on loan principals, interests or dividends.[87] It also maintains that in case the Project Company suffers significant economic loss due to China's policy changes, the Project Company will be allowed to raise the charging standard or extend the concession period.[88] Nevertheless, the Joint BOT Notice does not permit guarantees on the rate of return[89] and domestic financial institutions are not allowed to provide guarantees for the project's finance.[90]

1.3.5.2 Stock Company with Foreign Investment (SCFI)

A stock company with foreign investment (SCFI) is a company whose capital is made up of shares contributed by both domestic and foreign shareholders, with foreign shareholders owning no less than twenty-five percent of the company's total registered capital.[91] The company undertakes external liabilities with its total assets, and each shareholder undertakes the liabilities in proportion to the shares held.[92] The registered capital of a SCFI, ie, the total

[82] Point 1, the Joint BOT Notice.
[83] *Ibid.*
[84] *Ibid.*
[85] Point 1, the MOFCOM BOT Notice.
[86] *Ibid*, point 3.
[87] *Ibid.*
[88] Point 2, the Joint BOT Notice.
[89] In practice, this has not always been the case. In a reported case, the Chengdu Municipality government offered a 12% profit rate for a BOT water factory according to a co-operation agreement with a French company and a Japanese company. See *The First BOT Water Project Has Started to Provide Water*, posted at http://www.cctv.com (visited on 26 July 2001).
[90] Point 2, the Joint BOT Notice.
[91] Art 2, Provisional Regulations on Stock Companies with Foreign Investment.
[92] *Ibid.*

capital recorded with registering authority, shall be no less than 30 million RMB Yuan.[93] A SCFI may be established by means of promotion or public offer, but it must be in conformity with the national industrial policy towards foreign invested enterprises.[94]

1.3.5.3 Holding Companies with Foreign Investment (HCFI)

In 1995, the Ministry of Foreign Trade and Economic Co-operation (now the Ministry of Commerce, the MOFCOM) published an interim regulation on holding companies with foreign investment (HCFI),[95] with a view to encouraging large transnational corporations to make a series of investments in China. This interim regulation has been replaced by the Provisions on Holding Companies with Foreign Investment published in June 2003. According to the Provision, a HCFI may take the form of an EJV, CJV or WFE but must be incorporated as a limited liability company.[96] More than 160 HCFIs have been set up and their investment activities are continuously expanding.[97]

1.3.5.4 Merger and Acquisition (M&A)

As merger and acquisition (M&A) has become a major form of international investment and predicted to become the most important form of foreign investment in China in the future,[98] China has laid down regulations to facilitate its development.[99] According to Chinese law, there are two categories of M&As: 'Equity M&A' and 'Asset M&A'.[100] An 'Equity M&A' is that a foreign investor purchases the equity of a domestic enterprise and transform it to a

93 *Ibid*, Art 7.

94 *Ibid*, Arts. 4 and 5.

95 Namely, the Interim Provisions on Holding Companies with Foreign Investment, promulgated by MOFCOM Decree No. 4, 1995.

96 Article 2, *Provisions on Holding Companies with Foreign Investment*, MOFCOM Decree No. 1, 2003.

97 MOFTEC, *China's Attracting Foreign Investment Policy*, above note 63, at 1–2.

98 Worldwide, M&A occupy more than 70% of total flow of foreign direct investment. However, in China, it is estimated that by now less than 5% of FDI in China is realised by M&A. Nevertheless, it is anticipated that it will soon become the most popular mode of foreign investment in China. See Wu, Fuming and Xu, Shousong, 'M&A Is to Become the Major Form of FDI in Shanghai'; Yan, Lan, etc., 'M&A Becomes Popular in China', Yang Qing, 'Sharp Increase of Investment Opportunities in China for Transnationals', in (2003) 7 July, 9 Feb, 24 May *People's Daily* (overseas edition), at 2, at 5, and at 5 respectively.

99 The Interim Provisions on Merger and Acquisition of Domestic Enterprises by Foreign Investors, jointly promulgated by the MOFTEC (now MOFCOM), the State Tax Bureau, the State Industry and Commerce Bureau and the State Foreign Exchange Bureau in January 2003, implemented since 12 April 2003. For a proposal for a general law on merger and acquisition, see Hou, Huaixia and Zhong, Ruidong, 'Studies on the Law of Enterprise Merger and Acquisition', (1992) 2 *Chinese Legal Science*, at 29–38.

100 Article 2, the Interim Provisions on Merger and Acquisition of Domestic Enterprises by Foreign Investors, *ibid*.

FIE.[101] An 'Asset M&A' is that a foreign investor establishes an FIE and purchases assets of a domestic enterprise and operates those assets through that FIE, or that a foreign investor purchases assets of a domestic enterprise and establish an FIE with the purchased assets.[102] Again, a foreign investor should normally contribute no less than twenty-five percent of the equity in the FIE established after M&A and the M&A should be in conformity with national industrial policy.[103]

1.4 RECENT AMENDMENTS TO MAJOR FDI LAWS IN CHINA (2000–2001)

Since China's opening up is a gradual process, Chinese FDI laws are constantly changing.[104] However, the most massive and significant change so far is the one made during October 2000 through to July 2001, in which three basic FDI laws, namely the EJVL, the CJVL and the WFEL were revised. Two of the three implementing regulations of the basic laws, including the implementing regulations of the EJVL and WFEL, have both been modified.[105] The amendments have understandably drawn much attention in business and legal circles home and abroad.[106] The following sections examine the reasons underlying the amendments and the major points amended, and then analyse

[101] *Ibid.*

[102] *Ibid.*

[103] *Ibid*, Arts. 4 and 5.

[104] The author's Questionnaire shows that these changes are often unexpected. See Section 8.2.2.

[105] The third implementing regulation, that of the CJVL, has not been changed, probably because it was promulgated in 1995 and did not yet require updating.

[106] For related reports in English, see eg, *Chinese trade minister explains draft amendments to foreign enterprise laws*, Xinhua news agency domestic service, Beijing, in Chinese 0856 GMT 23 Oct 2000, BBC Monitoring, © BBC; *China: Congress drafts further changes to joint-venture law*, Xinhua news agency, Beijing, in English 0230 GMT 14 Mar 2001, BBC Monitoring, © BBC; *China: Congress passes amendment to joint venture law as commitment to WTO*, Xinhua news agency, Beijing, in English 0813 GMT 15 Mar 2001, BBC Monitoring, © BBC; *China: Congress drafts further changes to joint-venture law*, Xinhua news agency, Beijing, in English 0230 GMT 14 Mar 2001, BBC Monitoring, © BBC; *China drafts legislation easing restrictions on foreign investors*, Xinhua news agency, Beijing, in English 1335 GMT 31 Oct 2000, BBC Monitoring, © BBC; *China: Premier Zhu Rongji signs bills to revise foreign-funded enterprise laws*, Xinhua news agency for Hong Kong, Beijing, in Chinese 0642 GMT 23 Oct 2000, BBC Monitoring, © BBC; *Chinese State Council eases regulations on foreign investment*, Xinhua news agency domestic service, Beijing, in Chinese 0439 GMT 2 Aug 2001, BBC Monitoring, © BBC.

For reports in Chinese, see eg, *FIEs Welcome the Amendments to the FIE Laws*, at http://www.pu-dong.com/jjxx/200012/jjxx_001204.htm (visited on 12 December 2000); *The Amendments to the EJVL will Benefit Hong Kong Investors Significantly*, at http://news.china.com/zh_cn/hmt/1004/20010317/145251.html (17 March 2001); Lu, Cairong and Zhang, Bingsheng, *NPC Deputies Discuss the Proposed Amendments to the 'China-Foreign Equity Joint Venture Law'*, at http://dailynews.sina.com.cn/c/207560.html (14 March 2001); Liu, Jiangfeng, *Combining the Three FIE Laws, or Including Them into the Company Law?*, at http://finance.sina.com.cn/g/43903.html (visited on 15 March 2001); Wu, Yu, *China Has Generally Finished the Checking-up and Amendments of Its Laws and Regulations Related to Foreign Trade and Economic Relations*, at http://finance.sina.com.cn/g/61985.html (visited on 18 May 2001).

the implication of these amendments to the improvement of the general FDI law system.

1.4.1 Background to the Amendment

The reason underlining the recent amendments is twofold. On the one hand, China was required to make amendments to fulfil the promises it made to the World Trade Organization (WTO) members when its membership was pending.[107] For example, in the China-US bilateral Market Access Agreement, China agreed to abolish, upon joining the WTO, all trade-related investment measures (TRIMs) prohibited by the 1994 Agreement of Trade-Related Investment Measures (TRIMs Agreement), including local content requirements, trade balancing requirements, and export performance requirements.[108] Therefore, immediate measures must be taken by China to make its FDI law in harmony with WTO rules and its promises.

However, on the other hand, the internal need for further reform and opening-up has also played an equally, if not more, important role in this legal change. This can be easily seen with a closer look at the contents of this amendment. The amendments to the EJVL, the oldest and most important FDI law, are an example. These amendments have mainly touched three issues: the production and operation plan, the right to amend the EJVL, and the purchase of domestic materials. As explained by Mr. Gu Angran in the National People's Congress before the amendments were passed,[109] the first change, the deletion of the requirement of EJVs to submit their production and operation plan to the authorities concerned and to carry them out 'by means of economic contracts', was made because China had already shifted from a centrally planned economy to a socialist market economy.[110] The second change, changing the right to amend from the NPC to its Standing Committee, is made solely in order for the Standing Committee of the NPC to have the power to amend the law when reform and opening-up policy so require it.[111] In other words, the first two changes are both responses to the

[107] See eg, *China: Congress passes amendment to joint venture law as commitment to WTO*, Xinhua news agency, Beijing, in English 0813 GMT 15 Mar 2001, BBC Monitoring, © BBC. China formally applied for the membership in 1986 and was not finally accepted until 11 December 2001. See Williams, Frances, 'China and Taiwan Join World Trade Today', Financial Times, 12 November 2001. For details of the background of China's progress towards Geneva, see Leonard, Sean, *The Dragon Awakens: China's Long March to Geneva* (Cameron May, 1999).

[108] '*US-China WTO Market Access Agreement*', available at http://www.uschina.org/public/wto/market/227–237.pdf (visited on 21 August 2001). Among these performance requirements that China promised to remove, the export performance requirement is beyond the WTO rule, as the TRIMs Agreement does prohibit export performance requirement in general. See US International Trade Commission, *Assessment of the Economic Effects on the United States of China's Accession to the WTO*, Publication No. 3229, Sept. 1999, at xiii.

[109] Gu, Angran, 'The Amendments to the China-Foreign EJVL is to Adapt to the Development of Circumstances', (2001) 10 Mar *People's Daily* (overseas edition), at 2.

[110] *Ibid.*

[111] *Ibid.*

economic reform and opening-up, and are not directly related to the WTO membership. Although it appears that the third amendment, the deletion of domestic purchase priority requirements, was made to conform to the national treatment requirement in the TRIMS Agreement,[112] it was also based on the need to establish a market economy. Mr. Gu said,[113]

> 'The main consideration of this amendment is that, under socialist market economy, enterprises should be able to decide the purchase of supplies, based on market situations and the principle of fairness and reasonableness. The Government shall not interfere. Foreign invested enterprises, like other national enterprises, shall have such purchasing rights. Meanwhile, according to TRIMs Agreement of the WTO and Article 1 of its Annex 'Illustrative List', Members shall not by any means restrict enterprises to purchase, use products produced locally or there originated from. Our Government has made commitment to abolish 'local content requirement' during the WTO admission negotiations...'

Here it can be seen that the internal need for China to carry on reform and opening-up, and in the end to establish a 'Socialist Market Economy', are deeper and more fundamental reasons for these amendments. If China was not committed to establish a market economy, it would not have made these commitments to WTO members.

Nevertheless, it is necessary to stress that the two sides, the internal reasons for establishing a market economy and the external reasons for entering the WTO are in harmony rather than contradiction. Both of them are market and rule based. Moreover, the Chinese reformers may use the WTO as a powerful instrument to carry out massive, and maybe radical economic and social changes.

1.4.2 The Changed Rules

This amendment of FDI laws and regulations started in October 2000, when the 18th Session of the Ninth National People's Congress (NPC) Standing Committee reviewed and passed the amendments to the WFEL and the CJVL. In April, the State Council approved the modifications to the Implementing Regulations of the WFEL accordingly. In March 2001, the 4th Meeting of the Ninth NPC reviewed and passed the amendments to the EJVL. Subsequently, in July 2001, the State Council approved the amendments to the Implementing Regulations of the EJVL. The biggest changes were made to the Implementing Regulations of the EJVL. Forty-five changes were made in total and 19 article and provisions were deleted.[114] According

[112] For details about TRIMs, see Section 3.2.2.3.

[113] Gu, Angran, above note 109, at 2.

[114] For details, see *The State Council Decision Concerning Amendment of the 'Equity Joint Ventures Law Implementing Regulations'* promulgated and entered in to force on July 22, 2001, came into force on the date of promulgation, as reprinted at *People's Daily* (overseas edition), 6 August 2001, at 5.

to officials from MOFCOM (then MOFTEC) and other government departments concerned, these amendments to the 'Implementing Regulations' can be classified into four main groups:[115]

Firstly, there are amendments in accordance with the changes to the EJVL. These include deletion of production and operational plans reporting requirements, domestic purchase priority requirements, foreign exchange balance requirements, export performance requirements and domestic sales restrictions.

Secondly, there are amendments of clauses inconsistent with WTO rules and China's external commitments.[116] Deleted from the 'Implementing Regulations' is the requirement that machines and equipment contributed as investment by the foreign investor should be import-substituting machines and equipment, and the requirement that industrial property rights contributed as investment by the foreign investor should produce exports. It is added that the allowed areas of foreign investment will be provided for in the Investment Guidance and the Guiding Catalogue.

Thirdly, there are amendments of clauses clearly inconsistent with laws, administrative laws and regulations and relevant State Council rules currently in effect. These have mainly amended the provisions on industrial and commercial registration, land use right acquisition and transfer, tariff and industrial and commercial consolidated tax reduction or exemption, labour management and the joint venture term of EJVs, and the liquidation of EJVs to keep the 'Implementing Regulations' in conformity with those relevant laws and administrative laws and regulations. The provision that EJVs shall not reduce their registered capital, provisions on accounting in foreign currency and financial and accounting reports, provisions on income clearing and tax payment by Sino-foreign joint ventures, and the provision on the power of interpreting the 'Implementing Regulations' have also been amended to bring them into conformity with the Company Law, the 1999 Accounting Law, the FIEs and FEs Income Tax Law, and the Law of Legislation.

Finally, there are amendments of some provisions clearly unsuitable to new circumstances in reform and development. In accordance with the reform of government institutions and the change of their functions, the provisions on a 'department in charge' (*zhuguan bumen*) of an EJV have been deleted. Also deleted are provisions on channels through which foreign investors may seek cooperative partners, on EJVs' capital construction plans and funds, on goods and materials supply, and on marketing channels for products, to suit the requirements of a market economy. In light of the structural

115 *MOFTEC and State Council Legislative Affairs Bureau Officials Answer Questions Raised by Journalists on the Amendments to the Implementing Regulations of the EJVL*, *People's Daily* (overseas edition), 13 August 2001, at 5.

116 This is how the Chinese officials classified the changes. Indeed, it is obvious that most changes of the first category are also relevant to China's WTO commitment.

reforms of foreign exchange control and financial administration, the provisions on foreign exchange rates, on account opening and foreign exchange receipts and expenses administration, on loans, and on outward remittances have been amended. In addition, since enterprises have already enjoyed the right to fix product prices themselves, the provision for price control on EJVs has been deleted.

1.4.3 An Evaluation of the Amendments

The amendments to these FDI laws and regulations are, naturally, warmly welcomed by foreign investors in China, as they entitle FIEs to more freedom in activities such as production planning, purchasing and sales.[117] It is also a positive sign which demonstrates that China is treating its WTO commitments seriously and positively. However, the amendments are only tactical and represent technical changes rather than a fundamental shift, and their limitations are therefore obvious. In the first place, some changes are made merely to repeat the changes that have already taken place in practice.[118] As Mr. GU Angran mentioned in his report, for instance, as a result of market economy reform, FIEs were no longer, in practice, required to submit their production and operation plans as required by previous laws and regulations.[119] Second, the amendments have not addressed many important aspects of FDI law, some of which have been raised by the NPC deputies. During NPC discussions on the amendments to the EJVL, for instance, some deputies proposed that Chinese joint venture partners should also include individuals; that joint ventures should also take the form of shareholding companies; that the proportion of the investment contributed by the foreign joint venture partner does not have to be no less than 25 per cent; and that the president, vice-president, general manager and deputy general managers need not necessarily be the joint venture partners.[120] The Law Commission of the NPC,[121] however, 'considering the complexity and the number of problems involved, and considering that some questions have to do with CJVL and WFEL', believes that 'more thorough investigations and fuller discussions are required' before a decision can be made. In the authors'

[117] See eg, *China: Congress passes amendment to joint venture law as commitment to WTO*; *FIEs Welcome the Amendments to the FIE Laws*; *The Amendments to the EJVL will Benefit Hong Kong Investors Significantly*, above note 101.

[118] See eg, *FIEs Welcome the Amendments to the FIE Laws*, above note 106.

[119] Gu, Angran, above note 109, at 2.

[120] *China: Congress amends Chinese-Foreign Equity Joint-Venture Law*, Xinhua News Agency Domestic Service, Beijing, in Chinese 0324 GMT 14 Mar 01/BBC Monitoring/© BBC. See also *'The Three Laws Two Regulations' May Need to be Further Modified* (author unknown) posted at http://www.etisu.com.cn/zgwmxh/tongxun/00126.02–0126-WTO1.htm (visited on 28 June 2003).

[121] The Law Commission of the NPC is a special department in charge of the preparation and reviewing of laws within the NPC.

opinion, these changes are all sensible, necessary and important, though they may need to be considered together with the changes in the FDI legal framework, which are discussed below. Lastly, changes in the general FDI legal framework proposed by some scholars and legislators have not been made.[122] In other words, only details have been changed, not the general regime: 'new wine has been put in an old bottle' (Jiuping Zhuang Xinjiu), as a Chinese person might put it. The problem, for example, of the application of Company Law to FIEs has not been touched at all, which has caused difficulty for judges and officials handling FIE cases.[123]

1.5 FURTHER REFORM OF THE CHINESE FDI LAW SYSTEM

It is therefore argued that China should further reform its FDI legal system, with a view to unifying and codifying the various FIE laws and regulations and applying Company Law to all FIE companies.[124]

1.5.1 A Unified FDI Code

It has been argued that China should consolidate its three basic FDI laws (ie, EJVL, CJVL and WFEL) and their implementing regulations to make a unified FDI law.[125] Meanwhile, the special regulations necessary to suit the special needs of every form of investment may be maintained, either in the form of special sections within the unified FDI law, or as separate regulations. In other words, the core of the new Chinese FDI legal system could take the form of either a single FDI Code with special rules for different forms of FIEs integrated therein, or be an FDI Code plus a number of individual regulations on different forms of foreign investment.

The author is of the view that the unification and codification of FIE laws and regulations are necessary, based on the following reasons. Firstly, a united law will remove the aforementioned repetitions that are prevalent in the three laws and regulations, which are a waste of legal resources, and are reflections of the immaturity of legislative skills. Secondly and more importantly, a united law will fill the gaps in the current Chinese FDI law system. A United FDI Code will include a chapter of general rules on the purposes of law, on definition of FIEs, general standards of treatment and on expropria-

122 Liu, Jiangfeng, *Combining the Three FIE Laws, or Including Them into the Company Law?*, at http://finance.sina.com.cn/g/43903.html (visited on 15 Mar 2001). See also Yang, Zhongxiao, above note 42.

123 *Ibid.*

124 *Ibid.*

125 Cao, Jianming and He, Xiaoyun, 'WTO Accession and China's Foreign Economic Legislation', (2000) 1 *Chinese Legal Science* (*zhongguo faxue*), at 12; Zhang, Mei, above note 46, at 70–74.

tion and compensation. This will in turn make the law more comprehensive and coordinated. Moreover, the legal vacuums which have become apparent with practice within the current FDI legal system may be cured by a new united law. Thirdly, a united FDI Code will help to consolidate and streamline the numerous FDI laws and regulations. At the moment, there are voluminous FDI laws and regulations in China and they are not always consistent.[126] The large number of FDI laws and regulations add substantially to the legal cost of investing in China, especially because they are not readily accessible. After accession to the WTO, China has amended thousands of laws and regulations related to foreign investment and trade.[127] Still, the number of FDI laws and regulations remain huge. While it may be impossible to include all details of the numerous existing laws and regulation into a single FDI code, it will at least consolidate some generic rules. In this sense, the codification of the united Contract Law would offer great experience.[128] Finally, a collective FIE legislation approach has been adopted in most complementary FDI laws and regulations since 1986.[129] For example, the regulations about investment directions, capital contribution, contracting operation and liquidation are aimed at all FIEs. Furthermore, many newly promulgated FDI-related laws apply to both FIEs and domestic investors and their enterprises. Since 1994, China has adopted a new tax system which addresses all enterprises in China in the same way. The RFEA applies to all financial institutions, FIEs, and other institutions and individuals in China. The recently amended Contract Law applies not only to domestic transactions, but also to foreign transactions, including joint venture contracts, which used to be governed by a special contract law, the 1985 Foreign Economic Contract Law. The FDI laws and regulations should therefore be unified to be in agreement with these laws and practices. The experience of the unification of these laws and regulations might aid the unification of FDI laws and regulations.

In short, a united FDI Code is justifiable as it will eliminate the repetitions, avoid contradictions and legal loopholes, consolidate and streamline rules and be in harmony with other relevant laws and practices. However, some may consider these changes to be only transitional and may prefer more radical changes, eg, to abolish the FDI laws and regulations altogether and apply Company Law universally to companies.

[126] The inconsistency between the two BOT notices serve as a good example of the problem of legal coherence. See Section 1.3.5.1.

[127] According to an interview with Minister SHI Guangsheng, the then Minister of MOFTEC (now MOFCOM), by June 2002, the Chinese government had identified more than 2300 regulations to be cleaned up. Among them, 830 were to be abolished and 325 modified. Gong, Wen, 'Changes after WTO: Interview with Minister SHI Guangsheng', (2002) 10 July *People's Daily* (overseas edition), at 1.

[128] The *Contract Law* Promulgated in 1999 not only united the former *Economic Contract Law*, *Foreign Economic Contract Law* and the *Technology Contract Law*, but also consolidated and combined many related regulations and rules, which have regarded as a success.

[129] Cao and He, above note 125, at 12.

1.5.2 A Universally Applied Company Law

As discussed above, the Company Law only applies to SCFIs while most FIEs are incorporated under their respective FIE laws and regulations even though they are in the form of a 'Limited Liability Company (LLC). Therefore, many scholars argue that in future, China should abolish the LLC model of FIEs altogether and let the Company Law govern all companies in China including LLC FIEs.[130] However, it has also been argued that, however old fashioned it might be, this design has its own values and should be kept as an option.[131] They argue that this management model not only allows the investment partners to have direct control over the management, but also serves the 'public purpose' of the Chinese partners by directly participating in company management learning advanced management skills from the foreign managers.[132]

In the author's opinion, it may not be necessary to keep this company form as an option if the Company Law is to govern all LLC FIEs. Firstly, it is not a good idea to have several kinds of LLC within a single legal system, which complicates the law and confuses investors. Also, decades of attracting FDI experience has made it much less important to learn management skills by directly participating in management. Lastly, investors who still want to learn from the other co-operation partners and take direct control over the enterprise may use the form of partnership, which is governed by the Partnership Law.

1.5.3 An FDI Code plus a Universally Applied Company Law

However, if the Company Law were to apply to all FIEs in the form of companies, would it lead, as some people have suggested, to a total abolishment of all FDI laws and regulations? The answer is in the negative, at least for the time being. FDI laws, as they are in many developing countries, are mainly laws of government regulation over FDI, rather than laws of corporate governance, ie FIE laws. More precisely, the FDI Code should contain provisions on such aspects as investment admission and approval, treatment, protection including expropriation and compensation, incentives, management and dispute settlement.[133] In China, the reason FDI laws served as FIEs laws for decades is that originally there was no Company Law at all. Therefore, the application of Company Law to FIEs simply reshapes the FDI laws as they should have been and will not necessarily cause FDI laws to disappear. Nevertheless, with the company law sections removed, the unification and codification of FDI laws and regulations will be much easier. If this is the case,

[130] Yang, Zhongxiao, above note 42.
[131] See Xu, note 44 above, at 131–2, 136.
[132] *Ibid*, at 132.
[133] Cao and He, above note 125, at 12–13.

it is anticipated that a universally applied Company Law will go hand in hand with a FDI Code as China marches towards a real market economy and further integrates into the world.

1.6 CONCLUSION

The Chinese legal system for inward investment, or the Chinese FDI law system, is a result of the Chinese 'Open-Door' policy adopted in 1978 and carried out ever since. The opening up of China has been a gradual process, as has been the formation of the FDI law system. The Chinese FDI law system is currently three-tier with constitutional provisions on the top, national laws and regulations as the body in the middle and sub-national regulations at the bottom. Some of the national laws and regulations are foreign invested enterprises (FIE)-specific whilst the others are FIE-related only. Under these laws and regulations, various forms of foreign investment are allowed. EJV, CJV, WFE and are the traditional vehicles, while BOT, SCFI, HCFI and M&A are the major new forms of foreign investment.

The current Chinese FDI legal system, as represented by the basic FDI laws and regulations, has three main features: foreign, enterprise-oriented and unsystematic. Firstly, laws and regulations are specially designed to regulate foreign investments. Secondly, they are laws and regulations of certain forms of foreign invested 'enterprises', where a large proportion of the provisions in those laws and regulations deal with FIE corporate governance. Thirdly, the current Chinese FDI legal system is scattered, uncoordinated and therefore unsystematic. The recent amendments to the major FDI laws and regulations, albeit massive in terms of scale, are only technical and tactical changes to bring them in line with the WTO agreements and completed economic reform programmes. The basic structure of FDI law still remains unchanged.

It is therefore argued that, in order to attract foreign—including EU—investment, China should further reform its FDI legal system. A unified FDI Code (or Law) should be adopted, to consolidate and coordinate all the existing laws and regulations. Special rules for different forms of investment could either be incorporated into the FDI Code, or into separate individual regulations. Corporate provisions in the current FIE laws and regulations could be removed and the Company Law applied to all FIE adopting any form of company prescribed therein. The application of Company Law to FIE companies will not necessarily lead to the outright abandonment of all FDI laws and regulation, but will facilitate the codification of FDI laws and regulations. Therefore, a unified FDI Code may well go hand in hand with a universally applied Company Law.

2

EU Law on Outward Investment

EU law of outward investment plays a role in facilitating and promoting EU investment in China. Indeed, promoting outward investment has long been one of the top priorities of the EU and its Member States. As a result, restrictions on outward investment have been very rare in the laws of both the EU and its member states. On the contrary, both the EU and its member states have developed schemes to promote investment outflow. However, at this stage, the power to regulate FDI issues is shared between the EU and its member states and the precise distribution of external investment competence between the EU and its member states still remains ambiguous. This Chapter will, therefore, first make an in-depth investigation of the law and practice of the EU's competence on external investment issues, and then proceed to identify the laws of outward investment at both the EU and its member state levels. It concludes that the Community should be given exclusive competence on investment issues and a common Community investment policy should be established.

2.1 THE EU'S EXTERNAL INVESTMENT COMPETENCE

On the world stage, trade and investment are inextricably intertwined as the lifeblood of the emerging integrated international production systems.[1] Accordingly, the development of trading systems must coordinate with that of investment regimes. However, it appears that this has not happened within the framework of the European Community (the EC or the Community). While the Community's exclusive competence on trade has long been well established, its competence on FDI remains vague and is often ignored, despite the European Commission (the Commission)'s persistent efforts.[2] This section intends to look closely at the issue of the EU's external investment competence. Following Professor Alan Dashwood's formula,[3] it first

1 See *World Investment Report 1996—Investment, Trade and Investment Policy Arrangements: Overview*, UNCTAD/DTCI/32 (Overview), at 16.

2 For EC's practice in investment matters, see Section 2.2.2.

3 The distinction between 'existence question' and 'exclusivity question' was first drawn by Professor Alan Dashwood, in his contribution on '*Implied External Competence of the EC*', in

discusses the question of the existence of such competence, and then analyses its exclusivity.

2.1.1 The Existence of EC's External Investment Competence

Generally speaking, EC's competence derives from the Treaty Establishing the European Community (the EC Treaty or the Treaty), as well as the objectives set forth therein.[4] This principle of the attribution of powers (or of 'conferred powers') applies to both actions by the Community in the sphere of international law and actions taken within the internal legal order.[5] However, according to the European Court of Justice (hereinafter the Court or the ECJ), the requisite authorisation for the acceptance of international commitments by the community need not be expressly given by the specific provisions relied on as the legal basis (*express external power*): it may be implied from these provisions (*implied external power*).[6]

Such an implication would be drawn where the community institutions had been given powers within the internal order to pursue a specific objective, as to the possibility of entering into the international commitments *necessary* for the attainment of that specific objective.[7] In other words, if the community has been conferred internal power to pursue certain specific objectives and it is necessary to extend that power to international order for the same objectives, the Community may enjoy the external power by implication, i.e., without the express conferment of that power by the Treaty.

In short, to determine whether the EC has external competence in a certain field, it is first necessary to look to the Treaty for provisions conferring express external powers. Failing this, one should determine whether that power exists by implication, ie, if the EC has conferred power for the same objectives in internal legal order and if it is necessary to extend this to international commitments.

Koskenniemi, Martti (ed.) *International Law Aspects of the European Union* (Kluwer Law International, 1997), at. 113. See Dashwood, Alan, *The Attribution of External Relations Competence* (hereinafter '*Attribution*'), in Dashwood, Alan, and Hillion, Christophe (ed.), *The General Law of EC External Relations* (Sweet & Maxwell, 2000), at 115, note 1.

[4] Article 5 (ex Article 3b) states that 'the Community shall act within the limits of the powers conferred upon it by this Treaty and of the objectives assigned to it therein'. Article 5, EC Treaty.

[5] Dashwood, *Attribution*, above note 3, at 117. See also *Opinion 2/94 (Re ECHR)* [1996] ECR 1–1759, at para. 24. Other important Court decisions and opinions related to external competence include *Case 22/70 Commission v Council (ATER)* [1971] ECR 263, *Joined cases 3, 4 and 6/76 Cornelis Kramer* [1976] ECR 1279, *Opinion 1/76 (Re inland waterway vessels)* [1977] ECR 741, *Opinion 2/91 (Re ILO Convention)* [1993] ECR 1–1061, *Opinion 2/92 (Re OECD National Treatment Instrument)* [1995] ECR 1–521 and *Opinion 1/94 (Re WTO)* [1994] ECR 1–5267.

[6] *Opinion 2/94*, *ibid*, para. 26.

[7] Dashwood, above note 3, at 117.

2.1.1.1 Express Competence

So far the EC Treaty has vested in the Community external competence in fields such as common commercial policy, research and technological development co-operation, environment matters, development co-operation, association agreements and monetary and foreign exchange regimes.[8] Admittedly, all of them, especially common commercial policy (CCP), monetary and foreign exchange regimes and association agreements, are closely related to investment issues and are therefore analysed below.

Firstly, the CCP has significant implications for FDI activities. Most foreign invested companies will import materials or technologies, and export their products or services. Furthermore, investment is particularly relevant to trade in services, which, according to the definition in the General Agreement on Trade in Services (GATS) embraces any 'commercial presence',[9] ie, foreign funded companies or their subsidiaries or branches. At most, based on a broad definition of the CCP, it may, as the Commission[10] and the European Parliament (EP)[11] have proposed, include all investment issues. However, this broad interpretation has been rejected by the Court in Opinion 1/94 and then in Opinion 2/92. In Opinion 1/94, the Court ruled in particular that services through 'commercial presence' were not covered in the CCP.[12] More recently, in its Opinion 2/92, the Court held that the national treatment rule, which was basically a rule on FDI activities, related only partially to international trade with non-member countries and therefore Article 113 (now art. 133) could not be used as the legal basis for the exclusive Community competence thereon.[13]

During the Intergovernmental Conference 2000 (IGC 2000), a proposal was put forward by the European Parliament, to change the 'the conclusion of tariff and trade agreement' in article 133 (1), into 'the conclusion of tariff and trade agreements relating to trade in goods and services, investment and intellectual property'.[14] As a result, however, in the Treaty of Nice, this pro-

[8] Dashwood, *Attribution,* above note 3, at 119–24. See also Macleod, I, Hendry, ID and Hyett, Stephen, *The External Relations of the European Community* (Clarendon Press, Oxford, 1996), at 45–7.

[9] According to GATS, 'commercial presence' means any type of business or professional establishment, including through (i) the constitution, acquisition or maintenance of a juridical person, or (ii) the creation or maintenance of a branch or a representative office, within the territory of a Member for the purpose of supplying a service. See Article 28, GATS

[10] In Part 11 (2) of the Commission Opinion on the 1996 Intergovernmental Conference, the Commission said that the common commercial policy should be clarified, so as to 'take account of the radical changes in the structure of the world economy, in which services, intellectual property and direct foreign investment play an increasingly important role'.

[11] See Brok, Elmar, and Tsatsos, Dimitrios, Representatives of the European Parliament at the Intergovernmental Conference, *IGC 2000—Commercial Policy and International Agreements*, CONFER 4759/00, Brussels, 11 July 2000. It proposed to extend the CCP to include investment as well as services and intellectual property.

[12] *Opinion 1/94*, above note 5, para. 36–53. See also Section 2.2.3.2.

[13] *Opinion 2/92*, para. 18–28.

[14] See Brok and Tsatsos, above note 11.

posal has only been partly accepted. While it did extend the application of Article 133 Paragraphs 1–4 to 'the negotiation and conclusion of agreements in the fields of trade in services and the commercial aspects of intellectual property rights',[15] it did not accept that investment agreements should be treated in the same way. It is clear therefore that, unless the Treaty has been further amended, the EC cannot rely on Article 133 to establish its competence on investment matters.

Secondly, as monetary and foreign exchange regimes play an important role in investment activities, the EC's competence in this field can to a certain extent justify its competence on investment issues. Nevertheless, foreign investment does not only mean monetary and foreign exchange, but also relates to many other matters, such as right of establishment, employment, purchase and sale, taxation, etc. Hence, it is unlikely that the EC can establish its competence on this single legal basis.

Lastly, association agreements may cover investment issues. An example of this is the EC's co-operation with the ACP countries based on the Lomé Conventions, which beginning with the second Convention has included extensive investment clauses.[16] However, again, the Community probably cannot claim a general investment competence simply based on its practice of an association agreement, which, as the Court said, creates 'special, privileged links with a non-member country, which must, at least to a certain extent, take part in the Community system'.[17]

To summarise, the EC probably cannot establish its power on external investment relations *simply* on the ground of express Treaty provisions, as interpreted by the Court. Although these provisions may be closely related to investment, none of them has been sufficiently developed, or clearly identified by the Court, to cover investment issues in general. Therefore, no provision alone may be relied on as a single legal basis for Community competence on investment aspects. Neither do all those provisions combined seem to have that effect. Therefore, it is necessary to take into account the principle of implied power to justify the EC's general competence on investment matters.

[15] It must be noted that, however, the Community's competence in these 'new CCP' fields are different from that in traditional CCP areas, ie, trade in goods areas. Firstly, express competence has only been granted to the negotiation and conclusion of international agreement, not the adoption of autonomous measures. Secondly, the EC's power to enter into international agreement in these areas is not exclusive, but shared with member states. Finally, unanimity is required when negotiating horizontal agreements in these areas or specific agreements in a certain areas. See 2000 Treaty of Nice (Amending the Treaty of European Union, The Treaties Establishing the European Communities and Certain Related Acts), Article 2 (8), OJC 80/1 (10.3.2001). For insightful comments on the new CCP rules, see Cremona, Marise, 'The External Dimension of the Single Market: Building (on) the Foundations', in Barnard, Catherine and Scott, Joanne (eds), *The Law of the Single European Market: Unpacking the Premises* (Hart, 2002), at 351–93, particularly 370–80.

[16] For details see Part III.2.B of the Convention.

[17] See *Case 12/86 Demirel v Stadt Schwabisch Gmund*, [1987] ECR 3719, at para. 9.

2.1.1.2 Implied Competence

2.1.1.2.1 Articles 56 and 57. To identify the EC's implied external competence on investment matters, Chapter 4 of the EC Treaty on capital and payment, particularly Article 56 (ex art. 73b) and 57 (ex art. 73c) are of primary importance[18]. Article 56 states that,

> 1 'Within the framework of the provisions set out in the Chapter, all restrictions on the movement of capital between Member States and between Member States and third countries shall be prohibited.
> 2 Within the framework of the provisions set out in the Chapter, all restrictions on payments between Member States and between Member States and third countries shall be prohibited.'

Actually, the Treaty does not treat the movement of capital[19] and payments between member states and third countries in the same way as those between member states, in that the former is subject to certain extra restrictions set forth in the Chapter. Nevertheless, the absolute terms used distinguished them from those used in preceding Chapters on the right of establishment and services. As observed by the court in Opinion 1/94, the sole objective of the chapters on the right of establishment and on freedom of providing services is to secure the right of establishment and the freedom to provide services 'for nationals of member states'.[20] They do not contain express provisions extending the competence of the Community to 'relationships arising from international law'.[21] Nor does Chapter 2 have provisions on the right of first establishment of a non-member country national, or on their access to self-employed activities.[22] By comparison, Article 56 not only expressly extends the freedom of capital movement and payments from those between member states to those between member states and third countries, but also,

[18] Within the EC framework, the achievement of freedom of capital movement was a gradual process. In the original 1957 EEC Treaty (the Treaty of Rome) (Art 67), member states were only required to progressively abolish restrictions between them on capital movement belonging to member state residents and any 'discrimination based on nationality or on the place of residence...' To that end, a few Council Directives were made successively. The most recent one among them was Directive 88/361, which according to Juillard, is still effective. For detail of these Directives, see Directive 60/921, OJ L43 12 July 1960, at 921; Directive 72/156, OJ L91, 18 April 1972 at 13; Directive 86/566, OJ L332, 26 November 1986, at 22; Directive 88/361, OJ L178, 8 July 1988, at 5. See also, Juillard, Patrick, 'Freedom of Establishment, Freedom of Capital Movements, and Freedom of Investment', (2000) 15 *ICSID Review—FILJ*, at 331–32.

[19] As observed by Juillard, here 'movement of capital' should be interpreted as including direct investment. Further, this is confirmed in the EC Directive 88/361, which defines 'movement of capital' to cover, first of all, direct investment. See Juillard, *ibid*, at 325. For details of the Directive, see Council Directive of 24 June 1988 for the implementation of Art 67 (88/361/EEC), OJ L178/5.

[20] *Opinion 1/94*, above note 5, para. 81.

[21] *Ibid.*

[22] *Ibid.*

in absolute terms, put them in parallel. The terms may imply that the Community has powers over internal capital movement and payments, as well as external ones. This is confirmed in the next provision, Article 57 (2) (ex art. 73c), which reads:

> 'Whilst endeavouring to achieve the objective of free movement of capital between Member States and Third Countries to the extent possible and without prejudice to the other Chapters of this Treaty, the Council may, acting by a qualified majority on a proposal from the Commission, adopted measures on the movement of capital to or from third countries involving direct investment—including investment in real estate—establishment, the provision of financial services or the admission of securities to capital markets. Unanimity shall be required for measures under this paragraph which constitute a step back in Community law as regards the liberalization of the movement to or from third countries.'

Most importantly for the present purposes, this provision directly empowers the Community to adopt 'measures' to facilitate the flow of direct investment. Here the 'measures' were not defined, but from the wording of Articles 56 and 57, it appears to embrace internal measures in the functioning of the internal market, as well as external measures 'arising from international law'. This is shown by the fact that this Article was used by the EC as a legal basis for the conclusion of WTO agreements including GATS and TRIMs Agreement as well as the 1994 Energy Charter Treaty (ECT) and other co-operation and partnership agreements with third countries.[23]

Such power as that conferred by Article 57 (2) is, however, subject to certain exceptions stipulated in Article 57 (1) and Article 58 (ex art. 73d). Article 57 (1) permits all the restrictions on the external movement of capital involving direct investment existing at the end of 1993. It is therefore observed that the Community is given power to act only in those areas where the Treaty itself does not automatically require existing restrictions to be eliminated by the Member States.[24] Exceptions under Article 58 include, among others,[25] national taxation law and restrictions on the right of establishment, which are both of great importance to FDI. Thus a closer look at the relevant Treaty provisions is merited.

[23] See Section 2.2.3.2. See also the Letter from Mr. Carlo Pettinato of the European Commission to the author, dated August 14, 2000.

[24] Usher, JA, *The Law of Money and Financial Services in the EC*, 2nd edition (Oxford University Press, 2000), at 232.

[25] Including 'all requisite measures to prevent infringements of national law and regulations, in particular in the field of taxation and the prudential supervision of financial institutions, or to lay down procedures for the declaration of capital movements for purposes of administrative or statistic information, or to take measures which are justified on grounds of public policy or public security.' See Art 58 (1) (b), the EC Treaty.

2.1.1.2.2 National taxation law and the right of establishment. Chapter 2 of Title VI (ex Title V) deals specifically with national taxation law. Article 93 (ex art. 99), in particular, states that the Council shall adopt provisions for

> 'the harmonization of legislation concerning turnover taxes, excise duties and other forms of indirect taxation to the extent that such harmonization is necessary to ensure the establishment and the functioning of the internal market'.

Therefore, according to the Court, the Community might have competence on indirect taxation, once such harmonisation has been achieved. Nevertheless, it only covers forms of indirect taxation, rather than direct taxation such as income tax, which is also very important for FDI operations. In other words, the Community has limited competence over national taxation laws.

Regarding the right of establishment, as the Court has made clear in Opinion 1/94, the Treaty contains neither provisions on the first establishment of nationals of non-member countries nor rules on their access to self-employed activities. It therefore follows that the Community does not have express competence over the right of establishment of non-member country nationals.

2.1.1.2.3 Articles 94, 95 and 308. These deficiencies of competence, however, may be helped by Article 94 (ex art. 100), 95 (ex art. 100a) and finally Article 308 (ex art. 235). As a general entitlement, Articles 94 and 95 confer the Council the right to adopt measures for the approximation of the provisions laid down by law, regulation or administrative action in member States 'which have as their object affected the establishment and functioning of the internal market'. Thus the Community may take actions on FDI-related issues, such as direct taxation, and such actions will have the effect of depriving member states of their powers.[26] Also, more generally, Article 308 grants the Community power to take appropriate measures

> 'if action by the Community should prove necessary to attain, in the course of the operation of the common market, one of the objectives of the Community and this Treaty has not provided the necessary powers'.

For instance, in Opinion 1/94, the Court stated that,

> '[a]lthough the only objective expressly mentioned in the chapters on the rights of establishment and the freedom to provide services is the attainment of those freedoms for nationals of the member states, it does not follow that the Community institutions are prohibited from using the powers conferred on them in that field[27] in order to specify the treatment which is to be accorded to nationals of non-member countries.'[28]

Instead, according to Opinion 1/94, the Community may adopt such meas-

[26] *Opinion 1/94*, above note 5, para. 88.
[27] Here it means internal powers concerned only.
[28] *Opinion 1/94*, above note 5, para. 90.

ures, and once they are adopted it acquires (exclusive) external competence in the sphere covered.[29]

In conclusion, based on Article 57 (2) and other related provisions mentioned, it would be tempting to argue that the EC should have, in general, external competence on investment matters. The participation of the EC in investment-related treaties such as WTO agreements and the ECT serves as practical example.[30]

2.1.2 The Exclusivity of the EC's External Investment Competence

However, is the EC's external investment competence exclusive, ie, do Member States still possess external power on investment issues, given that the Community has external competence in this field? To answer this question, it is necessary to look at the general criteria of the exclusivity of Community external competence. The EC Treaty says nothing explicitly on the nature of the EC's external competence. The criteria of the exclusivity of external competence have been developed by the Court in its opinions and judgements. Despite the inconsistencies in these opinions and judgements, it seems the general idea is, as stated by Advocate General Jacobs, that the Community shares its competence with the Member States unless there is 'any indication to the contrary'[31]. In other words, shared competence is the general principle while exclusive Community competence is the exception. According to the Court case law, the Community's external competence may be regarded as exclusive in the following cases:[32]

A. Exclusive Community competence flows from the Treaty provisions from which the competence derives. (*Exclusivity by the Treaty*) For instance, in the EC Treaty, the Community's competence is exclusive, as the Court has made clear, under the articles establishing the common commercial policy and the protection of fishery stock. For the 12 Euro Countries, the common monetary policy also falls within the EC's exclusive competence. It is, moreover, also argued that the Treaty articles on competition confer exclusive competence on the Community.[33]
B. Exclusive Community competence exists where internal powers can be effectively exercised only concurrently with external powers (*Exclusivity by Nature*). In Opinion 1/76, it would have been impossible to achieve the Community's objective of rationalizing the inland waterways sector in the

[29] *Ibid*, para. 91–96.
[30] For details of Community practice in investment related treaties, see Section2.2.3.
[31] Opinion of Jacobs AG in *Case C-316/91 Parliament v Council* [1994] ECR 1–625, at para. 40.
[32] Macleod, Hendry and Hyett, above note 8, at 56–61.
[33] *Ibid*, at 56–57.

Rhine and Moselle basins, without involving a third country in the scheme envisaged. Therefore, 'the conclusion of an international agreement is necessary in order to achieve Treaty objectives which cannot be attained by the adoption of autonomous rules'.[34] Under these circumstances, the Community can acquire exclusive competence even in the absence of any internal measures being adopted.

C. In other cases, exclusive Community competence may only flow from the scope of measures adopted by the Community Institutions (*Exclusivity By Measures Adopted*). According to the Court, 'each time the Community, with a view to implementing a common policy envisaged in the Treaty, adopts provisions laying down common rules, whatever form these may take, the Member States no longer have the right, acting individually or even collectively, to undertake obligations which affect those rules.'[35] This constitutes the famous '*AETR principle*', which has precipitated much debate.[36] It is notable that this principle is applicable even where Community legislation is not complete or 'exhaustive'.[37] For example, in the ILO case, Part III of the Convention in question was considered within an area 'which is already covered *to a large extent* by Community rules... adopted...with a view to achieving an ever greater degree of harmonization'.[38] The Court nevertheless ruled that the Community competence in these matters was exclusive. Moreover, the principle is neither confined to the 'common policies' identified by that term in the EC Treaty, but applies 'in all the areas corresponding to the objectives of the Treaty'.[39]

D. In a special case of *Exclusivity by Measures Adopted,* exclusive community competence may arise from an express power in an internal act (*Exclusivity by Acts*). In Opinion 1/94, the Court stated that 'whenever the Community has included in its internal legislative acts provisions relating to the treatment of nationals of non-member countries or expressly conferred on its institutions powers to negotiate with non-member countries, it acquires exclusive competence in the sphere covered by those acts.'[40] However, the practice of this kind of exclusive competence is yet to be seen.

The following paragraphs are to examine the exclusivity of the EC's external investment competence, using the criteria explored above.

[34] *Opinion 2/92*, above note 5, para. 32.
[35] *Case 22/70*, above note 5, para. 17.
[36] Macleod, Hendry and Hyett, above note 8, p. 58.
[37] *Ibid.*
[38] *Opinion 2/91*, above note 5, para. 25.
[39] *Ibid*, para. 10.
[40] *Opinion 1/94*, above note 5, para. 95.

2.1.2.1 Exclusivity by the Treaty

The most likely means by which investment issues can become the exclusive competence of the EC under express provisions of the Treaty is by including them in the common commercial policy. However, as observed above, this would not be the case unless the Treaty had been modified accordingly.

2.1.2.2 Exclusivity by Nature

This seems inapplicable to investment, in accordance with the Court's Opinion 1/94 and 2/92. In the former Opinion, the Court said,

> 'That application of Opinion 1/76 to GATS cannot be accepted...attainment of freedom of establishment and freedom to provide services for nationals of member states is not inextricably linked to the treatment to be afforded in the Community to nationals of non-member countries or in non-member countries to nationals of member states of the Community.'[41]

In the latter, Opinion 2/92 on the National Treatment Instrument, the Court again held that

> 'it is undisputed that that (a situation where the conclusion of an international agreement is necessary in order to achieve Treaty Objectives which cannot be attained by the adoption of autonomous rules) is not the case here.'[42]

2.1.2.3 Exclusivity by Measures Adopted and Exclusivity by Acts

According to the Council Decision on agreements reached in the Uruguay Round Negotiations, no act in Community law has been adopted on the basis of Article 57 (ex art. 73C).[43] The Court observed, in its Opinion 2/92, that

> 'although the Community has adopted measures capable of serving as basis for an exclusive external competence in accordance with the aforesaid case-law and falling in particular within the scope of Articles 57(2), 75, 84 and 100a of the EC Treaty, it is undisputed that those measures do not cover all the fields of activity to which the Third Decision relates.'[44]

Accordingly, the Court ruled out the Community's exclusive competence on it, though in general it upheld the existence of the EC's competence.[45] There-

[41] *Opinion 1/94*, above note 5, at para. 84–6.
[42] *Opinion 2/92*, above note 5, at para. 32.
[43] OJL 336/1 (23 December 1994).
[44] *Opinion 2/92*, above note 5, at para. 34.
[45] *Ibid*, at para. 35. It reads that 'It follows that the Community is competent to participate in the Third Decision, but that such competence does not cover all the matters to which that decision relates.'

fore, the exclusive Community competence on investment activities cannot flow from either an express power in an internal act, or the scope of measures adopted by the Community Institutions.

In conclusion, at present the EC has not yet attained exclusive external competence on investment issues. What it has is a 'shared competence' or 'joint competence', which it shares with the Member States. It is therefore necessary to look at both the EU law and its member state laws to draw a complete picture of the governing law on outward investment within the EU.

2.2 EU LAW AND PRACTICE ON OUTWARD INVESTMENT

At the Community level, although there is neither an established external investment policy nor Commission Officials dealing purely with external investment issues, many investment-related Community rules exist and a range of EU Directorates handle FDI matters.[46] Within the EU, the EC Treaty is the most important law governing internal as well as external investment relations, including outward investment. Besides which, the Community has also adopted some polices and measures concerning outward investment issues. The Community has also been very keen to conclude international agreements related to external investment matters beyond the internal legal order of the EU.

2.2.1 The EC Treaty

For outward investment, the most important provisions in the EC Treaty are Articles 56–60 (ex Article 73), particularly Article 56, which is potentially the general legal basis for a Community code on FDI.[47] As mentioned above, Article 56 requires, in absolute terms, that 'all restrictions' on the movement of capital and payments between member states and third countries be prohibited. Article 57 (2) further provides that the Council may adopt measures on the movement of capital to and from third countries involving the establishment of *direct investment* including investment in real estate, the provision of financial services or the admission of securities to capital markets. Nevertheless, these articles are subject to the exceptions prescribed in Articles 57 (1) and 58–60. Article 57 (1) permits all the restrictions on the external movement of capital involving direct investment existing at the end of 1993 (grandfather clause). Articles 58–60 provide for various exceptions to the freedom of capital movement, including general exceptions such as public

[46] Brewer, Tomas L, and Young, Stephen, 'European Union Policies and the Problems of Multilateral Enterprises', 29 *Journal of World Trade*, 1995, No. 1, at 41.

[47] Brewer, Tomas L, and Young, Stephen, *The Multilateral Investment System and Multilateral Enterprises* (Oxford University Press, 1998), at 179.

policy or security, safeguard measures, or special exceptions such as tax law, right of establishment or prevention of infringement of national laws and regulations, particularly in the field of taxation and prudential supervision of financial institutions or in setting out procedures for the declaration of capital movements for the purposes of administrative or statistical information.[48] Most of these special exceptions are related to inward investment. It may therefore be concluded that under the EC Treaty, restrictions on outward investment are generally prohibited and eliminated.

2.2.2 EU Policies and Measures on Outward Investment

The Community by contrast has adopted numerous policies and measures to promote outward investment to third countries, particularly developing countries.

2.2.2.1 General Policy: From the 1972 Proposal to the 2000 Approach

The Community's interest in promoting outward investment dates back as early as 1972 when the Commission initiated a proposal to the Council for a Regulation establishing a Community guarantee system for private investments in third countries (the 1972 Proposal).[49] Since then, the Commission has made persistent efforts on the protection and promotion of Community investment in third countries.

The Commission made another Communication to the Council in 1978 based on the 1972 Proposal on the 'Need for Community action to encourage European investment in developing countries and guideline for such action'[50] (the 1978 Communication). The change of application scope from 'third countries' to 'developing countries' did not make any significant difference as the protection and promotion of FDI among developed countries had already been guaranteed, by the OECD Codes of Liberalization of Capital Movements and Liberalization of Current Invisible Operations (the OECD Codes).[51] In this Communication, the Commission argued that two categories of Community action were needed. The first one involved the negotiation of agreements (or of clauses to be concluded in global agreements) between the Community and developing countries or groups of developing countries, on basic rules relating to the treatment of foreign

[48] For further discussion of these exceptions and other restrictions, see Peers, Steve, 'Free Movement of Capital: Learning Lessons or Slipping on Spilt Milk?', in Barnard, Catherine, and Scott, Joanne (eds), *The Law of the Single European Market: Unpacking the Premises* (Hart, 2002), at 335–36.

[49] COM (72) 1461 final. The European Parliament also produced a detailed Report on this proposal in 1973, see PE 33.931/fin (Document 208/73).

[50] COM (78) 23 final.

[51] See Section 2.3.1.1.

investment. The second involved specific projects selected on the ground of particular interests, the conclusion of specific protection agreements on a project-by-project basis, and the granting of guarantees and measures to promote investments.

In 1980, the Commission made a report[52] to the Council (the 1980 Report) in which it summarized the investment promotion and protection clauses in agreements between the Community and various categories of developing countries since 1978, and set forth the guidelines for joint action in the future. In the report, the Commission concluded that the two categories of action proposed in the 1978 Communication were necessary, and that certain guidelines had emerged from the Community's actions in this sphere. In particular they include:

> 'a the utility of raising the subject of investment with all partner developing countries;
> b the desirability of incorporating the basic rules on investment or other measures in an agreement distinct from the overall co-operation agreement;
> c the potential importance of the instrument comprising specific agreements for individual projects, preferably supplemented by financial guarantees; and
> d the Community's specific interest in negotiating investment clause with groups of developing countries.'[53]

In the 1980s and 90s, the Community seemed to have not produced any new policy on outward investment, while it signed numerous co-operation agreements, partnership agreements or multilateral agreements including investment clauses.[54] At the same time, the Community was very keen on the formation of a world-wide multilateral investment agreement. For instance, in the preparation for the Millennium Round negotiations, the Community very actively advocated a multilateral framework on investment under the aegis of the WTO.[55]

2.2.2.2 Unilateral Measures: From ECIP Facility to Asia Invest Programme

Apart from the general policies, the EC had taken some concrete unilateral measures to promote outward investment. The most significant two had been the European Community Investment Partners (ECIP) facility launched in 1988 and the Asia Invest Programme launched in 1995.

2.2.2.2.1 The ECIP Facility. The ECIP facility, or European Community International Investment Partners (EC–IIP) as it was originally called, was

52 COM (80) 204 final.
53 *Ibid*, at 17.
54 See Section 2.2.3.
55 See Settle Conference preparation: EC approach to trade and investment, at http://europa.eu.int/comm/trade/2000-round/1806ti.htm (visited on 22 May 2000).

launched in 1988 at the initiative of the Commission with the support of the European Parliament.[56] Initiated as a pilot project, ECIP has been the object of two successive Council Regulations and three independent evaluations.[57]

ECIP aimed to promote investment by private economic operators from the Community in the form of joint ventures with operators in eligible developing countries, to the mutual interest of both parties.[58] Eligible developing countries must be from Asia, Latin America or the Mediterranean. It was subsequently extended to South Africa.[59] ECIP offered four types of financing facilities to cover various phases of the investment process:[60]

a identification of projects and partners;
b feasibility studies and other operation prior to the decisions to invest;
c capital requirements of the joint venture; and
d training and assistance for the management of an existing joint venture.

Among them, only facility 'a' consists of outright grants, while the other facilities involve equity loans and equity holdings.[61]

The management of ECIP schemes was decentralised. Economic operators in EU member states and/or eligible developing countries must first send their financing applications to a financial institution that has signed a framework agreement with the European Community. The financial institutions then evaluate the application and forward them to the Commission for final decisions.[62]

According to the final beneficiaries and the financial institutions who have received funds, ECIP has proven to be an effective investment and development promotion instrument.[63] Also, it has strengthened the Commission's development policy and reputation both within and outside the EU. However, it came to an end in 1999 as its management became more bureaucratic and new instruments with similar functions had come into being.[64] One of these instruments is the Asia Invest Programme.[65]

2.2.2.2.2 The Asia Invest Programme. Launched by the Commission in 1997,

[56] See Report from the Commissions to the Council and the European Parliament: European Community Investment Partners (ECIP) Report 1999, COM (2000) 439 final, at 2.

[57] The two Regulations are Regulation (EEC) 319/92 of 3 February 1992 and Regulation (EEC) 213/96 of 29 January 1996. The three evaluation were conducted in 1990, 1994 and 1999 respectively. COM (2000) 439 final, *ibid*, at 3.

[58] Communication from the Commission on the 'EC-International Investment Partners' Facility for Latin America, Asia and the Mediterranean, COM (90) 575 final, at 4.

[59] COM (2000) 439 final, at 2.

[60] COM (90) 575 final, at 5.

[61] *Ibid*, at 6.

[62] *Ibid*.

[63] COM (2000) 439 final, at 3.

[64] *Ibid*, at 3–6.

[65] Other instruments include ALINVEST, MEDA, JOP, JEV and the instruments addressed to the ACP countries. *Ibid*, at 5.

the Asia-Invest Programme is one of the most important initiatives within the European Community for promoting and supporting mutually beneficial economic co-operation between the European Union and South and South East Asian countries.[66] This Programme aims to promote business co-operation between companies in the European Union and Asia, through providing a range of grants and supporting measures to help companies to research new markets, to do business in unfamiliar cultural environments, to meet and evaluate potential partners and to identify investment opportunities.[67] In particular, it has three main instruments:[68]

a The Business Priming Fund helps Asian and European companies to forge alliances through three schemes: marketplace monitoring, language and business culture familiarisation and technical assistance;
b The Asia-INTERPRISE and Partenariat schemes cover a range of business to business (BtoB) events to help companies find partners. These events include Asia-INTERPRISE, Asia-Invest Business Meeting, Asia-Partenariat and Europatenariat;
c The Asia Investment Facility finances country-wide or sector specific studies which provide European companies with key information on Asian economies.

The Asia Invest Program covers a five-year period and has a budget of EUR 45 million.[69] To benefit from an Asia-Invest grant, a project must be submitted by an organisation acting on behalf of a group of companies, eg a chamber of commerce, sector or professional association, whose role it is to run the project for the group. Such organisations are invited to submit projects that could be considered for co-funding in response to the calls for proposals published by the European Commission. The Commission's Evaluation Committee evaluates the proposals and decides whether a grant should be awarded.[70]

China has been the primary beneficiary of this Programme, as China is involved in forty six percent of all the projects co-financed under the programme.[71] As *Table 6: China's Asia-Invest Record* shows, Asia-Invest has approved 49 proposals involving China and 10 from China, and the success rates have been rather high (47.5 per cent and 25 per cent respectively).

[66] Asia-Invest: *About Us*, at http://europa.eu.int/comm/europeaid/projects/asia-invest/newhtml/aboutus.html (visited on 2April 2002).

[67] *Ibid.*

[68] *Asia-Invest: Unlocks Partnership Opportunities for European and Asian Companies*, Office for Official Publications of the European Community, May 2000, at 5.

[69] Asia-Invest: *About Us*, at http://europa.eu.int/comm/europeaid/projects/asia-invest/newhtml/aboutus.html (visited on 2April 2002).

[70] *Ibid.*

[71] Asia-Invest News: *Liberal Investment Incentives in Bangladesh*, Office for Official Publications of the European Community, June–August 2001, at 14.

Table 6: China's Asia-Invest Record

Projects	No. of proposals received	No. of proposals approved	Success rate
Project involving China	103	49	47.5%
Projects from China	40	10	25%

Source: Asia-Invest News: *Liberal Investment Incentives in Bangladesh*, Office for Official Publications of the European Community, June–August 2001, at 14.

These policies and measures show that the EU has been enthusiastic in promoting the outflow of investment, particularly to developing countries. They also confirm that the Community has competence on investment issues.

2.2.3 Community Practice in Concluding International Investment-Related Agreements

Apart from adopting internal legislation, policies and measures, the Community is very active in engaging in international investment-related agreements, both bilaterally and multilaterally. A summary of the Community's involvement in these agreements follows.

2.2.3.1 Bilateral Agreements

So far the Community has not successfully concluded an agreement specialised in investment protection and promotion, despite the Community's efforts as reflected in the 1978 Communication and the 1980 Report. In the late 1970s, the EC Member States had, surprisingly, reached a consensus within the framework of the Euro-Arab dialogue (EAD), on a draft for a comprehensive investment protection agreement, after their views on the principles had been co-ordinated with those on the Arabian side. The document was 'a fully worked-up and detailed legal text'[72] containing provisions on rights and obligations of the Member States of both the Arab League and the EC.[73] Unfortunately, this convention seems not to have been concluded. In 1984, when the Community was to conclude a co-operation agreement with China,[74] the European Parliament had proposed to sign another individual agreement with China on investment and intellectual property Protection.[75] Again, nothing seems to have been produced. Nevertheless, the

[72] COM (80) 204 final, at 2.

[73] Voss, Jurgen, 'The Protection and Promotion of European Private Investment in Developing Countries—An Approach Towards a Concept for a European Policy on Foreign Investment: A German Contribution', (1981) 18 *Common Market Law Review*, at 364.

[74] OJ L250/1 (19–09–85).

[75] See the European Parliament's Resolution on economic and commercial relations between China and the EEC, OJ C 127/210, 1984.

Community has managed to insert an investment clause or sometimes a whole chapter on investment into various framework agreements with third countries, mainly developing countries. These framework agreements include, among others, co-operation agreements (eg, co-operation agreements with China, India, ASEAN, Brazil, etc.), partnership agreements (eg, the 2000 EC-ACP Partnership Agreement), and free trade agreements (eg, the 2000 EC-Mexico Free Trade Agreement).[76]

2.2.3.2 Multilateral Agreements

In addition to signing bilateral agreements, the EC is very active in multilateral investment law making. This can be seen from its participation in the WTO agreements, the Third Revised Decision of the Organization for Economic Co-operation and Development (OECD) on National Treatment (the Third Decision), and the 1998 Multilateral Agreement on Investment (MAI) negotiations.[77]

2.2.3.2.1 WTO Agreement. The EU was one of the leading players of the Uruguay Round negotiations which created the WTO. As a matter of fact, the Council and the representatives of the governments of the member states approved the Punta del Este declaration,[78] which launched the negotiations. In order to ensure the maximum consistency, the Council decided that the Commission alone on behalf of the Community and the member states conducted negotiations.[79] The Council nevertheless stated in the minutes of the meeting at which the Punta del Este declaration was approved, that this decision 'does not prejudice the question of the competence of the Community or the member states on particular issues.'[80]

On 6 April 1994, some days before the WTO agreements were to be signed, the Commission submitted to the Court a request for an opinion on the exclusivity of the Community competence to conclude all the WTO agreements. In November that year, the Court delivered the lengthy Opinion 1/94, which confirmed the Community's exclusive competence to conclude the Multilateral Agreement on Trade in Goods, pursuant to Article113 (now art. 133) of the EC Treaty, but it ruled that the Community had to share with its member states the competence to conclude the GATS and the 1994 Agree-

[76] For further details please see Shan, Wenhua, 'Towards a Common European Community Policy on Investment Issues', (2001) 2 *Journal of World Investment* 603, at 616–18.

[77] Some other multilateral instruments that the EU has participated are also of some importance. For instance, EU signed the Energy Charter Treaty (ECT), along side with its Member States, which is closely related to investment issues. For further details of EU's involvement in the ECT, see Shan, Wenhua, above note 76, at 621.

[78] See Part III of the *Opinion 1/94*, above note 5, on the 'Negotiation and signature of the WTO Agreement'.

[79] *Ibid.*

[80] *Ibid.*

ment on Trade-Related Intellectual Property Rights (TRIPs Agreement). On GATS, in particular, the Court said that only services provided through cross-border modes of supply were covered by Article 113 (now art. 133) and therefore fell within the exclusive competence of the Community. Of other forms of services, including those supplied through 'commercial presence', which fall outside the common commercial policy, it said that the Community did not have sole competence and had to share the power with its Member States.[81] This implies that the EC's power to regulate direct investment in services sectors is shared rather than exclusive.[82]

Surprisingly, it seemed that the TRIMs Agreement, a sub-agreement specifically addressing investment issues under the Multilateral Agreement on Trade in Goods (MATG), had not raised any question at all during the proceedings. Nor did Opinion 1/94 even specifically mention the TRIMs. From the Opinion, a logical conclusion would be that the Community should have sole competence over TRIMs, as it is included in the MATG, which as a whole falls within the Community's exclusive competence. However, this conclusion is ambiguous and could be dangerous. While it may be clear that the listed measures fall within the sole Community competence, it would be doubtful whether the follow-up investment-related activities also do. For instance, does the Community have exclusive power to participate in the WTO reviews and negotiations on all investment-related aspects,[83] and more disputably, can the Community alone take part in the possible negotiations on a multilateral investment agreement under the aegis of the WTO? If the answers are positive, it would contradict the spirit of Opinion 1/94, which rejected the broad interpretation of Article 133 on CCP as covering all trade-related economic issues. If the answers are negative, a finer line must be drawn on the scope of the TRIMs. Nevertheless, it should have been clear that at least certain investment measures regulated by the TRIMs fell into the EC's exclusive competence.

2.2.3.2.2 The Third Decision. The Third Decision is a binding OECD instrument, which concerns a procedure for notification and examination of measures relating to national treatment. In December 1991, when the Third Decision was adopted by the Council of the OECD, the Commission

[81] *Opinion 1/94*, above note 5, at para. 36–53

[82] The Treaty of Nice has made some progress on this in that it extends the application of Art 133 to trade in services. In other words, now that EC has the express competence in concluding international agreements in services. Nevertheless, it appears that the power to regulate trade in services is still shared with member states. See Section 2.1.1.1 and above note 15.

[83] In fact, most of the reviews and negotiations scheduled for the early years of the WTO concerned investment issues and several of them had the potential for significant expansion of the WTO's coverage of investment matters. Also, the 1996 Singapore Ministerial Conference created three new working groups, among which one was to investigate the relationship between trade and investment and the possibility to conclude a multilateral agreement on investment within the WTO framework. See Brewer and Young, above note 46, at 139. See also WTO: *Trading into the Future*, 2nd edition (WTO, 2001), at 50.

representative stated that the Community intended to accede to the Third Decision, based on Article 57 and 113 of the EC Treaty. At the same time, the Netherlands representative expressed his concern that the Community Member States would be bound by it after the accession by the Community.[84] Hence in December 1992, Belgium submitted its request to the Court for an opinion on the legal basis of the EC's participation in the Third Decision.

The Court delivered its opinion (Opinion 2/92) in March 1995, maintaining that neither Article 113 (now art. 133) nor the Opinion 1/76 applied to this case. It also said that since the Community measures adopted so far did not cover 'the fields of activity to which the Third Decision relates', the Community possessed only partial competence thereon.[85] At the end, it ruled that the Community was competent to participate in the Third Decision, but must do so jointly with Member States. As the first Court Opinion on an instrument dedicated to international investment issues, Opinion 2/92 shows that the Community has non-exclusive competence on investment matters.

2.2.3.2.3 MAI. Soon after the Opinion 2/92 was delivered, the member countries of the OECD, including the EC Member States, decided to negotiate a binding MAI.[86] The MAI was a detailed, high-standard agreement on investment protection and promotion. In order to co-ordinate actions of the Community and its member states, a framework for co-operation was finally agreed a year later. The framework was adopted as a series of non-binding Council of Minister's Decisions, and it had four components[87] as follows:

a the Community negotiated in areas of EC competence on the basis of directives from the Council and in consultation with appropriate Council committees;
b the negotiators for the commission, Council and Member States met before each OECD negotiation session;
c a Working group of government officials assisted the Commission and worked to ensure co-operation between the EC and the member governments; and
d 'modelities' structured participation and confirmed the obligation to cooperate in accordance with the treaties and the Court case law.

This framework turned out to be unsuccessful. In early 1998, when public opposition was mounting, a number of participating governments doubted the value of the agreement and were concerned about the constraints it would

[84] *Ibid.*
[85] *Ibid.*, above note 10, at para. 28, 32, 34.
[86] Young, Alasdair R, 'The Adaptation of European Foreign Economic Policy: from Rome to Seattle', (2000) 39 *Journal of Common Market Studies*, at 108–11.
[87] *Ibid.*

impose on them.[88] Later the French government first asked to suspend the talks to allow time for domestic consultation and then withdrew from the talks without formally consulting its Community negotiating partners.[89] This left the other EC Member States with the worst of both worlds. On the one hand, because the Community's co-operation was characterised by 'soft institutions' they could not prevent the French withdrawal. On the other hand, since some aspects of the negotiations fell within the exclusive competence of the EC, other governments could not carry on the talks without France, even if they had wanted to do so.[90] It may be argued that the failure of the MAI proposal within the OECD demonstrates that the vaguely defined 'shared competence' of the EC on investment issues cannot keep up with the needs of the ever integrating Community and the fast globalising world economy.

To summarise the Community has successfully concluded a number of investment related agreements, bilaterally and multilaterally. This has not only confirmed that the Community has external investment competence but has also demonstrated that it has great enthusiasm for entering into international investment agreements. Furthermore the failure of the OECD MAI proposal has implied that a further clarification of the power attribution between the Community and its Member States on investment matters is needed.

2.3 EU MEMBER STATE LAW ON OUTWARD INVESTMENT

At the member state level, restrictions on outward investment[91] have been very rare except, for instance, notification or authorisation requirements in several countries and the 50 per cent foreign-currency requirement in Greece.[92] On the contrary, EU member states have established a variety of schemes and mechanisms to promote outward investment.

2.3.1 The Liberalisation of Outward Investment within EU Member States

The liberalisation of outward investment regimes in EU member states is a result of EU laws and regulations, as described above. It also owes to the legal instruments of the Organisation of Economic Co-operation and Develop-

[88] *Ibid.*
[89] *Ibid.*
[90] *Ibid.*
[91] There are, however, still a variety of controls in member states, principally on inward FDI. These rules are permissible exemptions to the OECD and are mainly related to take-overs from outside the Country of the EU, or sectoral measures in regulated or sensitive industries. See Brewer and Young, above note 46, at 41.
[92] For details about EU Member State policies on investment issues, see OECD: *EU Member State Policies on FDI in the 1980s*, as reprinted in 29 *Journal of World Trade* 1, at 42–3.

ment (OECD), whereby all EU member states are members. The OECD has made efforts since 1961 to dismantle barriers to investment flows, particularly in inward investment. The most influential legal instruments it has produced so far are the Codes of Liberalisation and the Declaration on International Investment and Multinational Enterprises.

2.3.1.1 The OECD Codes of Liberalisation

The OECD Codes of Liberalisation include the Code of Liberalisation of Capital Movement and the Code of Liberalisation of Invisible Operations, which were firstly laid down in 1961.[93] The two Codes take the form of Council Decisions of the OECD and are therefore legally binding on all member states.[94] The Code of Capital Movements covers all long- and short-term capital movements between residents of OECD member states. This includes the right of establishment and foreign direct investment, eg, the acquisition of existing companies by foreign enterprises or establishment of subsidiaries by multinational corporations.[95] The Invisible Operations Code covers cross-border trade in services between residents of OECD member states, particularly banking and financial services, insurance, professional services, maritime and road transport, travel and tourism, etc.[96] Although covering different areas, the two Codes are governed by similar general principles and monitoring procedures.[97] The key idea is set out in Article 1 of both Codes, which requires member states to eliminate any existing restrictions between one another on capital movement and invisible transactions.[98] Other provisions provide for a framework by which member states must work towards that goal, including:[99]

a the right to proceed gradually towards liberalisation through lodging and maintaining reservations;
b non-discrimination obligation;
c public order and security exceptions;
d derogations in cases of temporary economic difficulty;

[93] For an official overview of the Codes, see OECD Directorate of Finance, Fiscal and Enterprise Affairs: *Overview to the OECD Codes of Liberalisation* (hereinafter 'Overview'), June 2002, available at http://www.oecd.org/pdf/M00031000/M00031423.pdf (visited on 1 August 2002); for the text of the Codes, see OECD Directorate of Finance, Fiscal and Enterprise Affairs: *Code of Liberalisation of Capital Movements* and *Code of Current Invisible Operations*, May 2001, available at, respectively, http://www.oecd.org/pdf/M00007000/M00007320.pdf and http://www.oecd.org/pdf/M00007000/M00007322.pdf (visited on 1 August 2002). For a scholarly discussion of the Code, see Muchlinski, Peter, *Multinational Enterprises and the Law* (Blackwell Publishers, 1995), at 247–50.

[94] Muchlinski, *ibid*, at 248.

[95] OECD, above note 93, Overview, at 4.

[96] *Ibid*.

[97] Muchlinski, above note 93, at 248.

[98] OECD, Overview, above note 93, at 3.

[99] *Ibid*, at 3–4.

e procedures to ensure compatibility of regional economic integration arrangements such as the EU and its special processes;
f a system of notification, examination and consultation run by the Committee of Capital Movements and Invisible Transactions (CMIT), a special OECD committee.

The OECD Codes of Liberalisation are compatible with the EU regulations because from the beginning they provided for regional economic integration organisations such as the EU.[100] As an exception to the non-discrimination obligation, the EU may liberalise more rapidly and more widely than the OECD,[101] without extending the liberalising benefits to non-EU OECD member states. However, the CMIT will examine and determine whether EU regulations and directives are otherwise compatible with its member states' obligations under the Codes. In particular, harmonisation and liberalisation within the EU may not raise new barriers to transactions with non-EU OECD members.[102] Moreover EU member states are still required to be committed to the overall objectives of the Codes. Restrictions removed within the EU should also eventually be removed in relation to other OECD member states, if they fall within the coverage of the Codes.[103]

The EU regulations and the OECD Codes have therefore played a crucial role in the liberalisation of FDI regimes in EU member states. It can be argued that EU investment in China may also have benefited from such liberalisation, because such liberalisation is achieved by member states adopting unilateral measures and thus may not necessarily discriminate against non-OECD countries. In addition, China has signed BITs with most EU member states, which entitle China and its EU counterparts to mutual most-favoured-nation treatment.[104]

2.3.1.2 The OECD Declaration on International Investment and Multinational Enterprises

Apart from the Codes of Liberalisation, investments between the EU and non-EU OECD member states are also facilitated by the OECD Declaration on International Investment and Multinational Enterprises (hereinafter the

[100] OECD, Overview, at 8.

[101] A particular example is the Second EU Banking Directive, which has introduced a single licence to provide banking services across the EU, which is a special advantage that has not been fully extended to all OECD member states. OECD, Overview, at 8. See also second Council Directive 89/646/EEC of 15 December 1989 on the coordination of laws, regulations and administrative provisions relating to the taking up and pursuit of the business of credit institutions, OJ L 386, 30.12.1989, p. 1.

[102] This may happen when a EU member state with a highly liberal investment regime is required to adopt more restrictive measures in a particular area, as a result of the harmonisation effort made by the EU. See OECD, Overview, above note 93, at 8.

[103] *Ibid.*

[104] For details about most favoured nation treatment in China EU BITs, See Section 5.2.2.1.

'OECD Declaration'),[105] a broad political commitment adopted by the OECD Governments in 1976. The OECD Declaration comprises four instruments for international co-operation: the Guidelines for Multinational Enterprises, the National Treatment instrument, an instrument on Conflicting Requirements; and an instrument on International Investment Incentives and Disincentives.[106]

Among these four instruments, the National Treatment instrument has been most important for investment liberalisation, as it requires member states to treat foreign investors in the same way as they do their own nationals in similar situations. However, the most extensive instruments is the OECD Guidelines on Multinational Enterprises (hereinafter 'the OECD Guidelines'). The OECD Guidelines, which are contained in an Annex to the Declaration, form the only comprehensive code of business conduct that are multilaterally endorsed by countries that are the source of most of the world's direct investment flows and home to most multinational enterprises.[107] The Guidelines are recommendations addressed by governments to multinational enterprises operating in or from Adhering countries (the OECD members plus Argentina, Brazil and Chile).[108] They provide voluntary principles and standards for responsible business conduct, in a variety of contexts including employment and industrial relations, human rights, environment, information disclosure, competition, taxation, and science and technology.

The OECD Guidelines are not legally binding or enforceable. However, Muchilinski argued that they are an example of 'soft law' and could 'harden' into public international law, provided that they are generally accepted and frequently applied by governments in their dealing with MNEs.[109] He further pointed out that the OECD countries appear to prefer an extension of investment protection standard rather than strengthening the restrictive provisions contained in the OECD Guidelines.[110] Nevertheless, as the only existing multilateral instrument on MNE conducts, the OECD Guidelines may serve as a reference, for host governments' handling MNEs issues, and in particular, for future international law making on investors' responsibilities. A further discussion of sources of international law and 'soft law' is contained in Chapter 3.[111]

105 For text, commentary and clarifications of the OECD Declaration, see http://www.oecd.org/pdf/M00021000/M00021070.pdf. See also Muchlinski, above note 93, at 478–592.

106 OECD: *The OECD Declaration and Decisions on International Investment And Multinational Enterprises: Basic Texts*, DAFFE/IME(2000)20, 'Foreword', at 2, available at: http://www.olis.oecd.org/olis/2000doc.nsf/c5ce8ffa41835d64c125685d005300b0/c125692700623b74c1256991003b5147/$FILE/00085743.DOC.

107 OECD Website: *The OECD Guidelines for Multinational Enterprises: Frequently Asked Questions*, at: http://www.oecd.org/EN/document/0,EN-document-93-nodirectorate-no-21-18096- 9,00.html (1 August 2002)

108 *Ibid*.

109 Muchlinski, above note 93, at 578.

110 *Ibid*.

111 See Section 3.1 , in particular, Section 3.1.7.

2.3.2 The Promotion of Outward Investment in EU Member States

While liberalising inward and outward investment flow, several EU Member States have developed schemes to promote and encourage outward investments. France, Germany, Britain and Sweden provide loan facilities for outward investments through various forms of development financial corporations, such as 'Caisse Centrale de Co-operation Economique' in France, 'German Finance Company for Investment in Developing Countries', British 'Commonwealth Development Corporation' and the 'Swedish Fund for International Co-operation with Developing Countries'.[112] Additionally, 10 of the 15 EU member states have established national political risk insurance schemes to encourage outward investment.[113] Tuearbeit AG of Germany for instance, is one of world's largest political insurance agencies.[114] Administered by the German federal government, Tuearbeit AG offers insurance for investments, loans with equity features and guarantees for services contracts in the petroleum sector.[115] Its insurance covers risks associated with nationalisation, measures equivalent to expropriation, wrongful failure to act by public authorities, war, other armed conflicts, revolution and insurrection, blockage of payment, moratorium on payment, and bans on currency convertibility or transfer.[116]. In the UK, political insurance is offered through the Export Credits Guarantee Department (ECGD), against risks related to expropriation, political violence and currency inconvertibility. Furthermore, all EU member states have signed the Convention Establishing the Multilateral Investment Guarantee Agency (hereinafter 'the MIGA Convention').[117]

EU member states have signed numerous bilateral investment treaties (BITs) with third countries.[118] Indeed, the first BIT in the world was signed between West Germany and Pakistan in 1959. So far, 14 of the 15 member states within the EU have concluded BITs with China.[119]

[112] Zeng, Huaqun, *International Investment Law* (*Guoji Touzi Faxue*) (Peking University Press, 1999), at 134–35.

[113] These member states include Austria, Belgium, Denmark, Finland, France, Germany, Italy, Netherlands, Portugal, Sweden and the UK. See Rowat, Malcolm D, 'Multilateral Approaches to Improving the Investment Climate of Developing Countries: The Cases of ICSID and MIGA', (1992) 33 *Harvard International Law Journal*, at 138. See also Zeng, Huaqun, above note 112, at 141–43; Comeaux, Paul, and Kinsella, N Stephan, *Protecting Foreign Investment under International Law: Legal Aspects of Political Risks* (Oceana Publications Inc., 1997), 179–81.

[114] Comeaux and Kinsella, *ibid*, at 151.

[115] *Ibid*, at 179.

[116] *Ibid*.

[117] For more details of the MIGA Convention, please refer to Section 3.2.2.2 and Section 7.5.2.

[118] One of the conditions that an investment guarantee scheme is dependent on is that the host country of the guaranteed investment project agrees that the home country or its investment guarantee can subrogate the rights and claims from the guaranteed investor. Therefore, one of the key functions of a BIT is to attain such a state consent on such subrogation or rights and claims.

[119] See Section 3.2.1.2.

2.4 TOWARDS A COMMON COMMUNITY INVESTMENT POLICY

It has been concluded from the preceding investigations that the EC has competence on investment issues. However this competence is generally regarded as a competence shared with the member States, rather than an exclusive competence. Moreover, the Community practice has also proved that the vaguely defined 'shared competence' may put the Community as well as its Member States into awkward and difficult situations when negotiating international investment agreements.

In fact the ambiguous division of competence between the Community and its Member States and the lack of a Community FDI policy, when the Community is entering into international negotiations, slows deliberations,[120] frustrates other countries and enables rivals such as the US and Japan to play off member States against each other.[121] It also results in problems when the Community deals with internal relations, such as relationships between different Community Directorates, between the Community and its Member States and even between different Member States.[122] For instance, the Community investment policies and policy-making are handled at the Directorate level but there is no framework for ensuring a coherent approach to all relevant policies. Therefore, overlap, contradiction and gaps in policy coverage may happen frequently, which will affect the effectiveness and efficiency of their administrative operations.

A common Community investment policy (CIP) and a sole Community investment competence will, to a considerable extent, facilitate the efficient functioning of the EC, and, at the same time, place the EU in a much more favourable position in future bilateral or multilateral investment law-making. Moreover, this could eventually secure the equal treatment among the European investors internally and externally. Last but not least, the European multinational enterprises, the major investment players in the Europe now belonging to the Community rather than a single member state, will benefit most from this scheme.

To achieve this goal, it may be necessary, first of all, to coordinate and harmonise the laws and regulations existing in Member States on investment promotion and protection, and to create a common Community policy thereon. It would help if the EC established an External Investment Unit (EIU) under the Directorate General for Trade of the Commission.[123] Its aims

120 An interview by the author with an EC official dealing with investment issues reveals that unanimity and consensus is needed in negotiating such agreements. This indeed makes it much more difficult than negotiating a trade agreement. See Interview No. 6 in the author's file.

121 Brewer and Young, above note 46, at 46.

122 For a detailed list of possible problems in different policy areas, see Brewer and Young, *ibid*, at 45.

123 Now the Commission has established a Unit dealing with investment and other issues under Directorate F of Directorate-General for Trade. However, in order to achieve harmonisation and coordination, it is necessary to have a Unit exclusively devoted to investment issues.

would be to facilitate information exchange between the Community and its member states, to conduct research, to provide a forum for discussing internal and external investment issues and to furnish an FDI input into the policies of the EC Directorates, and perhaps more specifically, to draft model investment agreements at the Community level, based on the co-ordination based on the 1978 Communication and the 1980 Report.

Meanwhile, a Community program on investment guarantees should also be established, to facilitate the EC outward investment flow to third countries, especially developing countries.[124] Although by now many EU Member States have established their investment guarantee projects, it is preferable to have such a mechanism at the Community level, because of its larger coverage, bigger size, higher credit and therefore higher efficiency. In this sense, the EC could learn from various experiences of the Multilateral Investment Guarantee Agency (MIGA) and the national investment insurers in the EU Member States.

When the time comes, the EC should promulgate Community FDI Guidelines to direct the internal harmonisation and co-ordination of FDI-related laws and regulations, which could be converted to be a Community FDI Regulation based on Article 57 (2) when the co-ordination and harmonisation have been achieved. In the end, it would be necessary to clarify the common Community policy and competence, particularly its exclusive external competence on investment aspects, in the EC Treaty, preferably by amending and extending the coverage of Article 133 (ex art. 113). As noted above, the Treaty of Nice has only extended the application of Article 133 Paragraphs 1–4 to 'the negotiation and conclusion of agreements in the fields of trade in services and the commercial aspects of intellectual property rights', not in the field of investment as proposed by the European Parliament.[125] In the draft constitution of the European Union, another attempt has been made to extend the CCP to cover FDI issues.[126] In June 2004 the draft Treaty was adopted by leader of the 25 member states and CCP was extended, finally to cover FDI, alongside with trade in services and commercial aspects of intellectual property rights.[127] Once it is ratified by the 25 member states, the EU will acquire exclusive competence on external investment issues and consequently a common investment policy (CIP) will probably be established.

[124] One should recall that the first proposal specifically addressing investment issues, by the Commission, was a proposal to establish a Community investment guarantee system (the 1972 Proposal). See Section 2.2.2.1 for further details.

[125] See Section 2.1.1.1.

[126] The draft Constitution also clarifies the different categories of EU competences. For details, see the Draft Treaty Establishing a Constitution for Europe, available at http://european-convention.eu.int/docs/Treaty/cv00850.en03.pdf (visited on 31 January 2004)

[127] Article III–217, Provisional Consolidated Version of the Draft Treaty Establishing a Constitution for Europe). For more about the treaty, see http://www.fco.gov.uk/servlet/ Front?pagename=OpenMarket/Xcelerate/ShowPage&c=Page&cid=1007029392727 (visited on 29 August 2004).

2.5 CONCLUSION

The law within the EU governing outward investment includes both EU law and member state law, because the Community has not yet attained exclusive competence on external investment issues, despite the continuous efforts made by the Commission since the early 1970s. Under the EC Treaty, and particularly Articles 56 and 57, all restrictions on investment to and from third countries, inward and outward alike, are prohibited within the framework of the EU. On outward investment in particular, virtually no restriction has been maintained at the EU level. On member state level very few such restrictions exist in practice. The liberalisation of outward investment achieved in EU member states is the result of both EU regulations and OECD Codes and instruments. Meanwhile, both the EU and its member states have developed policies and measures to promote outward investment, particularly in developing countries. At the Community level, the EU has initiated ECIP and Asia-Invest Programmes, which are useful and highly successful in promoting EU investment to third countries, particularly to Asian countries including China. At member state level the most frequently used mechanism to promote outward investment has been investment guarantee schemes that exist in a number of EU member states.

As far as entering into international investment agreements is concerned, EU member state have been very keen in concluding BITs and most of them have signed such agreements with China. At the community level, although the Community has not yet signed any bilateral agreement devoted to investment issues, it has managed to conclude some bilateral agreements that bear implications on external investment. At the same time the Community has participated in a number of multilateral instruments that are closely related to investment matters, and has played a full part in the negotiation of the MAI draft, a multilateral framework for investment protection and liberalisation sponsored by the OECD. The Community's involvement in international investment instruments has confirmed its competence over investment issues and has demonstrated its long standing enthusiasm in international investment law-making.

However the Community practice in international investment law-making, particularly in the ill-fated MAI negotiations, has proved that the vaguely defined 'share competence' may put the Community as well as its Member States into awkward and difficult situations when negotiating international investment agreements. It is therefore argued that a common Community investment policy (CIP) and a sole Community investment competence will, to a considerable extent, facilitate the efficient functioning of the EC, and, at the same time, place the EU in a much more favourable position in future bilateral or multilateral investment law-making. Furthermore, it would eventually secure the equal treatment among the European investors internally and externally and greatly benefit the European multinational enterprises. In this regard, the Treaty Establishing a Constitution for Europe will mark a significant breakthrough. It is also argued that setting up a Community investment guarantee scheme would help to promote EU investment in developing countries including China. Although some EU member states have their own investment insurance schemes and the MIGA can insure all EU investment in China, it would still be desirable to have an EU investment guarantee scheme.

3

International Law Governing EU Investment in China

International law plays an important role in protecting and promoting EU investment in China. Compared with Chinese law and EU law, international law offers higher certainty and predictability as it cannot be changed unilaterally. This Chapter explores the structural aspects of the international law governing EU investment in China, including the sources of applicable international law, the major international agreements and the interaction between international treaties and Chinese law.

3.1 SOURCES OF INTERNATIONAL LAW GOVERNING EU INVESTMENT IN CHINA

The sources of international law governing EU investment in China mainly refer to traditional sources, such as international treaties, customary international law, general principles of law, judicial decisions and publicists' writings.[1] Additionally, they may refer to United Nation Resolutions and 'soft law', which have been argued as new or 'proper' sources of international investment and economic law.[2] A discussion of these sources follows.

[1] See Art 38 (1) of the *Statute of the International Court of Justice (ICJ Statute)* reads, 'The Court, whose function is to decide in accordance with international law such disputes as are submitted to it, shall apply:
(a) international conventions, whether general or particular, establishing rules expressly recognised by the contesting States;
(b) international customs, as evidence of a general practice accepted as law;
(c) the general principles of law recognised by civilised nations;
(d) subject to the provisions of Art 59, judicial decisions and the teachings of the most highly qualified publicists of the various nations, as subsidiary means for the determination of rules of law.'
Although Art 38 does not directly refer to 'sources' of international law and therefore may not be regarded as straightforward enumeration of the sources, it is generally regarded as an authoritative statement of the sources of international law, as it reflects state practice and previous practice of arbitration tribunals. See Jennings, Robert and Watts, Arthur, *Oppenheim's International Law*, 9th edition (Longman, 1992), at 24; See also, Brownlie, Ian, *Principles of Public International Law*, 4th edition (Oxford University Press, 1998), at 3.

[2] Seidl-Hohenveldern, for example, separates UN resolutions and international economic 'soft

3.1.1 International Treaties

It is undisputed that international treaties are of the most important sources of international law.[3] So far there has been no universal international convention on international investment, despite continuous attempts, usually made by developed capital-exporting countries.[4] As a result, regional and bilateral treaties play important roles in the protection and promotion of foreign investment. For EU investment in China in particular, although there has been no applicable regional agreement, some applicable bilateral and multilateral agreements on investment do exist. The EU has bilaterally signed a co-operation agreement with China in 1985[5] (the 'EC-China Co-operation Agreement'), which touched upon investment issues. At member state level, 14 of the 15 EU member states have signed bilateral investment treaties (BITs)

law' from traditional sources of international law, in his discussions on sources of international economic law. Whilst rejecting the binding force of UN resolutions, he considers international economic 'soft law', among other, as 'proper' source of international economic law. However, Verma considers UN resolutions a new source of international law. See Seidl-Hohenveldern, Ignaz, *International Economic Law*, 3rd edition (Kluwer, 1999), at 29; Verma, DP, 'Rethinking about New International Law-Making Process', (1989) 29 *Indiana Journal of International Law*, , at 48. See also Qureshi, Asif H, *International Economic Law* (Sweet & Maxwell, 1999), at 17; Fox, Hazel, *International Economic Law and Developing States: An Introduction* (The British Institute of International and Comparative Law, 1992), at 20–4. Moreover, Jennings and Watts note that the list of sources of international law by the ICJ Statute is not necessarily exhaustive and new sources may be added up thereto. *Oppenheim's International Law*, *ibid*, at 45.

[3] For instance, Brownlie writes that, international treaties and international custom are 'obviously the important sources' and the priority of international treaties is 'explicable by the fact that this refers to a source of mutual obligation of parties'. However, he also notes that international treaties is not a source of general application and may be void or avoidable if they are contrary to a custom or to a general principle part of the *jus cogens*. Brownlie, above, note 1, at 3–4. Similar view is also expressed in *Oppenheim's International Law*, *ibid*, at 25–6.

[4] The first effort as such was the unsuccessful Charter of the International Trade Organisation drafted immediately after the World War II, which included rule of international investment. One of the recent attempt is the draft Multilateral Agreement on Investment (MAI) negotiated among the OECD countries launched in 1995 with the intention to become a universal, comprehensive code of international investment. However, the negotiations of such a MAI draft were suspended in 1998. Now it is hoped that a general agreement on investment might be concluded eventually under the auspices of the World Trade Organisation (WTO), as its Doha Ministerial Declaration has shown such a possibility. For a good survey of earlier attempts to create a multilateral investment agreement, see Tschofen, Franziska, 'Multilateral Approaches to the Treatment of Foreign Investment', in Shihata, Ibrahim (ed), *Legal Treatment of Foreign Investment: The World Bank Guidelines* (Martinus Nijhoff, 1993), 267 onwards. For further information about the MAI negotiation, see Engering, Frans, 'The Multilateral Investment Agreement', (1996) 5 *Transnational Corporations*, at 147 onwards; Witherell, William H, 'The OECD Multilateral Agreement on Investment', (1995) 4 *Transnational Corporations*, at 1 onwards. See also The World Trade Organisation: *Ministerial Declaration adopted by the Fourth Session of the Ministerial Conference at Doha* on 9–14 November 2001 (hereinafter '*Doha Ministerial Declaration*'), at para 20. WT/MIN(01)/DEC/W/1 (14 November 2001), posted at http://www.wto.org/english/thewto_e/minist_e/min01_e/mindecl_e.htm (visited on 18 January 2002). The initiative of an investment agreement within WTO will be further discussed in Section 9.3.1.1.

[5] Officially the 1985 Agreement on Trade and Economic Co-operation between the European Community and the People's Republic of China. See OJ L250 (19/9/85).

with China. China and the EU and/or all of its Member States have been parties to several multilateral agreements that have substantial bearings on investment matters, such as the MIGA Convention, the ICSID Convention and the WTO Agreement. These bilateral and multilateral agreements constitute the core of international law which governs EU investment in China. They are further discussed in the immediately following sections.

As a general rule of law, international treaties do not normally bind third parties.[6] In general, therefore other important regional or multilateral investment agreements, such as the 1992 North American Free Trade Agreement (NAFTA) Chapter 11, ECT, do not bind the EU and China. This book will refer to them from time to time, as evidence of principles and standards to which the EU in particular or developed countries in general have submitted.

3.1.2 Customary International Law

Customary international law is the original and oldest source of international law.[7] As a result, apart from being separately applied as one of the principal formal sources of international law,[8] it is very often used to interpret treaty provisions in doubtful cases.[9] Furthermore, it may prevail over treaty provisions if it embodies a rule of *jus cogens* with which the treaty provisions are in conflict.[10] In establishing customary international law, there are two recognised criteria, namely state practice (or *usus*) and *opinio juris*.[11] According to the jurisprudence of the International Court of Justice (ICJ), the state practice must be 'constant', 'extensive' and 'uniform'[12] and the *opinio juris* requires a

[6] The International Law Commission considered this an almost universal rule, which is based on both the law of contract and on the sovereignty and independence of states. See *Oppenheim's International Law*, above, note 1, at 1260.

[7] *Oppenheim's International Law*, *ibid*, at 25.

[8] It is widely accepted that treaties and custom are two principal sources of international law. See eg, Brownlie, at 3; Cassese, Antonio, *International Law* (Oxford University Press, 2000), at 117.

[9] *Oppenheim's International Law*, above, note 1, at 25.

[10] *Oppenheim's International Law*, *ibid*. Brownlie considers the principle of permanent sovereignty over natural resources a rule of *jus cogens*. In contrast, Seidl-Hohenveldern considers that it is not. See Brownlie, above, note 1, at 515; Seidl-Hohenveldern, Ignaz, 'Hierarchy of the Norms Applicable to International Investment', in his *Collected Essays on International Investment and International Organisations* (Kluwer, 1998), at 201.

[11] Cassese, above, note 8, at 119. See also *Oppenheim's International Law*, above, note 1, at 27; Brownlie, above, note 1, 4–5.

[12] In the *Asylum* case, the ICJ used the words 'constant and uniform' to define the state practice required. In *North Sea Continental Shelf cases*, the Court used 'both extensive and virtually uniform' to define the state practice element. See *Asylum* case, ICJ Reports 1950, at 276–77; and *North Sea Continental Shelf cases*, ICJ Reports, 1969, at 43. However, as Brownlie pointed out by referring to *Fisheries* and *Genocide* cases, no complete uniformity or universality of practice is necessary, but substantial uniformity and generality are. See Brownlie, *ibid*, at 5–6. See also *Anglo-Norwegian Fisheries* case, ICJ Reports, 1951, at 131; *Case Concerning the Application of Genocide Convention (Bosnia-Herzegovina v. Yugoslavia (Serbia and Montenegro)) (Provisional Measures)* ICJ Reports, 1993, at 25.

'general recognition that a rule of law or legal obligation is involved'.[13] Further, a wide range of materials can be used as evidence of customary international law.[14]

Customary international law plays an important role in international investment law. It is thus a customary international law that, subject to overriding treaty commitments, a State has the right to admit or reject a foreign investment, to ban or limit capital transfer related to a foreign investment out of the state, or and to expropriate or nationalise foreign assets.[15] In case there is a dispute between a foreign investor and the host state, customary international law requires local remedies to be exhausted before any international remedies are resorted to.[16] In many cases however customary international law on international investment is characterised by uncertainty and ambiguity.[17] A classical example is the debate on the customary international law of compensation in cases of expropriation of foreign assets. Capital exporting countries insist that, in such cases, customary international law requires 'adequate, prompt and effective' compensation. By contrast, capital importing countries have vigorously rejected this standard of compensation and have endeavoured to create a new rule of customary international law.[18]

It may sometimes be particularly difficult to establish rules of customary international law in the context of EU investment in China against such a background.[19] On the one hand, since EU countries are all developed coun-

[13] *North Sea Continental Shelf* cases, ICJ Reports, 1969, at 43. Jennings and Watts note that, although a practice and indeed its acceptance as law must be general in order to constitute an international custom, a practice does not have to be either observed or accepted as law, expressly or explicitly, by every state. *Oppenheim's International Law*, 9th ed., above, note 1, at 29. Nevertheless, they have noticed that Marxist/Socialist theory has an emphasis on the need for consent to rules of international law, which, in turn, has led to a strong preference for treaties over customary international law. *Oppenheim's International Law*, above, note 1, at 29.

[14] The International Law Commission (ILC) produced a non-exhaustive list of the forms that state practice may take: treaties, decisions of international and nation courts, national legislation, diplomatic correspondence, opinions of national legal advisors and the practice of international organisations. Further evidence may include, as Brownlie suggests, policy statements, press release, official manuals on legal questions, executive decisions and practices, orders to naval forces, etc. and comments by governments on drafts produced by the ILC. Apparently, the value of those evidences varies and much depends on the attending circumstances. Harris, David, *Cases and Materials on International Law* (Sweet and Maxwell, 1998), at 25–26; Brownlie, above, note 1, at 5.

[15] See Sections 4.1, 5.4 and 6.2.2.2 for further discussions.

[16] See Section 7.2.1.

[17] For instance, Fatouros noted that, 'customary law in matters of foreign direct investment rarely posses a high degree of clarity and specificity.' Fatouros, AA, Towards An International Agreement On Foreign Direct Investment?, *ICSID Review—Foreign Investment Law Journal* Vol. 12, No. 2, 1995, at 189. In the general areas of international economic law, it has been observed that international customs are all passive, 'soft' in legal nature and are focusing on the extremes of economic behaviour, or in Qureshi's summary, they all have the features of negativity, extremity and ambiguity. See Zamora, S, 'Is There Customary International Law?' (1989) 32 *German Yearbook of International Law* No. 9, at 41. See also, Qureshi, above, note 2, at 21.

[18] For further discussion of the controversy over the general international law of expropriation and compensation, see Section 6.1.

[19] Indeed, Sornarajah has argued that there exist but few general customary international law

tries and are familiar with customary international law rules, which are arguably Europe-centred, the EU and its member states are more than willing to use these rules to support their outward investors. On the other hand, as a developing country and a country with a socialist legacy,[20] China has long been very suspicious and cautious of the concepts of customary international law, as it has never had an opportunity to shape these customs and it often believes that they are adverse to its interests. In an early article on sources of international law, a Chinese international lawyer writes,

> 'Bourgeois international law scholars say that custom is also one of the principal sources of international law. The so-called custom refers to those customs formulated by external practices of big capitalist powers...the bourgeoisie has never considered and will never consider as customs the resistance of weak and small countries and colonies, the colonist countries' anti-aggression and anti-imperialist wars and opposition to imperialist intervention in internal affairs of other countries, and other just actions, and has never given support to these activities.'[21]

Chinese textbooks on international investment law likewise consider customary international law as of marginal importance.[22] In their discussions on rules of expropriation and compensation, Chinese lawyers have vigorously rejected the allegation that 'prompt, adequate and effective' compensation represents customary international law.[23] It can therefore be argued that, compared with international treaties, the role that international custom plays as an applicable source of international law governing EU investment in China is rather limited.[24]

3.1.3 General Principles of Law

According to Article 38 (1)(c) of the ICJ Statute, general principles of law[25] recognised by civilised nations are a source of international law. According to

rules on international investment. See Sornarajah, M., *The International Law on Foreign Investment* (Cambridge University Press, 1994), at 74.

20 For example, Jennings and Watts note that Marxist theory emphases state consent to any rule of international law, which has led to a strong preference for treaty over customary law. *Oppenheim's International Law*, above, note 1, at 29 note 22. For a critique on Communist approaches to expropriation and compensation, see Seidl-Hohenveldern, 'Communist Theories on Confiscation and Expropriation: Critical Comments', in Seidl-Hohenveldern, above, note 10, at 281 onwards.

21 See T'ao, Ying, 'Recognize the True Face of Bourgeois International Law from a Few Basic Concepts', included in Jerome Alan Cohen and Hungdah Chiu, *People's China and International Law: A Documentary Study* (Princeton University Press, 1974) vol. 1, at 71.

22 See eg, Yu, Jinsong, *International Investment Law* (in Chinese) (Law Press, 1994), at 13.

23 A further discussion on this follows in Section 9.4.3.

24 However, there are signs that China has become more willing to accept the concept of customary international law. For example, in the Sino-Morocco BIT, China has agreed to adopt 'principles of international law', which probably imply customary international law, as one of applicable laws to any investment disputes. For further details, see Section 7.2.2.

25 However, among international lawyers, there are various views with regard to the meanings

Oppenheim's International Law, '[T]he intention is to authorise the courts to apply the general principle of municipal jurisprudence, insofar as they are applicable to relations of states.'[26] It is also noted that general principles of law can play an important part in providing rules in areas beyond both the normal scope of national private law and the traditional scope of international law. These areas include certain transactions of states (particularly in their dealing with private corporations) on essentially private law matters.[27]

Indeed, general principles of law are sometimes resorted to in international judicial and arbitration practice to support the existence of certain rules of international law on foreign investment, despite the argument that they play only a very limited role as a source of international economic law.[28] For example, when justifying the full compensation for expropriation, notions of acquired rights, unjust enrichment and equity are often used.[29] Sometimes it is argued that the rule that compensation has to be paid *per se* is a general principle of law.[30] In contrast, developing country scholars have been cautious about using these principles. For instance, while acknowledging the usefulness of general principles of law in the development of international investment law, Sornarajah pointed out that the use of these principles is subject to a very high degree of subjectivity.[31] As a matter of fact, he has observed that arbitration tribunals have used the general principles of law in a manner that may not be acceptable to host states.[32] Often, they choose rules that favour the promotion of investment protection and are detrimental to the interests of host countries.[33]

In China, international economic lawyers have vigorously refuted the application of principles such as 'acquired rights' or 'unjust enrichment' in justifying full compensation.[34] YU argued for instance that these two prin-

of such a source. For further discussions of the various interpretations, see Shaw, M, *International Law*, 4th edition (Cambridge University Press, 1997), at 78–79; Judge Wang, Tieya, *International Law* (in Chinese) (Law Press, 1995), at 17.

26 *Oppenheim's International Law*, above, note 1, 36–37. Brownlie shares the view, see Brownlie, above, note 1, at 16.

27 *Oppenheim's International Law*, above, note 1, at 39.

28 Qureshi, above, note 2, at 22; Sornarajah, above, note 19, at 77; Seidl-Hohenveldern, above, note 2, at 34.

29 Sornarajah, above, note 19, at 77–78

30 In the *Chorzow Factory Case*, the Permanent Court of Justice said that 'it is a general conception of law that every violation of an engagement involves an obligation to make reparation.' See *Chorzow Factory Case*, [1928] PCIJ Series A No. 17, at 29. See also Sornarajah, above, note 19, at 78 note 129.

31 Sornarajah, above, note 19, at 78.

32 Sornarajah, above, note 19, at 78.

33 For instance, Sornarajah observed that while there have been general principles of law that support unilateral dismissal of state-investor contracts, arbitration tribunals tend to discard them and adopt only those favourable to investors. Sornarajah, above, note 19, at 78. Also, Harris has noted that the majority of arbitrators in arbitration awards supporting an 'international minimum standard' on the treatment of aliens tend to be from developed countries. Harris, above, note 14, at 523.

34 Yu, above, note 22, at 316–18; Yao, Meizhen, *International Investment Law* (in Chinese) (Wuhan University Press, 1987), at 381–83. Zeng, Huaqun, *Introduction to International Economic Law* (in Chinese) (Law Press, 1997), at 185–87.

ciples should apply only to tort or *sine causa* actions. Actions of expropriation based on the host country's sovereign rights are completely lawful and so should not be subject to these principles.[35] Moreover, he pointed out that these principles are principles of national law, rather than those of international law and so should not be applied at all.[36] Chinese discussions of sources of international investment law likewise normally do not refer to general principles of law.[37]

It is therefore very difficult to establish general principles of law that apply to the investment relations between the EU and China. Accordingly, as a source of international law governing EU investment in China, they are only of marginal importance.

3.1.4 Judicial Decisions

Formally, according to Article 38(1)(d) of the ICJ Statute, judicial decisions are subsidiary sources of international law.[38] In practice however decisions by courts and tribunals have become a most influential factor in the development of international law.[39] In the area of international investment, there have been two important decisions made by the ICJ, namely the *Barcelona Traction Case*[40] and the *ELSI Case*,[41] which respectively concern diplomatic protection and the expropriation of foreign investment.[42] Both the Court judgements and the separate opinions contain valuable discussions of international investment law.[43] Another form of 'judicial' decision is arbitration awards made by either *ad hoc* or institutional arbitration tribunals on international investment issues. These awards, particularly those made by tribunals constituted under the ICSID Convention, may be evidence of possible norms that are useful for the interpretation of rules of international law on foreign investment.[44] The Iran-US Claims Tribunal is a special case in this field. The Tribunal was set up by the two states in accordance with the Algiers Accord, which also provided for the enforcement of the awards.[45] Although it

[35] Yu, *ibid*, at 318.

[36] *Ibid*.

[37] See eg, Yu, above, note 22, at 11–15; Zeng, Huaqun, *International Investment Law* (*Guoji Touzi Faxue*) (Peking University Press, 1999), at 12–25.

[38] Art 38 (1)(d), ICJ Statute, above, note 1.

[39] In fact, Fitzmaurice has criticised the classification of judicial decisions as merely evidence of international law. See *Oppenheim's International Law*, above, note 1, at 41 and note 3; Brownlie, above, note 1, at 19 and note 116.

[40] *Barcelona Traction, Light and Power Co. Case*, ICJ Reports 1970 p 3.

[41] *ELSI Case*, ICJ Reports 1989, p 14.

[42] Sornarajah, above, note 19, at 79.

[43] *Ibid*.

[44] Sornarajah, *ibid*, at 80. Sir Elihu Lauterpacht and Rayfuse also consider that ICSID cases can contribute significantly to both the substance of international investment law and the procedures of international arbitration. Lauterpacht, Sir Elihu, and Rayfuse, R, 'Introduction', in *ICSID Reports*, Volume 1 (Grotius, 1993), at ix.

[45] Sornarajah, above, note 19, at 80.

has been argued that this Tribunal was specially designed to deal with special types of problems in the context of a special situation and thus do not have much value in the creation of principles of general validity,[46] the case law created by the Tribunal[47] and the extensive literature thereon have certainly had an impact on the development of international investment law.[48]

So far, the Chinese government has not been involved in an investment case before an international court or arbitration tribunal. Consequently, there has been no special case that could be singled out in the context of EU-China investment relations. Moreover, as in most European legal systems, cases within the Chinese legal system, do not have binding legal force. Nevertheless, it can be argued that, in future, the jurisprudence drawn from these judicial decisions will play a more and more important role in the development of applicable international rules governing EU investment in China, given that China has become more and more open to international courts and tribunals[49] and that EU-China investment relations are growing.

3.1.5 Writings of Publicists

The ICJ Statute recognises writings of highly qualified publicists as subsidiary sources of international law.[50] As Brownlie has pointed out, although the opinions of publicists are widely used, they must be treated with caution, as individual writers tend to reflect national and other prejudices, and other motivations.[51] Sornarajah also argues that in the field of international investment, publicists' writings cannot make any significant contribution to the development of international law, as most writers are from capital-exporting countries and, as such, their views lack impartiality.[52] This view is probably

[46] *Ibid.*

[47] Cases of this Tribunal have been published by the *Iran-US Claims Reports*, by Grotius, and Cambridge University Press.

[48] For example, in drafting the *Guidelines on Treatment of Foreign Investment*, the World Bank experts investigated the awards by this Tribunal. See Shihata, Ibrahim F. I., above, note 4, at 355–56. Amerasinghe has examined many cases of the Tribunal and has found that some cases were purportedly decided on the basis of customary international law. However, he has further observed that many cases applied a standard of compensation which was incorporated in the Treaty of Amity between the US and Iran, and in cases decided on the basis of customary international law, it had been held that the treaty standard and the customary standard were similar, if not identical. See Amerasinghe, CF, 'Issues of Compensation for the Taking of Alien Property in the Light of Recent Cases and Practice', (1992) 41 *International and Comparative Law Quarterly* 22, at 41–42. Westburg also has examined the Tribunal cases and has come to more or less the same conclusion. See also Westberg, John A, 'Compensation in Cases of Expropriation and Nationalisation: Awards of the Iran-United States Claims Tribunal', (1990) 5 *ICSID—Foreign Investment Law Journal* 256, at 278–80.

[49] Since 1990 when China signed the ICSID Convention, Chinese BITs have become more and more open to the use of international tribunals and international law in settling investment disputes. For details, see Section 7.2.

[50] Art 38 (1)(d), ICJ Statute.

[51] Brownlie, above, note 1, at 24.

[52] Sornarajah, above, note 19, at 80–81.

shared by Chinese writers on international investment law, who normally simply ignore the writings of publicists as a subsidiary source of international law on foreign investment.[53] Nevertheless, as Professor Judge WANG Tieya wrote, publicists' writings, especially the authoritative and scientific ones, can 'provide reliable materials, and are helpful in explaining principles and rules of international law'.[54] In this sense, writings on international investment law do not constitute direct and binding sources but are still useful materials in identifying and interpreting international law in this area.

3.1.6 United Nations General Assembly Resolutions

Although not legally binding[55] resolutions adopted by the United Nations General Assembly (UNGA) may demonstrate the views of the majority of the international community, and therefore may serve as important evidence for customary international law.[56] Since the 1960s the United Nations General Assembly (UNGA) has passed a series of resolutions on international eco-

[53] Yu, above, note 22, at 11–13; Zeng, Huaqun, above, note 37, at 12–25.

[54] Judge Wang, above, note 25, at 18. Jennings and Watts also expressed similar views, see *Oppenheim's International Law*, above, note 1, at 43.

[55] The Charter of the United Nations (UN Charter) only empowers the UNGA to make 'recommendations' to member states on any questions of matters within the scope of the Charter or relating to the powers and functions of the any organs provided for therein. However, as pointed out by Judge Sir Hersch Lauterpacht, UNGA resolutions addressed to the organs of the UN are endowed with legal validity and effect, while resolutions addressed to the administering authorities are in the form of recommendations. He also said that, these resolutions, 'however rudimentary, elastic and imperfect, is nevertheless a legal obligation and constitutes a measure of supervision. The state in question, while not bound to accept the recommendation, is bound to give it due consideration in good faith. ... These obligations appear intangible and almost nominal when compared with the ultimate discretion of the Administering Authority; they have been acknowledged as such by the Administering Authorities.' Furthermore, Judge Elias has argued that all UNGA resolutions should have binding force: 'If there is unanimity in the Assembly during the vote, all are bound, provided that the subject falls within the Assembly's competence. If the votes are divided, then those states that voted for a particular resolution by the requisite majority are bound on the grounds of consent and of estoppel. Those that abstain are also bound on the ground of acquiescence and tacit consent, since an abstention is not a negative vote; while those voted against should be regarded as bound by the democratic principle that the majority view should always prevail when the vote has been truly free and fair and the requisite majority has been secured...This is the raison d'être of the overwhelming trend towards consensus which is an expression of the judicial conscience of the world community.' See Art 10, the Charter of the United Nations; Brownlie, Ian, *Basic Document in International Law*, 5th edition (Oxford University Press, 2003), at 5; *Separate Opinion of Judge H. Lauterpacht in the Advisory Opinion of 7 VI 55 on Voting Procedure on Questions Relating to Reports and Petitions Concerning the Territory of South-West Africa*, ICJ Reports, 1955, at 118; Elias, TO, 'Modern Sources of International Law', in *Transnational Law in a Changing Society—Essays in Honour of Philip C. Jessup* (Columbia University Press, 1972), at 51.

[56] Brownlie writes, 'In general these resolutions are not binding on member states, but, when they are concerned with general norms of international law, then acceptance by a majority vote constitutes evidence of the opinion of governments in the widest forum for the expression of such opinion.' Also, he listed UN resolution as one form of evidence of customary international law. See Brownlie, above, note 1, at 14 and 5. He further treated the legal effects of UN resolutions at pp 515, 542–49 of the same book.

nomic relations.[57] The most important ones concerning international investment are Resolution 1803 of 1962[58] (hereinafter 'Res 1803') and Resolution 3281 of 1974 (hereinafter 'Res 3281' or the 'Economic Charter').[59]

The debate on the evidential weight of theses two resolutions is long and intense.[60] Developed countries tend to think that only Res 1803 reflects customary international law.[61] Developing countries however consider that Res 3281 states the new rule of law—'an emergent principle, applicable *ex nunc*',[62] which overrides Res 1803 as an earlier and unsatisfactory compromise between developed and developing countries.[63] Since the debate is centred upon the law on compensation for expropriation, it is further discussed in Section 6.1 on expropriation.

3.1.7 'Soft' Law

'Soft' law refers to those instruments that command respect but are not legally binding or enforceable.[64] Although not directly binding, 'soft' law is helpful in interpreting current rules of law and in shaping the law of the future.[65] In this sense, there are a number of international instruments that may be classified as 'soft' international investment law.[66] Over the past

[57] These UNGA Resolutions include Resolution 1803 (1962), 2158 (1966), 2386 (1968), 2692 (1970), 3016 (1972), 3171 (1973) and 3201 (1974) and 3281 (1974). For further details, see Aréchaga, Eduardo Jiménez de, 'State Responsibility for the Nationalisation of Foreign Owned Property', (1978) 11 *New York University Journal of International Law and Politics* 179, at 179.

[58] Declaration on Permanent Sovereignty over Natural Resources, UNGA Res 1803 (XVII), UN Doc. A/RES/1803 (XVII), 19 December 1962, reprinted in ILM (1962, Vol. 2), at 223.

[59] Charter of Economic Rights and Duties of States, UNGA Res 3281 (XXIX), UN Doc. A/RES/3281(XXIX) (1975), reprinted in 14 ILM 251 (1975).

[60] It has been noted that the legal effect or legal significance varies considerably, depending on their attending circumstances. Accordingly, the legal effect of the aforementioned resolutions on international investment 'must be weighed in evidential terms accordingly to its merits.' See Brownlie, above, note 1, at 14–15 and 545. See also *Oppenheim's International Law*, above, note 1, at 48.

[61] See, eg, *Texaco Overseas Petroleum Co./California Asiatic Oil Co. v. Libya (the 'Topco case')*, 17 ILM 1 (1978), Award on the Merit, paras 88. For details on similar views, see Brownlie, above, note 1, at 545, note 105.

[62] Brownlie, above, note 1, at 545.

[63] For instance, Chen points out that, due to historical reasons, Res 1803 contains some elements that protect the 'acquired rights' of developed countries. Chen, An, *International Economic Law* (in Chinese) (Law Press 1999), at 16.

[64] It is observed that 'soft' law may have any one or more of the following elements: vagueness, imprecision, recommendatory language, strictly formulated obligations in a binding instrument but undermined by exceptions, strictly formulated obligations but contained in recommendatory non-binding instruments. Qureshi, above, note 2, at. 23.

[65] Qureshi holds that 'soft' law 'is both a sophisticated normative framework, as well as a pre-legal or legislative apparatus,' and it helps to 'shape opinion and practice, and thereby assist in the formation of General International Law'. See Qureshi, above, note 2, at 23.

[66] It must be noted that, in the traditional classification of sources of international law, all these legal instruments may also be regarded as *evidence* of general/customary international law. For

decades for example the UN and other major international organisations have adopted or drafted a few codes of conducts or guidelines that bear implications on international investment. These include the UN codes of conducts on transnational corporations (TNCs), technology transfer and restrictive business practices,[67] and the World Bank Guidelines on the Treatment of Foreign Investment (hereinafter the 'World Bank Guidelines'). While these rules are universal 'soft' law, there are also 'soft' laws for certain state groups or regions. Thus the Asia Pacific Economic Co-operation Organisation (APEC) Non-Binding Principles on Investment (hereinafter the 'APEC Principles') may be regarded as 'soft' law for China, whilst the OECD MNEs Guidelines and the MAI draft are so regarded for the EU and its member states.[68] These instruments, together with non-applicable formal treaties such as ECT and NAFTA, are sometimes referred to in this book as 'Multilateral and Regional Investment Instruments' (MRIIs).

3.2 APPLICABLE INTERNATIONAL TREATIES ON EU INVESTMENT IN CHINA

International treaties, as already stated, are the most important and least disputed sources of international law governing EU investment in China. They therefore merit a further elaboration. These treaties include mainly bilateral agreements[69] such as the co-operation agreement between the EU and China and the 13 BITs between China and EU member states, as well as multilateral agreements such as the MIGA Convention, the ICSID Convention and the WTO Agreement.

example, Brownlie's list of evidence of customary international law includes, inter alia, 'other international instruments' and 'practice of international organisations.' Brownlie, above, note 1, at 5.

[67] The codes of conducts on technology transfer and TNCs have never been adopted. They can, nevertheless, be regarded as useful references and evidence of the general opinion of the majority of the international community.

[68] Apart from the aforementioned guidelines and codes of conducts, Seidl-Hohenveldern considers UNGA resolutions are also a 'soft law'. See Seidl-Hohenveldern, above, note 2, at 39–40.

[69] Arguably, the Textile Agreement between China and the EU, as well as other agreements between China and EU member states on issues such as double taxation, economic and technology co-operation, are also of relevance to EU investment in China. However, they are not discussed in this book, as they only focus on investments in a special sector or certain aspects of foreign investment and therefore do not significantly affect the general framework of EU investment in China. See the 1988 Agreement between the European Economic Community and the People's Republic of China on Trade in Textile Products, OJ L380, 31/12/1988. For details of this agreement, see Hu, Yuanxiang, *Legal and Policy Issues of the Trade and Economic Relations between China and the EEC* (Kluwer, 1991), at 291–340.

3.2.1 Bilateral Agreements

3.2.1.1 The 1985 EC-China Co-operation Agreement

The 1985 EC-China Co-operation Agreement[70] is the framework agreement between the EU (at that time the EEC) and China on trade and economic co-operation in general. It replaces the EEC-China Trade Agreement signed in 1978.[71] Negotiations for a new agreement began in 1983 and were concluded in 1985. The EC-China Co-operation Agreement has four chapters. Chapter 1, 3 and 4 relate to trade co-operation, Joint Committee and final provisions, and are essentially identical to the EEC-China Trade Agreement. Chapter 2 is the only new chapter, which defines various forms of economic co-operation.

According to the EC-China Co-operation Agreement, Sino-EC economic co-operation is to be extended to every possible sphere,[72] particularly to industry and mining, agriculture including agro-industry, science and technology, energy, transport and communication, environmental protection and co-operation with third countries.[73] Both parties agree to endeavour to promote and facilitate various forms of co-operation, including joint production and joint ventures; common exploitation; transfer of technology; co-operation between financial institutions; visits, contacts and activities designed to promote co-operation between individuals, delegations, and economic organisations; organisation of seminars and symposia; consultancy services; and technical assistance, including the training of staff and continuous exchange of information relevant to commercial and economic co-operation.[74] The EC-China Co-operation Agreement also takes into account the different level of development between the EC and China and requires that the EC be prepared to continue, step up, and diversify its development activities in China, within the means at its disposal and in accordance with its rules.[75]

Most significantly for the purposes of this research, the EC-China Co-operation Agreement addresses investment issues. Article 12 of the EC-China Co-operation Agreement requires the two parties to promote and encourage greater and mutually beneficial investment. Furthermore the parties undertake to further improve the investment climate by encouraging the extension of BITs between China and the EC Member States.[76] Article 12 follows the Community's model of co-operation agreements with non-associated coun-

[70] Officially the Agreement on Trade and Economic Co-operation between the European Community and the People's Republic of China. See OJ L250 (19/9/85).

[71] For the text of the EEC-China Trade Agreement, see OJ L123 (11 May 1978).

[72] As long as they fall within the competence of the Community.

[73] Art 10 of the EC-China Co-operation Agreement.

[74] *Ibid*, Art 11.

[75] *Ibid*, Art 13.

[76] *Ibid*, Art 12.

tries and may have taken the mutual investment exchanges into account.[77] In fact, at the time the agreement was signed, there had been considerable EC investments in China, and most EC Member States had signed BITs with China.[78] Since this investment clause imposes no substantial obligation on the contracting parties but rather expresses their intention for future co-operation, it has a more symbolic than practical value. Nevertheless it lays down a general legal basis for future co-operation in this field.

Last but not least, a Joint Committee was set up under the Agreement to monitor implementation of the agreement and to examine various means and opportunities of further developing economic co-operation. It may also make recommendations to further the objectives of the Agreement in areas of common interest. If deemed necessary the Joint Committee may also set up working parties.

It is worth mentioning that although the Community has exercised its power to conclude economic co-operation agreements for a substantial period of time this power is not exclusive. Member States still hold the power to sign co-operation agreements with non-Member States. In order to decrease conflicts arising therefrom the Council adopted Decision 74/393.[79] This Decision requires Member States to hold prior consultation before the signing of any agreement of this kind and to inform the Commission of the agreement as well as the measures and commitments undertaken thereunder. Most EC Member States have in fact concluded economic co-operation agreements with China[80] in parallel with the EC-China Co-operation Agreement on the Community level. Further discussions of these economic co-operation agreements are, however, beyond the scope of this book.

3.2.1.2 Bilateral Investment Treaties between China and EU Member States

As has been already mentioned, China has so far concluded bilateral investment protection and promotion agreements with 14 of the 15 EU Member States.[81] The first BIT was concluded with Sweden on 29 March 1982. This was followed by BITs with Germany, France, BLEU, Finland, Italy, Denmark, UK, the Netherlands, Austria, Portugal, Spain and Greece (*Table 5: BITs between China and EU Member States*). Some of these states have successfully

[77] See Hu, Yuanxiang, above, note 69, at 116.

[78] At that time, 7 of the 10 EC Members had concluded BITs with China. The other three were Greece, Ireland and the United Kingdom.

[79] See Council Decision 74/393, OJ L 203/23,1974.

[80] For details of the economic co-operation agreement between China and EC Member States, see Hu, Yuanxiang, above, note 69, at 79.

[81] According to MOFTEC (now MOFCOM) officials, China had concluded 106 BITs by March 2003. See XU, Chunlin, *Investment Protection on Fast Track of Development in China*, posted at http://www.fdi.gov.cn/common/frnreport.jsp?id=CENSOFT0000000007375 (visited on 4 June 2003). For details of BITs signed by April 1998, see MOFTEC (now MOFCOM): *Collection of International Investment Treaties* (in Chinese and English) (Jingjuang Jiaoyu Press, 1998).

re-negotiated the BIT with China.[82] For example, Germany signed a new BIT with China on 1 December 2003.[83] Once the new BITs enter into force, the 'old' ones will expire. However, it seems that the newly concluded one have not yet been ratified, nor it there any indication of when they might be ratified. Thus the analysis of the substantive issues in these BITs will still be based on the existing BITs, although the new Sino-Germany BIT will also be referred to demonstrate the direction of change. As yet, Ireland is the only member state not to have signed such a treaty with China.[84] BITs between China and the EU Member States are the most important international legal instruments for EU investment in China, because they are the only legal instruments which provide general and substantial protection to EU investors.

The main purpose of these BITs is to promote and protect mutual investment, particularly investment in China. All of them therefore contain fundamental provisions relating to definitions, admission, treatment standards, expropriation and consequent compensation, war losses compensation, monetary transfers, subrogation, dispute settlement, and so forth. Details of these provisions will be discussed in the second part of the book on substantive issues of the legal framework.

3.2.2 Multilateral Agreements

3.2.2.1 ICSID Convention

The ICSID Convention, or the Washington Convention as it is sometimes called after its birthplace, was concluded in 1965 and came into force in October 1966 under the auspices of the World Bank. The ICSID Convention provides an institutional and procedural mechanism for the settlement of investment disputes between governments and foreign investors through conciliation and arbitration.[85] It establishes an International Centre for

[82] It is reported that both Germany and Holland have successfully signed a new BIT with China, in which they upgraded the investment protection clauses. However, the author only managed to find the new Sino-Germany BIT. See Dunham, Philip & Foster, George K, *Current Trends in Investment Treaty Arbitration*, posted at http://www.coudert.com/publications/articles/040515_5_ForeignArbitration_fe.pdf (19/09/2004).

[83] The text of this new BIT is available at MOFCOM website: http://tfs.mofcom.gov.cn/article/200405/20040500218063_1.xml (19/09/2004).

[84] China has also signed BITs with 9 of the 10 countries that are becoming member states of the EU in 2004, including Cyprus, the Czech Republic, Estonia, Hungary, Lithuania, Poland, the Slovak Republic, and Slovenia. Only Malta is an exception. Further, China has signed BITs with all the four other EU candidates, namely Bulgaria, Crotia, Romania and Turkey. For updated information about those BITs, see MOFCOM Official Website: http://tfs.mofcom.gov.cn/column/db.xml (visited on 2 September 2004); see also UNCTAD, *Bilateral Investment Treaties for China*, posted at http://stats.unctad.org/fdi/treaties/bits/China.htm (visited on 29 January 2004).

[85] ICSID Convention, Art 1. For discussions of the Convention and the Centre in Chinese please see Chen, An (ed), *Comments on ICSID* (Lujiang Press, 1990).

Settlement of Investment Disputes (ICSID or The Centre) which does not itself engage in conciliation or arbitration, but provides facilities for the conciliation commissions or arbitration tribunals constituted under the Convention to carry out these tasks.

The ICSID was established to satisfy the need for an apolitical mechanism to facilitate the arbitration of investment disputes between developing states and foreign investors.[86] Traditionally, host countries would not accept the jurisdiction of conventional commercial arbitration institutions such as the International Chamber of Commerce (ICC) or the American Arbitration Association (AAA), and inter-state arbitration tribunals like the Permanent Court of Arbitration are not normally open to private investors.[87] There was therefore, a lack of a widely recognised and accepted state-investor arbitration tribunal which resulted in a variety of creative solutions.[88] The creation of ICSID is perhaps the most successful solution so far.

The ICSID Convention has been widely accepted. As of 26 March 2003, 154 States had signed the ICSID Convention, 139 of which have already deposited their instruments of ratification.[89] Although not many disputes have been referred to the Centre, its caseload has increased significantly in recent years.[90] The fact that ICSID arbitration clauses are also commonly found in investment agreements between governments of member countries and investors from other member countries also suggests widespread adoption. Advance consents by governments to submit investment disputes to ICSID arbitration can be found in about 20 investment laws and in over 900 bilateral investment treaties.[91] Moreover, arbitration under the auspices of

[86] Jacobs, Kenneth, 'Reinvigorating ICSID With a New Mission and With Renewed Respect for Party Autonomy', (1992) 33 *Virginia Journal of International Law*, at 123.

[87] Ketcham, William T, *Arbitration between a State and a Foreign Private Party* (1961), 405–06. However, since 1990s, the PCA has adopted optional rules, allowing private parties to make use of its arbitration and conciliation facilities when they have disputes with a State or an international organisation. For details see *Permanent Court of Arbitration Optional Rules for Arbitrating Disputes between Two Parties of Which Only One Is a State* (effective July 6, 1993), *Permanent Court of Arbitration Optional Rules for Arbitration between International Organizations and Private Parties* (Effective July 1, 1996) and *Permanent Court of Arbitration Optional Conciliation Rules* (Effective July 1, 1996). All available at http://pca-cpa.org/BD/ (visited 3 December 2002).

[88] For example, the World Bank and the President of the Bank have assisted in mediation or conciliation of some investment disputes, such as the nationalisation of Anglo-Iranian Oil Company's assets in 1951 and 1952, and the nationalisation by each of the Suez Canal in 1956. See Rowat, Malcolm D, 'Multilateral Approaches to improving the Investment Climate of Developing Country: The Case of ICSID and MIGA', (1992) 33 *Harvard International Law Journal* 106.

[89] ICSID, *List of Contracting States and other Signatories of the Convention* (as of March 26, 2003), posted at http://www.worldbank.org/icsid/constate/c-states-en.htm (visited on 29 July 2003).

[90] By 29 July 2003, the ICSID has concluded 77 cases and 58 cases are still in process. Most of the cases are recent ones. For details, see *ICSID Cases*, at http://www.worldbank.org/icsid/cases/cases.htm (visited on 29 July 2003). See also ICSID, About ICSID, at http://www.worldbank.org/icsid/about/about.htm (visited on 29 July 2003).

[91] ICSID, About ICSID, at http://www.worldbank.org/icsid/about/about.htm (visited on 29 July 2003).

Table 7: ICSID, China and the EU

State	Signature	Deposit of Ratification	Entry into Force
China	Feb. 9, 1990	Jan. 7, 1993	Feb. 6, 1993
Austria	May 17, 1966	May 25, 1971	June 24, 1971
Belgium	Dec. 15, 1965	Aug. 27, 1970	Sep. 26, 1970
Denmark	Oct. 11, 1965	Apr. 24, 1968	May 24, 1968
Finland	July 14, 1967	Jan. 9, 1969	Feb. 8, 1969
France	Dec. 22, 1965	Aug. 21, 1967	Sep. 20, 1967
Germany	Jan. 27, 1966	Apr. 18, 1969	May 18, 1969
Greece	Mar. 16, 1966	Apr. 21, 1969	May 21, 1969
Ireland	Aug. 30, 1966	Apr. 7, 1981	May 7, 1981
Italy	Nov. 18, 1965	Mar. 29, 1971	Apr. 28, 1971
Lux'g	Sep. 28, 1965	July 30, 1970	Aug. 29, 1970
Neth'd	May 25, 1966	Sep. 14, 1966	Oct. 14, 1966
Portugal	Aug. 4, 1983	July 2, 1984	Aug. 1, 1984
Spain	Mar. 21, 1994	Aug. 18, 1994	Sept. 17, 1994
Sweden	Sep. 25, 1965	Dec. 29, 1966	Jan. 28, 1967
UK	May 26, 1965	Dec. 19, 1966	Jan. 18, 1967

Source: Compiled by the author according to List of Contracting States and other Signatories of the Convention, posted at http://www.worldbank.org/icsid/constate/c-states-en.htm (visited on 29 July 2003).

ICSID is one of the main mechanisms for the settlement of investment disputes under four recent regional trade and investment treaties, namely the NAFTA, the ECT, the Cartagena Free Trade Agreement and the 1994 Colonia Investment Protocol of Mercosur.[92]

The ICSID Convention is an important multilateral legal instrument for EU investment in China, as both China and all EU Member States are its contracting parties (See *Table 7: ICSID, China and the EU*). Most EU countries signed the Convention in the 1960s and 1970s whilst the remainder signed it in the 1980s and 1990s. China signed the Convention after careful consideration[93] in 1990 and ratified it in 1993.[94] Most of the 13 BITs that China

[92] *Ibid.*

[93] In 1986, Chinese publicists debated the acceptance of ICSID Convention by China, where very controversial views were presented. Some rejected immediate accession, as it would restrict Chinese sovereignty, while some others argued that China should join as soon as possible to improve the investment environment and speed up the 'opening up' process. A third voice purported that China investigate the ICSID mechanism thoroughly be fore making the decision. It seemed that the latter view had greater appeal as the Chinese government delayed accession to the Convention by 4 years. See Chen, An, *International Investment Disputes Arbitration—A Study on the ICSID Mechanism* (hereinafter '*ICSID Mechanism*') (Fudan University Press, 2001), at 25–41.

[94] In January 1966, the Taiwanese Government signed the Convention and ratified it in 1968.

concluded with the EU Member States refer to the ICSID Convention[95] and most of them provide that the arbitration tribunal established to settle a state-investor dispute shall determine its own procedures with references to the ICSID Convention.[96] Others require the negotiation of a supplementary agreement by the contracting parties to a binding system of dispute settlement within the framework of ICSID.[97] So far, however, China has never called upon the ICSID, nor has China been brought before the ICSID by any EU investor. Nevertheless, the possibility of taking the host country (China) before the ICSID must have helped to enhance the confidence of EU investors entering into the Chinese market.

3.2.2.2 MIGA Convention

As with the ICSID Convention, the MIGA Convention[98] (also known as the Seoul Convention) was concluded also under the auspices of the World Bank. Signed in October 1985 and entered into force in 1988, it created the Multilateral Investment Guarantee Agency (MIGA or the Agency), whose core mission is to promote the flow of FDI to and among developing countries[99] by providing insurance (including coinsurance and reinsurance) against political risks for investments made in a member developing country by another member state.[100] MIGA's aim is furthered by its complementary investment promotion activities, which include provision of programs, dissemination of information on investment opportunities and technical assistance to enhance the capability of national investment promotion agencies.[101] To a certain extent, MIGA's insurance programmes complement national insurance programmes which generally contain strict eligibility requirements that exclude many investors and investments.[102] Firstly, MIGA may insure investments which may not qualify for insurance under national insurance programmes such as the Overseas Private Investment Corporation (OPIC).[103]

However, its membership was revoked in October 1980 by the 14th Annual Meeting of the Administrative Council of ICSID, in the light of China's interest in joining in the Convention See Chen, An, above, note 93, at 21.

[97] Those include BITs between China and Sweden, Germany, France, BLEU, Finland, Italy, Austria and Denmark.

[96] See BITs between China and Germany, BLEU, Finland, Italy, Austria and Denmark.

[97] See Sino-France BIT and Sino-Sweden BIT.

[98] The MIGA Convention entered into force in April 12,1988. 24 ILM 1598. For detailed discussion of the Agency and the Convention, see Shihata, Ibrahim FI, *MIGA and Foreign Investment* (Martinus Nijhoff Publishers, 1988), and Chen, An (ed), *MIGA and China: Comments on the Multilateral Investment Guarantee Agency* (Fujian People's Press, 1995).

[99] Art 2, MIGA Convention,

[100] *Ibid.*

[101] *Ibid.*, Art 2 and Art 23.

[102] Shihata, Ibrahim FI, 'Factors Influencing the Flow of Foreign Investment and the Relevance of a Multilateral Investment Guarantee Scheme', (1987) 21 *International Lawyer* 671.

[103] Overseas Private Investment Corporation is a self-sustaining governmental agency of the US See *The Overseas Private Investment Corporation Act*, 22 USCA §§ 2191–220b (1990 & Supp.

Secondly, it can co-guarantee investments with national agencies via parallel or joint underwriting, and may provide re-insurance for these agencies.[104] MIGA also guarantees investments by investors originating from developing countries that do not have their own national insurance programs.[105]

MIGA has expanded significantly since its formation. It has so far issued more than 500 guarantees for projects in 78 developing countries.[106] By June 2001, its total coverage issued exceeded $9 billion, bringing the estimated amount of foreign direct investment facilitated since inception to more than $41 billion.[107] As of 25 June 2003, the number of member countries reached 162, and 8 additional countries were in the process of fulfilling the membership requirements.[108]

As the largest developing country and the largest FDI recipient in the developing world,[109] China has taken a positive attitude towards MIGA. As early as 1988, China signed and ratified the Convention. Since then, China has become the fifth largest shareholder in MIGA and the single largest shareholder among developing countries, possessing more shares than most EU Member States (see *Table 8: MIGA, China and The EU*). In 1991, China and MIGA entered into three Agreements concerning the local approval procedures, legal protection of MIGA guaranteed foreign investments and the use of local currencies respectively.[110]

MIGA has played, and will go on playing, an important role in encouraging and protecting investment in China. By the end of 1997 all EU Member States and China have become members of the MIGA Convention (*Table 8*). As EU members are developed countries and China is a developing country for the purposes of the Convention, all EU investments in China are in

1995). For further discussion on OPIC, see Vishny, Paul H, *Guide to International Commercial Law*, §§ 13.13, 13.14 (Shepard's/McGraw-Hill, 1994). For discussions in Chinese, see CHEN, An, *OPIC Case Studies* (Lujiang Press, 1986).

[104] Art 2, MIGA Convention. For instance, in 1995, MIGA issued $45 million in reinsurance coverage to the Export Development Corporation of Canada for CAMECO Corporations' investment in the Kumtor Goldmine in the Kyrgyz Republic. See *MIGA Press Release* (October 25 1995). See also Comeaux, Paul, and Kinsella, N. Stephan, *Protecting Foreign Investment under International Law: Legal Aspects of Political Risks* (Oceana Publications Inc., 1997), at 168.

[105] For example, in 1995, MIGA issued US$13.3 million of coverage to a Turkish beverage company (EFES Sinai Yatirim V Tikaret), for its equity investment in Coca-Cola Almaty Bottlers in Kazakhstan. See Comeaux and Kinsella, *ibid*, at 169.

[106] MIGA, *About MIGA*, posted at http://www.miga.org/screens/about/about.htm (visited on 29 July 2003).

[107] *Ibid.*

[108] MIGA, *MIGA Member Countries*, posted at http://www.miga.org/screens/about/members/members.htm (visited on 29 July 2003).

[109] China has been the largest FDI recipient among the developing since 1993 and became the largest FDI recipient in the world in 2002. See OECD: *Trends and Recent Developments in Foreign Direct Investment*, June 2003, posted at http://www.oecd.org/pdf/M00042000/M00042212.pdf (visited on 1 July 2003); *UNCTAD Predicts 27% Drop in FDI Inflow this Year and China May Outstrip US as World's Largest FDI Recipient*, UNCTAD Press Release TAD/INF/PR/63 (24/10/02).

[110] For details, see Chen, An (ed), *MIGA and China: Comments on the Multilateral Investment Guarantee Agency* (Fujian People's Press, 1995), at 689–94.

Table 8: MIGA, China and the EU

				Allocated shares				Subscribed shares		
				No. of shares			Amount	No. of shares		Amount
	Date signed	Date ratified	Membership date[a]	Initial capital	Capital increase	Total	In US$	Initial capital	Total	In US$[b]
China	04/28/88	04/30/88	04/30/88	3,138	2,392	5,530	59,834,600	3,138	3,138	33,953,160
Austria	04/29/97	09/17/97	12/16/97	775	591	1,366	14,780,120	775	775	8,385,500
Belgium	09/21/89	06/30/92	09/18/92	2,030	1,547	3,577	38,703,140	2,030	2,030	21,964,600
Denmark	08/27/86	08/18/87	04/12/88	718	547	1,265	13,687,300	718	718	7,768,760
Finland	05/13/88	12/28/88	12/28/88	600	457	1,057	11,436,740	600	600	6,492,000
France	07/22/86	12/28/89	12/28/89	4,860	3,705	8,565	92,673,300	4,860	4,860	52,585,200
Germany	07/24/86	10/06/87	04/12/88	5,071	3,865	8,936	96,687,520	5,071	5,071	54,868,220
Greece	07/18/86	05/24/89	08/30/93	280	213	493	5,334,260	280	280	3,029,600
Ireland	09/18/86	07/05/89	10/27/89	369	281	650	7,033,000	369	369	3,992,580
Italy	02/19/86	04/29/88	04/29/88	2,820	2,150	4,970	53,775,400	2,820	2,820	30,512,400
L'bourg	09/24/90	06/04/91	08/29/91	116	88	204	2,207,280	116	116	1,255,120
N'lands	02/03/86	10/09/87	04/12/88	2,169	1,653	3,822	41,354,040	2,169	2,169	23,468,580
Portugal	10/01/87	06/06/88	06/06/88	382	291	673	7,281,860	382	382	4,133,240
Spain	04/27/88	04/29/88	04/29/88	1,285	980	2,265	24,507,300	1,285	1,285	13,903,700
Sweden	04/02/87	12/31/87	04/12/88	1,049	800	1,849	20,006,180	1,049	1,049	11,350,180
UK	04/09/86	04/12/88	04/12/88	4,860	3,705	8,565	92,673,300	4,860	4,860	52,585,200

Source of information: Compiled by the author according to MIGA Capital Subscription Data, posted at http://www.miga.org/welcome.htm (visited on 10 December 1999).
[a]Investments from these countries into Category Two member countries are eligible for MIGA guarantees.
[b]Includes callable capital.

Table 9: MIGA Guarantees in China

Fiscal year	Guarantee holder	Project description	Maximum limit liability (US$ million)
1993	Non-Fluid Oil International	Glass Product	3.96
1994	American Cyanamid Company	Medical Product	7
1994	Continental Enterprise Limited (2 contracts)	Agriculture	4.4
1994	China Capital Development Corporation	Copper Product	5.4
1995	China Capital Development Corp.	Copper Products	2.7
1995	Citibank, N.A.	Banking	0.5
1995	Honeywell, Inc.	Petrochemicals	41.4
1995	Sunnen Products Co.	Machine Tools	1
1995	Pepsi-Co, Inc.	Silk Production	2.7
1995	Ratti Technologies S.r.L.	Silk Production	0.8
1995	Catalina Lighting Inc.	Lighting Fixtures	0.6
1995	Ingersoll-Rand China Ltd.	Machinery	14.4
1995	Shinwha Textile Company Ltd.	Silk Production	5.9
1996	Finance B.V.	Diesel Power Plant	16.7
1996	ING Bank N.V.	Silk Production	4
1997	Caribbean Mercantile Bank	Manufacturing	3.83
1997	Philips Electronics, N.V.	Banking	9
1997	Coastal Wuxi Power, Ltd.	Manufacturing	27
1997	Coastal Wuxi Power, Ltd.	Infrastructure	4.21
1997	Bank of Nova Scotia	Manufacturing	2.1
1998	Andre & Cie, S.A. Banco Santander S.A. Sithe International, Inc.	Agribusiness	1.7
1998	Banff Resources Ltd.	Infrastructure	17.7
1999	Coastal Nanjing Power Ltd.—Cayman Islands	Infrastructure	20.7
1999	BWF Unternehmensbeteiligungen GmbH (2 contracts)—Germany	Manufacturing	3.8
1999	Schmalbach-Lubeca AG—Germany	Manufacturing	5.9
1999	Interface Asia Pacific Inc.—USA	Manufacturing	3.2
1999	Coastal Guzu Heat and Power Ltd.—Cayman Islands	Infrastructure	10.8
1999	Interface Asia Pacific Inc.—USA	Manufacturing	6.3

Source: Compiled by the author according to *Guarantees Issued in FY 1995*, *Guarantees Issued in FY 1996*, *Guarantees Issued in FY 1997*, *Guarantees Issued in FY 1998* and *Guarantees Issued in FY 1999*, all available at MIGA website: http://www.miga.org/welcome.htm (visited on 29 October 1999). The information of fiscal year 1993 and 1994 are based on Lorin S Weisenfeld, 'The Co-operation between MIGA and China and its Potentials', in Chen, An (ed), *MIGA and China: Comments on the Multilateral Investment Guarantee Agency* (Fujian People's Press, 1995), 496–98.

principle eligible to be guaranteed by MIGA. MIGA has issued a number of guarantees for investments in China since 1993 when the first guarantee was issued.[111] MIGA had US$131.1 million worth of outstanding guarantees in China by June 1998, which accounted for 4.6 per cent of all guarantees issued by MIGA.[112] Most impressively, in the 1995 fiscal year, China hosted 9 of the 54 guarantees that MIGA issued in the year, valued at US$70.6, which accounted for 10.5 per cent of total MIGA guarantees. Many of those MIGA guaranteed investments in China were from the EU. For example, among the six MIGA guaranteed investments in China in the fiscal year 1999, two were from the EU (See *Table 9: MIGA Guarantees in China*).

3.2.2.3 WTO Agreement

In December 1993 the Uruguay Round trade negotiation drew to a conclusion and a comprehensive and powerful multilateral trading system was established. The WTO Agreement lies at the heart of the whole system and is now embraced in the Final Act Embodying the Result of the Uruguay Round of Multilateral Trade Negotiations. The WTO Agreement is the *de facto* charter of the World Trade Organisation (WTO). It defines its legal status and lays down its institutional basis. The operational rules of the WTO Agreement are contained in its four Annexes. Among these, three (Annexes I–III) are multilateral trade agreements[113] and one (Annex IV) includes four plurilateral trade agreements. Furthermore, the WTO is not just a set of static rules, it is a dynamic system. It evolves and develops through its other roles, as a platform for multilateral trade negotiations as a forum of trade dispute settlement and as a body of trade policy review.[114]

The 1947 General Agreement on Tariff and Trade (GATT) did not traditionally deal with investment issues, although the ill-fated Havana Charter[115] did encompass investment provisions. However, much effort has been made to include investment issues within the framework of the multilateral trade system because of the close link between trade and investment.[116] When

[111] Weisenfeld, Lorin S, 'The Co-operation between MIGA and China and its Potentials', in Chen, An (ed), above, note 110, at 496.

[112] See *MIGA Guarantees Outstanding*, in MIGA Annual Report 1998.

[113] They are Annex I, which includes Agreements respectively on trade in goods (GATT 1994), services (GATS) and trade-related property rights (TRIPs), Annex II—Understanding on Rules and Procedures Governing the Settlement of Disputes (DSU) and Annex III—Trade Policy Review Mechanism (TPRM).

[114] Art III, WTO Agreement.

[115] Officially the *Charter of the International Trade Organisation* (ITO), which is the underlying legal instrument of the GATT and which failed to enter into force and led to a 50-year-long 'provisional application' of the GATT.

[116] A simple but convincing indication of this link is the fact that approximately one-third of the total US$6.1 trillion total for world trade in goods and services in 1995 was trade within companies—for example between subsidiaries in different countries or between subsidiaries and its headquarters. See WTO Secretariat, *World Trade Organisation: Trading into the future*, 2nd edition (1998), at 50.

investment was put on the agenda for the Uruguay Round negotiation in 1986, it was regarded as one of several 'new issues'.[117] As a result, the WTO Agreement embraces an agreement called 'Agreement on Trade-Related Investment Measures' (the TRIMs Agreement) within its multilateral agreements on trade in goods. Although narrowly defined, the TRIMs Agreement may be regarded as a breakthrough in international investment law because it seeks to regulate investment explicitly and globally for the first time in history.[118] The GATS is another WTO agreement of significance for investment. It focuses mainly on the market access and national treatment of investment in service sectors. Other investment-related WTO agreements include the TRIPs Agreement, the 1994 Agreement on Subsidies and Countervailing Measures (SCMs), the Understanding on Rules and Procedures Governing the Settlement of Disputes (DSU) and the Trade Policy Review Mechanism (TPRM)). These are regarded as having continuous and direct relevance to FDI.[119] Indeed it could be argued that most of the WTO agreements and their implementation measures are related to FDI since they influence the FDI environment in its entirety. As such, the WTO Agreement as a whole is not only a breakthrough in the history of international trade law but also a significant advance in international investment law.[120]

All EU Member States and the EC itself are original members of the WTO. On 11 December 2001, China became a member of the WTO, marking a successful conclusion in its 15-year 'long march' towards Geneva. China's entry into the WTO will undoubtedly improve EU-China investment relations significantly, particularly the conditions for EU investment in China. In the Sino-US bilateral WTO Agreement concluded in November 1999, China made significant concessions in a large number of fields, notably in TRIMs measures and services sectors.[121] China offered further concessions in service sectors such as telecommunication, banking and insurance in the EU-China agreement made in May 2000, which undoubtedly 'will provide substantial new market opportunities for European companies selling to China or investing there'.[122] Substantive aspects of the TRIMs and GATS will be discussed in Section 4.2.2.

[117] The 'New Issues' are about GATS, TRIPs and TRIMs.

[118] On the contrary, it has been argued that this agreement is actually 'retrogressive' because it narrowed the scope of TRIMs that should be eliminated as required by the GATT. See Brewer, Tomas L., and Young, Stephen, *The Multilateral Investment System and Multilateral Enterprises* (Oxford University Press, 1998), at 124.

[119] See Brewer and Young, *ibid*, at 123.

[120] Shan, Wenhua, 'Comments on the International Investment Rules within the WTO Agreement', (1996) 2 *CASS Journal of Law* (*Faxue Yanjiu*).

[121] For details of the Sino-US Bilateral WTO Agreement, see http://www.uschina.org/ for a summary of the Agreement, see http://www.chinapntr.gov/bilatsumm.htm (visited on 22 May 2000).

[122] Statement on EU-China Trade Agreement by Romano Prodi, President of the European Commission, at http://europa.eu.int/comm/trade/bilateral/china/prodi.htm (visited on 22 May 2000). The author's Questionnaire also shows that EU investors firmly believe that the WTO accession will significantly improve China's investment climate. See Chart 4 for details.

3.2.3 An Assessment of the Applicable International Treaties

The aforementioned multilateral and bilateral agreements form the basis of the current international legal framework for the protection and promotion of EU investment in China. However, it can be argued that such a treaty network is neither complete nor coherent. The EC-China Co-operation Agreement serves as a framework agreement but does not provide any concrete principles or rules for the protection or promotion of investment flow. The BITs between China and a few EU member states do provide such concrete principles and rules, but in an incomplete and incoherent manner from the perspective of the EU as a whole. Ireland has not signed such a treaty for example, and therefore the BIT network cannot protect Irish investment in China. Moreover, as will be seen in Part II, the provisions in different EU-China BITs vary from one to another in important aspects such as treatment standards and monetary transfer, in spite of their general similarities.[123]

As far as multilateral agreements are concerned, none of the three applicable multilateral agreements provides a comprehensive solution for the protection or promotion of EU investment in China. Both the ICSID and the MIGA Convention are multilateral agreements on investment issues, dealing with investment issues from two specific points: the settlement of state-investor disputes and insurance against political risks. The WTO Agreement is not devoted to investment issues and covers some investment measures and the services sectors only. None of the multilateral agreements address investment issues in a general and comprehensive manner as a proper multilateral investment agreement (MIA) should do. Essential aspects of a proper MIA which these agreements failed to address, include the definition of 'investment', general rules of admission, treatment standards, expropriation and compensation. The three different dispute settlement mechanisms under the three agreements have not been harmonised. While investors can sue governments directly under the ICSID Convention, only members, not private parties, are eligible to take trade disputes before the dispute settlement body (DSB) of the WTO.[124]

The current international treaty network is therefore incomplete. It does not effectively protect and promote EU investment in China, and it follows that a new, comprehensive agreement on investment protection between the EU and China is necessary.

[123] A general comparison of these BITs can be found in Shan, Wenhua, 'Towards a New Legal Framework for EU-China Investment Relations', (2000) 35 *Journal of World Trade* 5, at 156–57.

[124] Whilst this is certainly an interesting topic of discussion, it is beyond the scope of this work and may be the subject of a PhD dissertation in its own right.

3.3 THE INTERACTION BETWEEN INTERNATIONAL TREATIES AND CHINESE LAW

It is necessary to discuss the general role of international treaties within the Chinese legal system in order to further investigate the role of international law in the legal framework for EU investment in China, the Chinese system being that within which these international agreements usually have to work.[125] There are three factors which must be examined in addressing this matter, namely the relationship between international treaties and domestic law, the integration of international treaties within the Chinese legal system and the direct applicability of international treaties by Chinese courts.

3.3.1 The Relationship between International Treaties and Municipal Law

No constitutional rules in China have been enacted as yet to govern the relationship between international treaties and domestic law. The Chinese Constitution merely provides for general rules on treaty making and ratification[126] but is silent on their legal status within the municipal legal system. Numerous laws and regulations do however provide that in case of conflict between international treaty and domestic law, international treaty provisions shall prevail. Thus the General Principles of Civil Law (GPCL) stipulate that,

> 'If an international treaty concluded or acceded to by the PRC contains provisions differing from those in the civil laws of the PRC, the provisions of the international treaty shall apply, unless the provisions are ones on which the PRC has made reservations thereon.'[127]

Similar provisions can be found in as many as 70 laws and regulations, ranging from civil law and civil procedures law to administrative procedures

[125] In theory, the interaction between international law and the law of EU and its member states is also relevant. However, given that the primary governing law of EU investment in China is Chinese law, this book discusses the relationship of Chinese law and international agreements only.

[126] The Chinese Constitution provides that the State Council shall sign treaties and agreements with other countries, while the Standing Committee of the National People's Congress (SCNPC) shall decide to ratify or abolish these treaties and agreements and, the Head of the State shall approve or abolish these treaties and agreements in line with the decisions of the SCNPC. The treaty making procedure is similar to the procedure for domestic legislation. Such similarity suggests that international treaties have the same legal effect as domestic legislation. See Arts 89, 67 and 81, *the Constitution of the People's Republic of China*. See also Judge Wang, above, note 25, at 33; Zeng, Lingliang, 'Application of WTO Agreements in China and a Revolution of China's Legal Construction', (2000) 6 *Chinese Legal Science* (*Zhongguo Faxue*), at 42.

[127] Art 142, *General Principles of Civil Law*.

law, patent law, wildlife preservation law, and postal administration.[128] The Regulations on Some Issues in Handling Foreign-related Cases, jointly promulgated in August 1987 by the Ministry of Foreign Affairs, the Supreme People's Court, the Supreme People's Procuratorate, the Ministry of Public Security, Ministry of State Security and the Ministry of Justice provide that,

> 'When domestic legislation or internal regulations are in conflict with obligations undertaken by China under an international treaty, rules of the international treaty shall be applied. Provisions of domestic legislation shall not be invoked as justification for the refusal to perform the obligations undertaken by China under the international treaty.'

These provisions have been cited as evidence that China has already accepted the superiority of treaties over all municipal laws and regulations,[129] but most Chinese international lawyers, including Judge WANG Tieya, believe that such provisions are merely an expression of China's willingness to accept the superiority of treaties within the legal hierarchy on specific areas, such as foreign-related civil and commercial, civil procedural and administrative procedural areas rather than over the entirety of Chinese law.[130] As a result it is unclear whether the overriding effect of international treaties over domestic law can be maintained in the absence of further constitutional clarification.[131]

Whether the aforementioned investment-related multilateral and bilateral agreements (hereinafter 'investment treaties') override domestic law is accordingly debatable. As a matter of fact, all major Chinese laws and regulations on foreign trade and FDI do not mention the status of international treaties vis-à-vis domestic law. Scholarly debates about the application of the WTO agreement in China have suggested that certain issues in the WTO Agreement relating to tariffs, anti-dumping, market access of financial services and trade-related investment measures are not subject to the principle of the superiority of international treaties over national law.[132] With regard to the general status of the WTO Agreement within the Chinese legal system, HE has argued that the place of WTO agreements should be equal to Laws made by the Standing Committee of the National People's Congress (SCNPC); ie higher within the overall legal hierarchy than Administrative Regulations and Local Regulations but lower than Constitution and Basic

[128] Chen, Hanfeng, Zhou, Weiguo and Jiang, Hao, 'The Relationship between International Treaties and Municipal Law and the Practices of China', (2000) 2 *Tribune of Political Science and Law* (*Zhengfa Luntan*), at 122; Judge Wang, above, note 25, at 33.

[129] See eg, He, Xiaoyong, 'On the Application of WTO Agreements in Chinese Courts', (2001) 3 *Journal of International Trade* (*Guoji Maoyi Wenti*), at 50.

[130] See eg, Judge Wang, above, note 26, at 33; Zeng, above, note 126, at 45; Chen, Hanfeng etc, above, note 128, at 122.

[131] It has been further pointed out that, given that the right to interpret rules on applicable laws rests in the hands of the Standing Committee of the National People's Congress (SCNPC), the general binding effect of the Regulations is debatable. See HE, above, note 129.

[132] He, above, note 129.

Laws made by the National People's Congress (NPC).[133] Zeng has further argued that should conflicts arise between WTO agreements and Laws the principles of *lex posterior derogate priori* or *lex speciali derogate generalis* ought to apply.[134]

Indeed, under international law and as restated in the Vienna Convention on the Law of Treaties[135] China may not 'invoke the provisions of its internal law as justification for its failure to carry out an international agreement'.[136] In other words China must guarantee that the treaties and agreements it concludes or to which it accedes have binding force in China. Furthermore as observed by Judge WANG Tieya the sheer fact that a series of laws covering a wide range of areas has adopted the principle of superiority of international treaties over domestic law indicates a clear legislative policy trend and has made it possible for the principle to become a general principle of law in China.[137]

3.3.2 The Reception of International Treaties within the Chinese Legal System

A survey of the state practice reveals that there are two basic approaches to giving effect to international treaties within a domestic legal system: incorporation or transformation.[138] 'Incorporation' is a process of integration whereby international treaties become a part of the domestic legal system and are directly applicable. This process may be achieved by enactment or amendment of constitutional provisions, the ratification and publication of treaties, or by judicial means. 'Transformation' means that an international treaty will not be binding and applicable until domestic legislation is adopted to accept or absorb the contents of the treaty within national law.[139]

The Chinese Constitution is silent on this issue and its sub-constitutional legislation varies. Contemporary Chinese legislative practice respecting international treaties may be classified as follows:

A Numerous Chinese laws and regulations allow international treaties to take precedence over domestic law where a conflict arises between the two. This suggests that international treaties are directly applicable even in absence of legislation to give such treaties effect under Chinese law.

[133] He, above, note 129, at 50–51.

[134] Zeng, above, note 126, at 45; See also HE, *ibid*, at 51.

[135] According to Chinese Ministry of Foreign Affairs, China deposited the protocol of accession on 3 September 1997, which took effect to China on 3 October 1997. See http://www.fmprc.gov.cn/chn/premade/8275/duobian.htm (visited on 4 December 2002).

[136] Art 26, Vienna Convention on the Law of Treaties.

[137] Judge Wang, above, note 25, at 33.

[138] Jiang, Guoqin, *Some Problems on International Law and International Treaties*, at http://www.peoplesdaily.com.cn (visited on 5 January 2001). For an extensive survey in English, see *Oppenheim's International Law*, above, note 1, at 54–81.

[139] Jiang, *ibid*.

B A few laws and regulations expressly provide that on certain specific issues international treaties must be applied. For example, Article 263 of the 1991 Civil Procedure Law requires that 'Requesting or offering judicial assistance shall go through the channels provided for by international treaties that China concluded or acceded to; in the absence of such international treaties, diplomatic channels shall be adhered to.'

C Sometimes China also lays down specific regulations for the application of certain international treaties. For instance, China acceded to the Vienna Convention on Diplomatic Relations and the Vienna Convention on Consular Relations in 1975 and 1979 respectively. China promulgated Regulations on Diplomatic Privileges and Immunities and Regulations on Consular Privileges and Immunities in 1986 and 1990[140] in order to implement them.

D In some other cases China promulgates municipal rules that include the contents of an international treaty as a preparatory step for formal accession to the treaty. In 1995 China enacted the 1995 Civil Aviation Law which reflects the rights of civil aircraft as they appear in the 1948 'Convention on the International Recognition of Rights in Aircraft'. The SCNPC formally acceded to the Convention[141] in October 1999.

It can be argued that China has adopted a 'mixed approach' towards the reception of international agreements. In the first two cases an 'incorporation approach' is employed; and in the latter two cases a 'transformation approach' is used.[142]

It has been made clear by a recent regulation stipulated by the Supreme People's Court (SPC)[143] that a 'transformation approach' has been adopted to the reception of international trade and investment agreements. The regulation provides that when adjudicating administrative cases involving international trade Chinese courts should apply only Chinese national and local laws and regulations.[144] The authority's explanations of the regulation clarify that this regulation also applies to international investment administrative cases.[145] Such a regulation is said to be compatible with the commitments that China made in the course of WTO accession negotiations.[146] It is therefore clear that, at least from a judicial point of view, international trade and investment agreements to which China is a party must be transformed into Chinese law before they can be applied and implemented.

140 Chen, Hanfeng etc., above, note 128, at 121.

141 *Ibid.*

142 Similar argument can be seen in Zeng, above, note 126, at 42.

143 The Provisions on Some Issues on the Adjudication of Administrative Cases Concerning International Trade (The Trade Cases Provisions), promulgated by the SPC on 29 August 2002.

144 Art 7 and 8, The Trade Cases Provisions, *ibid.*

145 Tian, Ji and Lin, Zhi, 'Judicial Review of Administrative Actions Involving International Trade', (2002) 7 Sep *People's Daily* (overseas edition), at 3.

146 *Ibid.*

Nonetheless the regulation also requires that the domestic laws and regulations implementing international trade and investment treaties should be interpreted in a manner consistent with international treaties if there should be more than one interpretations of any specific provision of those domestic laws and regulations.[147]

3.3.3 The Direct Applicability of International Treaties by Chinese Courts

The direct applicability of international treaties by local courts is closely linked to the approach by which a country chooses to give effect to international treaties. If the 'incorporation' method is used international treaties have direct applicability without the need for extra legislation. By contrast, if a state adopts the 'transformation' model, international treaties cannot be directly applied but need to be 'indirectly' applied via domestic legislation.[148]

There are no general rules in China on the direct applicability of international treaties before Chinese courts, where there are no constitutional provisions as such. However, as previously noted, the SPC's regulation has made clear that international trade and investment treaties are not directly applicable by Chinese courts.

3.4 CONCLUSION

The most important sources of international law governing EU investment in China are international treaties. Other formally applicable sources are customary international law and general principles of law, although they play only limited roles as they are difficult to establish, particularly within the context of EU-China investment relations. Although judicial decisions and publicists' writings are both regarded as subsidiary sources, the former possesses much more significant impact than the latter on the development of general international law on international investment relations. UN resolutions may also be important evidence of customary international investment law although their evidential weight is controversial, as are some 'soft law' international instruments about investment issues.

The applicable international treaties on EU investment in China are either bilateral agreements or multilateral agreements to which China and the EU (and/or all of its member states) are parties. Bilaterally the 1985 EC-China Cooperation Agreement provides a general framework for EU-China trade

[147] Art 9, the Trade Cases Provisions, above, note 143.

[148] Furthermore, the direct applicability of a specific international treaty may depend on its nature. For example, in the United States, domestic courts can only apply 'self-executing' treaty provisions. Shaw, Malcolm N, *International Law*, 4th edition (Cambridge University Press, 1998), at 118.

and economic cooperation, including investment exchanges. The BITs between China and 14 EU member states set forth conditions on all major aspects, such as admission, treatment, expropriation and compensation, subrogation, monetary transfer, and dispute settlement. Multilaterally the ICSID Convention enables all EU investors to bring their investment disputes with the Chinese government before an international arbitration tribunal. The MIGA Convention vests in them the rights to insure their investments in China against non-commercial risks; and the WTO Agreement, although a 'trade' agreement in name, contains principles and rules on investment issues, particularly on certain trade-related investment measures and investment in services sectors.

However, these bilateral and multilateral agreements do not provide a complete and coherent international legal framework for EU investment in China because the EC-China Cooperation Agreement does not have concrete provisions and the BITs are incomplete in coverage and inconsistent in content. All the multilateral agreements address only certain specific aspects or sectors of EU investment in China rather than addressing it in its entirety. A new international legal framework is surely necessary.

A study of the relationship between international agreements and Chinese law shows that China has put international treaties in a well-respected position even though the Constitution is silent on the relationship between international treaties and Chinese municipal law. On the one hand international treaties seem to have acquired a superior position vis-à-vis domestic law. On the other hand, China has adopted a 'mixed approach' towards the reception of international agreements. In some cases an 'incorporation approach' is employed and in other cases a 'transformation approach' is used. A recent judicial regulation has made clear that international trade and investment treaties cannot be applied unless they are transformed into domestic law first.

3.5 CONCLUSION OF PART I

Part I has explored the current legal framework governing EU investment in China. This includes the law of inward investment of China, ie the Chinese FDI law, the law of outward investment of the EU and its member states, and the applicable international law. It reveals that Chinese FDI law is a complex legal system with a large number of laws and regulations under which foreign investors may make their investment in a number of ways. The EU and its member states have greatly liberalised their investment regimes so that EU investors can freely invest in China. Also, international law, particularly the applicable international treaties, has played a significant role in protecting and promoting EU investment.

However it has also been concluded that the current legal framework is neither complete nor consistent. Despite the recent amendments the Chinese FDI law remains unsystematic, scattered as it is throughout Chinese laws and regulations. The EU has acquired shared international investment competence which prevents it from fully engaging in international co-operation on investment matters. The applicable international treaties are neither complete nor coherent, or they are either too general or too specialised.

It is therefore suggested that, firstly, China should adopt a unified FDI code and apply the Company Law to all business entities including FIEs. Secondly, the EU should establish a common Community Investment Policy (CIP) and an exclusive Community investment competence. Finally on the international level a new international legal framework is needed to effectively protect and promote EU investment in China.

PART II

The Current Legal Framework of EU Investment in China: Substantive Issues

This section will scrutinise the substance of the current legal framework governing EU investment in China, especially some of the most important and controversial legal aspects of EU investment in China including admission and establishment, post-establishment treatment, expropriation and compensation, and dispute settlement.[1] Among them, admission and establishment deal with the conditions of foreign investment market access; post-establishment treatment deals with the standard of treatment foreign investors receive once the investment is made. Expropriation and compensation deal with the legal conditions and remedies when a host country confiscates or takes the properties of a foreign investor. Dispute settlement focuses on the procedural aspects of dispute resolutions in case a foreign investor is in dispute with the host government. The following chapters will not only identify the currently applicable rules and principles on these issues, but also assess whether these rules and principles are adequate in protecting and promoting EU investment in China.

1 As a matter of fact, these aspects typically form the essential provisions of any international investment treaty, be it bilateral or multilateral.

4

Admission

4.1 ADMISSION OF FOREIGN INVESTMENT UNDER GENERAL INTERNATIONAL LAW

The issue of admission, establishment[2] or entry of foreign investment is concerned with whether and to what extent a country permits alien investors to make investments within its territory.[3] Under general international law, in absence of treaty obligations and contractual commitments, States enjoy the freedom to regulate the admission of foreigners in their territory, including the conditions and the extent of their carrying out investment activities, as a prerogative deriving from national sovereignty.[4] Such a freedom to regulate the entry of foreign investment is spelt out in a wide range of international legal instrument, such as the UNGA Res 1803[5] and UNGA Res 3281,[6] the

[2] The freedom of establishment is sometimes confused with the freedom of capital movement and the freedom of investment. For a good discussion and clarification of the three terms, see Juillard, Patrick, 'Freedom of Establishment, Freedom of Capital Movements, and Freedom of Investment', (2000) 15 *ICSID Review—FILJ*, at 322–39.

[3] Parra defines 'Admission' as 'the mere entry or making of foreign investment in the territory of a country'. Parra, Antonio R, 'Principles Governing Foreign Investment, as Reflected in National Investment Codes', in Shihata, Ibrahim (ed), *Legal Treatment of Foreign Investment: The World Bank Guidelines* (Martinus Nijhoff 1993), at 312.

[4] Subject to overriding treaty commitments, admission of foreign investors and their investments forms a part of the host country's general admission policy towards aliens, which, under customary international law, is a matter of discretion of the host country. See *Oppenheim's International Law* (by Jennings, Robert and Watts, Arthur), 9th edition (Longman, 1992), at 522; Shihata, Ibrahim FI, 'Recent Trends Relating to Entry of Foreign Direct Investment', (1994) 9 *ICSID Review—Foreign Investment Law Journal*, at 47; Sacerdoti, Giorgio, *Bilateral Treaties and Multilateral Instruments on Investment Protection,* in Hague Academy, Collected Courses, Vol. 269 (1997), at 321. United Nations Conference on Trade and Development, *Admission and Establishment*, UNCTAD/ITE/IIT/10/VOL.11, at 1.

[5] Art I (1–2) of the UNGA Res 1803 reads,

'1. The right of peoples and nations to permanent sovereignty over their natural wealth and resources must be exercised in the interest of their national development and of the well-being of the people of the state concerned;
2. The exploration, development and disposition of such resources, as well as the import of the foreign capital required for these purposes, should be in conformity with the rules and conditions which the peoples and nations freely consider to be necessary or desirable with regard to the authorisation, restriction or prohibition of such activities;...'

[6] Like UNGA Res 1803, while reiterating the host countries' 'full permanent sovereignty over

OECD project of a Convention on the Treatment of 1967 (Article 1 (b)), the United Nations project of a code of conduct for Transnational Corporations (1983) (Para. 48).[7] It is also generally implied by the OECD Code of liberalisation of capital movements and the IMF Articles of Agreement.[8] As a result, the policy of different groups of countries have varied substantially in this regard, from a complete ban of FDI in the formerly Soviet type of centrally planned economies, to a liberal approach adopted by industrial countries.[9] In practice, no national investment legislation has been free from limitations on the entry of foreign investment although the degree of openness towards foreign investment varies considerably.[10]

However such discretion of the host country on investment admission has been to some extent limited by international investment agreements which have proliferated in the past few decades. Typically in the negotiation of an investment agreement capital-exporting countries ask for the greatest possible measure of free admission; whilst capital-importing countries often argue for broad limitations.[11] Indeed, the issue of admission has also been among the most debated issues in both legal and economic literatures.[12] It has been noticed that the liberal approach has gained the upper hand in recent years and has been adopted by more and more national and international investment instruments.[13]

This chapter will examine the admission provisions in both the applicable international legal instruments[14] and Chinese FDI laws and regulations with a view to assessing whether such existing provisions have been sufficient in attracting and promoting EU investment in China.

4.2 ADMISSION OF EU INVESTMENT IN CHINA UNDER INTERNATIONAL TREATIES

International law plays a role in regulating the admission process of EU investment in China because it establishes the principles that China as the

all its wealth natural resources and economic activities', the UNGA Res 3281 states that each country shall have the right to regulate and exercise authority over foreign investment within its jurisdiction in accordance with it national objectives and priorities. Art 2. (2) (a), UNGA Res 3281.

7 Sacerdoti, above, note 4, at 321–22.

8 The IMF only requires its members to liberalise current account payment, not capital account payment (Arts VI & VII). See generally Sacerdoti, above, note 4, at 321, 322.

9 For further elaboration of the different approach in developed, developing and transition economies, see Sacerdoti, note 4 above, at 322–26.

10 Shihata, above, note 4, at 47–48.

11 Shihata, above, note 4, at 47.

12 Shihata, above, note 4, at 48.

13 The main feature of such an approach is imposing a combination of MFN and NT obligations on host states' discretion to regulate investment admission. Shihata, above, note 4; Fatouros, AA, 'Towards an International Agreement on Foreign Direct Investment?', (1995) 12 *ICSID Review-~~F~~ILJ*.

14 The law of the EU and its Member States do not directly deal with the admission of investment and therefore are not discussed here.

host country must follow when it enacts laws on investment admission. China has indeed significantly modified its domestic laws in recent years so that it can fulfil the international commitments it has undertaken under applicable international agreements (particularly the WTO Agreement). But not every international agreement identified in Chapter 3 has rules and principles on admission.[15] Admission has only been dealt with in the EU-China BITs and the WTO Agreement, which are discussed as follows.

4.2.1 EU-China BITs

As shown in *Table 10: Admission under EU-China BITs and MRIIs*, 11 of the 13 BITs between China and EU member states have a provision on investment admission.[16] Like most admission provisions in other European BITs[17] these provisions merely require the contracting parties to encourage and promote mutual investment and to admit investment in accordance with its legislation, laws, regulations, and administrative practices.[18] A representative provision may be found from the Sino-Germany BIT (both the old and the new), which reads,

> 'Either Contracting Party shall in its territory promote investment by investors of the other Contracting Party, permit such investment in accordance with its laws and regulations,...'[19]

The Sino-Britain BIT's wording differs slightly from other EU-China BITs in permitting investment 'subject to the right to exercise power conferred by its laws'[20] rather than 'in accordance with laws and regulations'. The Sino-BLEU BIT additionally provides that host countries shall permit investors to sign and execute licensing agreements business management agreements or technology assistance agreements.[21] In the Sino-Spain and Sino-Greece BITs[22]

[15] The 1985 EC-China Cooperation Agreement only states that the two sides agree to 'encourage and promote' greater and mutual beneficial investment. The ICSID Convention and the MIGA Convention only deal with post-admission issues—investment dispute settlement and investment insurance. Hence, all those agreements do not have concrete provisions on investment admission.

[16] Art 2, Sino-Germany BIT; Art 2, Sino-France BIT; Art 2 (1), Sino-BLEU BIT; Art 1, Sino-Italy BIT; Art 2, Sino-Demark BIT; Art 2, Sino-Netherlands BIT; Art 2 (1), Sino-Austria BIT; Art 2 (1), Sino-Britain BIT; Art 2, Sino-Portugal BIT; Art 2 (1), Sino-Spain BIT; Art 2 (1), Sino-Greece BIT.

[17] For a detailed elaboration of these European BITs, see Dolzer, Rudolf and Stevens, Margaret, *Bilateral Investment Treaties* (Martinus Nijhoff, 1995), at 50–56. See also Shihata, above, note 4, at 55–56.

[18] Art 2, Sino-Germany BIT; Art 2, Sino-France BIT; Art 2 (1), Sino-BLEU BIT; Art 1, Sino-Italy BIT; Art 2, Sino-Demark BIT; Art 2, Sino-Netherlands BIT; Art 2 (1), Sino-Austria BIT; Art 2, Sino-Portugal BIT; Art 2 (1), Sino-Spain BIT; Art 2 (1), Sino-Greece BIT.

[19] Art 2, Sino-Germany BIT, Art 2.1, Sino-Germany New BIT.

[20] Art 2.1 Sino-Britain BIT.

[21] Sino-BLEU BIT, Art 2.2.

[22] Sino-Greece BIT, Art 2.5; Sino-Spain BIT, Art 2.2.

Table 10: Admission under EU-China BITs and MRIIs

Legal instruments	No admission clause	In accordance with legislation/laws and regulations	Subject to right to exercise powers conferred by law	Right to regulate foreign investment	In accordance with the general economic policies	In accordance with NT/MFN standard
Sino-Sweden BIT	1	0	0	0	0	0
Sino-Germany BIT	0	1 (Art 2)	0	0	0	0
Sino-France BIT	0	1 (Art 2)	0	0	0	0
Sino-BLEU BIT	0	1 (Art 2 (1))	0	0	0	0
Sino-Finland BIT	1	0	0	0	0	0
Sino-Italy BIT	0	1 (Art 1)	0	0	0	0
Sino-Denmark BIT	0	1 (Art 2)	0	0	0	0
Sino-Netherlands BIT	0	1 (Art 2)	0	0	0	0
Sino-Austria BIT	0	1 (Art 2 (1))	0	0	0	0
Sino-Britain BIT	0	0	1(Art 2 (1))	0	0	0
Sino-Portugal BIT	0	1 (Art 2)	0	0	0	0
Sino-Spain BIT	0	1 (Art 2 (1))	0	0	0	0
Sino-Greece BIT	0	1 (Art 2 (1))	0	0	0	0
Total (13)	2	10	1	0	0	0
TRIMS (of WTO)						1 (NT) (Art 2)
GATS (of WTO)						1 (MFN)[a] (Art 2)
Energy Charter Treaty	1					
World Bank Guidelines			1 (Art II.3)			
NAFTA Chap. 11						1(Arts 1102 & 1103)
MAI Draft[b]						1(Art III)

[a]In GATS, national treatment is a 'specific commitment', rather than a generally applicable principle like MFN. See Article 17 of GATS.
[b]'The MAI Negotiating Text' of OECD of 24 April 1998.

host countries are required to offer assistance and facilities for obtaining visa and work permits, subject to their laws and regulations.

Despite the discrepancy in wording and technical details, however, it is clear from all these BITs between China and EU member states that the right to regulate the admission of investment falls within the discretion of the host countries. In other words, since these BITs put no limitation on the time nature or extent of the limitations that the host country may introduce, they 'effect no fundamental change on admission over what would have been the case had the BITs not been concluded'.[23] The approach adopted in the EU-China BITS on investment admission thus reflects the general practice of European BITs as well as existing customary international law on the matter.[24] It is followed in even the newest BIT signed between Germany and China, which clearly has not adopted the US pattern.[25]

4.2.2 WTO Agreement

The high level of discretion in the host country over investment admission is restricted by the WTO Agreement, which plays a very significant role in liberalising the conditions for admission.

Admission-related provisions can be found within the WTO Agreement in the annexed TRIMs Agreement and GATS. The TRIMS Agreement effectually eliminates certain PRs as trade-related investment measures (TRIMs), while the GATS deals with the admission of investment in services sectors as 'specific commitments' on 'market access' attached to the GATS.

4.2.2.1 TRIMs Agreement

The TRIMs Agreement requires that members do not apply any Trade-Related Investment Measures (TRIMs) which are inconsistent with the principles of 'national treatment' (Art 3 para 4) and 'the general elimination of quantitative restrictions' (Art 11 para 1) of GATT 1994.[26] Each member notifies the Council of Trade in Goods under the Agreement of all their inconsistent TRIMs within 90 days of the Agreement's entry into force, and eliminates them within a certain period of time.[27] To make matters clearer an illustrative list of those restrictive measures which 'are mandatory or enforce-

[23] Shihata, above, note 4, at 55.

[24] *Ibid*, at 56.

[25] Unlike US BITs, the new Sino-Germany BIT does treat pre-establishment and post-establishment together and apply national and most favoured nation treatment on both stages, but treat the two stages separately and leave the host country sufficient discretion in regulation investment admission. See Art 2.1 of the new Sino-Germany BIT.

[26] Art 2 of the TRIMs Agreement.

[27] The transition period is two years for developed countries, five years developing countries or seven years for least-developed countries. *Ibid*, Art 5, para 1–2.

able under domestic law or under administrative rulings or with which it is necessary to comply for advantage'[28] is annexed to the Agreement. These include:

- A requirement to purchase or use local products (the local content requirement).
- A limitation on the purchase or use of imported goods in an amount related to its exportation (a trade-balancing requirement).
- A quantitative restriction of importation of products for local production in general or to an amount related to its exportation (the general and trade-balancing importation restriction).
- A quantitative restriction of importation by restricting its access to forex an amount related to its forex contribution (the forex balancing requirement).
- A quantitative restriction of exportation or sale for export (an exportation restriction).[29]

According to the Protocol on the Accession of the People's Republic of China (hereinafter 'China Accession Protocol'), China's offers on PRs have been generous. Firstly China undertakes to comply with the TRIMs Agreement upon accession, without any transitional arrangement.[30] Secondly it not only commits itself to eliminating and ceasing to enforce trade and foreign exchange balancing requirements as well as the local content requirements required by the TRIMs Agreement, but also undertakes to abolish export or performance requirements, which goes beyond the TRIMS Agreement.[31] Moreover, China promises not to enforce provisions of contracts imposing such requirements.[32]

China also agrees that the allocation of permission of rights for importation and investment will not be conditional on performance requirements set by national or sub-national authorities. Nor will it be subject to secondary conditions covering, for example, the conduct of research, the provisions of offsets, or other forms of industrial compensation including specific types or volumes of business opportunities, the use of local inputs, or the transfer of technology. Permission to invest, import licenses, quotas, and tariff rate quotas, will be granted regardless of the existence of competing Chinese domestic suppliers.[33]

[28] This definition coincides with that of PRs as mentioned above, which suggests that they are basically the same thing with different names.

[29] See Annex: Illustrative List, to the TRIMs Agreement.

[30] World Trade Organisation Working Party on the Accession of China: *Report of the Working Party on the Accession of China* (hereinafter "*Working Party Report*"), WT/ACC/CHN/49 (1 October 2001), at 40, 76.

[31] *Ibid.*

[32] *Ibid.*

[33] *Ibid.*

As will be discussed, China has already substantially modified its FDI laws and regulations to ensure compatibility with the TRIMs Agreement. Local content, export performance and forex balancing requirements are all notably eliminated from these laws and regulations, which demonstrates that the TRIMS Agreement has indeed affected China's discretion to regulate foreign investment admission; and that China has been very seriously performing its international obligations.

4.2.2.2 GATS

GATS is another agreement in the WTO Agreement dealing directly with investment issues.[34] According to GATS trade is defined to embrace investment[35] since one of the four modes of trade in services is through 'commercial presence', which includes 'any type of business or professional establishment' either in the form of a juridical person or a branch or a representative office.[36] Some GATS's provisions on market access directly and specifically refer to joint ventures and limitations on the percentage of foreign ownership.[37] GATS may therefore be considered a set of 'Rules for Growth and Investment' or 'investor's agreement'.[38]

The substantive rules in GATS have three parts. The first part consists of the 'general obligations and disciplines', which include MFN, transparency, a number of traditional GATT-type exceptions, and competition, business practices, and government procurement.[39] The second part is entitled 'specific commitments'[40] and establishes the framework for a schedule of commitments from each member. A 'bottom-up' approach is taken herein that GATS applies only to the tabled or bound sectors established in the schedule and is subject to the terms conditions and limitations therein. There are three categories of commitments, namely limitations on market access, limitations on national treatment, and additional commitments. They are listed by modes of supply outlined in Article 1.2 of the GATS[41] and are

[34] The significance of GATS to FDI is in part due to the fact that in the recent years there has been rapid FDI growth in the services sector, more than in other sectors. See Brewer, Tomas L., and Young, Stephen, *The Multilateral Investment System and Multilateral Enterprises* (Oxford University Press, 1998), at 126. See also UNCTAD/World Bank, *World Investment Report 1994: Transitional Corporations, Employment and Workplace*, 1994, Tables 1.8 and 1.9, at 16–17.

[35] Brewer and Young, *ibid*, at 126.

[36] Any type of business or professional establishment, including through (i) the constitution, acquisition or maintenance of a juridical person, or (ii) the creation or maintenance of a branch or a representative office, within the territory of a Member for the purposes of supplying a service. See Art XXVIII of GATS, item (d).

[37] See Art XVI, para 2. (e)–(f), GATS.

[38] World Trade Organisation: *Trading into the Future*, 2nd edition, July 1998, at 21.

[39] Part II: 'General Obligations and Disciplines', GATS.

[40] *Ibid*, Part III.

[41] GATS does not give a compact definition of 'Trade in Services' but describes it as 'the supply of a service:

(a) from the territory of one Member into the territory of any other Member;

(b) in the territory of one member to the service consumer of any other Member;

summarised as cross-border supply, consumption abroad, commercial presence, and presence of natural persons. It is specifically stated that in sectors where specific commitments are undertaken the schedule must specify,

- terms limitations and conditions on market access;
- conditions and qualifications on national treatment;
- undertakings relating to additional commitments;
- where appropriate the time-frame for implementation of such commitments; and
- the date of entry into force of such commitments.

The third part of the substantive rules includes several articles on 'progressive liberalisation',[42] which deal with future negotiations on the various specific commitments to be included in the schedules.

The second part, the 'specific commitments' is of vital importance in defining members' rights and obligations under the GATS.[43] In particular, the 'specific commitments' on market access for admission of investment in services sectors are of paramount importance. China makes 'horizontal commitments' as well as 'specific commitments' in the Schedule of Specific Commitments on Services (hereafter 'the Service Schedule') as Part II of the Report of the Working Party on the Accession of China (the Working Party Report). HCs deal with commitments which apply to all sectors included in the schedule, while SCs only apply to the specific sectors or sub-sectors which they address. HCs specifically cover forms of investment, term limitations on land use, and entry and stay of key personnel with a service presence in China.[44] Specific commitments cover professional services, computing and related services, real estate services, other business services, communication services, construction and related engineering services, distribution, educational services, environmental services, financial services, tourism and travel related services, and transport services. There are also several annexes on basic telecommunication, distribution services, and insurance services.[45]

According to the Working Party Report the Chinese representative has made some further clarifications on issues such as service licensing, choice of partners, modification of the equity interests, prior experience requirements for establishment in insurance sectors, inspection services, market research,

(c) by a service supplier of one Member, through commercial presence in the territory of any other Member;
(d) by a service supplier of one Member, through presence of natural persons of a Member in the territory of any other Member.'

[42] Part IV, GATS.

[43] Jackson, John, *The World Trading System: Law and Policy of International Economic Relations*, 2nd edition (MIT Press, 1997), at 309.

[44] Schedule CLII-The People's Republic of China Part II—Schedule of Specific Commitments on Services, List of Art II MFN Exemptions, WT/ACC/CHN/49/Add.2, at 2–4.

[45] *Ibid*, at 5–48.

legal services, and minority shareholder rights.[46] These clarifications are, in line with the Part I 1.2 of the Protocol, integral parts of the WTO agreement and are thus binding on China as well as on other WTO members.[47]

Again, as will be seen, China has amended its domestic laws and made numerous new regulations to implement its 'specific commitments' on market access in services sectors. For instance, both the Investment Guidance and the Guiding Catalogue have been modified so as to accommodate investment in services sectors, and dozens of regulations have been promulgated to implement those commitments (See section 4.3.2 for further details of these legislative activities.) This further affirms that the 'liberal approach' adopted in the GATS has effectively restricted the discretion of China to regulate foreign investment, especially in services sectors. However it must also be noted that market access undertakings under the GATS are 'specific commitments', which means only those scheduled sectors will be bound and that they may still be subject to further conditions and limitations.

4.2.3 Summary

It can be concluded that two different approaches have been adopted in the applicable international law governing EU investment in China. The EU-China BITs adopt the traditional approach to deal with the investment admission issue, which leaves the host country (China) virtually unlimited freedom and discretion to adopt laws and regulations to regulate investment entry. By contrast the WTO Agreement, particularly the TRIMS and the GATS, reflect a new 'liberal approach' towards investment admission by imposing obligations on host countries to eliminate TRIMs and PRs and to liberalise market access for investment in service sectors. Nevertheless the TRIMs prohibited by the TRIMS Agreement are limited to a few measures, and the liberalisation of investment admission in services sectors are only 'specific commitments' rather than general undertakings. In total therefore the limitations imposed by the WTO Agreement on China's freedom to regulate investment admission are fairly limited. China still maintains the discretion to adopt measures and policies which restrict and regulate the admission of foreign investment in the vast areas not covered by the TRIMs Agreement and the GATS.

4.3 ADMISSION OF EU INVESTMENT IN CHINA UNDER CHINESE LAW

Chinese law plays for EU investors the most important role in regulating investment admission. As noted above, the EU-China BITs and other applic-

[46] *Working Party Report*, above, note 30, at 63–68.

[47] Protocol on the Accession of the People's Republic of China (*China Accession Protocol)*, Part I, Point 1.2.

able international agreements leave to the host country great discretion in regulating investment admission. All FDI projects under current Chinese law must be authorised specifically by the government before they can be carried out. This stringent approval system is the central point of the whole FDI regime in China. Getting through the Chinese investment scrutiny and approval system is therefore the first and most important step from the foreign investor's perspective towards any future success.

As a result, it is not surprising that there are quite a number of laws and regulations that deal with investment admission in China. Indeed all the three basic laws on EJV CJV and WFE contain some provisions on the procedures of investment admission. However, the most important regulations in this regard are the Investment Guidance and the attached Guiding Catalogue. They not only prescribe investments in which industries and sectors are encouraged prohibited or limited but also define the approval rights between the central government and their local counterparts. There are also two special catalogues aiming at promoting investment in the middle and western provinces of China and in high-tech industries. One is the Catalogue of Encouraged Industries for Foreign Investment in the Middle and Western Areas (hereinafter the 'Western Catalogue') and the other is the Catalogue of Encouraged High-Tech Products for Foreign Investment (hereinafter the 'High-Tech Catalogue'). Further, as a result of China's entry into the WTO China has promulgated a number of regulations on FIEs in services sectors, which include provisions on conditions of their establishment.[48] In July 2004, China's State Council passed a Decision on the Reform of the Investment Regime, with a view to streamlining both foreign and domestic investment admission regimes.[49]

Chinese law touches upon every aspect of foreign investment admission, which may be classified into three major elements. These are approval procedures, investment directions, and performance requirements. The first element defines the procedural part of the regime, including who is to make the approval decisions and how an approval application is filed and processed. The latter two elements deal, respectively, with the fields of FDI and the conditions of admission, and the substantive part of the investment admission regime.

[48] These include regulations on foreign invested travel agencies, insurance companies, telecommunication enterprises, financial institutions, cargo transportation agencies, foreign law firm representative offices, etc. See *The New Compilation of Laws, Regulations and Ministerial Rules on Foreign Trade and Economic Co-operation of the People's Republic of China* (hereinafter "*the New Compilation*"), edited by the Ministry of Foreign Trade and Economic Co-operation (now the Ministry of Commerce, the MOFCOM) (in Chinese) (Law Press, 2002), 120.

[49] State Council Decision on the Reform of the Investment Regime, passed on 1 July 2004, Guobanfa [2004] No. 20.

4.3.1 Approval Procedures

As observed by Parra, all countries, developing and developed alike, maintain the discretion to admit or reject foreign investment in accordance with their laws, although the degrees of discretion maintained varies greatly from country to country.[50] Unlike some developed countries that do not have specific laws on FDI admission most developing countries have laid down special codes to regulate FDI, and admission is one of the most important aspects of these codes.[51] Parra further noted that there are basically two categories of FDI codes in terms of investment admission: one having no special restriction on entry and the other requiring a special permission on entry.[52] Within the second category some FDI codes empower the government with high discretion while the others limit such discretion.[53]

Like many former socialist countries[54] China belongs to the group requiring special permission for every foreign investment project (FIP); and in deciding whether or not to grant such permits the authority's discretion is rather high. Indeed this approval process has long been criticised as inefficient, lacking in transparency, and frustrating.[55] Since the 1990s the Chinese government has made great effort to improve this, such as the 'one-stop shop' approval model which has been introduced in some localities.[56] But the most important result achieved for the purpose nationally is the promulgation of the Investment Guidance and the Guiding Catalogue. The Chinese government has recently promised to make the approval process more streamlined,[57] and has thus passed the State Council Decision on the Reform of the Investment Regime.

At present normal FIPs are either approved by the development and reform authorities (formerly named 'planning authorities') or the authorities in charge of commerce (departments of commerce) according to the Investment Guidance, while the FIP contracts and articles of association are

[50] Parra, above, note 3, at 317.

[51] Shihata, above, note 4, above, at 49. Parra, above, note 3, at 313.

[52] Parra, above, note 3, at 313–16.

[53] *Ibid*, at 314.

[54] Parra observed that former Socialist countries are more likely to adopt high-discretion admission policies. *Ibid.*

[55] See eg, *Getting Foreign Investments through the Approval Process*, EAER, April 15, 1997, at 1.

[56] In localities such as Shanghai, a joint office is normally established by local government authorities related to investment approval, including the foreign trade and economic co-operation commission, industrial and commercial administrative bureau, the customs and the environmental agency. Xu, Congli and Lin, Zhong, *Chinese Foreign Investment Law* (*Zhongguo Waizi Fa*) (Law Publishing House, 1998), at 49. However, it is reported that sometimes those 'one-stop shops' could not make final approval decisions and therefore become merely 'Mailing Centres'. See Hou, Zhiming, 'Do Not Let the 'One Stop Stops' Become 'Mailing Centres', (2002) 18 Apr *People's Daily* (overseas edition), at 2.

[57] See eg, *Opinions for Further Encouraging Foreign Investment*, jointly promulgated by 9 ministries and administrations and approved by the State Council, Guobanfa (1999) No. 73.

approved by departments of commerce.[58] There is a distribution of powers between these authorities of central government and their local equivalents in approving FIPs and their contracts and articles of association.[59] However it should be remembered that FIPs in services sectors are approved in accordance with the special state regulations and rules thereon.[60] The approval power on FIPs of financial institutions rests at the hands of the People's Bank of China,[61] for example, while the Ministry of Justice or its local equivalents hold the power to authorise the establishment of representative offices of foreign law firms.[62] Consequently the approval procedures of such FIPs vary considerably from each other. Furthermore, if an FIP involves quota or license, application for them must be made in advance to the departments of commerce.[63]

The following paragraphs will therefore only elaborate the approval authorities and procedures of a normal FIP, which is best represented by a manufacturing EJV project.

4.3.1.1 Approval Authorities

4.3.1.1.1 Authorities Involved. In China the approval process may normally involve, at various stages, the State Council, the State Development and Reform Commission (SDRC), the Ministry of Commerce (MOFCOM),[64] and, to a lesser extent, the State Asset Administration (SAA), the State Administration for Industry and Commerce (SAIC) and, the SAFE.[65] In general the SDRC and its local equivalents exercise the power to approve project proposals. The MOFCOM and its local equivalents are in charge of the approval of their joint venture contracts (if they are joint venture projects) and articles of association. MOFCOM is also in charge of the establishment of FIEs by large state owned enterprises (SOEs) and foreign investors for the purposes of upgrading the technological level of these SOEs, and it has the authority to approve project proposals of some of such FIEs. The SAIC and its local equiv-

[58] Art 12, the *Investment Guidance*.

[59] *Ibid*.

[60] *Ibid*.

[61] Arts 13 and 15, Regulations on Foreign Invested Financial Institutions (published on 20 December 2001 by the State Council).

[62] Art 6, Regulations on Representative Offices of Foreign Law Firms in China (published on 22 December 2001 by the State Council).

[63] Art 12, the *Investment Guidance*.

[64] In the past, the State Economic and Trade Commission (SETC)was charged with internal economic and commercial issues while the Ministry of Foreign Trade and Economic Cooperation (MOFTEC) with foreign trade and economic cooperation. In 2003, the new leadership reshuffled the government and a Ministry of Commerce (MOFCOM) was established to replace the SETC and the MOFTEC.

[65] See Xu, X and Chew, C, 'Foreign Investment Enterprises in China: A Comprehensive Guide to Approval Process (Part I)', (1995) Nov *EAER*, at 4.

alents are responsible for registration of and the issuance of business licence for all the approved FIEs.

If a Chinese party contributes or leases assets to an FIE an asset appraisal report must be made by an asset appraiser and approved by the SAA. The approved appraisal report forms the basis for calculating the Chinese party's capital contributions. From time to time the SAFE may be consulted for foreign exchange issues of FIEs.[66] Every joint venture previously had to have a 'department in charge', normally a ministry or commission of an industry or its local equivalent, to which the Chinese party belonged and which was consulted at the project proposal and feasibility study stages. In 2001, the law was changed and the 'department in charge' system was abolished,[67] so such consultations are no longer required.

4.3.1.1.2 Local and Central Approval Authorities. According to a series of regulations notices and provisions the distribution of power to approve foreign investment projects (FIPs) between local and central government depends on the nature of the FIE (production or non-production), the amount of total investment of the proposed FIE, and the relevance of the FIE to the allocation of resources under the state economic plans.[68]

Production FIEs

1 The project proposal for a production FIE whose total investment exceeds $100 million must be approved by the State Council in consultation with SDRC; and the joint venture contract and articles of association must be approved by MOFCOM.
2 The equivalents of SDRC or MOFCOM in provincial regions, Ministries and Commissions under State Council, SEZs, and Municipalities with separately listed plans, all possess delegated power to approve FIEs with total investment of up to $30 million when these are production FIEs not requiring allocation of resources under the state economic plan, whose equipment importation and products exportation are not subject to quota or licensing control. Except for projects falling within the Restricted Category of the Guiding Catalogue, the delegated authority may be further delegated to lower approval authorities.
3 Approval must be given by the SDRC or MOFCOM on the project proposal and MOFCOM on the JV contract and articles of association (AOA) to production FIEs with total investment between $30 million and $100 million, or to production FIEs whose total investment require the allocation of resources under the state economic plan.

[66] *Ibid*, at 1–2.
[67] See Section 1.4.2.
[68] See Xu, X, and Chew, C, '*Foreign Investment Enterprises in China: A Comprehensive Guide to Approval Process (Part II)*', (1995) Dec *EAER*, at 1–2.

Non-production FIEs

All Provinces, Ministries and Commissions under State Council, SEZs, and Municipalities with separately listed plans, are delegated the power to approve non-production FIEs that do not require the allocation of resources under state plan, regardless of the size of the total investment. However if the non-productive investment requires the allocation of resources under the state economic plan, approval from central approval authorities must be sought regardless of the size of their total investment. However it is observed that the line between a productive and a non-productive investment is sometimes difficult to draw, as it has not been defined in any of the relevant laws and regulations.[69]

Increases of total investment

Although it is prescribed that any increase in the registered capital of an FIE requires approval from the original approval authority, MOFCOM makes clear that its approval is needed if the total increase in investments has reached the $30 million threshold even when the initial investment was less than $30 million and might therefore have been approved by a local authority.[70]

Improperly approved FIPs

It has been noticed that normally the higher the authority to which the FIP applies the greater the scrutiny to which it is subjected and the longer the process takes.[71] So it is not uncommon that foreign investors may, encouraged sometimes by local governments, seek approval locally, even when their proposed FIPs are well beyond the $30 million mark. It is reported that MOFCOM has tolerated this practice and few, if any, of these improperly approved FIPs have been terminated. Problems may nevertheless arise when FIEs so approved deal with contractual issues, expansion of operations, import duties and VAT exemptions, financing, forex, etc.[72] The Investment Guidance also confirms that these improper approvals may result in termination of the FIP, the voiding of the JV contract and the articles of association, cancellation of business licence by the SAIC, and the rejection of import and export applications by the Customs.[73]

[69] It is, furthermore, observed that the definition on 'production FIE' in the Implementing Regulation of the FIEs and FEs Income Tax Law may not apply in this context. See Xu and Chew, Part I, above, note 65, at 2.

[70] See Xu and Chew, Part II, above, note 68, at 2–3.

[71] *Getting Foreign Investments through the Approval Process,* East Asian Executive Reports (EAER), April 1997, at 2.

[72] Xu and Chew, Part II, above, note 68, at 3–4.

[73] Art 13, the *Investment Guidance*.

Recent liberalisation

In 1999 several departments of the State Council jointly promulgated Opinions on Further Encouraging Foreign Investment. This stipulates that all FIPs belonging to the Encouraged Category which did not need the allocation of resources under the state economic plan could be approved at provincial level.[74] In other words only FIPs of Permitted and Restricted Categories may need approval from the central approval authorities if they fall within the jurisdiction as described above. Applications should be filed for the record to SDRC or MOFCOM, which should reply in a month if in disagreement. The Opinion also requires that central and local authorities further streamline the approval procedure and speed up the approval process.[75]

In July 2004, provincial governments' power in approving FIPs was further expanded by the State Council's Decision on the Reform of Investment Regime. It stipulates that provincial governments (planning authorities) can now approve FIPs of up to US$100 million (including increased investment) if they belong to the Encouraged or Permitted category in the Guiding Catalogue, and FIPs of up to US$50 million if they fall into the Restricted category of the Guiding Catalogue.[76] SDRC approval is required only for FIPs beyond such thresholds. Among them, approval from the State Council is required for Encouraged and Permitted FIPs with over US$500 million and Restricted FIPs with over US$100 million, as aclarified by the Provisional Regulations on the Approval of Foreign Invested Enterprises passed by the SDRC.[77] The Decision also confirms that MOFCOM and its local equivalents have the authoritiy to approve the establishment and changes of FIPs that are beyond stipulated amount and where foreign investment is restricted, and FIPs that involve quota and licensing regulation. MOFCOM also maintains the authority to approve the contracts and Articles of large FIPs, as well as important changes thereto, such as increase and decrease of capital, transfer of share and merger.[78] It is yet to see detailed rules on such approvals, in accordance with this new Decision.

[74] *Opinions for Further Encouraging Foreign Investment*, jointly promulgated by 9 ministries and administrations and approved by the State Council, Guobanfa (1999) No. 73.

[75] *Ibid.*

[76] Point 12 of the 'Catalogue of Investment Projects that Need Governmental Approval' attached to State Council's Decision on the Reform of Investment Regime, passed on 1 July 2004, Guobanfa [2004] No. 20.

[77] Art 3, Provisional Regulations on the Approval of Foreign Invested Enterprises, passed by the SDRC on 9 Oct 2004, SDRC Order No 22 (2004). These SDRC regulations were laid down in accordance with the aforementioned State Council Decision and the Administrative Licensing Law. The latter was promulgated in Aug 2003 and entered into effect on 1 July 2004.

[78] Point 12 of the 'Catalogue of Investment Projects that Need Governmental Approval' attached to State Council's Decision on the Reform of Investment Regime, passed on 1 July 2004, *Guobanfa* [2004] No 20.

4.3.1.2 Approval Process

In the past, the establishment of a normal EJV or a CJV goes through four stages: project listing, feasibility study, approval of contract, and articles and registration for a business licence. According to the State Council's Decision on the Reform of Investment Regime, approval authorities now only approve project proposal. It is no longer need to approve feasibility study report.[79]

Step 1: Approval of FIP Proposal [formerly known as 'Lixiang' (Project Listing)]

All proposed FIPs are required to be approved by the central or local planning department of the country and subsequently listed in the state economic plan,[80] a legacy of the planned economy that China has practised for more than half a century. It is normally the responsibility of the Chinese party to file the project listing application in the case of a joint venture, and to attain the approval. A project proposal, which sets out certain preliminary information relating to the project and reasons for listing,[81] is then submitted to the concerned authority for approval. However before the proposal is submitted the foreign party normally signs a non-binding letter of intent with the Chinese party on the basic principles of the proposed project. It is crucial for foreign investors to make sure that project listing approval has been attained before they proceed to further negotiations.[82]

According to SDRC regulations, the approval criteria include: (1) conformity with national laws and regulations including the Guiding Catalogue and the West Catalogue; (2) conformity with the middle and long term plans of the national economy and social development, industrial plans and industrial restructuring policy; (3) conformity with public interests and national antitrust regulations; (4) conformity with requirements in terms of land use, urban planning and environmental protection policies; (5) conformity with national technological standards; and (6) comformity with national regulations on the management of capital project and foreign debts.[83] A decision on the project proposal will be made within twenty days after receiving the application, with a possible extension of ten days, in which case reasons of extension will be given to the applicants.[84] However, it may take much longer than this if the SDRC refers such a proposal to a qualified consultant agency for evaluation, as the time taken for such evaluation will not be counted

[79] Art 2 (2), State Council Decision on the Reform of Investment Regime, passed on 1 July 2004 Guobanfa [2004] No. 20.

[80] Xu and Chew, Part I, above, note 65, at 5.

[81] Details of the contents of such a proposal, the required materials and the criteria of approval, see Arts 5 and 6 of the Provisional Regulations on the Approval of Foreign Invested Enterprises, passed by the SDRC on 9 October 2004, SDRC Order No. 22 (2004).

[82] Xu and Chew, Part I, above, note 65, at 5.

[83] Art 12, the Provisional Regulations on the Approval of Foreign Invested Enterprises, passed by the SDRC on 9 October 2004, SDRC Order No. 22 (2004).

[84] Art 10, the Provisional Regulations on the Approval of Foreign Invested Enterprises, passed by the SDRC on 9 October 2004, SDRC Order No. 22 (2004).

toward the time limit.[85] The decision will be given in writing, and if the FIP proposal is rejected, the reasons of rejection will be given and the applicants will be notififed of rights of applying for administrative reconsideration or litigation.[86]

Step 2: Approval of Contract and Articles

After obtaining the approval on the FIP proposal, the parties are normally negotiating on the terms of the JV contracts and the articles of association of the FIE.[87] The contract incorporates all understandings and terms from the letter of intent project proposal, though there could be some modifications made by mutual agreement.[88] Chinese law regards the JV contract as the fundamental document governing the rights and obligations of the parties to joint venture FIEs, similar to a shareholders' agreement in a Western corporation.[89] Articles of association in Chinese law are viewed as governing the company, rather like the bylaws or memorandum of association in other jurisdictions.[90] It should contain the basic information of the FIE—for instance, its name and address, business scope, total capital and organisation framework.[91]

The contract and AOA together with the project approval documents as attachments must be submitted to MOFTEC (now MOFCOM) or competent local authorities (Approval Authorities) for formal approval.[92] Chinese law requires that decisions on the formal application must be made within ninety days in the cases of EJV and WFE (forty five days in cases of CJV and SCFI) of receiving the documents. This only applies to complete applications. Any demand for further information may restart the clock.[93]

In some cases the JV contract may contain a provision to the effect that the annexed agreements are an integral part of and to the same legal effect as the contract.[94] These agreements may include technology transfer agreements, management agreements, and project contracting agreements. Some of them may require separate approvals, and, in such cases, the approval of the contract cannot be understood as the approval of the annexed agreements.[95]

Step 3: Registration for Business Licence

Upon receiving the formal certificate of approval the FIE must apply to the

85 *Ibid*, Art 9 and 10.
86 *Ibid*, Art 11.
87 *Getting Foreign Investments through the Approval Process,* EAER, April 1997, at 4.
88 *Ibid*, at 5.
89 Xu and Chew, Part I, above, note 65, at 6.
90 *Getting Foreign Investments through the Approval Process,* EAER, April 1997, at 5.
91 *Ibid.*
92 *Ibid.*
93 *Ibid.*
94 Xu and Chew, Part I, above, note 65, at 6.
95 *Ibid.*

SAIC or its local equivalent for a business licence. This step is sometimes regarded as a mere formality but problems may still arise if the business scope stated in the licence is different from that in the approval certificate, as sometimes happens.[96] The registration regulations stipulate that FIEs carry out business in accordance with the business scope as stated in the business licence. However it is argued that in this case the approval certificate shall precede the business licence, as the latter is or shall be based on the former.[97]

4.3.1.3 Summary

All FIPs in China are subject to an approval process by the government. FIPs are normally either approved by the development and reform (planning) authorities or the departments of commerce, while the FIP contracts and articles of association are approved by departments of commerce. There is a distribution of powers between these authorities of central government and their local equivalents in approving FIPs and their contracts and articles of association. FIPs in service sectors are approved in accordance with the special state regulations and rules thereon.

The process normally starts with the approval of the project proposal by a competent development and reform (planning) authority. Then the investment contract and the articles of association of the proposed FIE, together with the approved project proposal, are approved by MOFCOM or its competent local equivalent. A business licence will be issued by SAIC or its competent local equivalent in accordance with the approval by the competent approval authority.

MOFCOM may be involved in the project approval if the project involves the technological upgrading of an SOE or quota and licensing regulation, and SAA may be called to assess the Chinese contribution of capital if an SOE is involved. At every stage decisions on approval must be made within 3 months upon receiving a complete application.

It may be fair to conclude that, despite the government's effort to streamline the investment approval process, it still remains rather complicated and stringent. The approval authorities are many and the distribution of powers is unclear, particularly between the SDRC and MOFCOM, and between the central and local governments. As a result of local governments competing for FDI inflows, the effectiveness of such an approval system has been called into question. It has been reported that some local governments would accept foreign investments without examining whether they fit into the local circumstances, and sometimes investors with bad track records and backgrounds have been admitted and favourably treated.[98]

[96] *Ibid*, at 7.

[97] *Ibid.*

[98] It has been reported that sometimes FIPs harmful to public order have been approved by

However, it is notable that the Chinese government has recently announced a shift from the administrative approval approach to an approach of 'regulations, guidance and supervision' under the law[99] and has adopted a more relaxed approval system (Hezhun Zhi).[100] Whilst this simplifies the approval process, it does not change the stringent requirement that all FIPs are subject to approval. A selective approval system should arguably be introduced to replace the current 'one-by-one' approval system. Then only FIPs exceeding certain amounts of certain categories should be approved whist other FIPs would need only to be registered, without special approval.[101] In the long run it is advisable for China to adopt a registration system for FDI admission, so that normally FIPs do not need to be approved and can be established by simply registering with the registering authority. Indeed, in accordance with the State Council's Decision on the Reform of Investment Regime, China has already adopted such a selective approval system on domestic investment admission, under which only specifically listed investment projects are subject to governmental approval whilst most projects are only required to go through a registration process (Beian Zhi).[102] This obviously demands a further reform of the overall FDI law system, which has been discussed above in section 1.5.

4.3.2 Investment Directions

Given that every state retains the right to reject foreign investment it is of primary importance for an investor to determine the host country's attitude to the proposed FIP before taking any further action. Like many developing

some local authorities that are far too eager to attract FDI in their regions. See Zeng, Yabo, 'Attracting FDI Should Be Cautious of 'Three Irrespective' Theory', (2002) 7 Aug *People's Daily* (overseas edition), at 2.

99 Liu, Dongkai, 'China Changes Its Priorities in Utilising Foreign Investment', (2001) 25 Dec *People's Daily* (overseas edition), at 1.

100 Under the new approval system, the approval will be based on considerations on elements such as industrial policy, productivity planning, environmental protection, resources utilisation and monopoly. Aspects such as capital sourcing, technology use, marketing and reinvestment will no longer be examined by the approval authorities. See 'China is to Adopt an Authorisation System for FDI', (2004) 13 Jan *People's Daily* (overseas edition), at 6. Details please see State Council Decision on the Reform of Investment Regime, passed on 1 July 2004, Guobanfa [2004] No. 20.

101 See Xiao, Bin, *Legal Issues of the Foreign Investment Approval System* (in Chinese), paper presented at the 1996 Annual Conference of the China Association of International Economic Law, at 7–8. Zhong, Liguo, 'Codifying FDI Legislation to Improve Investment Environment', (1996) 4 *International Economic Cooperation* (in Chinese), at 46. See also Xu and Lin, above, note 56, at 50.

102 In accordance with the State Council's Decision on the Reform of Investment Regime, the government only requires large and important investment projects to be approved before making the investment. Other projects are only required to register with authorities concerned. State Council Decision on the Reform of Investment Regime, passed on 1 July 2004, Guobanfa [2004] No. 20.

countries China's main purposes in attracting FDI are to absorb foreign capital, skills, technology, know-how and experience, and to generate foreign exchange by the export of goods and services, or at least to substitute locally produced goods for imports to reduce foreign exchange expenditures.[103] In other words China does not welcome every FDI but only those beneficial to its economic and social development. In the case of a joint venture, foreign investors seeking to make investment in China should therefore study Chinese regulations on the directions of investment.

4.3.2.1 Investment Guidance and the Catalogues

It was very difficult until the mid-1990s to determine in advance what China's attitude to a proposed FIP might be because there were no published rules governing the directions of FDI in China. This inevitably led to criticism about the lack of transparency.[104] In an effort to increase transparency the Chinese Government issued the Investment Guidance and the Guiding Catalogue in 1995, which adopted the 'negative list' approach which is gaining in popularity among developing countries.[105] Both regulations are subject to periodic amendments and revisions.[106] The two documents classify all the FIPs into four Categories: the Encouraged, Restricted, Prohibited and Permitted Categories. The Encouraged,[107] Restricted[108] and Prohibited[109]

[103] Clifford Chance, *Planning a Foreign Investment Enterprise in China*, Memorandum to Clients and Professional Contacts of Clifford Chance, May 1997, at 5.

[104] Xu and Lin, above, note 56, at 51.

[105] Similar legislation may be the 1991 *Law on Spheres of Business Activities wherein Foreign Investment is Prohibited or Limited*, of Lithuania. Shihata, above, note 4, at 52–53.

[106] The latest revision was made in February 2002.

[107] According to the newly amended *Investment Guidance* (Art 5), FDI projects in the following areas are encouraged:
(a) new agricultural technology, comprehensive agricultural development, energy, transportation and essential raw materials industries;
(b) new and advanced technology, advanced and applicable technology, which can be used to improve a product, enhancing technological and economic efficiency of an enterprise, or to produce new equipment and materials, the demands of which cannot be satisfied by domestic industries;
(c) projects capable of meeting the needs of markets, upgrading products, developing new markets or enhancing international competitiveness of a product;
(d) new technology or equipment, which can save energy and raw materials, comprehensively utilises resources and renewable resources, and prevent and remedy environmental pollution;
(e) projects that can make use of the advantages of human and natural resources in the Middle and Western Areas of the country, and that compatible with State industrial policies; and
(f) other encouraged projects as stipulated by State laws and administrative rules and regulations. Details of these FDI projects are in the *Guiding Catalogue*.

[108] The new *Investment Guidance* (Art 6) provides for that the following FDI projects are limited:
(a) projects using outdated technology;
(b) projects unfavourable to save resources and improve ecological environment;
(c) exploration and exploitation of certain mineral resources that the State prescribed as to be protectively exploited;
(d) industries that the State opens up progressively;
(e) other projects stipulated by laws and administrative regulations. Details of these industries are also enlisted in the *Guiding Catalogue*.

[109] In accordance with Art 7 of the *Investment Guidance*, Prohibited FDI projects include:
(a) those endangering the state security public interest;

industries are specifically defined while all others are classified as Permitted industries by default.

FIPs in the Encouraged Category enjoy some special rights. They may enjoy tax incentives.[110] Some of them may be able to broaden their scope of business with approval from competent authorities.[111] FIPs in the Restricted Category are, on the contrary, subject to certain restrictions. Restricted FIPs are subject for example to more stringent approval procedures.[112] But classification is not absolute and FIPs of one category may be treated as those in a less restrictive category, depending on their performance. Thus, subject to approval, some Restricted Category FIPs may be treated as Permitted Categories if they export seventy per cent of their products.[113] Likewise Permitted FIPs may be automatically treated as Encouraged FIPs if they export all the products they make, without the need to seek approval.[114]

The Investment Guidance and the Guiding Catalogue attach additional requirements to investment in sensitive industries and sectors, such as 'JV Only', 'Chinese Partners Equity Control', or 'Chinese Partners Relative Equity Control'.[115] The two regulations have clarified the approval authorities and the distribution of the approval right of FIE projects between the authorities.[116] The new Guiding Catalogue includes in its Annex the commitments on the admission of investment in services sectors which China has undertaken to the WTO Members. Most of those service projects fall within the Restricted Category[117] although quite a few belong to the Encouraged Category.[118]

New incentives were recently adopted to encourage FDI in the vast area of

(b) those polluting the environment, damaging natural resources or harming human health;
(c) projects that request large tracts of farm land, unfavourable to the protection and development of land resources;
(d) those jeopardising to the safety and operational efficiency of military facilities; (e) projects based on the unique technology or know-how of China; and (f) other projects stipulated by laws and administrative regulations. Details of those industries are shown in the *Guiding Catalogue*.

110 For example, the FIEs and FEs Income Tax Law provides that Provincial Governments may decide to exempt or reduce local income tax on foreign investment in encouraged industries. Art 9, FIEs and FEs Income Tax Law.

111 Art 9, the *Investment Guidance*.

112 Art 12, the *Investment Guidance*.

113 Art 10, the *Investment Guidance*.

114 *Ibid.*

115 'JV Only' means that the forms of investment can only be EJV or CJV, while WFE is excluded. 'Chinese Partners Equity Control' requires all Chinese partners taken together control 51% or more of the total equity of the FIE, while 'Chinese Partners Relative Equity Control' only request all the Chinese partners taken together to have more equity than that any one of the foreign investors. Art 8, the *Investment Guidance*.

116 *Ibid*, Art 12. Details will be discussed later.

117 These include the establishment of transportation companies by bus, water and rail, telecommunication, distribution, retailing, whole sale and marketing, distribution of audio-visual products, etc. See Annex to the *Guiding Catalogue*.

118 These include venture exploitation and development of petroleum and natural gas, manufacturing of cars and motorcycles, international transportation by sea, multi-mode container transportation, cargo transportation, accounting and auditing services, etc. *Ibid.*

middle and western China.[119] The 'Western Catalogue'[120] was published to attract foreign investors to invest in certain industries in which the respective western provinces have comparative advantages.[121] According to the Investment Guidance, Permitted and Restricted FIPs listed in this 'Western Catalogue' may enjoy the same privileges as these granted to Encouraged FIPs.[122] The High-Tech Catalogue was published in July 2003 to attract FDI in high-tech industries.[123]

4.3.2.2 Observations

The promulgation of the Investment Guidance, together with the two Catalogues undoubtedly marked a significant step forward as it enormously increased the transparency of one of the most important aspects of the investment admission regime—the investment areas or directions. It also helped to curb the discretion of approval authorities in making approval decisions. But it should be noted that this only represents a modest step forward.

FIPs excluded from the 'negative list' are not subject to the screening process in some developing countries[124] but in China all FIPs have to go through the approval process and obtain a license from the approval authority. In other words Permitted and Encouraged FIPs may still be rejected until further conditions are met. Some of the further conditions are general ones. For instance the Implementing Regulations of the EJVL requires EJVs established in China to be conducive to the development of the Chinese economy and the improvement of scientific and technology standards.[125] They should also be beneficial to the socialist modernisation constructions.[126] FIPs will not be approved if they a) damage China's sovereignty, b) are against Chinese law, c) are incompatible with the needs of China's economic development, d) create pollution, or e) include investment agreements, contracts or articles of association which are apparently unfair and prejudicial to of the one parties.[127] Other conditions are specific 'performance requirements (PRs)'.

[119] MOFTEC (now MOCOM), http://www.moftec.gov.cn/moftec_cn/wzs/flfg2000_6_16.html (visited on 8 January 2002).

[120] The Western Catalogue was reprinted in MOFTEC (now MOFCOM), *New Compilation*, above, note 48, at 257–62.

[121] Dai, Lan, 'The Development of Western China is to Make a Substantial Move', (2000) 19 May *People's Daily* (overseas edition), at 1.

[122] Art 11, the *Investment Guidance*.

[123] See Tao Shian, '*The Catalogue of Encouraged High-Tech Products for Foreign Investment is Published*', (2003) 18 Jul *People's Daily* (overseas edition), at 4.

[124] Shihata, above, note 4, at 53.

[125] Art 3, the *Implementing Regulations of the EJVL*.

[126] *Ibid.*

[127] *Ibid*, Art 4.

4.3.3 Performance Requirements

The term 'performance requirements' (PRs) is normally regarded as an invention out of US BIT practice.[128] It is generally defined as certain commitments or obligations undertaken by foreign investors imposed by the host country as conditions for mere permission of investment entry or for enjoyment of certain special advantages or privileges.[129] PRs have two basic forms: either as a condition of admission (which may be called 'direct PRs'); or linked to an advantage (which may be called 'indirect PRs').[130]

Developing and transition countries viewed PRs for a long time as essential and effective tools to control FDI inflows, making sure that they are conducive rather than harmful to the national economy and society. However some developed countries, led by the US, take a liberal approach towards investment admission and attack the use of PRs and other screening measures as conservative and inward-looking, because they interfere with market forces and invite corruption. As a result of the insistence of developed countries some international investment agreements have included provisions to regulate the use of PRs. US BITs require certain direct PRs to be eliminated, and the NAFTA and MAI draft go further by prohibiting not only 'direct PRs' but also 'indirect PRs' listed in the texts.[131] ECT, following the TRIMS Agreement, regulates certain trade-related investment measures like local content requirements and export performance requirements. According to Shihata's survey of foreign investment codes of developing countries PRs remain widespread even in the newer codes.[132] Direct PRs are rare under current codes while indirect PRs remain extensive, most commonly as conditions for access to fiscal and other privileges, to encourage FIPs favoured by the country.[133]

In the case of China, PRs, both direct and indirect forms, have been exten-

[128] Zeng, Huaqun, *International Investment Law* (*Guoji Touzi Faxue*) (Peking University Press, 1999), at 424.

[129] Vendevelde, K, *United States Investment Treaties: Policy and Practice* (Kluwer, 1992), at 110.

[130] Also, PRs are sometimes divided into those imposed on the admission stage and those imposed on the operation stage. However, this division may prove to be false, since PRs imposed on admission stage will inevitably be carried onto the operation stage of a FIP, and, PRs imposed on the operation of a FIP may also be regarded as a part of the general conditions of investment admission—because admission of every foreign investment in every host country is conditional on foreign investors abiding by its laws and regulations, including those affecting investment operations. Therefore, in this book, they are all treated together, even though some of those (eg, local employment requirements) discussed are mainly concerned with investment operations. Gudgon also thinks that such a division is relative. See Gudgeon, Nancy, United States Bilateral Investment Treaties: Comments on their Origin, Purposes and General Treatment Standards, 4 *International Tax and Business Law* 1986, at 118, 120.

[131] Chen, Huiping, 'MAI and the International Investment Liberalisation', 3 *Chinese Journal of International Economics and Law* (Chinese), at 258–59.

[132] Shihata, above, note 4, at 53.

[133] *Ibid.*

sive.[134] The author's Questionnaire survey shows that most EU investors had had some sort of performance requirements imposed (*Chart 10: Frequency of Performance Requirements Encountered*). The most widely used was the transfer of technology requirements, with half of the surveyed investors having the requirement imposed. Other imposed performance requirements are as follows: export performance (36 per cent), local content (27 per cent), forex balance (27 per cent), compulsory JV (27 per cent), subsidiaries limitations (23 per cent) and local employment (14 per cent). About forty one per cent of EU investors had also experienced other forms of performance requirements. The recent amendments to major FDI laws nevertheless abolish some of the direct PRs, while indirect ones remain unchanged. A discussion of the PRs most frequently encountered by EU investors in China follows.

4.3.3.1 Local Content Requirements

Local content requirements have been a widely imposed PR in accordance with China's laws and policies. In some cases they are used as one of the conditions for the approval of some FIPs, as a result of China's 'Content Localisation' (*Guocanhua*) policy. A certain percentage of local content has been one of the prerequisites for approval of foreign invested car projects, the performance of which has been closely monitored by concerned authorities.[135] Another example is that only domestically purchased cars might be used in foreign invested car rental service companies under the old Guiding Catalogue.[136] In other cases local content requirements have been imposed in a softer form, as a priority rather than a necessity. Thus in some basic FDI laws there were requirements that foreign-funded enterprises make it a priority to purchase raw and semi-processed materials, fuels and auxiliary equipment in China.[137]

These local content requirements are clearly incompatible with the TRIMs Agreement of the WTO,[138] and the Chinese government has abolished them and has amended all these related laws and regulations.

[134] For general discussions on the PRs maintained in Chinese laws and regulations, see Shan, Wenhua, 'National Treatment and the Transformation of FDI Laws and Policies in China' (hereinafter 'NT and Transformation'), (2000) 1 *International Trade Laws and Regulations*; Mo, John, 'China, the World Trade Organisation and the Agreement on Trade-Related Investment Measures', 30 *Journal of World Trade* 5, at 106–12.

[135] As an example, Shanghai Santana is a Sino-Germany Joint Venture and the local content rate in the cars it produces has reached 85%. However, it should reach 90% in the future, according to the requirements of the government authority's involved. Xu and Lin, above, note 56, at 61.

[136] *Ibid.*

[137] See, eg, Art 15 of the old WFEL and Art 9 of the EJVL.

[138] One of the few clearly prohibited TRIMs in the Agreement is local content requirements. See the Illustrative List annexed to the TRIMs Agreement.

4.3.3.2 Export Performance Requirements

China has an 'export-oriented' foreign economic policy so export performance requirements have also been widespread in FDI laws and regulations. A statutory condition for establishing an WFE has been that it must export more than half of its products,[139] and the ratio of domestic and international sales must be included in the EJV or CJV contracts submitted to the government for approval.[140] There are also extensive regulations which link export performance to special advantages, like the State Council Provisions for Encouraging Foreign Investment (PEFI). The FIEs and FEs Income Tax Law and its Implementing Regulations entitle FIEs exporting more than fifty per cent of their products (the so-called 'product-exporting FIEs'[141] or 'product-for-export' FIEs) to a series of special tax and other privileges.[142]

Although export performance requirements are not expressly prohibited in the TRIMs Agreement, China is nevertheless committed to eliminate them as a result of its membership within the WTO. Export performance is no longer a condition of WFE admission or an issue to be included in the EJV or CJV contracts after the recent amendments to major FDI laws and regulations. However export performance requirements as indirect PRs are still maintained in major laws and regulations. While a compulsory requirement of export performance has been removed from FIE laws and regulations, for instance, China still expressly insists that it 'encourages' FIEs to export products to the international markets.[143] The special incentives offered to 'product-exporting FIEs' are also still in place.

It is unclear whether these incentives are inconsistent with China's undertaking to eliminate export performance requirements. That is made in the context of the TRIMs Agreement, which does not explicitly prohibit export performance requirements since it is not included in the illustrative list. Given that, even in NAFTA, export performance requirements linked to an advantage is not prohibited, it is probably safe to say that China may maintain these requirements.[144]

[139] Art 3 of the previous WFEL. This provision is now abolished.

[140] Art 14 of the previous EJVL and Art 12 of the previous CJVL. Now both of the provisions are eliminated.

[141] The PEFI defines it as 'production enterprises whose products are mainly for export, which have a foreign exchange surplus, after deducting the annual foreign exchange expenditures incurred in production and operation and the foreign exchange needed for the remittance abroad of the profits earned by foreign investors, from their total annual foreign exchange revenues.' Art 2, PEFI.

[142] For example, FIEs exporting 70% of their products (Product-Exporting FIEs) only need to pay half of the normal income tax and, if they are originally Restricted Category projects, they can be regarded as Permitted Category projects and enjoy extra freedom accordingly. See eg, Art 75 (7) of the Implementing Regulations of the FIEs and FEs Income Tax Law; Art 10 of the *Investment Guidance*; and Art 8 of the PEFI.

[143] Art 3 (1), the WFEL. See also, Arts 3, 45, 53, the Implementing Regulations of WFEL.

[144] See Annex: Illustrative List, TRIMs Agreement. See also Art 1106, NAFTA.

4.3.3.3 Foreign Exchange Balance Requirements

When China first decided to accept foreign investment in 1978, it had hardly any substantial foreign exchange reserves, owing to 30 years of isolation from the capitalist western world. As a result, the original basic FDI laws and regulations all required FIEs to maintain a forex balance themselves. Thus Article 75 of the old EJVL Implementing Regulations stipulated that EJVs should generally maintain the balance of foreign exchange revenue and expenditure. Similar provisions were found in Article 20 of the previous CJVL. Further, Article 16 of the former WFEL and Article 3 of its old Implementing Regulations required, as a condition for approval, that the WFEs must keep the balance of foreign exchange revenue and expenditure.

The forex balancing requirements proved to be one of most severe problems for FIE operations in China.[145] According to a survey by the Chinese authority dealing with foreign trade and economic issues done in 1988 among 4000 Sino-foreign JVs, only about one third (1300 JVs) maintained basic foreign exchange revenue and expenditure balances.[146] Most JVs, particularly those in the manufacture sectors, could not balance their forex.

Since 1996, China has abolished forex control on current transactions, which means that FIEs are no longer required to maintain forex balance on current transactions. After 2001, the aforementioned forex balance requirement provisions were abolished by the Chinese government, in order to bring those laws and regulations in line with the TRIMs Agreement provisions.[147]

4.3.3.4 Technology Transfer Requirements

Under the slogan 'Technology is the first production force', China emphasises the importation of foreign technology, and views FIEs as one of the most important vehicles of technology importation to China. Almost inevitably, FIEs which are involved in the production of goods, will involve the transfer of technology by foreign investors. According to the author's Questionnaire, technology transfer was the most frequently used performance requirement, and had been encountered by half of the surveyed EU investors.[148] In this context, 'technology' means intellectual property rights (IPRs) such as patents, trade marks, copyrights, as well as know-how that refers to technical

145 Yao, Meizhen, *Comparative Foreign Investment Law* (in Chinese) (Wuhan University Press, 1993), at 750.

146 Normally, two categories of FIEs can maintain forex balance. One category is some service FIEs, such as those in travel, hotel, restaurant industries, which earn forex directly from foreign visitors, tourists and other foreigners. The other category is export-oriented FIEs, which exported the majority of their products out of China and earned forex. Frisbie, John, 'Balancing Foreign Exchange', (1988) Mar–Apr *The Chinese Business Review*, at 24.

147 Forex balance requirements are also one of the few expressly listed quantitative restriction measures banned by the TRIMs Agreement. See 2 (b) of the Illustrative List annexed to the TRIMs Agreement.

148 See *Chart 10* for details.

processes, formulas, product design, quality control, technical services and management which has not been made public and is not necessarily protected by intellectual property laws.[149]

According to Chinese FDI laws, there are two main channels for FIEs to obtain foreign technology. One is that foreign investors may contribute technology as capital contribution to a JV, which is encouraged by the Chinese government through tax reductions and exemptions. The other is in accordance with a separate technology transfer contract between the technology provider and the FIE. In the latter case, the contract will need a separate approval, normally by MOFTEC (now MOFCOM) or its local equivalents, to make sure that the technology transferred is appropriate to China's needs and is supplied at a reasonable price.[150] In October 2001, China adopted new Regulations on Technology Import and Export (RETIE), which came into force from 2002. Under these regulations, China formulates, makes adjustments to and promulgates a catalogue of technology, defining the import of which categories of technology are prohibited or restricted. The Regulations introduce an approval system (Licensing administration) for the import of restricted technology, which is a condition for the contract to come into force.[151] For the import of unrestricted technology, the Regulations introduce a contract registration system, which is not a condition of the contract coming into force[152]. The approval procedure for investment projects in which the foreign investors use technology as part of its investment remains unchanged.[153]

As with export performance requirements, technology transfer requirements have been widespread. For WFEs, adopting advanced technology used to be one of the two prerequisites for their establishment.[154] Now the related law and regulations have been changed and China only 'encourages' establishing WFEs employing advanced technologies ('high-tech' WFEs).[155] In the same vein, 'high-tech' CJVs are also 'encouraged', in accordance with the CJVL.[156] The Investment Guidance regards all high-tech FIPs as 'Encour-

[149] Indeed, the Chinese system of intellectual property rights (IPR) protection is a major question related to technology transfer to China, an in-depth analysis of which is beyond the scope of this book. However, it is worthwhile to note that, on the one hand, China has established, in a rather short period, an IPR legal system including Patent Law, Trademark Law, Copyright Law and Regulations on the Protection of Computer Software and has joined in all the major international IPR conventions and agreement. On the other hand, the enforcement of these laws and conventions has continued to be a problem. In the author's Questionnaire, 58% of EU investors were dissatisfied by the Chinese system of IPR protection while only 7% replied positively. The other 35% were irrelevant to IPR, or did not know the answer, or did not have a clear answer. Nevertheless, it can be hoped that the accession to the WTO will bring significant improvement on this aspect.

[150] Clifford Chance, above, note 103, at 15.

[151] Art 10, RETIE.

[152] *Ibid*, Art 17.

[153] *Ibid*, Art 22.

[154] Art 3 of the original WFEL.

[155] Art 3, WFEL.

[156] Art 4, CJVL.

aged' FIPs[157] and the FIEs and FEs Income Tax Law expressly state that 'high-tech FIEs' (sometimes translated as 'technologically advanced' FIEs)[158] shall enjoy special privileges.[159] More concrete incentives for high-tech FIEs may be found in the State Council Provisions for Encouraging Foreign Investment (PEFI), which provides a range of special privileges in terms of land use fees, access to utilities, loans and tax, etc.[160] In short, it may be concluded that China has removed direct PRs on technology transfer but that indirect PRs on technology transfer still remain extensive.

4.3.3.5 Local Employment Requirements

Like most developing countries,[161] China generally requires that FIEs employ Chinese employees, although it allows FIEs to employ foreigners. The underlying reasons are both to increase the employment rate and to train domestic labour. As early as 1984, the Implementing Provisions of the Regulations on Equity Joint Ventures Labour Management provided that 'except representatives of foreign venture partners, EJVs should employ Chinese employees provided that the Chinese partners can provide them and that they are competent'.[162] The Foreign Invested Enterprises Labour Management Regulations, which replace the Regulations on Equity Joint Ventures Labour Management, continue to require that FIE should employ Chinese within China and employing foreigners must be approved by labour authority.[163] Likewise, the REON and the REOFF give priority to employing Chinese personnel for petroleum operations.[164]

4.3.3.6 Compulsory Joint Venture Requirements

As said above, in accordance with the Investment Guidance and the Guiding Catalogue, foreign investments in sensitive industries and sectors are only allowed to have a certain portion of local equity participation. Such compulsory JV requirements may vary from merely 'JV Only', to 'Chinese Partners Relative Equity Control' or even 'Chinese Partners Equity Control'. 'JV Only' means that the forms of investment can only be EJV or CJV, and WFE is

[157] Art 5, the *Investment Guidance*.

[158] This concept 'high-tech FIEs' may have first been introduced by the PEFI, which defines it as 'production enterprises possessing advanced technology supplied by foreign investors, which are engaged in developing new products, and upgrading and replacing products, so as to increase foreign exchange generated by exports or import substitution.' Art 2, PEFI.

[159] Art 6, FIEs and FEs Income Tax Law.

[160] All these advantages are equally applicable to 'product-exporting FIEs'. Arts 3–10, PEFI.

[161] Zeng, Huaqun, above, note 128, at 93–95.

[162] Art 12, Implementing Provisions of the Regulations on Equity Joint Ventures Labour Management.

[163] Art 6, Regulations on Equity Joint Ventures Labour Management.

[164] Art 21, REON; Art 13, REOFF.

excluded.[165] 'Chinese Partners Equity Control' requires that all Chinese partners together control fifty one per cent or more of the total equity of the FIE, while 'Chinese Partners Relative Equity Control' only requests all the Chinese partners together to have more equity than that any one of foreign investor.[166]

4.3.3.7 Special Performance Requirements on Services Investments

The aforementioned PRs are all general PRs that are applied to all sectors of foreign investment. In service sectors that are subject to progressive liberalisation, China has laid down special regulations which set out special requirements for the establishment of foreign investment. These requirements mostly cover business scale, scope of business, business background and expertise, etc. Thus, for instance, a foreign company that wishes to set up a JV trading company in China must have the following qualifications:[167]

- a turnover of over $5 billion in the year preceding the application;
- an average annual trade volume of over $30 million with China during each of the three years preceding the application; and
- a representative office that has been maintained in China for more than 3 years prior to the application, or an investment of over $30 million has been made in China.

Similar requirements can be found in the regulations related to foreign investment in sectors such as cargo transportation,[168] insurance, telecommunication, financial institution, printing, cinema, distribution, venture capital and leasing.[169]

4.3.3.8 Observations

China has maintained extensive PRs, both direct and indirect ones. As a result of China's recent amendment to major FDI laws and regulations, however, China has abolished some of the most commonly used PRs. Some of those abolished are specifically listed in the Illustrative list annexed to the TRIMs Agreement (eg, local content, forex balance), whilst others are beyond the

[165] Art 8, the *Investment Guidance*.

[166] *Ibid* According to the *Guiding Catalogue*, there are only few industries that are subject to 'Chinese Equity Control' and even fewer to 'Chinese Relative Equity Control'. Examples of the former are Printing of publications, rail transportation, construction and operation of cinema, surveying companies. Examples of the latter include construction and operation of comprehensive water projects and civil airports.

[167] Art 4 (1), Interim Provisions on the Experiment in the Establishment of Chinese-Foreign Trading Companies.

[168] 1995 Approval Measures on International Cargo Transport Agency Enterprises with Foreign Investment, Art 9.2.

[169] See MOFTEC (now MOFCOM), *the New Compilation*, above, note 48, at 282–346.

list, such as export performance and technology transfer requirements. Nevertheless, China still maintains indirect export performance and technology transfer requirements. Other commonly used PRs in China include compulsory JV requirements, or local equity requirements, and local employment requirements. Finally, PRs in the establishment of FIE in certain services sectors and industries have become prevalent in the numerous newly promulgated laws and regulations on services investments, in line with China's commitments under the WTO Agreement.

It may be concluded that while significant progress has been made in eliminating some most commonly used PRs, China still maintains extensive PRs, particularly in the form of indirect PRs. As a result of China's effort to progressively open the services sectors, new PRs on services investment have emerged and become widespread. It can be anticipated that for a considerable period, China will maintain these PRs, so as to maintain control over the introduction of FDI, although in the long run some may be gradually phased out.[170]

4.3.4 Summary

Chinese law deals with every aspect of the admission of foreign and EU investment in China: from substantive conditions to procedural requirements. In general, China has made only limited progress on both procedural and substantive aspects of the investment admission regime. From a procedural perspective, China has established a sophisticated system to screen foreign investment which involves a number of authorities. However, this system remains stringent. From a substantive perspective, China has significantly liberalised the admission conditions by introducing the Investment Guidance and a few accompanying Catalogues and by eliminating certain PRs. Nevertheless, the Investment Guidance can only offer guidance and does not replace the one-by-one approval regime. PRs, particularly the indirect ones, remain extensive in China.

It is therefore argued that further reforms of both the approval procedures and the substantives matters are needed to effectively attract EU investment in China. On the procedural side, a selective, more effective and accountable approval system is desirable. On the substantive side, although it will prove impossible to abolish all PRs in the near future, it would be desirable to gradually phase out some of them in a long run.

[170] Xu and Lin, above, note 56, at 57.

4.4 CONCLUSION

The current law governing the admission of EU investment in China is a combination of Chinese law and international law. Chinese law plays a major role as it covers every aspect related to investment admission, while applicable international law only covers limited areas, namely a few TRIMs and market access in services sectors. Also, there is an interaction between Chinese law and international law: in particular, China's commitments under the WTO, particularly the TRIMs Agreement and the GATS, have led to massive domestic legislative activities in China, which have significantly liberalised the market access conditions for EU investment in China. These liberalisations, however, are notably focused on the substantive aspects. For instance, an Investment Guidance was published, accompanied with three Catalogues, which enables foreign investors to discover China's attitude toward their intended investments in advance and therefore increases the transparency and efficiency of the admission process. Also, China has abandoned some of the most criticised PRs or investment measures, including local content, export performance and forex exchange balancing requirements, improving to a considerable extent market access conditions for foreign investors.

The current regime on admission of EU investment in China may yet be further improved, at both national and international law level. On the national law level, the Chinese investment screening regime remains too stringent to effectively attract EU investment. Meanwhile, there are still extensive PRs on investment admission, particularly indirect ones. At the international law level, although the WTO Agreement has brought about significant changes to the admission regime in China, its scope of application is limited to a few TRIMs and scheduled services sectors. The vast majority of investment fields remain unregulated by international law. It is therefore argued that, to further improve the conditions under which EU investment enters into China, the Chinese investment admission regime must be further reformed while the international law must be strengthened. To reform the Chinese investment admission regime, the effectiveness of the approval system must be improved. It is argue that a selective approval system should be introduced. Moreover, as China moves towards a market economy and increases its participation in the world economy, it should open more sectors to FDI, whilst progressively reducing remaining PRs.[171] On the international law level, because China's WTO admission has effectively improved investment access conditions, a comprehensive investment agreement between the EU and China with strengthened admission provisions[172] will contribute to liberalise the investment admission regime further.

[171] Xu and Lin, *ibid*, at 34–36, 56–157.
[172] This is further discussed in Section 9.4.1.

5

Treatment

5.1 STANDARDS OF TREATMENT OF FOREIGN INVESTMENT UNDER GENERAL INTERNATIONAL LAW

It is well settled that once a State admits foreign investors[1] it must grant them the necessary legal protection and ensure them a certain standard of treatment.[2] Indeed, since such standard of treatment define the general legal status of foreign investors in a host country, it constitutes the core of whole international investment legal regime.[3] However, the exact content of such duties, ie, the specific standard of treatment of the property of aliens in international law, is subject to debate.[4] In the landmark *Barcelona Traction Case*, the ICJ concluded that there were no generally accepted rules on the treatment of foreign investment internationally, as a result of 'an intense conflict of systems and interests'.[5] Beveridge has further observed that much of the history of international investment law concerns the efforts of developed countries to set and encapsulate therein minimum legal standards of treatment of foreign investment, and the efforts of developing countries to resist the imposition of these standards.[6] As a result, one has to resort to international treaties and domestic laws to ascertain the treatment that a foreign investor may enjoy in a certain host country.[7]

It is therefore unsurprising that general standards of treatment are spelt out in almost every multilateral and bilateral investment treaties. Applicable in all circumstances, these general standards do not directly specify their con-

[1] However, in recent years, new regional and multilateral investment agreements have managed to extend its coverage to investment admission as well.

[2] Sacerdoti, Giorgio, *Bilateral Treaties and Multilateral Instruments on Investment Protection*, in Hague Academy, Collected Courses, Vol. 269 (1997), at 341.

[3] Shan, Wenhua, 'National Treatment for Foreign Invested Enterprises and the Conditions for Its Implementation,' (1998) 5 *Social Sciences in China*, at 128.

[4] Sacerdoti, above, note 2, at 341.

[5] ICJ Reports (1970), Judgement of 5 February 1970, on *Case Concerning the Barcelona Traction, Light and Power Company Limited*, at 48. See also, Muchlinski, Peter, *Multinational Enterprises and the Law* (Blackwell Publishers, 1995), at 573; Dolzer, Rudolf and Stevens, Margaret, *Bilateral Investment Treaties* (Martinus Nijhoff, 1995), at 58.

[6] Beveridge, Fiona, *The Treatment and Taxation of Foreign Investment under International Law* (Juris Publishing, 2000), at 35.

[7] Dolzer and Stevens, above, note 5, at 58.

Table 11: Treatment under RMIIs

Legal Instruments	Fair and Equitable treatment	National treatment	MFN treatment	Non-discriminatory treatment	International standard treatment	More favourable treatment
Energy Charter Treaty	1 (Art 10.(1))	1 (Art 10.(3))	1 (Art 10.(3))			
World Bank Guidelines	1 (Art III.(2))	1 (Esta in/tors)[a] (Art III.3.(a))	1 (Esta in/tors) (Art III.3.(b))		1[b] (Art III.1)	
NAFTA Chap. 11	1 (Art 1105.(1))	1 (Esta in/tors) (Art 1102)	1 (Esta in/tors) (Art 1103)	1[c] (Art 1105.(2))	1 (Art 1105.(1))	
MAI Draft[d]		1 (Esta in/tors) (Art III)	1 (Esta in/tors) (Art III)			

[a]National Treatment covers not only investment at post post-establishment stage, but also 'investors' and at pre-establishment stage.
[b]As 'provisions of applicable international instruments' and 'firmly established rules of customary international law'. See Art III.1 of the Guidelines.
[c]Only with respect to measures the host country adopts or maintains relating to losses suffered by investments in its territory owning to armed conflict or strife.
[d]'The MAI Negotiating Text' of OECD of 24 April 1998.

tents but make reference to certain benchmarks developed in international practice.[8] The best known general standards include fair and equitable treatment (F&E), most-favoured-nation treatment (MFN), national treatment (NT), non-discrimination standard (ND) and international (minimum/law) standard (*Table 11: Treatment under MRIIs*). On the other hand, international investment treaties also prescribe *specific rights* of foreign investors in relation to operation, management, maintenance and conduct of the established enterprise, such as repatriation of profits and dividends, freedom of operation and access to public services and resources.[9] Needless to say, rules on expropriation and dispute settlement are all part of the treatment of foreign investment and are all detailed in international investment treaties.[10] It would therefore not be an exaggeration to say that all that BITs are trying to address is the question of the treatment of foreign investments.[11] The same is true with host country's investment laws and regulations. Although they tend not to set abstract, general standards as those in the BITs, they define the treatment of foreign investors by providing detailed rules as to how foreign investors may conduct their businesses in the host country.

8 Sacerdoti, note 2 above, at 340.

9 *Ibid.*

10 Whilst expropriations are now viewed as exceptional incidents unlikely to happen in current world, state interference with an investment operation during its normal life is seen as a real danger especially in economies in transition where authorise are unfamiliar with market operations. *Ibid.*

11 Zeng, Huaqun, *International Investment Law* (*Guoji Touzi Faxue*) (Peking University Press, 1999), at 426.

In the case of EU investment in China, the treatment is dealt with by both international agreements and Chinese law. Under applicable international treaties, particularly EU-China BITs, EU investors in China can enjoy MFN and F&E, whilst to a limited extent, they may also enjoy NT, ND or even international standards. In contrast, under Chinese law, EU investors (as well as other foreign investors) are being given special treatment, despite the government's recent decision to implement NT for foreign investment. The following sections discuss the relevant provisions in applicable international treaties and Chinese laws.

5.2 GENERAL STANDARDS OF TREATMENT OF EU INVESTMENT IN CHINA UNDER INTERNATIONAL AGREEMENTS

EU-China BITs are the main sources of international law governing the standards of treatment of EU investment in China, whilst the MIGA Convention and the WTO Agreement also contain such provisions.

As *Table 11* and *Table 12* shows, under those international agreements, the major standards of treatment that are applicable to EU investment in China are, to various extents, F&E, MFN, NT, ND, and more favourable (preferential) treatment.

5.2.1 Fair and Equitable Treatment (F&E)

Fair and Equitable Treatment (F&E)[12] is one of the most widely used standards of treatment by BITs worldwide.[13] It has been adopted in all the 13 BITs[14] and the MIGA Convention and its Operational Regulations.[15] In some BITs, variables such as 'equitable treatment' and 'equitable and reasonable treatment' are used.[16] An example of those F&E provisions is contained in Article 2 (1) of the Sino-Sweden BIT, which reads,

[12] An in-depth investigation of this standard is contained in UNCTAD, *Fair and Equitable Treatment*, UNCTAD/ITE/IIT/11 (Vol. III).

[13] Dolzer and Stevens observed that nearly all recent BITs require such a treatment. Dolzer and Stevens, above, note 5, at 58. See also Khalil, Mohamed I, 'Treatment of Foreign Investment in Bilateral Investment Treaties', in Shihata, Ibrahim (ed), *Legal Treatment for Foreign Investment: The World Bank Guidelines* (Martinus Nijhoff, 1993), at 233.

[14] Art 2, Sino-Sweden BIT; Arts 2, 3 and 8, Sino-Germany BIT; Arts 3 and 9, Sino-France BIT; Arts 2 and 8, Sino-BLEU BIT; Arts 3 and 4, Sino-Finland BIT; Arts 1, 3 and 9, Sino-Italy BIT; Art 3, Sino-Demark BIT; Arts 3 and 10, Sino-Netherlands BIT; Arts 2 and 3, Sino-Austria BIT; Arts 2 and 3, Sino-Britain BIT; Art 3, Sino-Portugal BIT; Art 3, Sino-Spain BIT; Arts 2 and 3, Sino-Greece BIT.

[15] See Preamble of the *MIGA Convention* and Art 3.1.6 of its *Operational Regulations*.

[16] Art 2, Sino-BLEU BIT; Art 3, Sino-Finland BIT; Art 1, Sino-Italy BIT; Art 3, Sino-Demark BIT.

Table 12: Treatment under EU-China BITs

Legal Instruments	Fair and Equitable treatment	National treatment	MFN treatment	Non-discriminatory treatment	More favourable treatment
Sino-Sweden BIT	1 (Art 2 (1))	0	1 (Excp)[a] (Art 2 (2))	0	0
Sino-Germany BIT	1 (Art 2)	0	1 (Excp) (Art 3 (1)–(3))	1 (DL)[b] (Art 3 (4))	1 (DL & IA)[c] (Art 8 (1))
Sino-France BIT	1(Art 3 (1))	0	1 (Excp) (Art 3 (2)–(3))	0	1 (DL & IA) (Art 9)
Sino-BLEU BIT	1 (E)[d] (Art 2 (1)–(2))	0	1 (Excp) (Art 2 (3)–(4))	0	1 (DL & IA) (Art 8)
Sino-Finland BIT	1 (E) (Art 3)	0	1 (Excp) (Art 4)	0	0
Sino-Italy BIT	1 (E&R)[e] (Art 1)	0	1 (Excp) (Art 3 (1)–(3))	0	1 (DL)[f] (Art 9)
Sino-Denmark BIT	1 (E&R) (Art 3 (1))	0	1 (Excp) (Art 3 (2)–(3))	1 (DL) (Art 3 (4))	0
Sino-Netherlands BIT	1 (Art 3 (1))	0	1 (Excp) (Art 3 (2)–(4))	0	1 (DL(Art 10)
Sino-Austria BIT	1 (Art 2 (2))	0	1 (Excp) (Art 3 (2)–(3))	1 (DL) (Art 3 (4), Prot 2)	0
Sino-Britain BIT	1 (Art 2 (2))	1(NL)[g] (Art3 (3))	1 (Excp) (Art 3 (1)–(2))	1 (DL) (Art 2 (2))	0
Sino-Portugal BIT	1 (Art 3 (1))	0	1 (Excp) (Art 3 (2))	0	0
Sino-Spain BIT	1 (Art 3 (1))	1 (NL) (Art 3 (4))	1 (Excp) (Art 3 (2))	1 (DL) (Art 3 (1))	0
Sino-Greece BIT	1 (Art 2 (2))	0	1 (Excp) (Art 3)	0	0
Total (13)	13	2	13 (Excp)	5 (DL)	5 (DL)

[a]Accompanied with exceptions based on customs union, free trade agreements, double taxation treaties, etc.
[b]Without prejudice to domestic legislation.
[c]More favourable treatment in accordance with both domestic legislation and international agreements are applicable.
[d]Equitable treatment only.
[e]Equitable and reasonable treatment.
[f]Only more favourable treatment derived from national laws is applicable.
[g]In accordance with the stipulations of its laws and regulations. See Art 3.3 of the Sino-Britain BIT.

> 'Each Contracting State shall at all times ensure fair and equitable treatment to the investment by investors of the other Contracting State.'

However, neither of those EU-China BITs agreements has defined this standard, which has led to different interpretations.[17] One school of thought believes that this standard is an independent standard,[18] while the other school believes that it is not an independent standard.[19] Among the latter school, some westerners consider that it refers to the minimum standard,[20] while some Chinese scholars think it means a combination of MFN and NT or MFN only.[21] Given that it has been used in parallel to MFN and/or NT and international standard, as in the case of Sino-BLEU BIT,[22] it is submitted here that F&E should be treated as independent standards.

A further controversy between the north and south countries with regard to this standard is on its applicable law. Developed countries tend to argue that such interpretation should be subject to international law, while developing countries insist that domestic law of the host country should be the applicable law.[23] In China, while most scholars hold to the latter, it has been argued that F&E might be interpreted according to general international law, provided that such 'general international law' is that of universal acceptability, rather than that special to western countries.[24] In the absence of such general international law, domestic law of the host country should be applied.[25] Given the controversies with regard to the existence and content of such international law on this issue, the actual result of this argument is the same as developing countries' common standpoint.

5.2.2 Most-Favoured-Nation Treatment (MFN)

MFN has been regarded as a cornerstone of international commercial transactions.[26] Likewise, it is one of the most commonly used standard of treatment for foreign investment.[27] Under this standard, the host country

[17] *Ibid*; Xu, Congli and Lin, Zhong, *Chinese Foreign Investment Law* (*Zhongguo Waizi Fa*) (Law Publishing House, 1998), at 37–38.

[18] Mann, FA, 'British Treaties for the Promotion and Protection of Investments', (1981) 52 *British Yearbook of International Law* 242; Dolzer and Stevens, above, note 5, at 58.

[19] See Dolzer and Stevens, above, note 5, at 59.

[20] *Ibid.*

[21] Yao, Meizhen, *Textbook on Foreign Investment Law* (in Chinese) (Law Press, 1994), at 13; Gao, Yongfu, *International Economic Law* (in Chinese) (Lixin Accounting Publications, 1993), at 234.

[22] Art 2 and Protocol point 7 of the Sino-BLEU BIT.

[23] Mo, John, 'Some Aspects of the Australia-China Investment Protection Treaties', (1991) 25 *Journal of World Trade Law* 43, at 52.

[24] Xu and Lin, above, note 17, at 40–41.

[25] *Ibid.*

[26] Jackson, John, Davey, William and Sykes, Alan, *Legal Problems of International Economic Relations*, 4th edition (West Group, 2002), at 415.

[27] Dolzer and Stevens, above, note 5, at 65. Khalil, above, note 13, at 233.

undertakes to grant investments from certain country treatments no less favourably than that accorded investment from any third country.[28] Thus, among all countries with which the host country has signed a BIT where MFN is normally provided, equal treatment is guaranteed. As MFN is contingent on the treatment that other countries receive, it is sometimes regarded as a 'relative treatment standard'.[29] MFN is often used together with NT, another 'relative treatment standard', which requires the host country to treat domestic and foreign investors in the same manner.[30]

The magic of MFN lies in its 'multiplying effect', which must be handled with caution. It is therefore generally agreed that MFN's scope of application should be restricted by the subject-matter of the treaty (*ejusdem generis*).[31] Thus, an MFN clause cannot have the effect of extending to beneficiary countries rights that may derive from treaties or instrument dealing with a different matter. Nor should it be extended to individual investment agreements between the host state and private foreign investors.[32] However, it is also observed that if a host country has provided NT in a BIT, the MFN clauses in the BITs it has signed with other countries shall have the effect of extending the NT to them, provided that the NT is more favourable.[33] Further, as confirmed in the Maffezini Case, the MFN clause can multiply not only provisions on substantive matters, but also provisions of procedural nature including dispute settlement.[34] Finally, MFN is subject to certain exceptions, such as customs unions, free trade areas, double taxation arrangements, etc.[35]

5.2.2.1 MFN Clauses in EU-China BITs

Like F&E, in all EU-China BITs, MFN is furnished (See *Table 12*), with common exceptions based on customs unions, free trade areas, frontier trade and avoidance of double taxation treaties.[36] Thus, for instance, Article 4 of the Sino-Finland BIT provides,

30 Dolzer and Stevens, above, note 5, at 65.

29 Another relative standard is NT. Vandevelde, KJ, 'US Bilateral Investment Treaties: the Second Wave', 14 *Michigan Journal of International Law*, at 69.

30 Vandelvelde, *ibid*, at 73; Khalil, above, note 13, at 233; Dolzer and Stevens, above, note 5, at 65.

31 This principle is dealt with in detail in the *Anglo-Iranian Oil Company Case (Jurisdiction)*, the *Ambatielos Case (merits: obligation to arbitrate)*, and more recently the *Maffezini Case*. See *Emilio Agustin Maffezini v. Spain Case*, ICSID Case No. ARB/97/7, paras 38–64. See also Dolzer and Stevens, above, note 5, at 66.

32 Dolzer and Stevens, *ibid.*

33 *Ibid.* See also Schwarzenberger, George, 'The Most-Favoured-Nation Standard in British State Practice', (1945) 22 *British Yearbook of International Law*, at 119.

34 See *Emilio Agustin Maffezini v. Spain Case*, ICSID Case No. ARB/97/7, paras 38–64.

35 For an elaboration of these exceptions, see Dolzer and Stevens, above, note 5, at 71–76.

36 See eg, Sino-Sweden BIT, Art 2 (2); Sino-Germany BIT, Art 3; Sino-France BIT, Art 3; Sino-Netherlands BIT, Art 3 (2)–(4;) Sino-Austria BIT, Art 3 (2)–(3); Sino-Britain BIT, Art 3 (1)–(2).

'(1) Neither Contracting party shall in its territory subject investments admitted in accordance with the provisions of this Agreement or returns of investors of the other Contracting Party to treatment no less favourable than that it accords, in like situations, to investment or returns of investors of any third State.
(2) The treatment mentioned in Paragraph (1) of this Article shall not include treatment accorded by either Contracting Party to investments or returns of investors of a third state based on agreements related to customs unions, free trade areas, or other forms of regional co-operation, economic union, avoidance of double taxation and frontier trade.'

5.2.2.2 MFN Clause in the GATS

Moreover, GATS has an MFN provision as a general principle. It requires each WTO Member to accord 'immediately and unconditionally' to services and service suppliers of any other Member, treatment no less favourable than that it accords to like services and service suppliers of any other country.[37] This general obligation is, also, subject to general exceptions prescribed in the GATS and special ones as listed in the Annex to this article.[38]

It can thus be concluded that MFN treatment for EU investment in China has been well established by these BITs and the GATS.

5.2.3 National Treatment (NT)

Under international law, National Treatment (NT) is a treatment standard for aliens which means that the host state must treat aliens as it does its own nationals. Under international investment treaties, NT requires the host country to accord foreign investors the same treatment as that enjoyed by its own nationals.[39] In BIT practice, NT provisions are often combined with MFN clauses. While the latter aims to tackle the problem of discrimination between different foreign investors in one host country, the former tries to eliminate discrimination between domestic and foreign investors.[40] Taken together, MFN and NT have the effect of creating a level playing field in the host country for all business players, irrespective of their national origin.[41]

Before the 1990s, NT was, as in most BITs, only applied to the post-establishment stage of investment. Now, the tendency has been that, as witnessed by the MRIIS, NT, together with MFN, are applied to the entire life of investment activities, before and after investment admission[42] (See *Table 11* for details).

[37] Art II (1), GATS.

[38] Art II (2) and (3), GATS.

[39] Dolzer and Stevens, above, note 5, at 63. For a thorough investigation of NT clauses in domestic and international legal instruments, see UNCTAD, *National Treatment*, UNCTAD/ITE/IIT/11 (Vol. IV).

[40] Shan, Wenhua, above, note 3, at 133.

[41] *Ibid.*

[42] The NAFTA signed in 1992 marked the change of trend in multilateral arena on this issue. Shihata, Ibrahim FI, 'Recent Trends Relating to Entry of Foreign Direct Investment', (1994) 9 *ICSID Review—FILJ*, at 59.

Nevertheless, NT has rarely been granted unfettered and various forms of limitations, and exceptions are often in place.[43] Thus many BITs provide that NT will apply only when the foreign and domestic investors are in 'identical' or 'similar' situations, or 'in like situations.' These provisions may also refer to 'similar enterprises', 'similar investments' or to investors 'with similar economic activities'.[44]

5.2.3.1 NT Provisions in EU-China BITs

In the case of EU investment in China, NT has rarely been adopted in applicable international instruments. Among the 13 BITs, only two (Sino-Britain BIT and Sino-Spain BIT) have NT provisions, which are substantially qualified. Thus Article 3 (3) of the 1986 Sino-Britain BIT states that,

> '...either Contracting Party shall *to the extent possible*, accord treatment *in accordance with the stipulations of its laws and regulations* to the investment of nationals or companies of the other Contracting Party the same treatment as that accorded to its own nationals or companies'.[45] (emphases added)

From China's perspective, this clause had marked a great concession and a significant step forward, as previously China had never agreed to refer to NT, even in a limited form, in any BIT it had concluded.[46] In a similar vein, the Sino-Spanish BIT signed in 1992 also makes reference to NT in accordance with the stipulations of its laws and regulations, although the phrase 'to the extent possible' is omitted.[47]

It must be noted that the qualifications that appear in both BITs on NT 'in accordance to the stipulations of its laws and regulations' are very substantial. Like the qualification on investment admission in the EU-China BITs,[48] they do not require existing discriminatory measures to be eliminated, nor do they prohibit new discriminatory actions from being taken, provided that they were in the form of domestic 'laws and regulations'.[49] In other words, these NT provisions impose no material restrictions on the manner in which a host country treats foreign investments.[50] As a result, one probably can argue that, in the two BITs, a NT 'principle' or 'standard' has not been established.[51]

However, it has been argued that the NT principle or standard for foreign

[43] Dolzer and Stevens, above, note 5, at 63; Vandevelde, above, note 29, at 71–76.

[44] Dolzer and Stevens, above, note 5, at 63.

[45] Art 3 (3), Sino-Britain BIT.

[46] Denza, Eileen, and Brooks, Shelagh, 'Investment Protection Treaties: United Kingdom Experience', (1989) 36 *International and Comparative Law Quarterly*, at 918.

[47] Art 3 (4), Sino-Spain BIT.

[48] See Section 4.2.1.

[49] Shihata, above, note 42, at 55.

[50] Li, Shishi, 'The Chinese Bilateral Investment Treaties', (1990) *Chinese Yearbook of International Law* (in Chinese), at 116. Shan, above, note 3, at 132.

[51] Shan, above, note 3, at 132.

investment might have been established by the Sino-Japan BIT signed in 1988. Unlike the Sino-Britain and Sino-Spain BITs, the Sino-Japan BITs introduces a standard NT provision in the text of the treaty, without the usual qualification 'in accordance with its laws and regulations', nor 'to the extent possible'[52] Also, it makes clear that this obligation applies to 'investment, returns and business activities related in connection with the investment' the latter of which include,

> '(a) [t]he maintenance of branches, agencies, offices, factories and other establishments appropriate to the conduct of business activities;
> (b) the control and management of companies which they have established or acquired;
> (c) the employment and discharge specialists including technical experts, executive personnel and attorneys, and other workers;
> (d) the making and performance of contracts.'[53]

Further, the Agreed Minutes state that such NT obligation shall also apply to measures restricting or impeding following activities, which are similar to the aforementioned PRs:

> 'the purchase of raw or auxiliary materials, of power or fuel, or of means of production or operation of any kind; the marketing of products inside or outside the country; the obtaining of loans inside or outside the country; the introduction of technology; and the establishment of branches or offices of resident representatives outside the country'.

Therefore, it can be said that the Sino-Japan BIT marks significant further progress towards the granting of NT treatment, from China's point of view. Nevertheless, such treatment is still substantially limited in the Protocol, which forms an integral part of the BIT. The Protocol points out that the NT obligation in the BIT does not prevent either Contracting Party from according discriminatory treatment,

> '*in accordance with it laws and regulations*, to national and companies of the other Contracting Party, in case it is really necessary for the reasons of public order, national security or *sound development of national economy*'.[54] (emphases added)

Here again, the qualification 'in accordance with its laws and regulations' emerges. Although permissible discrimination is limited to a few categories, the inclusion of 'sound development of national economy' as one of them suggests that the provision of NT is subject to the economic policy of the host country. Taken together, these two qualifications might have the same effect

[52] Art 3 (2), Sino-Japan BIT.
[53] Art 3 (3), Sino-Japan BIT.
[54] Point 3 of the Protocol, attached to the Sino-Japan BIT.

as those in the Sino-Britain and Sino-Spain BIT. Thus it may be concluded that although the Sino-Japan BIT has made further clarifications on the application of NT, it still has not substantially limited the host country's discretion and freedom to adopt discriminatory measures against foreign investment, and subsequently a NT 'principle' or 'standard' is still yet to be established.[55]

A further development on NT, however, is witnessed by the new Sino-Germany BIT. In Article 2 (2) of the BIT, NT is provided for without any qualification. The attached Protocol does qualify the application of NT *in China*, among other treatment standards such as fair and equitable treatment, MFN, constant protection and security and non-discrimination, by permitting all existing incompatible measure and their maintenance (grandfather clause).[56] The existing incompatible measure might also be modified, provided that such modification would not increase the degree of incompatibility.[57] Nevertheless, China has promised to phase out the incompatible measures.[58] The Protocol further defines the 'activities in connection with an investment' as to include but not limited to the 'management, maintenance, conduct, enjoyment and disposition' of an investment, particularly in relation to the 'procurement of raw material or auxiliary materials, of energy or fuel, or of means of production or operation of any kind, as well as any other measures with similar effect'.[59] This shows that regulation of investment admission or establishment is not subject to NT obligations. It is also made clear that such a NT obligation does not require the extension of a tax privilege, exemption of reduction to domestic investors to foreign investors,[60] which must be regarded as a substantial limitation on the application of NT.

The development of this BIT lies in the fact that since the entry into force of the new Sino-Germany BIT, China will no longer be able to adopt new discriminatory measure against foreign investors and investment, as it may do under previous BITs including the Sino-Japan and Sino-Korea BITs.[61] A clearer and firmer commitment in granting NT is therefore made by the Chinese government in this BIT. The existence of the 'grandfather clause' and other limitations, however, makes one hesitant to conclude that a NT principle is finally established by this BIT. Further, the new Sino-Germany BIT is yet to be ratified, which undoubtedly adds to the uncertainty.

[55] The same conclusion can be applied to the Sino-Korea BIT, which adopted the same provisions in the treaty text and protocol. Probably due to failing to see the protocol, some Chinese scholars have believed that an NT without substantial qualification has been granted by China therein 'by mistake'. See Art 3 (2) and Point 2 of Protocols of the Sino-Korea BIT. Xu and Lin, above, note 17, at 25.

[56] Point 3 (Re: Arts 2 and 3), Protocol to the new Sino-Germany BIT.

[57] *Ibid.*

[58] *Ibid.*

[59] Point 4 (Re: Art 3), Protocol to the new Sino-Germany BIT.

[60] *Ibid.*

[61] Discriminatory measures may still be adopted in the ground of some general exceptions, such as public order or security, and public health or morality. See Point 4 (Re: Art 3), Protocol to the new Sino-Germany BIT.

Indeed, as can be seen in the following discussions, as China had been practising a planned economy, it remains very difficult for it to implement a proper NT to foreign investors and their investment at this stage.[62] It would therefore be tempting to conclude that at the present stage, the NT provisions in the Sino-foreign BITs have more symbolic than substantial significance. Accordingly, although the 'multiplying effect' of MFN clauses in the 13 EU-China BITs may entitle most EU investors to the NT as prescribed in those BITs, it does not possess much substantial meaning for them.

5.2.3.2 NT Provision in the GATS

Under the GATS, NT, like admission or 'market access' in the GATS phrase, is a 'specific commitment', which applies only to the services sectors described in the host country's services schedule and which is subject to conditions set out therein.[63] Thus a 'bottom-up' approach is adopted. Again, it cannot be justified that a general obligation of NT has been established.

However, it is worth noting that in judging whether NT is afforded, GATS uses as criteria NT's actual effect on the 'condition of competition', rather than formal equality in applying such measures. In other words, even if a measure is equally applied to domestic and foreign service suppliers, it may be regarded as a violation of NT obligation, as it has in fact put foreign suppliers in a disadvantaged competitive position.

5.2.4 Non-Discrimination Treatment (ND)

Although general international law requires states to refrain from discriminatory treatment of aliens, it is unclear what such non-discrimination treatment (ND) is.[64] It has been argued that, in a narrow sense, ND means that the host country should not adopt special restrictions or limitation on foreign investors, whilst NT and MFN require that the host country extend the favourable treatment accorded to national investors or foreign investors from a third countries to the foreign investors.[65] Thus although they all address the issue of equality among investors from different countries, they do it from different perspectives and with different approaches: the ND takes a negative approach while the MFN and NT take a positive approach.[66] It is based on this understanding that the three standards of treatment may logically co-exist within a single legal instrument. On the other hand, if all of them are

[62] See Section 5.3.2.1.
[63] Art 17 (1), GATS.
[64] Dolzer and Stevens, above, note 5, at 61.
[65] Han, Depei, *Private International Law* (Wuhan University Press, 1989), at 112. See also, Schwarzenberger, above, note 33, at 118–19.
[66] Han, above, note 65.

broadly interpreted, ie, to include both the positive and negative aspects of treatment, they inevitably overlap. If this is the case, it may still be said that although they are addressing the same issue, their emphases are different: ND stresses the non-adoption of discriminatory measures whilst MFN and NT emphasise the extension of privileges.

It is probably based on the same understanding that Dolzer and Stevens have pointed out that, under international law, the non-discrimination treatment obligation will not be violated merely on the ground that there are differential treatments between nationals and aliens and between different groups of aliens.[67] ND is only violated if (a) a discriminatory measure has resulted in actual injury to an alien; and (b) the act were done with the intention to harm the aggrieved alien.[68]

ND clauses are a common feature of in BITs, even in those between developing countries.[69] However, for the same reasons as in NT, in the EU-China BITs or other Chinese BITs, it has not been very commonly used, and in the rare cases when it is used, it has been substantially limited. As shown in the *Table 12*, only five of the 13 EU-China BITs, have embraced such a provision.[70] All of them co-exist with MFN clauses and two with NT clauses. For example, Article 3 (4) of the Sino-Denmark BIT reads,

> 'Each Contracting Party guarantees that *without prejudice to its laws and regulations* it shall not adopt any discriminatory measures against any joint ventures with participation by shareholding nationals or companies of the other Contracting Party, or against investments made by nationals or companies of the other Contracting Party, including the management, maintenance, use, enjoyment or disposal of such investments.' (emphasis added)

The qualification that ND applies 'without prejudice to it laws and regulations' is universal in all five BITs (See *Table 12* for details). In some BITs, further limitations have been imposed. For instance, the Protocol of Sino-Germany BIT further defines 'discriminatory measures' as those restricting the procurement of raw material or auxiliary materials, of energy or fuel, or of means of production or operation of any kind, as well as any other measures with similar effect.[71] Measures taken 'for the reason of priority in the arrangement of its national economy within a period of time', but that are not directed specifically against investors or investment from the other Contracting Party, should not be deemed 'discriminatory measures'.[72] Also, discriminatory measures based on reasons of public order, or security, public

[67] Dolzer and Stevens, above, note 5, at 61–62.

[68] *Ibid.*

[69] *Ibid*, at 62.

[70] Art 3 (4), Sino-Germany BIT; Art 3 (4), Sino-Demark BIT; Art 3 (4) and Point 2 in the Protocol, Sino-Austria BIT; Art 2 (2), Sino-Britain BIT; Art 3 (1), Sino-Spain BIT.

[71] Point 3 (b) of the Protocol to the Sino-Germany BIT.

[72] *Ibid.*

health or morality, are exempted from ND obligations.[73] The new Sino-Germany BIT, however, has abandoned reference to domestic laws as the precondition of ND application.[74] It nevertheless limits the ND's application to only the 'management, maintenance, conduct, enjoyment and disposition' of an investment.[75] Its Protocol further limits ND's application *in China* by grandfathering existing incompatible measures.

It can be concluded that, at it stands, the standard or principle of ND has not actually been established, since its application is subject to very extensive and substantial qualifications. However, the future ratification of the new Sino-Germany BIT might have the affect to establish a ND principle, as a principle of post-establishment treatment of foreign investment.

5.2.5 More Favourable (Preferential) Treatment

No State should be compelled to grant preferential treatment to foreign investment. This principle is expressly set out in the UN Charter of Economic Rights and Duties of States.[76] However, this does not prevent sovereign states from adopting laws and regulations or entering into international agreements that confer certain special privileges to foreign investors. Thus some BITs explicitly state that the present treaty will not prevent foreign investors from enjoying any treatment that is more favourable according to any existing or future domestic legislation or international agreement. Such a clause is sometimes called 'preservation of rights' clause.[77]

In five of the EU-China BITs, such a clause has been included. Three refer to more favourable treatment deriving from both domestic law and international agreements,[78] while two refer to domestic law only.[79] (*Table 12*) Nevertheless, the MFN clause in the 13 BITs should make more favourable treatment available for all investors from the 14 EU countries.

5.3 TREATMENT OF EU INVESTMENT IN CHINA UNDER CHINESE LAW

The standards of treatment that China upholds under international law reflect the treatment that EU investors enjoy under Chinese law. Since Chinese domestic laws, policies and practices do not differentiate between investors from different foreign countries, it can be said that the MFN oblig-

[73] *Ibid*, Point 3 (c).
[74] Art 2.3 of the new Sino-Germany BIT.
[75] *Ibid*.
[76] Art 2 (2) (a), UNGA Res 3281.
[77] Dolzer and Stevens, above, note 5, at 82.
[78] Art 8 (1), Sino-Germany BIT; Art 9, Sino-France BIT; Art 8, Sino-BLEU BIT.
[79] Art 9, Sino-Italy BIT; Art 10, Sino-Netherlands BIT.

ation has been honoured. Corresponding to the substantially restrictive NT and ND clauses under applicable international agreements, China accords foreign, including EU, investors, as compared with national investors, special treatment: a treatment combined of special restrictions on the one hand and special privileges on the other. This special treatment may be called *non-national treatment*. However, a new policy of 'gradually implementing *national treatment* of FIEs' has been adopted and implemented since 1993.[80] This section therefore discusses both the current situation of special treatment for foreign investment and the progress and prospects of the implementation of NT in China.

5.3.1 Non-National Treatment for Foreign Investment

The non-national treatment (Non-NT) for foreign investment can firstly be seen from the legal structure for FDI: As discussed in Chapter 1, China has an independent legal system to deal with FDI issue, which is largely separate from that dealing with domestic investment. Such a separation of law naturally means a separation of treatment. In specific laws and regulations, furthermore, such a Non-NT takes the form of both 'superior-national treatment' (the special restrictions) and 'inferior-national treatment' (the special incentives or privileges) of FDI in China.[81]

5.3.1.1 Inferior-National Treatment

The inferior-national treatment (Inferior NT) refers to the special restrictions imposed upon foreign investors, which include those in the fields of investment, the special and stringent approval process, and the extensive performance requirements (PRs) imposed on both the admission and operation of foreign investment. Since those restrictions have been discussed at length in the Chapter on Admission, there is no need to repeat them here.

5.3.1.2 Superior-National Treatment

The superior-national treatment (Superior NT) refers to the special privileges and incentives (preferential treatment) that China grants foreign including EU investors, as compared with national investors. According to the author's Questionnaire, those investment incentives have played a very important role in attracting EU investors to China. It tells us that the vast majority of EU

[80] Zhang, Mo, 'China's Move toward National Treatment of Foreign Investors: New Shenzhen Regulations', (1996) 18 *East Asia Executive Report* 9, No. 11, at 9.

[81] Shan, Wenhua, 'Market Economy and the National Treatment for Foreign Invested Enterprises', (1994) 5 *Chinese Legal Science*, at 89.

investors (91 per cent) put investment incentives on a medium or higher position when deciding whether or not to invest in China. Forty one per cent of them consider incentives to be highly important factors in making their investment decision, while nine per cent considered it of top importance (*Chart 16: Importance of Incentives*). Some EU investors have expressed the opinion in the Questionnaire that abolishing investment incentives to FIEs would adversely affect the development of EU investment in China.

In order to attract foreign investment, China has over the last twenty years introduced and maintained numerous incentive measures. These investment incentives range from tax reduction, land fee discount, to access to public utilities or government loans. Some are more general in coverage, whilst some of them are more focused on certain geographical areas or industries. Therefore, they may be divided as General Incentives, Area-Specific Incentives and Industry-Specific Incentives.

General incentives

For all FIEs in China, the corporate income tax rate is thirty per cent on a taxable income basis, plus a three per cent local corporate income tax,[82] which is the same as that for domestic enterprises. However, unlike domestic enterprises, all 'Production FIEs'[83] of ten years standing or longer can enjoy a five-year tax holiday, including income tax exemption for the first two 'profit-making' years and a further three years of fifty per cent reduction.[84] If FIEs reinvest the profits they earn, the income tax they have paid on these reinvested profits may be refunded. Moreover, they are entitled to exemption from tariffs and value-added tax (VAT) for equipment imported for production or business operations and construction materials imported as a means of original or increased investment, and the vehicles and office equipment for use by the FIEs themselves.[85] Other general incentives include an automatic entitlement to import materials for production and to export products without the need to apply for licenses, autonomy in business operations and

[82] Art 5, the FIEs and FEs Income Tax Law.

[83] According to Art 72 of the FIEs and FEs Income Tax Law *Implementing Regulations*, 'Production FIEs' means FIEs engaged in the following industries:
(a) machine manufacturing and electronic industries;
(b) energy industries (excluding exploitation of oil and natural gas);
(c) metallurgical, chemical and building material industries;
(d) light industries and textiles and packaging industries;
(e) medical equipment and pharmaceutical industries;
(f) agricultural, forestry, animal husbandry, fishery and water conservation;
(g) construction industries;
(h) communication and transportation industries;
(i) development of science and technology, geological survey and industrial information consultancy directly for services in respect of production and services in respect of repair and maintenance of production equipment and precision instruments;
(j) Other industries as specified by the Tax Authorities under the State Council.

[84] Art 8, the FIEs and FEs Income Tax Law.

[85] For details, see the State Council Notice on the Adjustment of Tax Policy on Imported Equipment.

management, and the exemption from consolidated industrial and commercial tax for exports.[86]

Area-specific incentives

As said in the Introduction, China's opening-up structure is a multilevel model. In other words, while creating a generally favourable investment climate for FDI in the whole country, China also has introduced tremendous incentive measures to boost the development of certain special economic areas (SEAs). In China, those SEAs are many, including 6 SEZs,[87] 49 Economic and Technological Development Zones (EDTZs),[88] 15 Bonded Areas,[89] 14 Border Economic Co-operation Zones,[90] 15 Export Processing Zones,[91] 50 High-Tech Industries Development Zones, 12 National Tourist and Vacation Zones, 14 Coastal Open Cities (COCs) and a few Coastal Open Economic Regions.[92] FIEs established in these SEAs may enjoy reduction in income tax, turnover tax and, to a limited extent, customs duties. For example, the national enterprise income tax rate is thirty per cent, which is halved to fifteen per cent for FIEs established in the SEZs and ETDZs and is twenty four per cent in COCs.[93] In SEAs, foreign investors will also find more streamlined bureaucracy, better infrastructural services and other favourable treatment.[94] In an effort to tackle the problem of significant imbalance in terms of wealth and prosperity between the east and west of China, China recently launched a 'Great Western Development Strategy', which enables the FIEs established in the western provinces to enjoy the same as and, in some cases, even greater advantages than, those in the developed eastern provinces.[95]

[86] Arts 10–17, PEFI.

[87] Including Pudong New Area, which in fact enjoys the status of an SEZ.

[88] For an Introduction of the National-level ETDZs, see http://211.99.196.99:8080/fztdjj.asp (visited on 8 January 2002).

[89] Details available at: http://211.99.196.99:8080/kfqdh/kfqdh.asp?fc_types=102 (visited on 8 January 2002).

[90] Details available at: http://211.99.196.99:8080/kfqdh/kfqdh.asp?fc_types=103 (visited on 8 January 2002).

[91] Details available at: http://211.99.196.99:8080/kfqdh/kfqdh.asp?fc_types=104 (visited on 8 January 2002).

[92] Wang, Yongjun, *Investment in China: A question and answer guide on how to do business* (CITIC Publication House, 1997), at 27–43.

[93] For details of the incentives granted to FIEs established in those SEAs, see Wang, *ibid*, at 27–43.

[94] Clifford Chance, *Planning a Foreign Investment Enterprise in China (May 1997), at 6.*

[95] The Strategy was officially announced in January 2000. The policy to encourage investment in the western areas, however, was embarked on in 1996, when the Chinese government gave the central and western provincial authorities the power to approve foreign investment projects not exceeding US$30 million in value, as against the previous level of US$10 million. In late 1999, more preferential treatment was extended to FDI located in the inland regions. Foreign investment there, for example, may enjoy a 50% reduction of corporate income tax for another three years, after the existing preferential tax privilege expires. The 'great Western Development Strategy' launched in 2000 gave further incentives to FDI located in the central and western regions. For instance, priority will be given to applications for establishment in the west

Industry-specific incentives

In order to promote FDI in certain sectors or industries China deems of special importance to its economy, further Industry-Specific Incentives have been introduced. Thus technology and knowledge-intensive FIPs, energy, transportation and port construction FIPs, port and dock JVs, certain foreign banks and other financial FIPs are especially encouraged. Likewise, product-exporting and high-tech FIEs are also strongly encouraged.[96]

It must be noted that industry-specific incentives are indeed added on the top of the general and area-specific incentives. Therefore, according to the PEFI, product-exporting FIEs may continue to enjoy a fifty per cent reduction in income tax, provided that they export more than seventy per cent of their products, after the initial tax holiday granted to all FIEs.[97] Further, if they are established in a SEZ or an ETDZ where they are already taxed at 15 per cent, they can enjoy a further reduced tax rate of 10 per cent.[98] Again, while tax reduction is the main form of industry-specific incentives, other incentives may involve labour cost, land use fees, access to utilities such as water, electricity supply and transportation and communication facilities and short-term loans.[99]

5.3.1.3 Is the Existing Non-National Treatment Fair and Equitable?

It may be argued that the current non-national treatment is compatible with the F&E standard provided for in all EU-China BITs and the MIGA Convention, as it compensated for the special restrictions on FDI with special incentives.[100] Indeed, to judge whether the treatment a country has accorded foreign investment is fair and equitable, one must take into account not only the prevalent norms such as MFN and NT, but also the specific circumstances of that country, particularly the general economic system and the level of economic development. As discussed below, the implementation of NT is based on two economic conditions: a market economic regime and an adequately developed economy. Thus, in a highly developed market economy, as eg, in developed western countries, it would only be fair and equitable to provide MFN and NT to foreign investors. On the contrary, in a developing country such as China, which has not long practised a highly planned economy and has only begun to establish a market economy, it would be unfair if full NT

by foreign insurance companies or law firms. The limitations of foreign share in FIEs in infrastructure industries in the west will be more relaxed than in the east. See UNCTAD, *China: WTO Accession and Growing FDI Inflows*, 11 December 2002, at 14, posted at http://r0.unctad.org/en/subsites/dite/pdfs/PRChina.pdf (visited on 18 July 2003).

96 Art 73 (1), FIEs and FEs Income Tax Law *Implementing Regulations*.

97 Art 8, PEFI.

98 *Ibid.*

99 Arts 3–17, PEFI.

100 Same argument can be found in Zeng, Huaqun, above, note 11, at 442; Xu and Lin, above, note 17, at 38.

and ND obligations were imposed. However, as China progresses towards a market economy and economic power, it would be unfair if China did not implement NT and ND.

5.3.2 Implementing National Treatment for Foreign Investment in China

It is based on this understanding that China announced in 1992 its new policy to implement NT for FIEs, a standard of treatment it had resisted and denied for half a century.[101] The implementation of NT depends on two crucial economic conditions: a market economic system and a developed economy.

5.3.2.1 The Conditions

Market economy

The first reason for China's long resistance and denial of NT is that the centrally planned economy that the PRC had practised until the early 1990s intrinsically precluded the possibility of implementing NT, both in theory and in practice.[102] In theory, NT is based on the presumption that there is a unified national market where nationals and foreign investors can compete and cooperate.[103] However, a planned economy precludes such a market and the competition therein. Instead of the market, under a planned economy, the central plan allocates resources to economic entities. Accordingly, domestic economic entities, the 'nationals', are therefore merely passive recipients of national economic orders, rather than positive, independent companies seeking the maximisation of economic benefits. In other words, the nature and functions of 'nationals' under a planned economy are completely different from foreign investors which are run on a market economy basis.[104]

In practice, under the planned economy, there had been several forms of national invested enterprises ('nationals'), including state-run enterprises (SREs), collectively-owned enterprises, and some private enterprises, which were all treated differently. This raises the first difficult question of choosing a proper 'national' as the comparable 'national' to foreign investors.[105] Further, if the SREs, the dominant form of enterprise within the national

[101] For instance, in the China-US negotiation of a BIT, one of the stickiest points was the NT clause. See Steinert, Timothy A, 'If the BIT Fits: The Proposed Bilateral Investment Treaty between the United States and the People's Republic of China', (1988) 2 *Journal of Chinese Law*, at 434.

[102] Shan, Wenhua, 'National Treatment and the Transformation of FDI Laws and Policies in China' (hereinafter "NT and Transformation"), (2000) 6 *International Trade Laws and Regulations*, at 22–23.

[103] *Ibid.*

[104] *Ibid.*

[105] *Ibid.*

economy, were chosen as the comparable 'national', it would prove impractical to implement such 'national treatment'. For instance, on the one hand, in order to guarantee the implementation of the national plan, SREs undertook special obligations in terms of production, transaction and distribution. Obviously, these obligations could not be imposed on the foreign invested enterprises.[106] On the other hand, the Government gave SREs special support with respect to salaries, pricing, material supplies, financial loans and subsidiaries, as a return for their contributions to the national economy. Again, it would inappropriate to extend those forms of support to FIEs.[107] Therefore, there was no economic ground on which 'national treatment' could be implemented.

In the early 1990s, after a decade of market-oriented reform and opening-up to the outside, China had successfully transformed its economy from a purely planned one towards a 'socialist commodity economy with plans'. In 1993, 'Socialist Market Economy' was finally established as the goal of economic development for China, as included in the then revised Constitution.[108] Soon, the Chinese Government officially embarked on the plan to 'create facilities and conditions to implement the National Treatment for foreign-invested enterprises'.[109] This new move signalled a new era and a new approach in Chinese policy towards foreign investment. This policy moved from a FDI policy at the pre-mature stage featuring 'tax reductions', towards a FDI policy at relatively mature stage characterised by 'fair play'.[110]

Level of economic development

While a market economy is an important and necessary condition for implementing NT, alone it is not sufficient. The implementation of NT relies on the achievement of another important economic condition. The national economy in general must be sufficiently developed so that it is strong enough to compete fairly and freely with other countries.[111] In essence, NT means substantially eliminating both the protections for national industries and the restrictions on FDI. It therefore means that the national industries have to confront challenges from FDI without any protection.[112] Therefore, if the general economic power and the national industries of a country are adequately developed and sufficiently strong, the country can take full advantage of the FDI to supplement and enrich the internal market without the need to

[106] Kohona, Palitha TB, 'Investment Protection Agreements: An Australian Perspective', (1987) 21 *Journal of World Trade Law*, at 93.

[107] Shan, 'NT and Transformation', above, note 102, at 23.

[108] See Art 7, the 1993 Amendments to the Constitution of the People's Republic of China.

[109] See 'The Decision on Some Issues Related to the Establishment of the Socialist Market Economy by the Central Committee of the Chinese Communist Party', (1993) 7 Nov *People's Daily*, at 1.

[110] Shan, 'NT and Transformation', above, note 102, at 27.

[111] *Ibid*, at 26.

[112] *Ibid*.

worry about threats and injuries to the national economy. At the same time, national investors can make use of the NT arrangement to move freely in the world market, picking the best business opportunities and pursuing the greatest profits. This is actually why the major developed countries are keen on carrying out and promoting the NT standard around the world.[113] However, on the contrary, if a country has only weak national industries and little economic power, it is dangerous for it to afford aliens a proper NT.[114] Using Chinese phrases, it would be like 'introducing a wolf into one's home' (*Ying Lang Ru Shi*) or 'smashing a stone with an egg' (*Yi Ruan Ji Shi*). Such an insight is the very reason why the developing countries have refused to provide general NT for so long.[115]

From 1979 on, China implemented its market-oriented reform. In the national economy, the plan-controlled parts are getting smaller whilst the market-controlled parts are getting larger. In 1993, the principle of a 'Socialist Market Economy System' was finally set forth in the Constitution.[116] By then, the amount of the general economic power had accumulated considerably, and therefore the Chinese Government could announce its intention to grant NT to FIEs.[117] Nevertheless, it must be recognised that in China thus far a market economy has not been fully established, and the quality and efficiency of national industries and the national economy are still quite low.[118] In particular, there is still quite a long way to go to reform the State-Owned Enterprises (SOEs)[119] into real market entities and to establish the rule of law in China.[120] Therefore, one cannot expect an instant realisation of a proper NT, but can expect the Chinese Government to 'create facilities and conditions' to carry it out gradually but substantially.[121]

5.3.2.2 Progress and Prospects

Since 1993, China has passed a number of new laws and regulations and amended old ones, in accordance with the spirit of national treatment for FIEs. Several important changes should be mentioned here. Firstly, the 1993 Company Law now applies, in principle, equally to FIEs and non-FIEs, which

[113] *Ibid.*

[114] *Ibid.*

[115] For example, Dolzer and Stevens observed that developing countries tend to reject NT. Dolzer and Stevens, above, note 5, at 64.

[116] See above, note 108.

[117] Shan, 'NT and Transformation', above, note 102, at 27.

[118] *Ibid.*

[119] In the past, all state owned enterprises (SOEs) were run by the state and therefore called 'state run enterprise' (SREs). As a result of the market-oriented reform commencing in the economic reform in the early 1980s, SOEs are not necessarily directly run by government departments. Therefore, the name 'SREs' is no longer used.

[120] Shan, 'NT and Transformation', above, note 102, at 27.

[121] *Ibid.*

open up the possibility of the two categories of enterprises being treated equally in the future, even though the special rules contained in the special FIEs laws and regulations are still applicable.[122] Secondly, in late 1993, China decided to apply three revised tax laws equally to FIEs and non-FIEs.[123] These laws are the Provisional Regulations on Value Added Taxes, the Provisional Regulations on Consumption Taxes, and the Provisional Regulations on Business Taxes.[124] This decision marked the beginning of equal tax burdens on FIEs and non-FIEs. Thirdly, since 1994, 24 laws and regulations concerning safety in production have been applied to FIEs as well as non-FIEs.[125] Moreover, the 1994 Foreign Trade Law of the People's Republic of China provides the legal basis for China to grant national treatment in trade areas to foreign countries under certain circumstances. It explicitly provides that China grants MFN or NT in foreign trade under the international treaties or agreements that China has signed or acceded to, or on the basis of the principles of mutual benefit and reciprocity.[126] In addition, under Article 23 of the Foreign Trade Law, China will give market access and national treatment in the area of international trade in services in accordance with commitments China has made under international treaties or agreements to which it is a party.[127] Finally, since 2000, China has greatly modified its basic FDI laws and regulations and abolished the extensive PRs that are inconsistent with the NT obligations under the GATT 1994 and particularly the TRIMs Agreement, such as local content, export performance, forex balancing and technology transfer requirements[128]. Meanwhile, numerous laws and regulations have been promulgated to set up rules for the establishment of service FIEs.[129]

Implementing NT in China has not only brought about the reduction and elimination of restrictions, but also has decreased and phased out some incentives. However, so far, the progress in this direction has been slow. The only significant measure was adopted in early 1996, when China abolished the tax exemption for FIEs on the import of materials as means of capital contribution.[130] However, the tax exemption was reinstated in late 1997, as FDI influx dropped sharply in the two years,[131] partly due to this change in preferential tax policy and partly to the Asian financial crisis.

Nevertheless, the Chinese decision to implement NT to FIEs is a very

122 Art 18 of the *Company Law*. See also Section 1.5.2 for further discussions.

123 Cao, Jianming and He, Xiaoyun, 'WTO Accession and China's Foreign Economic Legislation', (2000) 1 *Chinese Legal Science* (*Zhongguo Faxue*), at 12–13.

124 *Ibid.*

125 *Ibid.*

126 Art 6, *Foreign Trade Law*.

127 Art 23, *Foreign Trade Law*.

128 See Section 1.4.2

129 See Section 4.3.3.7.

130 Phelan, Anne, '. . . But Tariff Exemptions Eliminated For FIEs', (1996) 18 *EAER*, at 4. See also 'Foreign Investment in China—I: Changing Trends and Policies', (1998) 20 *EAER*, at 8.

131 'Foreign Investment in China—I: Changing Trends and Policies', *ibid*, at 8.

significant move, the influence of which on China should not be underestimated.[132] On a most superficial level, such a decision means that, as has been seen, certain specific rules and regulations on FDI are to be adjusted—some restrictions may be removed and some certain preferential arrangements may be phased out or abandoned. On a more general level, this decision necessitates a material change of Chinese FDI policy, from the preliminary stage FDI policy that featured 'tax concession' towards the senior stage FDI policy that feature as 'fair play'. Thus, not only are the specific rules to be modified, but also the basic structure of Chinese FDI laws and policies are to be changed. The numerous FDI laws and regulations should be further tidied up and consolidated and a unified FDI code made, as argued in Section 1.5.1. Eventually, the dual system for FIEs and non-FIEs should be replaced by a single system of company laws and regulations.[133] However, the influence of this decision goes beyond FDI issues.[134] It has signalled a further reform of non-FIEs and national industries, especially the state-owned enterprises. Granting FDI the guarantee of NT, requires that these enterprises be restructured as real players at the market.[135] They will have to 'to find a solution through "the markets" instead of "the mayors"'.[136]

Needless to say, all these changes are far-reaching and therefore take time. Thus it would be impossible and unrealistic to expect China to implement a proper NT in the near future. However, in the long run, as China gets close to a real market economy and accumulates economic power, implementing NT for FIEs in China will be possible and desirable.

5.4 TRANSFER

One of the most important aspects of investment treatment is the transfer of funds out of the host country. It is important because it affects the feasibility, implementation and profitability of any investment project on the one hand, and the balance-of-payment (BOP) of the host country on the other.

Under customary international law, the host country has monetary sovereignty and can ban or restrict transfers as it deems appropriate.[137] Therefore domestic laws and regulations are the primary sources of law on this issue.

[132] Shan, 'NT and Transformation', above, note 102, at 27.

[133] See Section 1.5.2.

[134] Shan, 'NT and Transformation', above, note 102, at 27.

[135] *Ibid.*

[136] During the planned economy era, when in difficulties, the state-owned enterprise used to ask for help from the administrative authorities, normally 'the mayors' who were the best representatives. Now in the 'Socialist Market Economy', these enterprises have to solve their difficulties basically through 'the market'. Therefore there is a new saying that 'Looking for the mayors is less useful than looking for the markets.'

[137] Zeng, Huaqun, above, note 11, at 460. See also Dolzer and Stevens, above, note 5, at 85. On general issues in monetary law, see Mann, FA, *The Legal Aspects of Money*, 5th ed. (Clarendon Press, 1992).

Nevertheless, states may restrict such sovereignty by entering into international agreements. Thus capital transfer becomes one of the few most important issues addressed by BITs.[138] Unsurprisingly, in the negotiation of BITs, developed countries and developing countries have different interests on this point. As capital exporting countries, developed countries tend to seek broad and unlimited guarantees on the transfer of investment related assets, so that investors from their countries can promptly repatriate the profits earned from their investment. On the other hand, developing countries, which are normally in BOP difficulty and maintaining forex control, tend to maintain, to a certain extent, restrictions on such transfers. As a result, it quite often becomes one of the sticking points in BIT negotiations.

In the case of EU investment in China, the issue of transfer is mainly regulated by EU-China BITs, the TRIMs Agreement and Chinese law.[139] The TRIMs Agreement touches upon the issue of BOP, or forex balancing requirements, which has already been dealt with in Sections 4.3.3 and 4.2.2.1.

5.4.1 Transfer under EU-China BITs

In BITs, transfer provisions normally cover three aspects: types of transfer covered, restrictions and limitations, and convertibility and exchange rates.[140] This section discusses these aspects based on a comparison of transfer provisions in the existing EU-China BITs and other investment instruments.

5.4.1.1 Types of Payments Covered

As shown in *Table 13: Transfer under EU-China BITs and MRIIs*, all the 13 BITs have transfer provisions,[141] which cover payments of, eg, in the case of the Sino-Sweden BIT:

(i) The net profits, dividends, royalties, technical assistance and technical service fees, interest and other current income, accruing from any investment by an investor of the other Contracting Party ('returns' and 'license and other fees');

[138] Dolzer and Stevens, *ibid.*

[139] Although currency inconvertibility is one of the risks covered by the MIGA Conventions, it does not directly deal with the way host countries should regulate investment transfer. On the contrary, it may be said that it acknowledges host countries' rights to regulate this issue at will. For details about MIGA operations, see Sections 3.2.2.2 and 7.5.2.

[140] Dolzer and Stevens, above, note 5, at 86.

[141] Art 4, Sino-Sweden BIT; Arts 5 and 7 and Point 5 in the Protocol, Sino-Germany BIT; Art 5 and Point 3 of the Annex, Sino-France BIT; Arts 5 and 3 in the Protocol, Sino-BLEU BIT; Arts 6 and 7, Sino-Finland BIT; Arts 6 and 8, Sino-Italy BIT; Art 6, Sino-Demark BIT; Art 4, Sino-Netherlands BIT; Arts 5 and 7, and Point 4 in the Protocol, Sino-Austria BIT; Art 6, Sino-Britain BIT; Art 5, Sino-Portugal BIT; Art 6, Sino-Spain BIT; Art 6, Sino-Greece BIT.

(ii) The proceeds of the total or partial liquidation of any investment by an investor of the other Contracting Party ('proceeds of liquidation');
(iii) Funds in repayment of borrowings which both Contracting Parties have recognised as investment ('repayment of loans'); and
(iv) The earnings of nationals of the other Contracting States who are allowed to work in connection with an investment in its territory.[142]

Payments as compensation for expropriation are also covered in these BITs, though some of them express this in expropriation clauses rather than in transfer clauses. Other frequently included payments are capital or additional funds which include original investment and additional funds to maintain the operation of the invested project, contractual payments and management cost of the investment in the territory of the other Contracting Party (See *Table 13 for details*). The new Sino-Germany BIT expanded slightly from the current Sino-Germany BIT by adding 'payment relating to contracting projects' to the list of investment and returns subject to the transfer clause.[143]

This survey shows that coverage transfer provisions in EU-China BITs do not significantly deviate from general BIT practices.[144]

5.4.1.2 Currency Convertibility and Exchange Rate

As *Table 13* shows, most EU-China BITs require that transfers be made in convertible currencies at the official/prevailing rate of exchange and without delay. Some earlier BITs[145] do not touch upon the convertibility of currency, while some BITs add that the currency of the host country or the currency in which the investment was made is acceptable as well as (other) convertible currencies (as agreed by parties concerned). The Sino-Austria BIT requires the currency to be 'agreed upon by the parties concerned',[146] which probably will be the same currencies just mentioned. Only two of the BITs (Sino-Germany and Sino-Austria BITs) refer to the IMF in determining the exchange rate.[147] The new Sino-Germany BIT requires that transfers to be made in convertible currencies at the prevailing market exchange rate.[148] If such market rate does not exist, then reference shall be made to the IMF in determining

[142] Art 4, Sino-Sweden BIT.

[143] It covers primary or additional capital payment for the maintenance or expansion of the investment project; returns, proceeds of liquidation; repayment of loans; earnings of foreign nationals; and payment relating to contracting projects. See Art 6.1, the new Sino-Germany BIT.

[144] For a general picture of BIT provisions on transfer, see Dolzer and Stevens, above, note 5, at 90–94; UNCTC, Bilateral Investment Treaties, Graham and Trotman, 1988, at 59–61; Shihata, above, note 13, at 242–43.

[145] See eg, the Chinese BITS with Sweden, Germany, France, BLEU and Finland. For details please see *Table 13*.

[146] Art 7 (1), Sino-Austria BIT.

[147] Art 7, Sino-Germany BIT; Art 7 (2), Sino-Austria BIT.

[148] Art 6.3, the new Sino-Germany BIT.

Table 13: Transfer under EU-China BITs and MRIIs

Investment Instruments	(Free) transfer without delay of: i. returns, ii. repayment of loans, iii. Proceeds of liquidation, iv. license and other fees	Subject to domestic laws and regulations	Rate of exchange		In convertible currency
			official/ prevailing	IMF	
Sino-Sweden BIT (Art 4)	1+earnings of foreign employees	1	0	0	0
Sino-Germany BIT (Art 5 & 7, Prot.5)	1+ capital or additional funds	0 (China clause)[a]	1	1	0
Sino-France BIT (Art 5, Annex 3)	1+ compensation payments	0 (China clause)	0	0	0
Sino-BLEU BIT (Art 5, Prot. Art 3)	1+proceeds as compensation	0 (China clause)	0	0	0
Sino-Finland BIT (Art 6 & 7)	1+earnings of foreign employees	1	1	0	1
Sino-Italy BIT (Art 6 & 8)	1+additional funds, managements costs	1	0	0	1
Sino-Denmark BIT (Art 6)	1+ invested capital, earnings of foreign employees, payment of compensation	1	1	0	1 (or the currency of the original investment)
Sino-Netherlands BIT (Art 4)	1+ capital and additional funds, earnings of foreign employees, management fees	1	1	0	1 (or currency of the host country)
Sino-Austria BIT (Art 5 & 7 and Prot. 4)	1+ capital and additional funds, compensation	0 (China Clause)	1	1	1 (currencies agreed by parties concerned)
Sino-Britain BIT (Art 6 (1–4))	1	0 (China clause) (E)[b]	1	0	1 (currency of original investment or other agreed convertible currencies)
Sino-Portugal BIT (Art 5 (1–2))	1+ contractual payment, earnings of foreign employees, management fees	1	1	0	0

Sino-Spain BIT (Art 6 (1–6))	1+ contractual payments, earnings of foreign employees, management fees	1	1	0	1
Sino-Greece BIT (Art 6 (1–2))	1+ capital and additional funds	1	1	0	1
Total (13)	13	8	10	2	8
Energy Charter Treaty (Art 14)	1+ capital and additional funds, contractual payment, payments arising out of settlement of a dispute, payment of compensation	(E)	1 (market rate)		1
World Bank Guidelines (Art III. 6)	1+ earnings of foreign employees, contractual payment, payments of compensation and payments arising out of settlement of a disputes		1 (market rate)		1
NAFTA Chap. 11 (Art 1109)	1+ contractual payment, payments of compensation and payments arising out of settlement of a disputes	(E)	1 (market rate)		1
MAI Draft (Art IV. 4)	1+ capital and additional funds, contractual payment, payment arising out of settlement of a dispute, payment of compensation, earnings of foreign employees		1 (market rate)		1

[a] A special clause applicable to China, which requires that all transfers be made from the forex accounts of the FIEs and that China guarantees the provision of forex in certain cases as specifically prescribed where the FIE does not have sufficient forex in that account. See, eg, point 5 (Ad Art 5) of the Protocol of the Sino-Germany BIT.

[b] A contracting party may prevent the transfer through the non-discriminatory and in good faith application of its laws and regulations relating to certain exceptional cases as prescribed therein.

the exchange rate.[149] This new BIT reflects the changed foreign exchange regime in China since 1990, as can be seen below.

5.4.1.3 Restrictions and Limitations on Transfer

About half of these EU-China BITs, as can be seen from *Table 13*, have expressly made the right of investment-related transfers subject to the stipulations of domestic laws and regulations, which indicates that authorisation by or permission from the host country is required for such transfers.[150] The other half of the BITs contain a special clause applied to China (hereinafter the 'China Clause'). Such a 'China clause' is normally provided for in the Protocol or Annex to the formal text of the BITs, although it does appear in the text of Sino-Britain BIT. The 'China clause' reflects the Chinese forex regime in place when the BIT was signed. Thus it typically requires that all transfers be made from the 'forex account' of the FIE, and when the FIE does not have sufficient forex in its forex account for transfer, the Chinese Government undertakes to permit the conversion of local currency into convertible currencies for transfers in a number of specially listed cases. These cases cover the most likely forms of transfer,[151] such as, eg, in the Sino-Britain BIT,

(a) proceeds resulting from the total or partial liquidation of an investment;
(b) royalties derived from assets in Article 1 (1)(a)(iv);[152]
(c) payments made pursuant to a loan agreement in connection with any investment guaranteed by the Bank of China;
(d) profits, interests, capital gains, dividends, fees and any other form of return of national or company specifically permitted by the competent authority of the Peoples' Republic of China to carry out economic activities mainly in the territory of the People's Republic of China.

Thus, in essence, the 'China clause' still subjects transfers to the Chinese law of forex control, but has the merit of clarifying the applicable forex regime. However, on the other hand, such a clause may be misleading to foreign investors, as China has actually moved towards a more liberal regime, since the mid-1990s.[153]

In addition, a few BITs further require that transfer be made only after applicable tax and fees have been paid.[154] Finally, the Sino-Britain BIT expressly acknowledges that 'in exceptional balance of payment difficulty'

[149] *Ibid*.
[150] UNCTC, above, note 144, at 63.
[151] Denza and Brooks, above, note 46, at 920.
[152] They refer to 'copyrights, industrial property rights, know-how and goodwill'. Art 1 (1) (a) (iv), Sino-Britain BIT.
[153] See Section 5.4.2.
[154] Art 5, Sino-BLEU BIT; Art 6 (5), Sino-Spain BIT.

the host country may exercise equitably and, in good faith, powers conferred by its law. However, such powers should not be used to impede the transfer of profit, interests, dividends, royalties or fees. Moreover, with regard to investments and other forms of return, transfer of a minimum of twenty per cent per year should always be allowed.[155]

The new Sino-Germany BIT has signalled further liberalisation on the forex control, particular on the Chinese side. It has modified the 'China clause' existing the current Sino-German BIT, under which only two specific limitations are in place: One is that the transfer of proceeds of liquidation shall be subject to formalities required by current Chinese forex laws and regulations; the other is that the relevant loans must have been registered with the Chinese forex authority if they are to be transferred.[156] It also makes clear that such limitations would be abandoned if Chinese forex law so changes.[157] Furthermore, it has shortened the maximum period of allowed delay from six months as stipulated in the current Sino-Germany BIT to two months.[158]

It may thus be concluded that the EU-China BITs have adopted a measured liberal approach towards investment related transfers. On the one hand, they have adopted a broad interpretation of the transferable funds and interests. On the other hand, such transfers are subject to the laws and regulations of the host country (China). The new Sino-Germany BITs will have the effect to further relax the limitations imposed on transfer though the 'China clause' will still exist therein. It is therefore very important to take a close look at the Chinese law on transfers.

5.4.2 Transfer under Chinese Law

In China, the foreign exchange (forex) regime has undergone rapid changes since 1979,[159] and a rather liberal regime has existed since December 1996 when the RFEA were adopted. All the basic FIE laws and regulations have general guarantees on the rights of repatriation of investments and returns.[160] However, the operational rules in point are contained in the RFEA, together with the Regulations on Sale, Purchase of and Payment in Foreign Exchange.

Transfer of investment and returns, under Chinese law, may be divided into two interrelated aspects: the repatriation of foreign investments and returns and the convertibility of local currency into convertible currencies.

155 Art 6 (1), Sino-Britain BIT.
156 Point 5 (1) of the Protocol to the new Sino-Germany BIT.
157 *Ibid.*
158 Point 5 (2) of the Protocol to the new Sino-Germany BIT.
159 A brief outline of the history of China's forex regime reform can be found in the *Working Party Report*, at 5–6.
160 Details see below.

5.4.2.1 Repatriation of Foreign Investments and Returns

Chinese basic FIE laws and regulations normally guarantee that a foreign investor in an FIE can repatriate the net profits and the proceeds of the liquidation of the investment, in accordance with the RFEA.[161] Likewise, foreign employees of an FIE may remit their salary and other legitimate incomes out of China.[162] Since December 1996, China has formally accepted the obligations of Article VIII of the IMF Articles of Agreement, removing exchange restrictions on current account transactions.[163] Accordingly, the 1996 RFEA has freed all the payments and transfers of current transactions, which covers import and export transactions of the FIE, profits, dividends and interests of foreign investors and salaries and other legitimate income of foreign employees.[164] FIEs can purchase forex from designated forex banks or debit their forex accounts for any payment in current transaction, upon presentation of valid documents to the designated forex banks or the State Administration of Foreign Exchange (SAFE) for *bona fide* tests.[165]

Moreover, when an FIE is legally terminated, the foreign party may convert the RMB he/she may have, after due procedures of liquidation and taxation are cleared, into foreign currency and remit or carry it out of China.[166] FIEs may open forex accounts to hold foreign invested capital, and may sell from these accounts upon approval from the SAFE.[167] FIEs may also borrow forex directly from domestic and overseas banks, but are required to register with SAFE afterwards, and obtain approval by SAFE for debt repayment and services.[168]

Compared with the 'China clause' in the BITs, which requires all transfers to be made through FIEs' forex account, this has marked a great advancement as it is more favourable. In theory, this more favourable treatment can be enjoyed by all the 14 EU countries that have signed a BIT with China, even those with a 'China clause', as all the BITs have a MFN clause, and some of them accompanied by a 'preservation-of-rights' clause. Nevertheless, it would still be advisable to update the 'China clauses', so as to reflect the changed situation.

5.4.2.2 Currency Convertibility and Exchange Rate

RMB is fully convertible under current transactions. Thus FIEs can purchase forex from designated forex banks with the RMB they have, to pay the

[161] Art 11, EJVL; Art 19, WFEL.
[162] Art 12, EJVL, Art 19, WFEL.
[163] *Working Party Report*, at 6–7.
[164] Arts 21–25, Regulations on Sale and Purchase of and Payment in Foreign Exchange.
[165] *Working Party Report*, at 7.
[166] Art 26, Regulations on Foreign Exchange Administration (RFEA).
[167] *Working Party Report*, at 7.
[168] *Ibid.*

profits, dividends and interests of foreign investors and salaries and other legitimate incomes of foreign employees.[169] At the present, RMB is not yet convertible under capital transactions though official statements suggest that it will be in the future.[170] Nevertheless, the RFEA expressly prescribed that foreign investors may convert the RMB proceeds of liquidation of the investment into foreign currency and remit or carry them out of China. China unified the exchange rates in 1994 and adopted a single, managed floating exchange rate regime based on supply and demand. Since China has huge foreign reserves,[171] foreign currency is relatively freely available and the exchange rate is stable.[172]

An important issue related to investment transfer is the balance of foreign exchange requirements, which used to be a common condition on the establishment of FIEs[173] and which has indeed caused much difficulty in the operations of many FIEs. Since October 2000, as stated in Section 4.3.3.3, most FIE laws and regulations have been modified and the balance of forex requirements have been removed. For FIEs that generate little or no foreign currency, this is obviously a great relief.

5.5 CONCLUSION

The most important treaties dealing with the standards of treatment of EU investment in China are the BITs between EU member states and China, and to some extent, the MIGA Convention and WTO Agreement, particularly the TRIMs Agreement and the GATS. Under these international agreements, EU investments in China are entitled to fair and equitable treatment as well as MFN treatment. The MFN treatment standard notably has a 'multiplying effect', which is subject to certain restrictions and numerous exceptions. According to those international agreements, NT and ND are granted but are substantially qualified, so much so that one cannot say that they have been established as 'principles' of standards of treatment. The new Sino-Germany BIT has had the effect of preventing the adoption of any new measures incompatible with the NT and ND standards. Yet its ratification is still pending. In addition, some of the EU-China BITs expressly confer EU investors the rights to enjoy the more favourable treatment accorded in line with domestic laws or other international agreements.

169 Art 21–25, *Regulation on Sale and Purchase of and Payment in Foreign Exchange*.

170 Zhang, Weimin, 'Maintaining the Balance of International Payment, Proceeding to Full Convertibility of RMB', (2001) 15 Nov *People's Daily* (overseas edition), at 4.

171 By the end of June 2004, China has accumulated $470.6 billion foreign reserve. Official statistics of China's foreign reserve is now available at People's Bank of China website: http://www.pbc.gov.cn/baogaoyutongjishuju/2004S6.htm

172 Clifford Chance, above, note 94, at 10.

173 According to the author's Questionnaire, 27% of EU investors had been imposed with such requirement. See *Chart 10*.

The treatment accorded to EU investment under international agreements has been reflected in related Chinese law. Under Chinese law, MFN is generally guaranteed. At the moment, corresponding to the substantially qualified undertakings on NT and ND, the treatment towards foreign and EU investment under Chinese law features a combination of special restrictions and special incentives, which in essence may be called 'special treatment' or 'non-national treatment'. Thus there is 'inferior-national treatment' represented by restrictions on aspects such as areas of investment, approval process, extensive PRs, along with 'superior-national treatment' in the form of general or area-specific or industry-specific incentives. It can be argued that such a non-national treatment under Chinese law is fair and equitable, as China does not yet have the conditions to implement a proper NT and ND and the 'superior-national treatment' may have the effect of compensating the 'inferior-national treatment'.

The implementation of proper NT depends on two economic conditions: a market economy and a highly developed national economy. Before 1993, it had been impossible for China to effectively implement NT as it had not accepted a market economy. In 1993, China announced that it would 'create conditions, gradually implementing NT for FIEs', as it had formally established the constitutional status of a market economy and had accumulated considerable economic power. As a result, concrete measures have been taken since then to eliminate the restrictive PRs on the one hand and reduce overly extensive incentives on the other. However, China will still have a long way to go to implement a proper NT for FIEs, which possesses profound and far-reaching influence, not only on the FDI regime, but also on the non-FIE reform and the development of the national economy as a whole.

As a special issue of treatment, transfer of funds by EU investors in China is governed by EU-China BITs and Chinese law. The EU-China BITs have adopted a measured liberal approach towards investment-related transfers. They adopt a broad interpretation of transferable funds and interests on the one hand and subject such transfers to the laws and regulations of the host country (China) and other restrictions on the other. Within China, the law of forex control has undergone a rapid change, which has resulted in a rather liberal regime. Now no restrictions exist on current transactions, which include all the daily payments and transfers of FIEs and the repatriation of salaries of their foreign employees. Although capital transactions are still subject to forex control, the law nevertheless provides that proceeds of liquidation can be remitted or carried out of China.

Overall, it can be concluded that the treatment that EU investors in China are receiving is characterised by a combination of special restrictions and special incentives. Such a special treatment or non-national treatment system cannot create a level playing field for foreign and EU investment in China and therefore needs to be further reformed. The recent government initiative to implement national treatment for foreign investment is a desirable move, but its accomplishment will take a long time.

6

Expropriation and Compensation

6.1 EXPROPRIATION AND COMPENSATION UNDER INTERNATIONAL LAW

The issue of expropriation and its compensation is of the gravest concern to both investors and the host country. It by and large decides for the investors the extent of the risks involved in an investment project. For the host country it creates limitations on the exercise of sovereign rights. As a result, it has been one of the most controversial issues in modern international law[1] and a wealth of literature on the subject has been created by international lawyers.[2]

[1] Oscar Schachter wrote that 'apart from the use of force, no question of international law seemed to have aroused as much debate—and often strong feelings—as the question of the standard for payment of compensation when foreign property is expropriated'. See Schachter, Oscar, 'Compensation for Expropriation, Editorial Comment', (1984) 78 *American Journal of International Law* 121.

[2] The most important publications on this topic include *Oppenheim's International Law*, 8th edition (Lauterpacht, H, ed. Longmans, 1955), at 350–57, 9th edition (Jennings and Watts eds, Longman, 1992), at 910–27; Higgins, Rosalyn, 'The Taking of Property by the State: Recent Developments in International Law', (1982) 176 *Recueil des Cours* 263; Aréchaga, Eduardo Jiménez de, 'State Responsibility for the Nationalisation of Foreign Owned Property', (1978) 11 *NYU Journal of International Law and Politics* 179; Schachter, Compensation for Expropriation, id; Robinson, Davis R, 'Expropriation in the Restatement (Revised)', (1984) 78 *American Journal of International Law* 176; Mann, FA, 'British Treaties for the Promotion and Protection of Investments', (1981) 52 *British Yearbook of International Law* 241; Dolzer, Rudolf, 'New Foundations of the Law of Expropriation of Alien Property', (1981) 75 *American Journal of International Law* 553; Friedman, S, *Expropriation in International Law* (London, Stevens, 1953); Francioni, Francesco, 'Compensation for Nationalisation of Foreign Property: The Borderland between Law and Equity', (1975) 24 *International and Comparative Law Quarterly* 255; Sornarajah, M, 'State Responsibility and Bilateral Investment Treaties', (1986) 20 *Journal of World Trade Law* 79; Brower, Charles N, 'Current Developments in the Law of Expropriation and Compensation: a Preliminary Survey of Awards of the Iran-United States Claims Tribunal', (1987) 21 *International Lawyer* 639. For a four-volume collection of articles on this issue, see Lillich, Richard B, *The Valuation of Nationalised Property in International Law* (University Press of Virginia, 1972). More recent publications in English are Lauterpacht, Sir Elihu, 'International Law and Private Foreign Investment', (1996) 4 *Global Legal Studies Journal* 257; Westberg, John A, 'Compensation in Cases of Expropriation and Nationalisation: Awards of the Iran-United States Claims Tribunal', (1990) 5 *ICSID Review-Foreign Investment Law Journal* 256; Amerasinghe, CF, 'Issues of Compensation for the Taking of Alien Property in the Light of Recent Cases and Practice', (1992) 41 *International and Comparative Law Quarterly* 22; Shihata, Ibrahim, *Legal Treatment of Foreign Investment: The World Bank Guidelines*

The term 'expropriation' in general means the deprivation of a former owner of his property.[3] Other frequently used terms include 'nationalisation', 'confiscation', and 'taking'. Whilst the term 'taking' may be regarded as equivalent to 'expropriation',[4] 'nationalisation' and 'confiscation' seem to bear narrower meanings.[5]

From a historical point of view the controversies over expropriation and compensation date back before World War I, when capital exporting countries claimed the right to use military force to protect their foreign investment.[6] There was clearly not much of a role for international law to play at that time, but international law did become more and more important after World War I, when a few expropriation cases were brought before and adjudicated by international courts and tribunals.[7] The rule extracted and developed from these earlier international cases was later called the 'traditional' rule of international law, which was subsequently challenged by socialist and Third World countries. The following paragraphs are intended to give a brief history with a view to identifying the general international law on expropriation and compensation.

(Martinus Nijhoff 1993); Dolzer, Rudolf and Stevens, Margaret, *Bilateral Investment Treaties* (Martinus Nijhoff, 1995); Gagné, Gilbert, 'The Investment-State Provisions in the Aborted MAI and in NAFTA', (2002) 2 *JWI* 481; Starner, Gregory M, 'Taking a Constitutional Look: NAFTA Chapter 11 as an Extension of Member States' Constitutional Protection of Property', (2002) *Law and Policy in International Business*; Gudofsky, Jason L, 'Shedding Light on Art 1110 of the North American Free Trade Agreement (NAFTA) Concerning Expropriations: An Environmental Case Study', (2000) 21 *Northwestern Journal of International Law and Business* 243; Beauvais, Joel C, 'Regulatory Expropriations Under NAFTA: Emerging Principles & Lingering Doubts', (2002) 10 *New York University Environmental Law Journal* 245; Waren, William T, 'Paying to Regulate: A Guide to Methanex v United States and NAFTA Investor Rights', (2001) 31 *Environmental Law Reporter* 10986.

[3] *Oppenheim's International Law*, 9th Edition, above, note 2, at 916 note 9.

[4] *Ibid.*

[5] However, the precise definitions of these terms remain unclear. For example, Jennings and Watts consider 'nationalisation' as a transfer of property from private ownership to some form of state or public ownership, while Francioni goes further to distinguish it from individual expropriation by its 'political connotation' and 'the magnitude of the interests affected', as it is often carried out in the context of a broad-scale economic and social reform. By 'confiscation', Jennings and Watts think it means expropriation without compensation, whilst Sornarajah argues that it refers to taking of property by the ruler or the ruling coterie of the state for personal gain. Jennings and Watts ed., *Oppenheim's International Law*, above, note 2, at 916 note 9; Francioni, above, note 2, at 258; Sornarajah, M, *The International Law on Foreign Investment* (Cambridge University Press 1994), at 278.

[6] Vandevelde T, 'Sustainable Liberalism and the International Investment Regime' (herein after 'Sustainable Liberalism'), (1998) 19 *Michigan Journal of International Law* 373, at 378–79.

[7] Those cases include *Chorzów Factory case* (Germany v. Poland), 1928, PCIJ Series A, No. 13, at 63–64; *Case Concerning Certain Germany Interests in Polish Upper Silesia* (Germany v Poland), 1929, PCIJ Series A, No. 7, at 81–82; *Lena Goldfield*, 1930, (unpublished opinion), discussed in 36 *Cornell Law Quarterly* 1950, at 42; *Shufeldt Claim* (USA v Guatemala), 2 Rep. Int'l Arb. Awards, 1930, at 1080; *Norwegian Shipowners Claims* (Nor. v USA), 1 Rep. Int'l Arb. Awards, 1922, at 308. See Vandevelde, Sustainable Liberalism, above, note 6, at 379, note 44.

6.1.1 The 'Traditional' Rule

The most cited case reflecting the 'traditional' doctrine is probably the *Chorzów Factory case* decided by the PCIJ in 1928.[8] In its Judgement the Court distinguished lawful expropriations from unlawful dispossessions, as in the present case, which the Court found was contrary to the Geneva Convention.[9] The Court held that for a lawful expropriation the payment of 'fair compensation' or 'just price' would be sufficient, to be measured by 'the value of the undertaking at the moment of dispossession, plus interest to the day of payment'.[10] For an unlawful taking, however, restitution in kind or, if impossible, payment of compensation in place of it plus if necessary the damages for loss sustained should be the principles used to determine the amount of compensation.[11]

This judicial pronouncement was later synthesised by the US Secretary of State Cordell Hull[12] into the formula of 'adequate' or 'just' compensation ('Hull Formula', or 'Hull Rule') as an essential prerequisite of expropriation required by customary international law. The formula also requires that compensation be 'effective' and 'prompt', which essentially means that the payment should be made at the time of the taking or shortly thereafter in a convertible and freely transferable currency.[13] Since then this formula has been defended by many developed states as the 'traditional' rule of international law.[14]

[8] PCIJ Reports, Series A, No. 17 (Indemnity) (Merits) (1928).

[9] PCIJ Reports, Series A, No. 17, at 46–48.

[10] *Ibid.*

[11] *Ibid.*

[12] This first appeared in Hull's note to the Mexican Government in 1938 on the expropriation of assets of US nationals by the Mexican government. This note, together with the reply from the Mexican Government, can be found at Hackworth, Green H, US Department of State, Pub. No. 1708, 3 *Digest of International Law* 655–61 (1942).

[13] Aréchaga, above, note 2, at 180–81.

[14] For examples of insistence on this formula by developed countries, see the *Restatement of the Foreign Relations Law of the United States* (3rd revision) prescribes that, 'A state is responsible under international law for injury resulting from:

(1) a taking by the state of the property of a national of another state that
 (a) is not for a public purpose, or
 (b) is discriminatory, or
 (c) is not accompanied by provision for just compensation.'

Most recently, in the MAI drafted by OECD countries, expropriation issue was dealt with in a similar manner. See Section 712, The American Law Institute, *Restatement of the Foreign Relations Law of the United States*, 3rd revision, (hereinafter 'Restatement') Vol. 2, 1986; Art IV 2.1, OECD MAI Negotiating Text (as of 24 April 1998). Moreover, most Western publicists support this viewpoint. See eg, *Oppenheim's International Law*, 9th edition, above, note 2, at 919–21; Brownlie, Ian, *Principles of Public International Law* (4th edition, Oxford University Press, 1998), at 535. However, there are also some eminent western lawyers who believe that such a 'traditional' rule has never existed. For example, Friedmann wrote that, as quoted by the Second Circuit Court of Appeals in the *Banco Nacional case* and by Schachter, '[I]t is nothing short of absurd to pretend that the protestation of the rule of full, prompt and adequate compensation...in all circumstances is representative of contemporary international law.' See Friedmann, Wolfgang, 'National Courts and the International Legal Order', (1966) 34

The theoretical basis of such a 'traditional' view is the sanctity of property rights and respects for 'acquired rights' or 'vested rights',[15] a notion of property law deeply rooted in Western legal systems.[16] The application of the 'acquired rights' theory in expropriation and compensation may result in two conclusions: the extreme one being that the host state cannot expropriate foreign property at all (as applied in the *Chorzáw Factory* case and the Hull Note to the Mexican Government); the mild one being that the host state 'merely indemnifies the titleholder from complete and arbitrary destruction of their interest', as observed by Professor O'Connell.[17] Another often-mentioned principle is 'unjust enrichment', which requires host States to return in compensation all the benefits they have gained from the expropriation of foreign properties.[18]

6.1.2 Challenges to the 'Traditional' Rule

The 'traditional' or 'old' rule has received strong challenges, particularly from the former USSR Socialist bloc and the Latin American countries. The first major blow to the rule was posed by the socialist states which completely rejected the concept of private property.[19] The newly established Soviet Government of the USSR announced in 1917 that an alien who acquired property in another state did so subject to the national laws of the host state only, and thus international law imposed no obligation of compensation for expropriation of foreign investment by the host state.[20] This practice was followed by all other socialist countries, including Central and Eastern European countries and China.[21]

A second challenge to the 'traditional' rule was made by Latin American countries where the Calvo Doctrine prevailed.[22] Carlos Calvo, an Argentine diplomat and jurist, argued that foreign nationals should not be entitled to treatment in the host country more favourable than that accorded to its own nationals, and that all disputes arising therefrom should be subject to

George Washington Law Review 443 at 454. See also Schachter, above, note 1, at 124; *Banco Nacional de Cuba v. Chase Manhattan Bank*, 658 F. 2d 875 (2nd cir. 1981), at 892.

15 Francioni, above, note 2, at 258–59.

16 In the well-known *U.S. v. Perchman case*, for instance, Chief Justice Marshall stated, 'that the sense of justice and of right which is acknowledged and felt by the whole civilised world would be outraged, if private property should be generally confiscated and private rights annulled. The people change their allegiance; their relations to their ancient sovereign is dissolved; but their relation to each other, and their rights of property remain undisturbed.' *U.S. v. Perchman case*, 7 Peter's US Supreme Court Reports, 86, as cited in Francioni, above, note 2, at 259.

17 Francioni, above, note 2, at 261.

18 Aréchaga, above, note 2, at 181; Francioni, above, note 2, at 272, Dolzer, above, note 2, at 75.

19 Restatement, above, note 14, at 203.

20 Vandevelde, 'Sustainable Liberalism', above, note 6, at 380–81.

21 *Ibid*, at 383.

22 Restatement, above, note 14, at 203; Vandevelde, 'Sustainable Liberalism', above, note 6, at 379–80.

domestic law and the domestic jurisdiction of the host country. Diplomatic protection should be prohibited altogether.[23] This formed the core of the 'Calvo Doctrine'.[24] Under this theory special protection of foreign investment by the 'so-called' 'traditional' rule of international law was inconsistent with the prerogative of the host country to subordinate economic activities to the national interest, and therefore must be rejected.[25] In other words, if a state expropriated properties of both its own and foreign nationals and had not compensated its nationals, no compensation should be paid to the foreign nationals.

The Calvo Doctrine quickly received support throughout Latin America.[26] Some countries included it in their constitutions.[27] A best example of its application was probably the replying Note from the Mexican Government to the letter establishing the 'Hull Formula', which contended that Mexico was obliged to compensate foreign investors only to the extent required by its own law, because giving preference to foreigners would violate the principle of sovereign equality.[28]

6.1.3 Efforts to Create a New Rule

The efforts to challenge the 'traditional' rule of international law on expropriation were joined by another force—the newly independent states in Africa and Asia decolonised after World War II. These new states as Shaw points out were 'fiercely nationalistic' and resistant to being bound by an international legal regime that had been created without their participation.[29] Like the socialist and Latin American states they favoured extensive state regulation of economic activities and the redistribution of wealth from developed to developing states.[30] These three forces converged after World War II and formed a united front in the 1960s[31] in the UN, where they constituted the vast majority.[32]

23 Shea, Donald R, *The Calvo Clause: A Problem of Intern-American and International law and Diplomacy*, at 17–20 (Minneapolis, University of Minnesota Press, 1955).

24 *Ibid.*

25 Vandevelde, 'Sustainable Liberalism', above, note 6, at 380.

26 Shea, above, note 23, at 21.

27 *Ibid.*

28 Hackworth, above, note 12, at 658–59; Vandevelde, 'Sustainable Liberalism', above, note 6, at 380.

29 Anand, RP, 'Attitude of the Afro-Asian States towards Certain Problems of International Law', 15 (1966) *International and Comparative Law Quarterly* 55.

30 *Ibid.*

31 The establishment of such a united front was probably marked by the establishment of the United Nations Conference on Trade and Development (UNCTAD) and the Group 77 (G-77) in 1964, as they have both greatly facilitated the communication among the Third World and the socialist countries. This fact might help to explain the substantial difference between Res 1803 and Res 3281. See Chen, An, *International Economic Law* (Law Press, 1999), at 17.

32 Sir Elihu Lauterpacht observed an increase of UN membership from 82 in 1958 to 124 in 1970, most of the new members being newly independent countries from former colonies. Lauterpacht, Sir Elihu, above, note 2, at 264. See also, Restatement, above, note14, at 203. See

This majority pushed the UN to adopt a series of Resolutions to deal with international economic relations with a view to establishing the principle of permanent sovereignty over natural resources (PSNR), and then an NIEO.

The principle of PSNR was established in Res 1803[33] of 1962, whilst the principle of NIEO was pronounced in Res 3201[34] and Res 3281[35] of 1974. Res 1803[36] and Res 3281[37] deal with the issues of expropriation and compensation, although in a notably different way. The 'public purposes' requirement in Res 1803 was omitted in Res 3281,[38] and Res 3281 states that

also, Vandevelde, 'Sustainable Liberalism', above, note 6, at 384. Indeed, in 1945, the UN has only 51 member states. This number had increased dramatically to 138 by 1974. Most of the new member states were, understandably, newly independent states. For details of growth in UN member states since 1945, see United Nations, *Growth in United Nations Membership (1945-2003*), posted at http://www.un.org/overview/growth.htm (visited on 12 June 2003).

[33] *Declaration on Permanent Sovereignty over Natural Resources*, UNGA Res 1803 (XVII), UN Doc. A/RES/1803 (XVII), 19 December 1962, reprinted in ILM (1962, Vol. 2). This Resolution was adopted by 87 votes to 2 with 10 abstentions. France and South Africa voted against it; the Soviet bloc, Burma, Cuba and Ghana abstained. Harris, David, *Cases and Materials on International Law* (Sweet and Maxwell, 1998), at 549.

[34] *Declaration on the Establishment of a New International Economic Order*, GA Res 3201(S-VI), UN Doc A/RES/3201(S-VI) (1974), adopted without a vote. It is reprinted in 13 ILM 715 (1974).

[35] *Charter of Economic Rights and Duties of States,* UNGA Res 3281 (XXIX), UN Doc A/RES/3281(XXIX) (1975) [hereinafter Res 3281], reprinted in 14 ILM 251 (1975). It was adopted by 120 to 6, with 10 abstentions. The six states that voted in opposition were Belgium, Denmark, Federal Republic of Germany, Luxembourg, the United Kingdom and the United States. The ten states that abstained were Austria, Canada, France, Ireland, Israel, Italy, Japan, the Netherlands, Norway and Spain. See 14 ILM 265 (1975).

[36] The relevant paragraphs in Res 1803 reads, '4. Nationalisation, expropriation or requisitioning shall be based on grounds or reasons of public utility, security or national interest which are recognised as overriding purely individual or private interests, both domestic and foreign. In such cases the owner shall be paid appropriate compensation in accordance with the rules in force in the state taking such measures in the exercise of its sovereignty and in accordance with international law. In any case where the question of compensation gives rise to a controversy, the national jurisdiction of the state taking such measures shall be exhausted. However, upon agreement by sovereign states and other parties concerned, settlement of the dispute should be made through arbitration or international adjudication;...' See Paragraph 4 of the *Declaration on Permanent Sovereignty over Natural Resources*, UNGA Res 1803 (XVII), UN Doc A/RES/1803 (XVII), 19 December 1962, reprinted in ILM (1962, Vol. 2).

[37] Art 2 (2) (c) states that every state has the right, 'to nationalize, expropriate or transfer ownership of foreign property, in which case appropriate compensation should be paid by the State adopting such measures, taking into account its relevant laws and regulations and all circumstances that the State considers pertinent. In any case where the question of compensation gives rise to a controversy, it shall be settled under the domestic law of the nationalising State and by its tribunals, unless it is freely and mutually agreed by all States concerned that other peaceful means be sought on the basis of the sovereign equality of States and in accordance with the principle of free choice of means.' This Art was adopted by a separate vote of 104 to 16 with 6 abstentions. The sixteen negative votes were cast by Austria, Belgium, Canada, Denmark, Federal Republic of Germany, France, Ireland, Italy, Luxembourg, Japan, the Netherlands, Norway, Spain, Sweden, the United Kingdom and the United States. The six abstentions were by Australia, Barbados, Finland, Israel, New Zealand and Portugal. See 14 ILM 264 (1975).

[38] See Brower, Charles N, and Tepe, John B, Jr, 'The Charter of Economic Rights and Duties of States: A Reflection or Rejection of International Law?', (1975) 9 *International Lawyer* 295; Weston, Burns H, 'The Charter of Economic Rights and Duties of States and the Deprivation of Foreign Owned Wealth', (1981) 75 *American Journal of International Law* 437.

the relevant standard for compensation should, in principle, be decided by national tribunals based on the national law of the host State, and therefore eliminates explicit reference to international tribunals and international law in Res 1803.[39]

The legal value of Res 1803 and Res 3281 is subject to intense debate. Some scholars argue that Res 1803 reflects customary international law but Res 3281 does not because of the abandonment of the original intent to codify rules of international law thereon in the drafting of the latter, the votes against it by economically powerful states, and the recommendatory nature of UNGA Resolutions on the whole.[40] Others believe that Res 3281 has established new rules of customary international law on the ground that it had overwhelming support in the vote, that it was intended to be a binding legal document, that its title bore strong legal implications, and that it was the result of long consistent efforts to establish an NIEO.[41]

The author is of the view that the two resolutions should be read together and be regarded as evidence of an emerging rule of international law because they are *equivalent in form* and *essentially consistent in substance*. In form despite the slight difference in title[42] both were adopted by UNGA resolutions, which can be important evidence of international law although they are not directly binding.[43] A closer look at the votes of the two resolutions shows no significant difference between them. In both cases they were adopted by overwhelming majority votes (87 to 2 in Res 1803 and 120 to 6 in Res 3281), with only a few but important votes against (France and South Africa in Res 1803 and US, UK, Belgium, Denmark, Western Germany and Luxemburg in Res 1803); and a considerable number of abstentions (the entire Soviet bloc on Res 1803 and 10 industrialised countries on Res 3281). It is imprecise to say then that Res 1803 reflects the wills of 'all geographical areas' and 'all economic systems' whilst Res 3281 does not.[44] Res 3281 succeeded in substance to the *spirit* and *essence* of Res 1803, in that it reiterates the principle of PSNR,[45] the sovereign rights to expropriate, and the standard of 'appropriate compensation'.[46]

Res 3281 does admittedly differ from Res 1803 in that it does not directly refer to 'international law'. However this major difference is better under-

[39] Brower and Tepe considered this an 'utter rejection of international law'. However, Aréchaga believed that the UN Economic Charter did not rule out the applicability of international law and international remedy. Brower and Tepe, *ibid*, at 305; Aréchaga, above, note 2, at 186–88.

[40] See eg, Brower and Tepe, *ibid*, at 300–02.

[41] Dolzer, above, note 2, at 563–64; Weston, above, note 38, at 451–53.

[42] Indeed, it can be argued that the title used by Res 3281 ('Charter') suggest even stronger legal intent than that by Res 1803 ('Declaration').

[43] Section 3.1.4.1 in Chapter 3.

[44] *Texaco Overseas Petroleum Co./California Asiatic Oil Co.* v. *Libya* (*the "Topco case"*), 17 ILM 1 (1978), Award on the Merit, paras 84.

[45] Art 2 (1), Res 3281.

[46] Art 2 (2) (c), Res 3281.

stood as a further development in the same direction rather than as a significant change of direction. The omission of explicit reference to international law should not be considered as 'the utter rejection of international law'[47] but as a rejection of the 'old' or 'traditional' international law. The exclusion of the phrase 'in accordance with international law' in Res 3281, as Judge Aréchaga observes, merely expels 'its alleged identification with the doctrine of "prompt, adequate and effective compensation"'.[48] It does not root out the applicability of international law altogether.[49] If the host state had failed to provide 'appropriate compensation' the home state of the expropriated investor would be authorised under existing international law to make a claim on its behalf.[50] Indeed, such an international remedy is expressly recognised in the second sentence of Article 2 (2) (c), which states that, upon free and mutual agreement,[51] 'other peaceful means' of dispute settlement (than domestic remedies of the host state) may be resorted to. International law

> 'has come back through the window in the garb of an equitable principle which take into account the specific circumstances of each case and is more likely to be of assistance in the settlement of investment disputes through negotiation or, if the parties so agree, through adjudication'.[52]

Res 3281 has thus utterly rejected not international law as a whole but the 'traditional' rule on expropriation and compensation.[53] Its omission of explicit reference to international law does not preclude the application of international law. Rather, it serves to further clarify the 'appropriate compensation' standard pronounced in Res 1803 so that it could no longer be interpreted as *necessarily* equivalent to the 'Hull formula'.[54] Res 3281

[47] Brower and Tepe, above, note 38, at 305.

[48] It is noteworthy that some developed countries have interpreted the 'appropriate compensation' in Res 1803 as identical to 'adequate, effective and prompt' compensation they favour. For example, the US representative has declared that in its view the two standards are the same. See UN Doc. A/C.2/S.R. 850 at 327 (1962); Restatement, above, note 14, at 206. However, as Judge Aréchaga has noted, in drafting Res 3281, 'the vast majority of states categorically rejected the proposal to refer to 'prompt, adequate and effective compensation.' Indeed, a proposal to refer to 'just compensation' was also rejected by 87 to 19 with 11 abstentions. See Aréchaga, above, note 2, at 184; Harris, above, note 33, at 550, note 58.

[49] Aréchaga, above, note 2, at 186–88.

[50] *Ibid.*

[51] Aréchaga further considered this sentence is in conformity with the principle of 'free choice of means' established in the 1970 Declaration of Principles of International Law concerning Friendly Relations and Cooperation among State. Aréchaga, above, note 2, at 187.

[52] Aréchaga, above, note 2, at 188–89

[53] Aréchaga, above, note 2, at 186–89.

[54] Appropriate compensation takes into account 'all circumstances' and therefore cannot always be equivalent to 'full' compensation. However, it can be 'full' compensation if circumstances so justify. In the *Banco Nacional case,* the court adopted the standard 'appropriate compensation' but added that, '[B]ut the adoption of an appropriate compensation does not preclude the possibility that in some cases full compensation is appropriate.' See *Banco Nacional case,* above, note 14, at 892.

should be considered as a step further from Res 1803 also because it clarifies the relationship between domestic law and international law as the applicable laws to expropriation cases. A further discussion on this subject follows in Chapter 7, Section 7.1.

With regard to the legal implications of these resolutions, although it has been debated whether they have firmly *established or created* a new rule of customary international law, it is evident that they have effectively *destroyed or dismantled* the customary international law status of the 'Hull formula'.[55] The evidence of such derogatory effects of the resolutions is prevalent and clear. Firstly it has been supported by state compensation practice. The hundreds of lump sum agreements concluded after the Second World War almost invariably adopted 'partial compensation'.[56] In 1979, for example, China reached a lump sum agreement with the US in which China agreed to pay the US$80,500,000, forty one per cent of the US assets nationalised by the Chinese government.[57] Although there has been a debate on whether these agreements are able to contribute to general international law[58] it is evident that they do not support the 'Hull formula' and can be best explained by the principle of 'appropriate compensation'.[59]

Secondly, in some national codes on foreign investment, 'appropriate compensation' has also been accepted.[60] A few Chinese FDI laws and regulations provide that in case of expropriation of FIEs appropriate compensation shall be made.[61]

Thirdly, the 'appropriate compensation' standard has been supported in a few important international arbitration awards and domestic judicial decisions. Thus in both *Topco-Libyan* and *Aminoil* cases 'appropriate compensation' was referred to as the '*opinio juris communis*',[62] which that 'codifies positive principles'.[63] 'Appropriate compensation' has also found

[55] A few scholars have distinguished the derogatory effect on existing rules and the establishment of new rules. See Dolzer, above, note 2, at 563–64; Amerasinghe, above, note 2, at 25. See also Aréchaga, above, note 2, at 186–87.

[56] Lillich, R, *International Claims: Their Settlement by Lump-Sum Agreements* (1975), at 35. See also YU, Jinsong, *The Grounds for Compensation in Case of Expropriation under International Investment Law* (Social Sciences in China, No. 2, 1986), at 61; Wang, Xuan, 'The Permanent Sovereignty over Natural Resources of States', (1982) *Chinese Yearbook of International Law*, at 113.

[57] Yu, Jinsong, *ibid*. China has also signed similar agreement with the UK in 1987 and with Canada in 1981. See Lillich, R and Weston, BH, 'Lump Sum Agreements: Their Contribution to the Law of International Claims', 82 *American Journal of International Law* 69, in the Annex, at 78. Texts of the Sino-US and Sino-UK agreements are available at the UN Treaties, Nos 18180 and 28495 respectively.

[58] For a good survey of scholarly views thereon, see Lillich and Weston, *ibid*, at 73–77.

[59] Dolzer, above, note 2, at 560.

[60] *Banco Nacional case,* above, note 14, at 892.

[61] For details see Section 6.2.1.

[62] *Topco Case*, above, note 44, at 29.

[63] *Government of the State of Kuwait v American Independent Oil Co.* (*Aminoil case*), Award on the Merits, 21 ILM 976 (1982), at 976.

support in some US-Iran Claims Tribunal cases. Judge Lagergren decided in 1985, in the *INA* case, that,

> '[I]n the event of such large-scale nationalisations of lawful character, international law has undergone a gradual reappraisal, the effect of which may be to undermine the doctrinal value of any "full" or 'adequate' (when used as identical to "full compensation") standard as proposed in this case.'[64]

More than one Iranian judge of the Tribunal, albeit via dissenting opinions or special statements, has maintained that recent developments in the law of expropriation and compensation permitted the payment of 'less than full' or 'partial' compensation.[65] The most frequently cited domestic decision in this regard is the opinion of the court of appeals in the *Banco Nacional case* of 1982. Here the court reviewed much of the literature on the subject and concluded that

> 'it may well be the consensus of nations that full compensation need not be paid 'in all circumstances', '...and that requiring an expropriating state to pay "appropriate compensation"—even considering the lack of precise definition of that term—would come closest to reflecting what international law requires'.

Finally writings by some highly qualified publicists have pointed out that 'appropriate compensation' may be a better principle of compensation than the 'traditional' rule. Judge Aréchaga, a former President of the ICJ, prefers 'appropriate compensation' to 'adequate, prompt and effective' compensation, as 'it conveys better the complex circumstances which may be present in each case'.[66] Schachter has considered that the 'just compensation' requirement in the *Restatement of Foreign Relations Law* (3rd Edition) should now be replaced by 'appropriate compensation'. He further points out that since this standard has the support of a great many capital importing countries, it may have a practical advantage as these countries 'might then be more willing to accept international obligation and international procedures for dispute settlement'.[67]

In view of these practiced and well considered opinions it is tempting to

[64] *INA Corporation v the Government of the Islamic Republic of Iran* (*INA Case*), 8 Iran-US CTR (1985 I), at 378. Compare separate opinions of Judge Lagergren and Judge Holtzman, *ibid*, at 385, 391. Westburg has observed that 'appropriate compensation' was also referred to in the Sola Tiles case decided by the same Tribunal. See Sola Tiles Case (1987) 14 Iran-US CTR 223. See also Westburg, above, note 2, at 289.

[65] See eg, Judge Ameli, in the *INA case*, agreeing with Judge Lagergren, and Judge Shafeiei, in *Tippetts, Abbett, MaCarth, Stratton case*. Unfortunately, not much attention seems to have been paid on their opinions! See *INA Corporation v the Government of the Islamic Republic of Iran*, idem, at 415; *Tippetts, Abbett, MaCarth, Stratton v TAMS-AFFA Consulting Engineers of Iran, the Government of the Islamic Republic of Iran, et al.*, 6 Iran-US CTR, (1984 II), at 265–66.

[66] Aréchaga, Jiménez de, 'International Law in the Past Third of a Century', (1978) 159 *Recueil des Cours* 1, 302.

[67] Schachter, above, note 1, at 129.

conclude that the two resolutions, particularly Res 3281, have not only effectively *destroyed and dismantled* the legal status of the 'traditional' rule on compensation for expropriation, but have also *established or created* a new rule of customary international law, the standard of 'appropriate compensation'.

6.1.4 BIT by BIT:[68] Has the Proliferation of Investment Agreements Constituted a Complete Reversal to the 'Traditional' Rule?

The developed countries started to build up a network of bilateral investment agreements (BITs) as a result of the aforementioned UNGA resolutions with a view to protecting their overseas investments and to restoring the legal status of the 'traditional' rule.[69]

The proliferation of international investment agreements, particularly the BITs, is a phenomenon of the 1990s.[70] Vandevelde has observed that by the end of 1996 1330 BITs had been concluded, involving 162 countries, compared with less than 400 at the beginning of the 1990s.[71] A number of multilateral or regional legal instruments (eg, ICSID Convention, MIGA Convention, NAFTA, ECT, MAI draft and the WTO Agreement) have also come into being which are either specialised investment treaties or agreements containing substantial investment clauses (the 'MRIIs'). Naturally expropriation and compensation become the core clauses in those treaties, which often reflect the 'traditional' rule of 'adequate, effective and prompt compensation' (*Table 14: Expropriation and Compensation under MRIIs*). These clauses are almost unanimously based on model BITs drafted by developed countries, which, in turn, are based on the 1959 Abs/Shawcross Draft Convention on Investments Abroad and the 1967 OECD Draft Convention on the Protection of Foreign Property.[72]

The proliferation of investment treaties has led many Western scholars to

[68] This sub-title is borrowed from Salacus's article on BIT's impact on developing countries. See Salacuse, Jeswald W, 'BIT by BIT: The Growth of Bilateral Investment Treaties and Their Impact on Foreign Investment in Developing Countries', 24 *International Lawyer* No. 3, at 655–75.

[69] Vandevelde noted that, 'One of the most important, at least in the minds of the early proponents of these treaties (BITs), was to counter the claim made during the 1970s by many developing countries that customary international law no longer required that expropriation to be accompanied by prompt, adequate and effective compensation, if needed it ever had.' Vandevelde, KJ, 'US Bilateral Investment Treaties: the Second Wave', 14 *Michigan Journal of International Law*, at 625.

[70] UNCTAD: *World Investment Report 1997*, United Nations, 1997, at 19. See also, Vandevelde, KJ, 'The Economics of Bilateral Investment Treaties', (2000) 41 *Harvard International Law Journal* 469.

[71] Vandevelde, *ibid*, at 469. For an online list of BITs by 1996, see http://www.worldbank.org/icsid/treaties/treaties.htm (visited on 19 November 2002).

[72] Mann, above, note 2, at 109. For details of the two instruments, see Schwarzenberger, George, *Foreign Investment and International Law* (Stevens and Sons, 1969), at 109 and 153.

Table 14: Expropriation and Compensation under MRIIs

Investment Instruments	Rights to expropriate	Conditions				Standards of Compensation			
		Public interest	Non-dis-crimination	Due process of law	Compen-sation	Adequate, effective and prompt	Value of the expropriated investment + Interest	w/out delay, realisable and transferable	Evaluation methods
Energy Charter Treaty (Art 13 (1))	0	1	1	1	1	1	1 (fair market value)+1	0	0
World Bank Guidelines (Art IV.1)	0	1	1	1	1	1 (= 'appropri-ate')	1 (fair market value)	1	1 (detailed rules on the determination of 'fair market value')
NAFTA Chap. 11 (Art 1110 (1))	0	1	1	1 (incl. int. law)	1	0	1 (fair market value)	1	1 (valuation criteria shall include going concern value, asset value including declared tax value of tangible property, and other criteria, as appropriate)
MAI Draft (Art IV (2) (1))	0	1	1	1	1	1	1 (fair market value)	1	0

believe that a complete reversal of the paradigm on FDI has taken place, so that the 'traditional' rule of international law has regained its original status as the customary international law.[73] (They attribute this change to factors like the debt crisis in developing countries since early 1980, the modelling effect of the success of East Asian economies, the growing competition worldwide for FDI,[74] as well as the failure of the state-driven model of economic development, the collapse of communism, and the emergence of a new commercially-oriented middle-class challenging the NIEO-focused State classes in developing countries.)[75] The author wonders whether this conclusion has been over-optimistic when the following points are considered:

Firstly, as mentioned above, BITs as well as other investment agreements are the result of the demise of the old or 'traditional' rule of international law. Their existence signals the non-existence of such 'traditional' customary international law rather than the other way round. In other words if the 'traditional' rule actually had been re-established there would be no need for BITs or MRIIs.

Secondly, despite the general similarities, there are significant differences between one BIT and another. It can be seen from the survey of the 335 BITs conducted by the World Bank when drafting the World Bank Guidelines that the 'traditional' rule is not consistently supported by the BITs. On the conditions for expropriation, for instance, some 26 do not mention 'public purposes'. A majority of BITs do not require 'non-discrimination', and two BITs do not mention any conditions for expropriation but require the payment of compensation.[76] A substantial portion of these BITs (93) have adopted neither the 'adequate, prompt and effective' formula on the standards of compensation nor its potential equivalents such as 'just', 'full' or 'fair and equitable' compensation.[77] As Bernard Kishoiyian has rightly pointed out, after carefully examining many BITs 'there is no sufficient inconsistency in the terms of the investment treaties to find in them support for any definite principle of customary international law'.[78]

Thirdly, even if BITs had uniformly followed the Hull formula, (which is by no means the case, as observed above), this would not in itself be enough

[73] Lauterpacht, Sir Elihu above, note 2, at 263 and 265; Fatouros, AA, 'Towards an International Agreement on Foreign Direct Investment?', (1995) 12 *ICSID Review—FILJ*, at 187; Al-Nauimi and Meese eds, *International Legal Issues Arising under the United Nations Decade of International Law* (Kluwer Law International, 1995), at 1301 and 1335. Vandevelde used the word 'consensus' to describe the newly emerged paradigm towards FDI, see Vandevelde, 'Sustainable Liberalism', above, note 6, at 386.

[74] Vandevelde, 'Sustainable Liberalism', above, note 6, at 386–90; Lauterpacht, Sir Elihu, above, note 2, at 265.

[75] Al-Nauimi and Meese, above, note 73, at 1335.

[76] Shihata, above, note 2, at 256.

[77] *Ibid.*

[78] Kishoiyian, Bernard, 'The Utility of Bilateral Investment Treaties in the Formulation of Customary International Law', (1994) 14 *Northwestern Journal of International Law & Business* 327, at 372.

to prove the existence of the restoration of the Hull formula as customary law. It is an established general rule that repetitions of common provisions in bilateral agreements do not create or support an inference that those provisions reflect customary law.[79] To establish or restore a rule of customary law, one has to show not only that there is a extensive, constant and uniform state practice (*usus*), but also that the rules in these clauses are considered obligatory (*opinio juris*). With regard to the latter it is widely acknowledged that developing countries enter into BITs more for economic than for legal considerations.[80] In other words developing countries enter into BITs to offer higher investment protection, not because they believe the law 'is' or even 'should be' that expressed in the BITs but because they believe BITs to be useful tools for attracting FDI inflows.[81] Few developing countries have adopted the 'Hull formula' in their domestic legislation, where they are able to spell out their own convictions. Parra studied FDI codes of 51 developing countries when he was preparing the World Bank Guidelines, and found that none of them referred to 'adequate, effective and prompt' compensation. Only a few of them mentioned 'fair and equitable compensation' and most of them did not mentioned the standard of compensation at all.[82] In multilateral fora developing countries still aspire to the establishment of the NIEO and the implementation of the right to development spelled out in Res 3281.[83] This is initially witnessed by the speeches of leaders from developing countries in various multilateral fora.[84] It has also been decided within the WTO that the

[79] For example, extradition and air transit treaties are widely used and contain standard clauses, yet it is not claimed that these clauses are either declaratory or constitutive of customary law binding on third states. See Schachter, above, note 1, at 126; Amerasinghe, above, note 2, at 30.

[80] For instance, a few authoritative Western commentators have rightly pointed out that in return of the higher standard of protection and treatment to foreign investors, the host countries normally can receive benefits in the treaties themselves and in related trade and aid arrangements. Dolzer, above, note 2, at 553, 583–89; Schachter, above, note 1, at 127; Guzmán, Andrew T, *Explaining the Popularity of Bilateral Investment Treaties: Why LDCs Sign Treaties that Hurt Them?* Harvard Jean Monnet Working Paper 12/97, 1997, at 72.

[81] YU rightly pointed out that, 'Countries may be willing to accept certain rules in their BITs, but not as general rules of international law.' Yu, Jinsong, *International Investment Law* (in Chinese) (Law Press, 1997), at 246.

[82] Parra, Antonio R, 'Principles Governing Foreign Investment, as Reflected in National Investment Codes', in Shihata, above, note 2, at 325.

[83] Dolzer correctly has pointed out that, expropriation is viewed to be the central issue in the struggle for a NIEO. See Dolzer, above, note 2, at 556.

[84] For instance, in the 35th Annual Meeting of the Asian Banks held in May 2002, the then Chinese President Jiang Zeming pointed out that, 'The fundamental reason the world is not developing in a balanced manner is the failure in establishing a fair and reasonable NIEO. The unreasonable international financial and trade regime needs to be reformed and economic actors should be encouraged to move reasonably and orderly, so as to safeguard all countries, particularly developing countries rights of equal development under the new conditions of economic globalisation.' Likewise, during the 2002 World Summit on Sustainable Development held in Johannesburg, South Africa, President Thabo Mbeki, for example, convincingly urged the world to share the responsibility of sustainable development, particularly the development of developing countries. He said, 'I am also certain that we are of one mind that the imperative of human solidarity as well as actual experience demand that, together, we must strive for a

needs and interests of developing countries should be placed at the 'heart' of the Work Programme adopted by the Doha Ministerial Declaration.[85] Thus one cannot establish here the '*opinio juris*' required for the restoration of the 'traditional' rule.

Fourthly, there has so far been no global investment agreement put in place, and the value of other existing regional or multinational (trade and) investment is the same as the network of BITs. The MIGA Convention and the ICSID Convention are specialised investment agreements, but they do not touch on substantive issues such as the standards of treatment and rules on expropriation and compensation. NAFTA and ECT deal with those substantive issues but cover only a very limited number of developing countries in certain regions. The negotiation of the MAI under the auspices of the OECD was a major recent effort to draw up a global code on FDI. However, while this effort has again shown the uncertainty of existing international law, its failure has demonstrated that a consensus on such a 'high standard' multilateral investment agreement could not be achieved even within developed countries, let alone between them and developing countries.

Fifthly, those BITs and other investment agreements are not necessarily in conflict with Res 3281. As previously observed Res 3281 expressly provides that consensus established, States may resort to means other than domestic courts and tribunals. This implies the application of international law or at least treaty law.

The 'appropriate compensation' standard embraced in Res 3281 can also be compatible with the standard of 'just', 'full' or even 'prompt, adequate, and effective compensation.' Indeed, taking into consideration the pledges made in numerous multilateral fora to establish NIEO, developing countries engaging in BIT and other investment treaty practices are better explained as exercising economic sovereignty established by Res 3281 and an implementation of the Charter provision on special treaty arrangements dealing with FDI issues, rather than demonstrating a total change of attitude or a submission to the 'traditional' rule. In other words the proliferation of BITs and other investment agreements is better understood as a development within the paradigm of Res 3281 rather than a restoration to the 'traditional' rule. Nevertheless the rules established by the Economic Charter might be changed overthrown or reversed, if such a liberal trend continues and eventually leads to the conclusion of a new UNGA resolution or a multilateral investment agreement (MIA), with global coverage equivalent to that of the Charter.

shared prosperity. A global human society based on poverty for many and prosperity for a few, characterised by islands of wealth, surrounded by a sea of poverty, is unsustainable.' See *People's Daily* (overseas edition), 11 May 2002, at 1 and 4, and *Opening Statement by President Thabo Mbeki at the World Summit on Sustainable Development*, available at: http://www.un.org/events/wssd/statements/openingsae.htm (visited on 1 January 2003).

[85] The World Trade Organisation: *Ministerial Declaration adopted by the Fourth Session of the Ministerial Conference at Doha on 9–14 November 2001* (hereinafter "*Doha Ministerial Declaration*"), WT/MIN(01)/DEC/W/1 (14 November 2001), posted at http://www.wto.org/english/thewto_e/minist_e/min01_e/mindecl_e.htm (visited on 18 January 2002).

6.2 THE LAW OF EXPROPRIATION AND COMPENSATION OF EU INVESTMENT IN CHINA

The law of expropriation and compensation is mainly composed of two categories of law in the context of EU investment in China: the EU-China BITs and Chinese law.[86] While the latter only provides general principles, the former lays down more detailed rules.

6.2.1 Chinese Law

China cherishes expropriation as an inalienable and indispensable sovereign right, so it has been very cautious in passing legislation concerning nationalisation, expropriation, and compensations. When the EJVL was first adopted in 1979 silence was the 'policy' of choice to deal with this important issue. When China adopted the REOFF in 1982, it stated in Article 26 that '[I]n the course of war, threat of war or other emergencies, the Chinese Government has the right to requisition or expropriate a part or all of the oil that the foreign contractors earn or buy.' China did not formulate its general prototype of expropriation clauses until 1986, when the WFEL was published. Article 5 of the WFEL, which has been followed by other major basic FIE laws and regulations (except the CJVL),[87] stipulates that:

> 'China does not conduct expropriation or nationalisation of WFEs. Under special circumstances, in public interest, WFEs can be expropriated in accordance with legal procedures and appropriate compensation will be provided.'

Chinese law therefore pledges that under 'normal circumstances' China would not take expropriatory measures, which can only be resorted to under 'special circumstances'. What are the special circumstances? There is no further clarification. One scholar argues that 'special circumstances' should refer to war, threat of war, other emergencies, as well as *force majeure* situations such as severe natural disasters.[88] However this interpretation might have been too restrictive. It can be particularly argued that the state should be exempt from the obligation of compensation if expropriation is conducted in a *force majeure* situation.

Another key concept here is 'appropriate compensation', which again is not further defined in Chinese law. A reasonable interpretation of this stand-

[86] The MIGA Convention deals with the expropriation and compensation as a category of political risk to be guaranteed but not touches upon the substance of this issue. On the other hand, the ICSID Convention sets up an international mechanism to handle investment disputes, including expropriation disputes, but, again, does not deal with the substantive issues thereof. Therefore, they are not discussed here.

[87] See eg Art 2 (3) of EJVL as amended I 1990, Art 5 of REON.

[88] See Zeng, Huaqun, *International Investment Law* (*Guoji Touzi Faxue*) (Peking University Press, 1999), at 36.

ard may be that in case there is an applicable BIT to the expropriation, the standard of compensation should be compatible with the compensation clauses stipulated in that BIT.[89] In other cases, 'appropriate compensation' requires the amount of compensation to be determined, taking into account 'all circumstances' China considers 'pertinent', as provided for in Res 3281. Those circumstances may include, as Judge Aréchaga forcefully argued,

> 'Whether the initial investment has been recovered, whether there has been undue enrichment as a result of colonial situation, whether the profits obtained have been excessive, the contribution of the enterprise to the economic and social development of the country, its respect for labour laws and its investment policies.'[90]

This interpretation of 'appropriate compensation' is certainly based on domestic law and is thus far from the interpretation of some Western countries, which equates this standard of compensation with the 'Hull Formula'.[91] Chinese law does not go any further in defining expropriation, its conditions, and the standard of compensation. Reference must therefore be made to applicable BITs to find a clearer answer on these elements.

6.2.2 The EU-China BITs

The EU-China BITs are the most important sources of law on the issue of expropriation and compensation for EU investment in China. Each of the 13 BITs contains separate clauses dealing with this issue. Like most other BITs they approach the expropriation issue from three perspectives: constitution of expropriation, conditions of expropriation, and compensation of expropriation.

6.2.2.1 The Constitution of Expropriation

Expropriation may take many forms.[92] Apart from outright deprivation of property (sometimes called 'direct expropriation'), there may be various forms of 'indirect expropriation', or 'creeping expropriation', or, in the terms of BITs, 'measures equivalent/tantamount to expropriation'.[93]

As *Table 15* shows, the existing BITs between China and the EU (EU-China

[89] Zeng, Huaqun, *ibid*; Shan, Wenhua, *The Development of Theories and Practice on the Compensation for Expropriation and China* (Law Science, No. 4, 1995), at 72.

[90] Aréchaga, above, note 821, at 185.

[91] For instance, the US vote in favour of the UN Res 1803 and asserted that in its view the 'appropriate compensation' therein was equivalent to the 'Hull Formula' it had advocated since 1938. See Restatement, above, note 14, at 206.

[92] *Oppenheim's International Law*, 9th edition, above, note 2, at 916.

[93] For a good survey of laws and practices on 'indirect expropriation', see Dolzer, R, 'Indirect Expropriation of Foreign Property', (1986) 1 *ICSID Review—Foreign Investment Law Journal*.

Table 15: Constitution of Expropriation under EU-China BITs

Investment Instruments	National-isation	Expropria-tion	Measures having equivalent/similar effects
Sino-Sweden BIT (Art 3 (1))	1	1	1
Sino-Germany BIT (Protocol 4 (a))	1	1	1
Sino-France BIT (Art 4 (2)	1	1	1
Sino-BLEU BIT (Art 4 (1))	1	1	1
Sino-Finland BIT (Art 5 (1))	1	1	1
Sino-Italy BIT (Art 4 (2))	1	1	1
Sino-Denmark BIT (Art 4 (1))	1	1	1
Sino-Netherlands BIT (Art 5 (1))	1	1	1
Sino-Austria BIT (Art 4 (1))	0	1	1
Sino-Britain BIT (Art 5 (1))	1	1	1
Sino-Portugal BIT (Art 4 (1))	1	1	1
Sino-Spain BIT (Art 4 (1))	1	1	1
Sino-Greece BIT (Art 4 (1))	1	1	1
Total (13)	12	13	13

BITs) adopt a broad definition of 'expropriation', which covers 'nationalisation' 'expropriation' and 'measures having equivalent effects'[94] (*Table 15: Constitution of Expropriation under EU-China BITs*). The new Sino-Germany BIT covers 'direct and indirect expropriation, nationalisation or measures having equivalent expropriation and nationalisation effects'.[95] However when it comes to the interpretation of 'indirect expropriation' disagreements between China and the EU can be anticipated. As a group of capital-exporting countries with a liberal tradition on investment regulation the EU will probably submit to a broad interpretation of indirect expropriation.

In the ninth edition of *Oppenheim's International Law*, for example, the list of measures that may 'amount to expropriation' include imposition of stringent currency control regulations, the non-payment or annulment of the state's contractual debts or claims against it, the imposition of exorbitantly high rates of taxation, currency devaluation, the requisition of an enterprise leading to its bankruptcy, the absorption of property into cooperatives under state control, the enforced but illusory 'sale' of property, and the annulment

[94] See Art 3 (1), Sino-Sweden BIT, Protocol 4 (a), Sino-Germany BIT; Art 4 (2), Sino-France BIT; Art 4 (1), Sino-BLEU BIT; Art 5 (1), Sino-Finland BIT; Art 4 (2), Sino-Italy BIT; Art 4 (1), Sino-Denmark BIT; Art 5 (1), Sino-Netherlands BIT; Art 4 (1), Sino-Austria BIT; Art 5 (1) Sino-Britain BIT; Art 4 (1), Sino-Portugal BIT; Art 4 (1), Sino-Spain BIT and Art 4 (1), Sino-Greece BIT.

[95] Art 4.2, the new Sino-Germany BIT.

of judicially recognised rights or the imposition of extensive control of property or on the exercise of the normal rights of the ownership.[96] The OECD interpretation of 'indirect expropriation', as expressed in the Commentary to Article 3 of the OECD Draft Convention on the Protection of Foreign Property (Paris 1967), is that it should include

> 'excessive or arbitrary taxation; prohibition of dividend distribution coupled with compulsory loans; imposition of administrators; prohibition of dismissal of staff; refusal of access to raw materials or of essential export or import license'.[97]

China, as a capital-importing country with a planned economic legacy, is reluctant to accept such a broad interpretation. In Chinese literature authorities almost unanimously take the view that 'indirect expropriation' should not be excessively broadly defined and must be treated with caution.[98] Professor YAO wrote that regulatory measures such as currency deflation, forex control, tax increase, and export control were not at all measures depriving foreign investors of their property rights but were exercises of the normal regulatory power acknowledged by international law.[99] Further, he pointed out that according to state practice some measures were permissible even though they had indirect impact on foreign investors' property rights.[100]

Examples of these measures include change of contractual conditions, local content requirements, and measures to arrange workers to participate in enterprise management.[101] Finally he concluded that 'indirect expropriation' is a concept of 'traditional' international law, whose use should be restrained.[102]

Indeed as Dolzer and Stevens indicate there is no clear definition of the concept of 'indirect expropriation' in spite of many decisions from international tribunals. The boundary line between regulation and expropriation is difficult to identify.[103] Each case is therefore likely to be decided on the basis of its attending circumstances.[104] Jennings and Watts also point out that '[T]he question (of the constitution of expropriation) cannot be answered in the abstract but only on the basis of particular circumstances and in the context of particular purposes.'[105]

[96] *Oppenheim's International Law*, 9th edition, above, note 2, at 916–17.

[97] As cited in Dolzer and Stevens, above, note 2, at 100, note 270.

[98] Chen, An, *International Investment Law* (Lujiang Press, 1987), at 87; YAO, Meizhen, *Comparative Foreign Investment Law* (in Chinese) (Wuhan University Press, 1993), at 774–82; Zeng, Huaqun, above, note 88, at 448; Xu, Congli, *The Controversial Issues in International Investment Law and China's Countermeasures* (Social Sciences in China, No. 1, 1994).

[99] Yao, *ibid*, at 781.

[100] Yao, *ibid*.

[101] Yao, *ibid*.

[102] Yao, *ibid*, at 782.

[103] Dolzer and Stevens, above, note 2, at 100. Dolzer, Rudolf, 'Indirect Expropriation of Alien Property', (1986) 1 *ICSID Review—Foreign Investment Law Journal*, at 59.

[104] Dolzer and Stevens, *ibid*.

[105] *Oppenheim's International Law*, 9th edition, above, note 2, at 916–17.

It must moreover be realised that eventually the definition of the scope of expropriation is an issue of the boundary between the host State's right to regulate and the foreign investors' property rights which can go beyond the context of north-south relations. Recent history has witnessed the governments of developed countries defending their rights to regulate FDI activities against the accusation of abusive expropriation by foreign investors. A few 'frivolous' expropriation cases against governments of NAFTA members have been brought before international tribunals under NAFTA Chapter 11 since 1997.[106] Developed states, such as the US and Canada, suddenly found themselves in the position of being accused of expropriation after taking measures they considered to be 'normal regulatory activities'—eg, measures to protect the environment.[107] The *Globe and Mail*, a pro-business Canadian newspaper, reported that since 1997 'companies have lined up to use the investment chapter of NAFTA to sue Ottawa'.[108] This has led to proposals of amendments to NAFTA expropriation clauses by the Canadian Government. NAFTA members have expressed concerns over the abuse of expropriation clauses in the MAI negotiations.[109] Ironically this time it was Mexico, a developing country famous for vigorously rejecting the 'Hull Rules' which opposed the amendment proposals.[110]

It can be argued that the interpretation of 'expropriation' should not be excessively broad. A relatively conservative approach may be desirable in defining expropriation, particularly 'indirect expropriation', with a view to balancing the needs and rights of host governments to regulate FDI activities and to the respecting of investors' property rights. Every country in practice maintains the rights to restrict and interfere with private property rights, including those of aliens, especially those connected with taxation, measures of policy, public health, the administration of public utilities, and the planning of urban and rural development.[111] These measures closely relate to the basic functioning of the government and should, in any case, be immune from the possibility of being accused of expropriation. Other 'normal regulatory activities', such as currency devaluation, forex control, restrictions on profit repatriation, import and export licensing, environmental protection etc, are all measures well established under general international law and should not in principle be viewed as expropriatory measures.[112]

[106] For a good survey of the dozen earliest cases, see Gagné, above, note 2.

[107] For in-depth studies on some of the cases, see Beauvais, Joel C, 'Regulatory Expropriations Under NAFTA: Emerging Principles & Lingering Doubts', (2002) 10 *New York University Environ- mental Law Journal* 245; Waren, William T, 'Paying to Regulate: A Guide to Methanex v. United States And NAFTA Investor Rights', (2001) 31 *Environmental Law Reporter* 10986, .

[108] *The Globe and Mail*, 16 February 1999, B6.

[109] Gagné, above, note 2, at 483, 501–05.

[110] *Ibid*, at 503.

[111] *Oppenheim's International Law*, 9th edition, above, note 2, at 917.

[112] Akehurst considered those measures were all lawful unless they are ill conceived or motivated. See Akehurst, M, *Akehurst's Modern Introduction to International Law*, Chinese translation (Chinese Social Sciences Press, 1981), at 110. In 2000, a NAFTA tribunal decided that,

6.2.2.2 Conditions of Expropriation

It is now well established that a sovereign state has the right to expropriate foreign property,[113] but the question remains whether such a right is subject to the fulfilment of certain conditions. As noted, Western countries hold that 'traditional' international law requires nationalisation or expropriation to be non-discriminatory, for public purposes, in accordance with legal procedures, and, most importantly, accompanied by the payment of 'adequate, prompt and effective', 'full', or 'just' compensation. Otherwise, the expropriation is unlawful, state responsibility may be invoked, and the principle of restitution should apply.[114]

Developing countries argue that the right to expropriate foreign assets is inherent in the sovereignty of states and that they should be able to regulate and control the use of foreign property within their territories.[115] They argue that since few if any could afford to pay full compensation, insistence on this standard would in effect deprive them of their sovereign rights to expropriate, or of the benefit that they might otherwise have received from such actions.[116] Some eminent Chinese lawyers have argued that these conditions

'The general body of precedent usually does not treat regulatory action as amounting to expropriation under Art 1110 of the NAFTA, although the Tribunal does not rule out the possibility.' It went on to distinguish regulation from expropriation, 'Expropriations tend to involve the deprivation of ownership rights; regulation a lesser interference. The distinction screens out most potential cases of complaints concerning economic intervention by a state and reduces the risk that governments will be subject to claims as they go about their business of managing public affairs.' See Tribunal Final Merits Award of the *S.D. Myers, Inc. v. Government of Canada case*, in a NAFTA Arbitration under the UNICITRAL Rules (hereinafter the '*Myers case*'), Para 281, 282, decided on 13 November 2000.

113 This has been confirmed by, eg, the Joint Declaration by French, British and US Governments in 1956 on the nationalisation of the Suez Canal. It is also expressed in Art 2 (2) (c) of the UN Economic Charter, which clearly states that 'Each State has the right to...nationalise, expropriate, or transfer ownership of foreign property...' In addition, international lawyers now unanimously acknowledge that sovereign right of states. See eg, Aréchaga, above, note 2, at 179; Sornarajah, above, note 5, at 315; Dolzer and Stevens, above, note2, at 97; *Oppenheim's International Law*, 9th edition, above, note 2, at 918; Brownlie, above, note 14, at 535.

114 In the famous 1928 Chorzów Factory case, the PCIJ ruled that, 'The essential principle contained in the actual notion of a illegal act—a principle which seems to be established by international practice and in particular by the decision of arbitration tribunals—is that reparation must, as far as possible, wipe out all the consequences of the illegal act and re-establish the situation which would, in all probability, have existed if that act had not been committed. Restitution in kind, or if this is not possible, payment of a sum corresponding to the value which a restitution would bear; the award, if need be, of damages for loss sustained which would not be covered by restitution in kind or payment in place of it—such are the principles which should serve to determine the amount of compensation due for an act contrary to international law.' PCIJ Reports, Series A, No. 17, at 46–48.

Further, the latest version of the Draft Arts on State Responsibility by the UN International Law Commission (ILC), 'Every internationally wrongful act of a State entails the international responsibility of that State.' Meanwhile, restitution is prescribed as the primary form of reparation for injuries caused by internationally wrongful acts. For details of these Arts, see Crawford, James, *The International Law Commission's Articles on State Responsibility: Introduction, Text, and Commentaries* (Cambridge University Press, 2002).

115 Lauterpacht, Sir Elihu, above, note 2, at 265.

116 *Ibid.*

Table 16: Conditions of Expropriation under EU-China BITs

Investment Instruments	Conditions			
	Public interest	Non-discrimination	Due process of law	Compensation
Sino-Sweden BIT (Art 3 (1))	1	1	1	1
Sino-Germany BIT (Art 4 (1))	1	0	1	1
Sino-France BIT (Art 4 (2)	1	1	1	1
Sino-BLEU BIT (Art 4 (1))	1	1	1 (domestic)	1
Sino-Finland BIT (Art 5 (1))	1	1	1	1
Sino-Italy BIT (Art 4 (2))	1	0	0	1
Sino-Denmark BIT (Art 4 (1))	1	1	0	1
Sino-Netherlands BIT (Art 5 (1))	1	1	1	1
Sino-Austria BIT (Art 4 (1))	1	0	1	1 (appropriate)
Sino-Britain BIT (Art 5 (1))	1	0	0	1 (reasonable)
Sino-Portugal BIT (Art 4 (1))	1	1	1 (domestic)	1
Sino-Spain BIT (Art 4 (1))	1	1	1 (domestic)	1
Sino-Greece BIT (Art 4. (1))	1	1	1 (domestic)	1
Total (13)	13	9	10	13

and the limitation of expropriation and nationalisation were either unnecessary or unreasonable. They believe that expropriation and nationalisation are an attribute of sovereignty which should not be limited. They particularly oppose the imposition of compensation as a condition of expropriation because they think that compensation should be a result of expropriation rather than a precondition.[117] As a result of this North-South debate, the UN Economic Charter adopted in 1974 confirms that host countries have the

[117] See eg, Yao, Meizhen, *International Investment Law* (in Chinese) (Wuhan University Press 1987), at 379–80; YAO, above, note 98, at 771–74; Chen, An, *International Investment Law* (in Chinese) (Lujiang Press, 1987), at 88–92. Wang, Guiguo, *International Investment Law* (in Chinese) (Peking University Press, 2002), at 214–16.

right to expropriate, in which case compensation 'should' be paid. The author believes that these principles, as spelled out in the Charter, still represent general international law. It represents the view of the vast majority of the international community, and it does not prevent States from entering into special treaty arrangements to restrict their right of expropriation by attaching some conditions to it.

Thus all EU-China BITs (as shown in *Table 16: Rights and Conditions of Expropriation under EU-China BITs*) accept that expropriation should be made in the public interest and accompanied by compensation.[118] Most also stipulate that non-discrimination and the due process of law should be additional conditions for expropriation[119]. On the standard of compensation, most EU-China BITs merely mention 'compensation' as a condition without specifying its standard, though 'reasonable compensation' and 'appropriate compensation' are mentioned in Sino-Britain BIT and Sino-Austria BIT respectively[120] (*Table 16*).

Taking into account the MFN clauses in the EU-China BITs, it can be concluded that EU investment would not be expropriated until four conditions are fulfilled. These are public interests, due process of law, non-discrimination and compensation. The standard of compensation will be discussed below.

6.2.2.3 Compensation for Expropriation

The issue of compensation may be divided into two: the standard of compensation and the evaluation of compensation

6.2.2.3.1 The Standard of Compensation. Historically, as Section 6.1 shows, there have been three arguments on the standard of compensation: 'prompt, adequate and effective' or 'just' and 'full' compensation advocated by developed countries, no compensation by socialist and Latin American countries, and 'appropriate compensation' as prescribed by the UN Economic Charter.[121]

In the earlier years of the new China, the Chinese government followed in the footsteps of the USSR and nationalised foreign properties without payment of compensation.[122] In other words China submitted to the no compen-

[118] See Art 3 (1), Sino-Sweden BIT, Art 4 (1), Sino-Germany BIT; Art 4 (2), Sino-France BIT; Art 4 (1), Sino-BLEU BIT; Art 5 (1), Sino-Finland BIT; Art 4 (2), Sino-Italy BIT; Art 4 (1), Sino-Denmark BIT; Art 5 (1), Sino-Netherlands BIT; Art 4 (1), Sino-Austria BIT; Art 5 (1) Sino-Britain BIT; Art 4 (1), Sino-Portugal BIT; Art 4 (1), Sino-Spain BIT and Art 4 (1), Sino-Greece BIT.

[119] Sino-Italy BIT, Sino-Denmark BIT and Sino-Britain BIT do not mention 'legal procedure' as a condition for expropriation. Further, Sino-BLEU BIT, Sino-Portugal BIT, Sino-Spain BIT and Sino-Greece BIT make clear that the condition of legal procedure refer exclusively to 'domestic' legal procedure. See Art 4 (1), Sino-BLEU BIT; Art 5 (1), Sino-Portugal BIT; Art 4 (1), Sino-Spain BIT; Art 4 (1), Sino-Greece BIT.

[120] See, in particular, Art 4 (1), Sino-Austria BIT and Art 5 (1) Sino-Britain BIT.

[121] Francioni, above, note 2, at 255–56.

[122] See the Introduction part of this book for details of China's earlier practice of expropriation.

sation model. Since 1979 when China re-opened its doors to the outside world the expropriation policy has been changed and 'appropriate compensation' has been adopted as the new standard of compensation.[123] Nevertheless Chinese scholars have vigorously rejected the 'Hull Formula' because the terms 'adequate, prompt and effective' 'have long been used in capitalist countries for *extorting* compensations for liquidated assets'.[124]

Accordingly, none of the 13 EU-China BITs refer to the Hull Formula of 'prompt adequate and effective' payment of compensation (*Table 17: Compensation for Expropriation under EU-China BITs*). As mentioned above most of them merely mention 'compensation' as a condition of expropriation while only two of them refer to general formula such as 'reasonable' and 'appropriate'.[125]

However on a technical level China seems to be ready to pay compensation in a way similar to the general BIT practice. As *Table 17* shows, all these BITs have required the payment of compensation to be made without (undue) delay, to be (fully/effectively) realisable, and freely transferable.[126] All investment-related transfers (including transfer of compensation for expropriation) will be in convertible currency (or other agreed currencies) on the basis of the prevailing rate of exchange at the time, as *Table 13* shows.[127] Twelve BITs provide that the compensation shall be *equivalent to* the (actual)/(real) value of the expropriated investment immediately before the date on which the actual or threatened expropriation has been publicly known.[128] Four BITs also expressly state that the amount of compensation must include interest.[129] The new Sino-Germany BIT also stipulates that the compensation shall be equivalent to the value of expropriated investment, plus interest.[130] All these provisions on the amount of compensation in the EU-China BITs are thus rather similar to general BIT practice.[131]

123 See eg, EJVL, Art 2.

124 See Gu, Ming, *Investment Environment Seen as Favorable*, Beijing Review, July 16, 1984, at 16, as cited in Steinert, Timothy A, 'If the BIT Fits: The Proposed Bilateral Investment Treaty between the United States and the People's Republic of China', (1988) 2 *Journal of Chinese Law*, Fall, note 251. At that time, Gu was a Deputy Secretary-General of the State Council of China.

125 See Section 6.2.2.2.

126 Art 3 (1), Sino-Sweden BIT; Art 4 (1) and point 4 (c) in the Protocol, Sino-Germany BIT; Art 4 (2) and point 2 in the Protocol, Sino-France BIT; Art 4 (1) and Art 2 in the Protocol, Sino-BLEU BIT; Art 5 (2), Sino-Finland BIT; Art 4 (2), Sino-Italy BIT; Art 4 (1), Sino-Denmark BIT; Art 5 (2), Sino-Netherlands BIT; Art 4 (1), Sino-Austria BIT; Art 5(1)(2), Sino-Britain BIT; Art 4 (2), Sino-Portugal BIT; Art 4 (2), Sino-Spain BIT and Art 4 (2), Sino-Greece BIT.

127 See also Section 5.4.1.

128 See Art 4 (1) and point 4 (c) in the Protocol, Sino-Germany BIT; Art 4 (2) and point 2 in the Protocol, Sino-France BIT; Art 4 (1) and Art 2 in the Protocol, Sino-BLEU BIT; Art 5 (2), Sino-Finland BIT; Art 4 (2), Sino-Italy BIT; Art 4 (1), Sino-Denmark BIT; Art 5 (2), Sino-Netherlands BIT; Art 4 (1), Sino-Austria BIT; Art 5 (1) (2), Sino-Britain BIT; Art 4 (2), Sino-Portugal BIT; Art 4 (2), Sino-Spain BIT and Art 4 (2), Sino-Greece BIT.

129 See Art 5 (2), Sino-Finland BIT; Art 4 (1), Sino-Denmark BIT; Art 5 (2), Sino-Netherlands BIT and Art 5 (1) (2), Sino-Britain BIT.

130 Art 4.2, the new Sino-Germany BIT.

131 For surveys of standard compensation clauses in BITs, see Khalil, Mohamed I, 'Treatment of Foreign Investment in Bilateral Investment Treaties', in Shihata, above, note 2, at 256–59. See Dolzer and Stevens, above, note 2, at 108–12.

Table 17: Compensation for Expropriation under EU-China BITs

Investment Instruments	Value of the expropriated investment + Interest	Adequate, effective and prompt	w/out delay, realisable and transferable	Evaluation of value
Sino-Sweden BIT (Art 3 (1))	0	0	1	1 (To place the investor in the same financial position as if not expropriated)
Sino-Germany BIT (Art 4 (2) and Protocol 4 (c))	1	0	1	0
Sino-France BIT (Art 4 (2) and Protocol (2))	1	0	1	1 (Should be specified in advance)
Sino-BLEU BIT (Art 4 (2) and Protocol Art 2)	1	0	1	0
Sino-Finland BIT (Art 5 (2))	1+1	0	1	0
Sino-Italy BIT (Art 4 (2))	1	0	1	0
Sino-Denmark BIT (Art 4 (1))	1+1	0	1	1 (reviewable)
Sino-Netherlands BIT (Art 5 (2))	1+1	0	1	0
Sino-Austria BIT (Art 4 (1))	1 (appropriate)	0	1	0
Sino-Britain BIT (Art 5 (1–2))	1 (reasonable)+1	0	1	1 (judicially reviewable)
Sino-Portugal BIT (Art 4 (2))	1	0	1	0
Sino-Spain BIT (Art 4 (2))	1	0	1	0
Sino-Greece BIT (Art 4 (2))	1	0	1	1 (to place the investor in the same financial position as without the expropriation, and on the basis of generally accepted international methods.
Total (13)	12+4	0	13	5

The only perceivable difference is that these EU-China BITs have not used '(fair) market value', which is prevalent among general BITs. As observed by Stevens and Dolzer, this avoidance of 'market' may result from the planned economy that China has long implemented.[132] When China determined to establish a 'Socialist Market Economy' after 1993, it has started to use 'market value' as a reference to the amount of compensation in its newly signed BITs.[133] It is also noted that 'real value' and 'actual value' can be regarded as variations of 'market value'.[134] It maybe concluded that the *actual* standard of compensation in EU-China BITs is not significantly different from general BIT practice, even though most of them do not define the general standard.

6.2.2.3.2 The Valuation of Compensation. Professor Sir Elihu Lauterpacht has rightly pointed out that, whilst the establishment of the standard of compensation payable is a *legal* question of primary importance, the actual valuation should be an *objective and separate* process.[135] It is not surprising that, as Stevens and Dolzer have observed, so far virtually no BITs have made reference to valuation methods in their expropriation clauses.[136]

As *Table 17* shows none of the 13 EU-China BITs have included a provision on the specific methods of determining the value of the expropriated property. However the Sino-Sweden BIT and the Sino-Greece BIT provide general principles on the valuation of compensation, which shall be 'to place the investor in the same financial position as that in which the investor would have been if the expropriation or nationalisation had not taken place'.[137]This is more like a clause of standard than a clause of valuation methods, but it has been argued that this formula may fail to take into account 'non-financial' aspects of the investment, such as goodwill and long-term benefit.[138] In other BITs some procedural requirements have been included in several of these BITs. Thus the Sino-France BIT requires that the valuation methods shall be specified before the expropriation takes place; and both Sino-Denmark BIT and Sino-Britain BITs provide that expropriated companies may request a review on the valuation of compensation. The new Sino-Germany BITs has gone step further to allow investors to request a judicial review not only on the valuation of the amount of compensation, but also the *legality* of

[132] Dolzer and Stevens, above, note 2, at 110. See also, Denza, Eileen, and Brooks, Shelagh, 'Investment Protection Treaties: United Kingdom Experience', (1989) 36 *ICLQ*, at 919.

[133] See eg, Sino-South Korea BIT, Art 5 (3); Sino-Morocco BIT, Art 5 (1). It has been argued, however, that the understandings of '(fair) market value' are 'fundamentally different' between developed countries and developing countries, as the latter rejects the concepts of 'goodwill' and 'anticipated profits'. Zeng, Huaqun, above, note 88, at 456. About rejection to these concepts by Chinese scholars, see also YAO, above, note 117 (1987), at 393–97.

[134] UNCTC, *Bilateral Investment Treaties* (Graham and Trotman 1988), at 80.

[135] Lauterpacht, Sir Elihu, above, note 2, at 267.

[136] Dolzer and Stevens, above, note 2, at 110.

[137] See Art 3 (1), Sino-Sweden BIT and Art 4 (2), Sino-Greece BIT.

[138] Bergman, Mark S, 'Bilateral Investment Protection Treaties: An Examination of the Evolution and Significance of the U.S. Prototype Treaty', (1983) *New York University Journal of International Law and Politics* Fall, at 32. See also Dolzer and Stevens, above, note 2, at 110.

the expropriation.[139] It also requires the host country to make appropriate preparation for the compensation and its payment before conducting expropriation.[140]

It must be stated that there is a significant gap between Chinese and EU countries on the understanding of the scope of compensable 'values', which, again, has not been dealt with by the BITs. While EU countries, like most other developed countries, think that they should include both direct damage (*damnum emergens*) and indirect losses such as 'future profit loss' (*lucrum cessance*) and 'good will',[141] Chinese scholars believe that only direct damage as reflected in the 'book value' should be compensated.[142] They particularly oppose the inclusion of 'future profit loss' and 'good will', as they could amount to numerous multiples of the 'book value', so that the damages become 'extorting' rather than fair.[143]

Because the BITs do not provide guidelines for the valuation of compensation it would be left to the discretion of the judges, probably with help from accounting experts, to decide the amount of compensation payable, taking into account all the attendant circumstances.[144]

6.3 CONCLUSION

The general or customary international law on expropriation has undergone significant changes over the last century. The 'traditional' rule of 'adequate, prompt and effective' compensation for expropriated foreign property has been continuously challenged by socialist, newly independent, and developing countries. The adoption of a series of UNGA resolutions, particularly Res 1803 and Res 3281 (the Economic Charter), has marked the emergence of new standards of international law on expropriation and compensation. This states that expropriation is an inherent right of a state and only 'appropriate compensation', taking into account all relevant circumstances, is required in the case where an expropriation takes place. The recent proliferation of BITs and other investment agreements, albeit large in number and similar in content, does not constitute a complete reversal of the 'traditional' rule but rather illustrates developments within the Economic Charter framework.

The expropriation of EU investment in China is subject both to Chinese law and EU-China BITs. Whilst Chinese law provides general principles

[139] Art 4(2), the new Sino-Germany BIT.

[140] *Ibid.*

[141] An example of this Western understanding can be found in the Restatement, above, note 14, at 208.

[142] Xu, Congli and Lin, Zhong, *Chinese Foreign Investment Law* (*Zhongguo Waizi Fa*) (Law Publishing House, 1998), at 177.

[143] Xu and Lin, *ibid*. See also Yao, above, note 117, at 393–98.

[144] In this sense, the World Bank Guidelines may prove to be rather useful to help making the valuation, as they provide both general principles and specific methods for such valuation. See *World Bank Guidelines*, Art IV 4–6.

thereon the EU-China BITs offer more detailed rules. Under Chinese law China undertakes not to expropriate foreign investment, and should expropriation have to take place under 'special circumstances' it must be conducted in the public interest, in accordance with legal procedures, and 'appropriate compensation' should also be paid.

Under EU-China BITs expropriation is broadly defined to embrace 'nationalisation', 'expropriation' and measures having equivalent effects, which suggests 'indirect expropriation', although Chinese scholars tend to hold to a narrower interpretation of the latter than Western scholars do. The EU-China BITs also require the exercise of such a right to be conditional on public purpose, due process of law, non-discrimination, and compensation.

As far as the standard of compensation is concerned most of the EU-China BITs only refer to 'compensation', whilst two of them add 'reasonable' and 'appropriate' to qualify it. None of these BITs have referred to the 'Hull Formula' of 'adequate, prompt, and effective' compensation. However the specific provisions on the amount of compensation as well as the time and forms of the payment thereof show no significant deviation from general BITs practices. A few EU-China BITs have prescribed general principles of and procedural requirements for the valuation of compensation, but none of them have mentioned any specific methods. Nevertheless a significant gap exists between Chinese and Western understanding of the scope of compensable 'values', particularly of the compensability of 'future profit loss' and 'good will'.

On the whole it can be said that the legal protection against expropriation provided by the Chinese law and the EU-China BITs is substantial but not ideal. The relevant Chinese law extends 'appropriate compensation' but fails to define this and other key concepts such as 'special circumstances' and the legal procedures concerning expropriation and compensation. Although the specific provisions in the EU-China BITs are similar to most BITs worldwide, the gap of understanding between Chinese and Western scholars on essential concepts like 'indirect expropriation', 'appropriate compensation' and the scope of compensable 'values' suggest that the interpretation of those terms is still controversial and, as such, needs further clarification.

7

Settlement of Disputes

7.1 SETTLEMENT OF INVESTMENT DISPUTES

A proper mechanism to settle investment disputes is required for the protection and promotion of foreign investment. As Steinert correctly pointed out, without a fair and effective dispute settlement mechanism, the substantive provisions of a BIT would be meaningless.[1] However, while its importance is universally accepted, the understanding of the term 'investment disputes' may vary significantly. A broad definition of this term may cover all sorts of disputes on, about or related to foreign investment, including state-state disputes, state-investor disputes and disputes between an investor and a non-state party. State-state disputes may arise when, for example, the home state of an investor exercises its right to diplomatic protection, or two contracting states of an investment treaty (eg, a BIT) disagree on the interpretation and implementation of that treaty. In turn, state-investor disputes refer to disputes between, normally, the host state and the foreign investor, over investment issues such as expropriation of property or unjust treatment.[2] The third category of investment disputes are mainly between different investment partners in a joint venture, joint exploitation or other joint investment activities.[3] In a narrow sense, 'investment disputes' only refer to state-investor disputes,[4] which are the most complex and difficult to handle,[5] as they are

[1] Steinert, Timothy A, 'If the BIT Fits: The Proposed Bilateral Investment Treaty between the United States and the People's Republic of China', (1988) 2 *Journal of Chinese Law*, at 405.

[2] YAO observed that, in practice, apart from contractual disputes, state-investor disputes mostly arise out of regulatory activities of or other political events within the host country, which have caused injuries to foreign investors. They include:

a. disputes over nationalisation and expropriation;

b. disputes over the regulatory activities by the host country, eg, forex control, tax increase or intervention to operations of the foreign investment;

c. disputes arisen out of special event of the host country such as domestic riot, revolution and war. See Yao, Meizhen, *Comparative Foreign Investment Law* (in Chinese) (Wuhan University Press, 1993).

[3] *Ibid.*

[4] Rubin, S, and Nelson, R, *International Investment Disputes: Avoidance and Settlement* (West Publishing Co., 1985), at 63–64; Dolzer, Rudolf and Stevens, Margaret, *Bilateral Investment Treaties* (Martinus Nijhoff, 1995), at 119.

[5] Yao, above, note 2, at 940.

'transnational disputes' involving a sovereign State on the one hand and a private party on the other. Among those state-investor disputes, disputes over expropriation, and in particular, the amount of compensation, are often singled out as a special category, which is frequently dealt with separately in BITs. In this book, unless other wise specified, 'investment disputes' refer to state-investor disputes only.

The settlement of investment disputes may take many forms. In the past, it is not unknown that powerful states used armed forces to protect overseas investment and to collect unpaid private loans.[6] Nowadays, however, settlement of investment disputes usually mean the peaceful means of dispute settlement. These means may include non-legal (diplomatic) means such as negotiation, mediation and conciliation, as well as legal means such as arbitration and adjudication.

On the issue of legal settlement of investment disputes, traditionally, opposing views have been held by developed and developing countries, as to whether there should be an international dimension thereon, by, in particular, resorting to an international forum applying international law. Developed countries tend to believe that investment disputes should be decided by an international court or tribunal in accordance with international law, as they involve 'international elements' and therefore may not be impartially adjudicated by domestic courts.[7] Based on 'territorial supremacy' and the 'Calvo Doctrine', developing countries, on the contrary, argue that investment disputes fall exclusively within the jurisdiction of the host country and the applicable law should be only its domestic law.[8]

The UN resolutions related to NIEO have dealt with the settlement of investment disputes, particularly disputes over compensation for expropriation. UNGA Res 1803 represents a compromise between the two groups of countries, which reads,

> 'in any case where the question of compensation gives rise to a controversy, the national jurisdiction of the state taking such measures shall be exhausted. However, upon agreement by sovereign states and other parties concerned, settlement of disputes should be made through arbitration or international adjudication…'[9]

Thus, in principle, investment disputes *shall* be settled under domestic jurisdiction. Resorting to international fora is possible only if there is an agreement between sovereign states and other parties concerned. The sentence immediately before the cited ones further provides that compensation

[6] For instance, Vandevelde has noted that, before World War I, 'Economic nationalist states, who linked the protection of their citizen's property with the national interest, proved all too willing to use military forces to collect loans,' and 'to protection foreign investment'. Vandevelde, 'Sustainable Liberalism and the International Investment Regime' (hereafter "Sustainable Liberalism"), (1998) 19 *Michigan Journal of International Law* 373, at 378–79.

[7] Xu, Congli, *The Controversial Issues in International Investment Law and China's Countermeasures* (Social Sciences in China, No. 1, 1994), at 31.

[8] *Ibid.*

[9] Art 1 (4), UNGA Res 1803.

for expropriation should be paid in accordance with both domestic law of the host country and international law. It is thus clear that Res 1803 intends to close the gap between developed and developing countries on the settlement of compensation disputes, among other issues, by combining their preferences together. However, such a combination has undoubtedly left huge ambiguity and uncertainty. The most significant ambiguity is the hierarchy in case there is a conflict between applicable domestic law and international law.

The ambiguity in Res 1803 was *clarified* (at least from the viewpoint of the vast majority of the members of the international community) in Res 3281 (the UN Economic Charter) favoured by the vast majority of the international community and rejected by the major capital exporting countries, which states,

> 'in any case where the question of compensation gives rise to a controversy, it shall be settled under domestic law of the nationalising State and by its tribunals, unless it is freely and mutually agreed by all States concerned that other peaceful means be sought on the basis of the sovereign quality of Sates and in accordance with the principle of free choice of means'.[10]

Unambiguous as it is, it does not bring an end to the controversy and the uncertainty of international law on this issue still remains, because, as mentioned in Section 6.1.3, the legal effect of this resolution has been a subject of controversies. Further, by concluding bilateral, regional and multilateral agreements on investment, capital exporting countries have built up a treaty network of investment protection, with which international arbitration becomes the most frequently used means of investment dispute settlement and international law is often referred to (*Table 18: Dispute Settlement under MRIIs*).[11] Nevertheless, for the same reasons mentioned in Section 6.1.4, the author holds that such a treaty network itself cannot be relied on as sufficient evidence of the restoration of the 'traditional' rule of customary international law; on the contrary, the proliferation of investment treaties shows that no customary international law has been genuinely established and widely accepted.

Against such a background, it is important to investigate the international and domestic laws governing EU investment in China, to establish the applicable rules for the settlement of dispute arising from such investments. In this context, again, the EU-China BITs play the most important role, whilst ICSID Convention and Chinese law are also of vital importance. Thus the next three sections deal with the dispute settlement rules contained in the three categories of laws, followed by a discussion on subrogation and investment insurance, as a special solution for investment disputes.

[10] Art 2 (2) (c), UNGA Res 3281.

[11] For a good survey of the dispute settlement provisions in these investment agreements, see Parra, A, 'Provisions on the Settlement of Investment Disputes in modern Investment Laws, Bilateral Investment treaties and Multilateral Instrument on Investment', (1997) 12 *ICSID Review—Foreign Investment Law Journal*, at 287–364.

Table 18: Dispute Settlement under MRIIs

Investment Instruments	Jurisdiction	International Arbitration				Applicable law	
		Ad hoc	Institutional			Domestic law (of the host country)	International law
			ICSID	Other institutions (selective)	Automatic State Consent		
Energy Charter Treaty (Art 26)	1. Courts or administrative tribunals; 2. Previously agreed dispute settlement procedures; and 3. International arbitration and conciliation procedures provided for in the ECT. (Art 26 (2))	A sole arbitrator or ad hoc arbitration tribunal established under the UNCITRAL Arbitration Rules.	ICSID arbitration	AISCC (Stockholm)	To ICSID Convention, New York Convention and the UNCITRAL Arbitration Rules.		This Treaty and applicable rules and principles of international law.
World Bank Guidelines (ArtV)	1. National courts; 2. Other mechanisms including conciliation and binding independent arbitration as agreed between the host and home states or between the host state and the investor.	As agreed	Encouraged to use the ICSID facilities				

NAFTA Chap. 11 (Art 1120, 1122 & 1131)		Arbitration under the UNICITRAL Arbitration Rules, as modified by this Section of NAFTA (detailed procedural rules). (Art 1120 (1))	ICSID and its Additional Facilities (Art 1120 (1))		To ICSID Convention and its Additional Facilities Rules, New York Convention and Inter-American Convention. (Art 1122 (2))	This Agreement and applicable rules of international law (Art 1131 (1))
MAI Draft (Art V D)	1. Courts or administrative tribunals of host countries; 2. Previously agreed procedures; and 3. Arbitration under MAI (Art V. D (2))	Arbitration under UNCTRAL rules. (Art V.D (2))	Under ICSID Convention or its Additional Facilities Rules (Art V.D (2))	Under ICC Rule of Arbitration	Unconditional consent to the submission of a dispute to international arbitration. Together with investors' written submission, this constitutes a written agreement required by all related arbitration procedural rules. (Art V.D (3)(a))	1. Issues concerning any general obligation under this Agreement: This Agreement, as interpreted and applied in accordance with the applicable rules of international law. (Art VD (14)) 2. Issues concerning any specific obligation under government authorisation and agreement: Rules of law as agreed by the parties to the dispute. In the absence of such agreement, such issues shall be decided according to the law of the Contracting Party, the law governing the authorisation or agreement and such rules of international law as may be applicable. (Art V.D (14))

7.2 SETTLEMENT OF INVESTMENT DISPUTES UNDER EU-CHINA BITs

Like other BITs, all the 13 EU-China BITs have provisions dealing with the settlement of investment disputes.[12] There are two categories of disputes: those between contracting parties (state-state disputes) and those between an investor and a contracting party—the host country (state-investor disputes). On state-state disputes, as shown in *Table 19: Dispute Settlement in EU-China BITs*, these EU-China BITs provide that amicable settlement (negotiation or conciliation) must be pursued for a period of six months before an arbitration application can be submitted. These BITs also describe how such tribunals are constituted. In short, these BITs are essentially identical and are similar to most BITs concluded by other countries. However, *Table 19* also shows that the provisions of state-investor dispute settlement in these BITs vary from each other. This section therefore focuses on the state-investor dispute settlement rules in the existing EU-China BITs, particularly rules on jurisdiction and applicable law.

7.2.1 Jurisdiction

7.2.1.1 Domestic or International Jurisdiction

Under most EU-China BITs, state-investor disputes are normally subject to domestic jurisdiction, while resorting to international arbitration is possible only for disputes arising out of the amount of compensation in the event of expropriation.[13] In this regard, the Sino-BLEU BIT is a good example. It stipulates that state-investor disputes should be subject to jurisdiction of the host country and should be 'amicably' settled as far as possible under the laws and regulations of the host country. However, as an exception, a dispute over the amount of compensation for expropriation, which has not been resolved within six months of notification, may be submitted by the investor to either a judicial body of the host country or an international arbitration.[14]

However, the Sino-Greece BIT, the latest one among the 13 signed in June 1992, has marked a significant step forward on this point. It no longer strictly limits disputes that can be submitted to international arbitration to those over

[12] Art 6 and the Protocol, See Sino-Sweden BIT; Art 10 and the Protocol, Sino-Germany BIT; Arts 8, 9 and the Protocol, Sino-France BIT; Art 12 and the Protocol, Sino-BLEU BIT; Art 9 and the Protocol, Sino-Finland BIT; Art 11 and Protocol, Sino-Italy BIT; Arts 8 and 9, Sino-Denmark BIT; Arts 9 and 13, Sino-Netherlands BIT; Arts 4, 10 and the Protocol, Sino-Austria BIT; Arts 7, 8 and the Exchange of Notes, Sino-Britain BIT; Arts 7 and 8, Sino-Portugal BIT; Arts 8, 9 and 12, Sino-Spain BIT; and Arts 9, 10 and 12, Sino-Greece BIT.

[13] See eg, Protocol (4) c–d, Sino-Germany BIT; Art 9 and point 4 in the Protocol, Sino-France BIT; Art 4 (4) and point 3 in the Protocol, Sino-Austria BIT; Art 8 Sino-Denmark BIT; Arts 5.4 and point 4 in the Protocol, Sino-Italy BIT.

[14] Art 10, Sino-BLEU BIT.

the 'amount of compensation', but also includes other state-investor disputes by mutual consent. The expanded scope of disputes subject to international arbitration in this BIT demonstrates China's new confidence in international arbitration and coincides with China's declared intention to submit non-amount-of-compensation issues to ICSID for arbitration.[15] In accordance with the MFN clauses in all the EU-China BITs, this should enable most EU (except Irish) investors to submit non-amount-of-compensation disputes to international arbitration.

7.2.1.2 International Arbitration and the Use of ICSID

As far as the specific form of international arbitration is concerned, most EU-China BITs only provide *ad hoc* arbitration, rather than institutional arbitration. Two BITs set forth several alternative forms of arbitration.[16] For example, in the Sino-Britain BIT concerned parties in a state-investor disputes may agree to refer to the dispute either to:

> (i) 'an international arbitrator appointed by the party to the dispute; or
> (ii) an *ad hoc* arbitration tribunal to be appointed under a special agreement between the parties to the dispute; or
> (iii) an *ad hoc* arbitration tribunal established under the Arbitration Rule of the United National Commission on International Trade Law.'[17]

In the EU-China BITs, ICSID mechanism has been mentioned in various ways. Firstly, most (8 of 13) BITs refer to ICSID procedures as the arbitration procedures to be used by the *ad hoc* arbitration tribunal[18] (*Table 19*). Secondly, some earlier EU-China BITs require that contracting parties negotiate a supplementary agreement on the use of ICSID arbitration, in case China becomes a member of the ICSID Convention.[19] A third approach was adopted in some EU-China BITs after China signed the ICSID Convention in February 1990, namely the Sino-Spain and Sino-Greece BITs.[20] Under these two BITs, direct submission to ICSID for arbitration of state-investor disputes became legally possible, when China formally became a member of the ICSID Convention, which took place in February 1993 when the Convention came

[15] Mu, Zili, *Chinese Government is to enact regulations to implement obligations under the ICSID Convention*, Arbitration and Law Communication (Published by the Chinese International Economic and Trade arbitration Commission-CIETAC), No. 1 1997, at 3.
[16] See Art 8, 9, the Sino-Spain BIT; Art 7 (2), Sino-Britain BIT.
[17] Art 7(2), Sino-Britain BIT.
[18] See Art 10 and the Protocol, Sino-Germany BIT; Art 12 and the Protocol, Sino-BLEU BIT; Art 9 and the Protocol, Sino-Finland BIT; Art 11 and Protocol, Sino-Italy BIT; Arts 8 and 9, Sino-Denmark BIT; Arts 9 and 13, Sino-Netherlands BIT; Arts 4, 10 and the Protocol, Sino-Austria BIT; Arts 7 and 8, Sino-Portugal BIT; and Arts 8, 9 and 12, Sino-Spain BIT.
[19] See the Protocol, Sino-Sweden BIT; the Exchange of Notes dated May 30, 1984, Sino-France BIT; and the Exchange of Notes No. 1 and 2, Sino-Britain BIT.
[20] Art 9 (2), Sino-Spain BIT; Art 10 (1) and (4), Sino-Greece BIT.

Table 19: Dispute Settlement under EU-China BITs

Investment Instruments	State-state disputes: Negotiation/ consultation + ad hoc int'l arbitration	State-Investor disputes							Future supplementary agreement on ICSID arbitration
		Jurisdiction				Applicable law			
		Exclusive domestic jurisdiction	International Arbitration			Domestic law (of the host country)	Provisions of the present Agreement	(Generally accepted) Principles of international law adopted by both parties	
			Ad hoc		Submission to ICSID arbitration				
			No reference to ICSID procedures	Reference to ICSID procedures					
Sino-Sweden BIT (Art 6, 7 and Protocol)	1	0	0	0	0	0	0	0	1
Sino-Germany BIT (Art 10 & Protocol 4.c–d)	1	1 (except cases on amount of compensation—AoC)	0	1 (AoC)	0	0	0	0	0
Sino-France BIT (Art 8, 9, Annex 4 and Ex Lett)	1	1 (except AoC)	1 (AoC)	0	0	0	0	0	1
Sino-BLEU BIT (Art 10,12 and Protocol 6.3)	1	1 (except AoC)	0	1(AoC)	0	1	1	1	0
Sino-Finland BIT (Art 9 & Prot Art 2)	1	1 (except AoC)	0	1(AoC)	0	0	0	0	0

Sino-Italy BIT (Art 11 and Prot 4)	1	1 (except AoC)	0	1(AoC)	0	1	1	1	0
Sino-Denmark BIT (Art 9 & 8)	1	1 (except AoC)	0	1(AoC)	0	0	0	0	0
Sino-Netherlands BIT (Art 13 & 9 (1–3) & Prot 3)	1	1 (except AoC)	0	1(AoC)	0	1	1	1	0
Sino-Austria BIT (Art 10, 4. (4–5) & Prot 3)	1	1 (except AoC)	0	1(AoC)	0	0	0	0	0
Sino-Britain BIT (Art 8, 7 & Ex of Notes Nos 1–2)	1	1 (except AoC)	1(AoC)	0	0	0	0	0	1
Sino-Portugal BIT (Art 7 & 8)	1	1 (except AoC)	0	1(AoC)	0	1	1	1	0
Sino-Spain BIT (Art 8, 9 (1–3) & 12)	1	1 (except AoC)	0	1(AoC)	1 (in case both parties become ICSID members)	0	0	0	0
Sino-Greece BIT (Art 9, 10 (1–4) & 12)	1	1 (except AoC and other disputes with mutual consent)	1 (AoC and other disputes with mutual consent)	0	1 (in case both parties become ICSID members)	0	0	0	0
Total (13)	13	12	3	9	2	4	4	4	3

into force in China. Whilst the Sino-Spain BIT still limits the disputes submitted to ICSID arbitration to those concerning the amount of compensation, the Sino-Greece BIT extends it to cover all 'disputes between an investor of a Contracting Party and the other Contracting Party concerning an obligation of the latter under this Agreement, in relation to an investment of the former'.[21] Nevertheless, state consent is still required for any ICSID arbitration to be initiated, in accordance with these two BITs.[22]

However, such special state consent requirement has been removed in some recent Chinese BITs. For instance, the Sino-Morocco BIT signed in 1995 provides that an investor may choose to submit a state-investor dispute either to a competent domestic court or to the ICSID for arbitration.[23] Both Contracting Parties thereby give irrevocable consent on the submission of disputes concerning the amount of compensation to the ICSID arbitration. Mutual consent from parties concerned, nevertheless, should still be sought if other disputes are to be submitted to the ICSID arbitration.[24] Similar provisions can also be found in the Sino-Israel BIT.[25] Again, with the MFN clauses in the EU-China BITs, most EU (except Irish) investors may choose to submit to ICSID arbitration, without the need to seek China's written consent.

The preceding survey on jurisdiction clauses in the EU-China BITs shows that, on the one hand, local remedies are still the default remedies for most investment disputes, as only disputes over the amount of compensation could be automatically submitted to an international forum. On the other hand, however, a shift in attitude of China in accepting international jurisdiction in general and ICSID arbitration in particular in its BIT practice, has taken place since the early 1990s. Before China signed the ICSID Convention in 1990, only disputes on the amount of compensation could be submitted to an international forum (normally an *ad hoc* arbitration tribunal, rather than an international institution such as the ICSID), which was subject to mutual consent by the parties concerned. After 1990, and especially after 1993 when China ratified the ICSID Convention, all state-investor disputes may be submitted to an international forum. Disputes over the amount of compensation can now be 'automatically' submitted to the ICSID, ie, without the need to seek specific consent from the parties concerned. Referral of other state-investor disputes to ICSID arbitration is also possible, but subject to agreement by the parties concerned. The recent developments in Sino-foreign BITs

[21] *Ibid.*

[22] The Sino-Greece BIT provides that, in case both contracting parties become member of the ICSID Convention, state-investor disputes may be submitted to ICSID for conciliation or arbitration 'by mutual consent'. Similarly, the Sino-Spain BIT provides that an investor and the host country 'may agree' to refer the disputes to, among other fora, the ICSID, in case both contracting parties become member of the ICSID Convention. See Art 10 (4), Sino-Greece BIT; Art 9(2), Sino-Spain BIT.

[23] Art 10 (2), Sino-Morocco BIT.

[24] *Ibid.*

[25] Art 8 (1), Sino-Israel BIT. However, the Sino-Israel BIT does not mention that other disputes can be submitted with mutual consent.

also show that all EU-China BITs are now outdated, particularly in their dispute settlement provisions.

The 2003 Sino-Germany BIT, however, has marked another significant step forward. According to this new BIT, 'any dispute arising out of investment' can be submitted, at the foreign investors' request, to the ICSID for arbitration, if the dispute cannot resolved within six months by amicable consultation.[26] Dispute may also be submitted to *ad hoc* arbitration set up in accordance with the UNCITRAL Arbitration Rules or other arbitration rules.[27] The Protocol to the BIT, nevertheless, adds a further limitation on the submission of investment disputes for arbitration by German investors in China. The Protocol requires that German investors in China first submit the disputes for administrative reconsideration procedures before they submit it for international arbitration.[28] They may not submit the case for international arbitration unless the dispute still exists after three months since they submitted for administrative reconsideration procedure.[29] The Protocol also requires them to withdraw the case from the Chinese court if they have submitted it to a Chinese court, before they submit it for international arbitration.[30] Despite such 'exhaustion of local remedies' requirement in the Protocol, the new Sino-Germany BIT signals a significant progress in China's acceptance of international arbitration, as it has made it possible for all investment disputes to be automatically submitted for international arbitration.

7.2.2 Applicable Law

The issue of applicable law governing state-investor disputes is closely linked to the issue of jurisdiction. As a matter of fact, domestic courts tend to apply municipal laws, while international arbitration tribunals tend to apply international principles and rules. In this context, given that EU-China BITs have established that state-investor disputes should be, in general, subject to domestic jurisdiction, it can be argued that municipal law should be the governing law of such disputes unless applicable international agreements provide otherwise.

As shown in *Table 19*, most EU-China BITs do not specifically stipulate the applicable law of investment disputes, which may imply that domestic law should apply (and of course the applicable BIT). Four of these BITs clearly provide that these disputes should be governed by the domestic law of the host country, provisions of the present BIT and (generally accepted) princi-

[26] Art 9.1–3, the new Sino-Germany BIT.
[27] Art 9.3, the new Sino-Germany BIT.
[28] Point 6 (re: Art 9), Protocol to the new Sino-Germany BIT.
[29] *Ibid.*
[30] *Ibid.*

ples of international law *adopted by both parties*.[31] The qualifying phrase of 'adopted by both parties' before 'general principles of international law' clearly shows that 'traditional' rules of international law, the making of which China had not participated in, would not be applied. Nevertheless it may indicate that rules and principles adopted in other international agreements, to which both parties are contracting parties, are also applicable.[32]

However, recent Chinese BITs have moved further on the applicability of general international law. For example, the Sino-Morocco BIT signed in 1995 provides that the international arbitration tribunal should make its decision in accordance with the domestic law of the host country, the present Agreement, provisions of the special agreement for the investment and 'principles of international law'.[33] This development can be of great significance, as it shows that China has become more confident in and more willing to accept general international law. However, it is still unclear what 'principles of international law' it refers to. Nevertheless, through the 'multiplying effect' of the MFN clause in EU-China BITs, general 'principles of international law' should now be applicable to investment dispute between China and non-Irish EU investors.

This recent development also demonstrates that the existing EU-China BITs need to be updated. Interestingly, the new Sino-Germany BITs does not provide for the applicable law to state-investor disputes. This may be partly explained by the facts that it prefers ICSID arbitration and the ICSID Convention has already contained a rather liberal rule on the applicable law.

7.2.3 Summary

The EU-China BITs have witnessed the impact that China's accession to the ICSID Convention has brought about on the settlement of investment disputes. Before 1990, when China signed the ICSID Convention, only disputes about the amount of compensation may have been submitted to an ad hoc international tribunal, which was subject to mutual consent of the parties concerned. Since 1990, the restrictions have been gradually eliminated. Now, disputes over the amount of compensation may be submitted to the ICSID without the need to seek the consent of the parties concerned. Other investment disputes may also be submitted to the ICSID and other international fora, with agreement of parties concerned, ie, both the Chinese government and the foreign investors. In other words, investment disputes on issues other than amount of compensation are, in principle, dealt with by Chinese courts

[31] See Art 12 and the Protocol, Sino-BLEU BIT; Art 11 and Protocol, Sino-Italy BIT; Arts 9 and 13, Sino-Netherlands BIT; Arts 7 and 8, Sino-Portugal BIT.

[32] For instance, if a multilateral investment agreement (MIA) is to be signed by both China and the EU, among other countries, the rules and principles established in this MIA may be applicable as well.

and tribunals. The provisions on the applicable law have also been under change since the early 1990s. Now state-investor disputes are not only governed by the domestic law of the host country and provisions of the present BIT, but also governed by general principles of international law. The preceding investigations also show that all the existing EU-China BITs have become outdated, particularly in their dispute settlement provisions. As a result, the new Sino-Germany BIT has not only updated the dispute settlement provision of the current Sino-Germany BIT, but also made a breakthrough in that it make it possible for all state-investors disputes to be automatically submitted for international arbitration, preferably the ICSID arbitration. However, it is yet to be ratified and therefore uncertain whether or when it may enter into force.

7.3 SETTLEMENT OF INVESTMENT DISPUTES UNDER THE ICSID CONVENTION

As said in Chapter 3 Section 3.2.2.1, the ICSID Convention is an important multilateral legal instrument for EU investment in China since both China and all EU Member States are its signatories (*Table 7)* and, as mentioned above, most EU-China BITs referred to ICSID arbitration.

It should be noted that the International Centre for the Settlement Investment Disputes between States and Nationals of other States (hereinafter the ICSID or the Centre) established by the ICSID Convention does not engage in conciliation or arbitration by itself but provides facilities the Conciliation Commissions (CCs) or Arbitration Tribunals (ATs) constituted according to the Convention. The Centre thus maintains two panels: one for conciliators and one for arbitrators. Contracting States and the Chairman have overall responsibility for the designation of the two panels of conciliators and arbitrators.[34] Moreover, ICSID awards are binding and final. They are not subject to any appeal or to any other remedy except as provided for in the Convention.[35] Every Contracting State must recognise an ICSID award in its courts as if it were a final judgement of that State.[36]

A comprehensive study on the ICSID Convention is beyond the scale of

[33] Art 10 (4), Sino-Morocco BIT.

[34] Each Contracting State may designate 4 Conciliators and 4 arbitrators to the Panels, while the Chairman can designate 10 to each panels. See Art 13, the ICSID Convention. All EU member states have designated conciliators and arbitrators to the ICSID. In 1993, China decided to designate 4 conciliators and arbitrators to the Centre. However, for some reason the process has not been finalised and no Chinese conciliators or arbitrators have appeared in the two Panels yet. For details, see http://www.worldbank.org/icsid/pubs/icsid-10/icsid-10.htm (visited on 10 August 2002). Chen, An, *International Investment Disputes Arbitration—A Study on the ICSID Mechanism* (hereinafter "*ICSID Mechanism*") (Fudan University Press, 2001), at 70. Professor Chen was among the list of arbitrators designated by the Chinese Governments.

[35] Art 53 (1), ICSID Convention.

[36] *Ibid*, Art 53(1), 54 (1).

this book. Rather, it will focus on two of the most important elements of ICSID mechanism, namely its jurisdiction and applicable law.

7.3.1 Jurisdiction[37]

The most important breakthrough that the ICSID has made lies in its jurisdiction provisions, which make it possible for an international institution to conciliate and arbitrate state-investor disputes that were previously almost exclusively reserved to domestic courts.[38] According to Article 25 (1) of the ICSID Convention,

> 'The jurisdiction of the Centre shall extend to any legal disputes arising directly out of an investment, between a Contracting State (or any constituent subdivision or agency of a Contracting State designated to the Centre by that State) and a national of another Contracting State, which the parties to the dispute consent in writing to submit to the Centre. When the parties have given their consent, no party may withdraw its consent unilaterally.'

Therefore, four conditions must be satisfied before the Centre can assume jurisdiction over a dispute.

Firstly, the dispute must involve a Contracting State and a national of another Contracting State. In other words, both the host and home states of an investor must have signed and ratified the Convention.[39] This limitation is in keeping with the purpose of the creation of the Centre, as a new international forum for handling exclusively state-investor disputes, rather than state-state or private-private disputes that have already been dealt with by existing international courts and arbitration tribunals. The 'Contracting State' here includes 'any constituent subdivision or agency of a Contracting State designated to the Centre by that State', the consent of which shall

[37] As noted by Broches, the term 'jurisdiction' here is open to objection, on the ground that the Centre is not a court but an administrative organ under whose auspices conciliation commission and arbitration tribunal may be established and proceedings conducted. However, he argues that precedent of this kind of usage could be found in the Hague Convention for the Pacific Settlement of International Disputes of 1907 which created the Permanent Court of Arbitration, an administrative framework to facilitate arbitration proceedings. See Broches, Aron, *The Convention on the Settlement of Investment Disputes: Some Observations on Jurisdiction,* in Broches, Aron, *Selected Essays: World Bank, ICSID, and Other Subjects of Public and Private International Law* (Martinus Nijhoff Publishers, 1995), at 166.

[38] Sir Elihu Lauterpacht observed that the ICSID Convention represented 'striking and significant' developments in international law, as it 'put an end to myth, so prevalent until the end of the Second World War, that only States are subjects of international law and that individuals cannot possess rights or bear duties under international law.' Lauterpacht, Sir Elihu, 'International Law and Private Foreign Investment', (1996) 4 *Global Legal Studies Journal* 257, at 274.

[39] In 1978 the Centre added an 'Additional Facility', which allowed recourse to the main Centre mechanism even if only one party met the requirement, provided that both parties had so agreed. See Lauterpacht, Sir Elihu, *Foreword*, in Schreuer, Christoph H, *The ICSID Convention: A Commentary* (Cambridge University Press, 2001), at xi.

be subject to the approval of that state until the State notifies otherwise.[40] 'National of another Contracting State' could be a natural person or a juridical person having the nationality of a Contracting State other than the Contracting State party, on the date on which the parties consented to submit the dispute to the Centre.[41] In addition, a juridical person possessing the nationality of the Contracting State party can be qualified as a 'national of another Contracting State' if the parties agree to this on the grounds of foreign control.[42]

As a result, all EU investors in China, regardless of whether they are natural persons or juridical persons, are 'nationals of another Contracting State' under the Convention and can make use of the ICSID regime to settle their investment disputes with the Chinese Government. Furthermore, foreign invested enterprises (FIEs) controlled by these EU investors may also be treated as 'nationals of another contracting state' and may therefore be able to make use of the Centre mechanism, provided that both the FIE and the Chinese Government so agree.[43]

Secondly, the dispute must 'arise directly out of an investment'. There is no definition on 'investment' within the ICSID regime. During the negotiations, several definitions of 'investment' were considered and rejected.[44] It was accepted in the end that a definition could be dispensed with 'given the essential requirement of consent by the parties.' [45] In other words, the requirement that investment disputes must arise out of 'investment' can be inferred by a party's consent. Thus, the parties' agreement that a dispute is an 'investment dispute' will be given great weight in establishing the Centre's jurisdiction over a particular case, even though it might not be controlling.[46]

Thirdly, the dispute must be a 'legal dispute'.[47] Again, there is no definition of 'legal dispute' in the Convention. According to the Executive Report, the term 'legal dispute' indicates that while conflicts of rights would fall within the Centre's jurisdiction, mere conflicts of interests would not. Furthermore, 'the dispute must concern the existence or scope of a legal right or obligation, or the nature or extent of the reparation to be made for breach of a legal obligation'.[48]

[40] Art 25 (3), the ICSID Convention.

[41] *Ibid*, Art 25 (2). Broches believes that on this point, the parties should be given the widest possible latitude to agree on the meaning of 'nationality' and that any stipulation of nationality made in connection with a conciliation or arbitration clause which is based on a reasonable criterion should be accepted. Broches, above, note 37, at 207.

[42] *Ibid.*

[43] According to Chinese FDI laws, most FIEs are 'Chinese legal persons' and therefore are not *per se* 'national of another contracting state'.

[44] Broches, above, note 37, at 168.

[45] See *Report of the Executive Directors on the Convention on the Settlement of Investment Disputes between States and Nationals of Other States* (*Executive Report*), ICSID Doc 2, March 18, 1965, at para 27.

[46] Broches, above, note 37, at 168.

[47] Executive Report, above, note 45, at para 26.

[48] *Ibid.*

Finally and most importantly, both parties to the dispute must agree to submit the dispute to the Centre for conciliation or arbitration. 'Consent' is regarded as the 'cornerstone' of the jurisdiction of the Centre, which must be given by both parties and in writing.[49] As for the manner in which the consent may be given, the Executive Report offers a broad interpretation:

> 'Consent may be given, for example, in a clause included in an investment agreement, providing for the submission to the Centre of future disputes arising out of that agreement, or in a compromise regarding a dispute which has already arisen. Nor does the Convention require that the consent of both parties be expressed in a single instrument. Thus, a host State might in its promotion legislation offer to submit disputes arising out of certain classes of investments to the jurisdiction of the Centre, and the investor might give his consent by accepting the offer in writing.'[50]

Moreover, Article 25 (4) of the Convention provides that a Contracting State may, when or after ratifying, accepting or approving the Convention, notify the Centre of the class or classes of disputes that it would or would not consider submitting to the jurisdiction of the Centre, though such notification shall not constitute 'consent', as required by the Convention.[51]

On acceding to the Convention, China declared that, in accordance with Article 25 (4), the Chinese government agreed only to refer disputes about the amount of compensation arising from expropriation or nationalisation.[52] However, China is considering expanding the scope of disputes to be referred and is enacting the implementation of regulations for the Convention.[53] In some newly-signed BITs, China has agreed to refer to the Centre disputes other than those on the amount of compensation for expropriations, if both parties to the dispute so agree.[54] It can be argued that, according to the Most Favoured Nation (MFN) clause of the BITs between China and EU member states, EU investors shall also be able to refer non-compensation issues to the ICSID, if they obtain consent from the Chinese Government.

It may be worth mentioning here that the Convention also indicates that Conciliation Commissions and Arbitration Tribunals shall be the judges of their own competence. Hence, if a case is brought before them, they can decide, inter alia, whether the specific dispute falls within the jurisdiction of the Centre. ICSID jurisdiction is exclusive, ie, parties' consent to its jurisdiction excludes any other remedy, unless otherwise agreed to by the parties.[55] However, a Contracting State may require the exhaustion of local administra-

[49] Executive Report, *ibid*, para 23.

[50] *Ibid*, at para 24. However, it is unclear, in the third case, when the investor shall give the acceptance and in what form. For further discussion on this issue see Broches, above, note 37, at 168–74.

[51] Art 25 (4), the ICSID Convention.

[52] Mu, above, note 15, at 3–4.

[53] *Ibid.*

[54] See eg, Art 9 (3) of Sino-Korea BIT and Art 10 (2) of Sino-Morocco BIT.

[55] Art 26, the ICSID Convention.

tive and judicial remedies as a precondition of its consent to ICSID arbitration.[56] It may also provide for diplomatic protection or bring an international claim in respect of such a dispute when another Contracting State has failed to abide by and comply with the award rendered therein.[57]

7.3.2 Applicable Law

The provisions of applicable law[58] in the ICSID Convention are also distinctive. Article 42 (1) of the Convention provides,

> 'The tribunal shall decide a dispute in accordance with such rules of law as may be agreed by the parties. In the absence of such agreement, the Tribunal shall apply the law of the Contracting State party to the dispute (including its rules on the conflict of law) and such rules of international law as may be applicable.'

This core provision on applicable law has two features. On the one hand, it allows parties to choose the governing 'rules of law' rather than 'the law'. This may mean, according to Shihata and Parra, that the parties can submit different issues to rules of different legal systems, to submit disputes to rules common to more than one legal systems, to combine national and international legal systems, and to submit to laws of a nationalised system frozen on a set date.[59] On the other hand, if the parties fail to choose the applicable rules of law, the Convention requires the arbitration tribunal to apply 'the law of the Contracting State party to the dispute (including its rules on conflict of laws) and such rules of international law as may be applicable'.[60] Thus both domestic and international laws are applicable. Although this provision was regarded as a 'considerate balance of interests between investors and host countries', it does not make clear the relationship between applicable domestic law and international law.[61] Some Western commentators believe that international law supplements domestic law of the host country, whilst others

[56] *Ibid.*

[57] *Ibid*, Art 27.

[58] The term 'applicable law' should include both procedural law and substantive law as applicable. However, in this book, it means only applicable 'substantive law'. As for applicable procedural law, the Convention basically provides that it shall be autonomous. To be precise, unless the parties agree otherwise, the Conciliation Commission or the Arbitration Tribunal shall apply procedural rules of the Convention and the effective Conciliation Rules and the Arbitration Rules adopted by the Centre and shall decide the questions that are not covered by these rules mentioned. See Arts 33 and 44, the ICSID Convention.

[59] Shihata, IFI and Parra, A, 'Applicable Substantive Law in Disputes between States and Private Foreign Parties: The case of Arbitration under the ICSID Convention', (1994) 9 *ICSID Review—Foreign Investment Law Journal* at 189. Although agreeing on this literal interpretation, at least one Chinese commentator writes that, for the sake of clarifying the rights and duties of parties involved, host country's law should be selected. Chen, An, *ICSID Mechanism*, above, note 34, at 133.

[60] Art 42 (1), the ICSID Convention.

[61] See Zeng, Huaqun, *International Investment Law* (*Guoji Touzi Faxue*) (Peking University Press, 1999), at 604–08.

argue that international law not only fills the gaps left by domestic law, but also takes precedence over domestic law where the two are in conflict.[62] Chinese scholars, in general, tend to support that view that international law should play a supplementary rather than a supervisory or overwhelming role and the definition of 'international law' should be limited to those accepted by the host country.[63] In practice, it seems that in most ICSID cases arbitrators tend to apply international law and stress its precedence over national law.[64]

In Article 42 (2), the Convention also ruled out the possibility of the tribunal bringing a finding of *non liquet* on the grounds of silence or the obscurity of the law.[65] Broches believes that this reflects the view that existing international law provides international judges or arbitrators with sufficient elements for a legal resolution of disputes, contrary to earlier positivist opinions purporting to argue that the international legal order was incomplete. Leading Chinese scholars also consider this provision reasonable in both legal and economic terms.[66]

Finally, in Paragraph 3 of Article 42, the Convention empowers the tribunals to decide a dispute *ex aequo et bono* if the parties so agree.[67] This is held as, in the words of O'Connell, 'an authorisation to decide without reference to the rules of law'.[68] However, as Hudson commented on the same provisions in the Statute of the Permanent Court of Justice (PCIJ),

> 'It cannot act capriciously and arbitrarily...It must proceed upon objective consideration of what is fair and just...The tribunal cannot be justified in reaching a result which could not be explained on reasonable grounds.'[69]

In ICSID cases, the power to decide *ex aequo et bono* is based on the agreement of the parties, and quite often, the tribunal will still take into account

[62] For example, Broches thinks that international law applies when: a. domestic law so requires; b. the issue is governed by international law, and c. domestic law or actions violate international law. Shihata believes that here domestic law of host country should be applied, supplemented by international law. Sir Elihu Lauterpacht wrote, however, that here international law should be applied at all times. See eg, Broches, above, note 37, at 228–30; Lauterpacht, Sir Elihu, 'The World Bank Convention on International Dispute Settlement', in *Recueil d'etudes de droit international en hommage a Paul Guggenheim*, at 642, 660–61 (Geneva, 1968); Shihata, in *News from ICSID*, 1985 Winter, at 2.

[63] For Chinese views, see, Chen, An, *ICSID Mechanism*, above, note 34, at particularly 156, 159, 160.

[64] However, it is argued by some Chinese scholars that ICSID arbitration is dominated by western ideas since most arbitrators are from developed (capital exporting) countries, and the President of the Administrative Council tend to designate western scholars as Chairmen of arbitration tribunals and *ad hoc* committee members who could annul the awards. See Zeng, Huaqun, above, note 61, at 604–08. See also Chen, An, *Commentary on the ICSID Convention* (in Chinese) (Lujiang Press, 1989), at 125–26.

[65] Art 42 (2), the ICSID Convention.

[66] Zeng, above, note 61, at 608–09.

[67] Art 42 (3), the ICSID Convention.

[68] O'Connell, Manley Ottmer, *International Law* (London: Stevens, 1970), at 14.

[69] Hudson, *The Permanent Court of International Justice (1920–1942)*, (New York: Macmillan, 1943), at 620.

laws that might have been applicable. Issues that are decided purely *ex aequo et bono* are normally only issues about the evaluation of compensation for expropriation.[70]

In the context of EU investment in China, therefore, the applicable law of an investment dispute referred to the Centre could be chosen by the parties by agreement, but if no agreement is reached, the tribunals may decide such disputes in accordance with both Chinese law and applicable rules of international law. If both parties agree, the tribunals may also give awards *ex aequo et bono*.

7.3.3 Summary

Further to the EU-China BITs, the ICSID Convention provides for detailed rules under which the EU investors may refer a dispute it may have with the Chinese government to the ICSID for arbitration. The Centre exercises its jurisdiction if four conditions exist: that the dispute must be a state-investor dispute; that it must arise out of 'investment'; that it must be about a 'legal' issue and that the State involved must have given its consent to such arbitration. In case of disputes between China and most (except Irish) EU investors, because of the existing EU-China BITs, it is understood that automatic consent has been given by the Chinese Government on the submission of disputes about the amount of compensation to the ICSID arbitration. Nevertheless, special consent by China will still be required for referring other investment disputes to the Centre. The rules on applicable law in the ICSID convention have proved to be rather liberal and distinctive. Under the ICSID Convention, parties to a dispute are allowed to choose the applicable *rules of law*, which suggest a wider interpretation than the law of a given jurisdiction. In case no such agreement exists, the arbitration or conciliation tribunal may apply both domestic law of the host country and applicable rules of international law. Furthermore, if the parties agree, the tribunal may decide a dispute *ex aequo et bono*, which may imply an authorisation to decide without reference to the rules of law. These rules on jurisdiction and applicable law in the ICSID Convention, therefore, further strengthens the principles set forth in the EU-China BITs.

7.4 SETTLEMENT OF INVESTMENT DISPUTES UNDER CHINESE LAW

Chinese law regarding dispute settlement, particularly its administrative procedures, plays a very important role in settling the investment disputes

[70] Zeng, Huaqun, above, note 61, at 611.

between the EU investors and the Chinese authorities, as the EU-China BITs leave most investment disputes to be, by default, decided by domestic courts or tribunals. Normally, in China, state-investor disputes are handled through administrative channels, for instance, by complaining to the authority at a higher level for reconsideration (Fuyi) or by bringing an administrative law suit. It might also be possible to submit a state-investor case to a Chinese arbitration tribunal, including the China International Economic and Trade Arbitration Commission (CIETAC), China's most prominent international arbitration authority. As mentioned above, recent BITs including the new Sino-Germany BIT require that foreign investors exhaust the local administrative reconsideration (review) procedures before they can be submitted for international arbitration.[71] Also, if a foreign investor has submitted a dispute to a local court, the foreign investor must withdraw from such court procedures before he/she submit it to international arbitration.[72] If the local court procedures have been completed and a final ruling has been made, then the investor cannot resort to international arbitration.[73]

7.4.1 Administrative Reconsideration and Litigation

Since 1989, the promulgation of the Administrative Procedures Law (APL) has made it possible for all citizens, juridical persons and other organisations to bring an action before a court against 'specific administrative acts' by administrative authorities. Such actions are rather broadly defined, to cover all 'specific' regulatory activities by the government authorities on foreign investment. They are:

(1) An administrative sanction, such as detention, fine, rescission of a licence or permit, order to suspend production or business or confiscation of property, which one refuses to accept;
(2) A compulsory administrative measure, such as restricting freedom of the person or the sealing up, seizing or freezing of property, which one refuses to accept;
(3) Infringement upon one's managerial autonomy as defined by the law;
(4) Refusal by an administrative organ to issue a permit or licence, which one considers oneself legally qualified to apply for, or its failure to respond to the application;
(5) Refusal by an administrative organ to perform its statutory duty of pro-

[71] Point 6 (re: Art9), Protocol to the new Sino-Germany BIT. Similar provision can been found in other recent BITs, such as Art 9, Sino-Cote d'Ivore BIT; Art 8, Sino-Bosnia Herzegovina BIT; Art 9, Sino-Benin BIT; Art 9, Sino-Latvia BIT and Art 9, Sino-Guyana BIT.
[72] *Ibid.*
[73] *Ibid.*

tecting one's rights of person and of property as one has applied for, or its failure to respond to the application;

(6) Cases where an administrative organ is considered to have failed to issue a pension according to the law;

(7) Cases where an administrative organ is considered to have illegally demanded the performance of duties; and

(8) Cases where an administrative organ is considered to have infringed upon other rights of the person and of property.[74]

Likewise, the Administrative Reconsideration Law of 1999 (formerly the Administrative Reconsideration Regulations of 1990 which was modified in 1994) enables citizens, legal persons and other organizations to resort to higher administrative authorities to review any specific administrative acts conducted by administrative authorities. Unless stipulated otherwise by the law, the citizen, legal person or organization concerned may challenge the decision made by the reconsideration authority and bring an administrative lawsuit to a Chinese court of law. A longer list that that in the Administrative Procedure Law is provided to define the scope of application of this law, including the following acts:

(1) an administrative sanction, such as warning, fine, confiscation of illegal gains or property, order to suspend production or business, suspension or rescission of license or permit, administrative attachment, which one refuses to accept;

(2) a compulsory administrative measure, such as restriction of personal freedom or the sealing up, seizing or freezing of property, which one refuses to accept;

(3) an administrative decision of altering, suspending or discharging certificates, such as a license, permit, credit certificate, credential, which one refuses to accept;

(4) an administrative decision of confirming ownership or right to use of natural resources, such as land, mineral resources, rivers, forests, mountains, grasslands, unreclaimed land, beaches, maritime waters, which one refuses to accept;

(5) infringement upon one's managerial decision-making power, which, one holds,has been perpetrated by an administrative organ;

(6) cases where an administrative organ, which has altered and nullified one's agricultural contract, is considered to have infringed upon one's rights and interests;

(7) cases where an administrative organ is considered to have illegally raised funds, levied property, apportioned charge, or demanded the performance of duties;

[74] Art 11, the Administrative Procedures Law.

(8) cases where an administrative organ is considered to have illegally handled issuing a certificate, such as a permit, license, credit certificate, or credential, or examining and approving or registering relative items, which one considers oneself legally qualified to apply for;
(9) cases where an administrative organ is considered to have failed to perform its statutory duty, according to law, of protecting one's rights of the person and of property, and one's rights to receive education, as one has applied for;
(10) cases where an administrative organ is considered to have failed to issue a pension, social insurance money or minimum maintenance fee for living according to law; and
(11) cases in which other specific administrative acts of an administrative organ are considered to have infringed upon other lawful rights and interests.[75]

However, *abstract administrative acts* such as administrative regulations, rules, or decisions and orders with general binding force formulated by administrative organs, are not subject to administrative proceedings. Although China undertakes, in its admission Protocol to the WTO, to allow individuals and entities to 'bring to the attention of the national level' cases of non-uniform application of the trade regime, and to maintain judicial review of 'all administrative actions' related to the implementation of laws, regulations, judicial decisions and administrative rulings of general application referred to in GATT, GATS and TRIPs Agreement,[76] it has been confirmed by the Supreme Court that, in international trade area, that still only '*specific administrative acts*' are allowed be challenged by individuals.[77] Further, in accordance with the APL, if these specific administrative acts have caused damages, the injured person may claim compensation.[78] The State Compensation Law was formulated in 1994 to deal with claims of damages.

Since most FIEs are incorporated as 'Chinese juridical persons', they are all entitled to resort to such administrative remedies. Even foreigners, stateless persons and foreign organisations are also entitled to the same rights and obligations as Chinese citizens and organisations in terms of administrative procedural rights.[79] Thus branches or representative offices of foreign business entities may also use such remedies.

[75] Art 6, Administrative Reconsideration Law of the People's Republic of China (Adopted at the Ninth Meeting of the Standing Committee of the Ninth National People's Congress on April 29, 1999, promulgated by Order No.16 of the President of the People's Republic of China on April 29, 1999, and effective as of October 1, 1999.).

[76] WTO: Protocol on the Accession of the People's Republic of China (*China Accession Protocol*), Section 2 (A) 4 and (D) 1.

[77] Art 3, the Trade Cases Provisions, promulgated on 27 August 2002, by the Supreme Court of China.

[78] Art 12, the Administrative Procedures Law.

[79] Art 70, the Administrative Procedures Law.

7.4.2 Recent Cases

It seems, however, that FIEs have rarely used such administrative remedies until recently when some disputes between foreign investors and local governments surfaced. A best example is the *Changchun Huijin (CWC) Case*, which is reportedly the first litigation case between an FIE and a local government.[80] This case involved a contractual joint venture (CJV) and the People's Government of Changchun City (the Changchun Government), the capital city of Jiling Province in northern China. The CJV involved was the Changchun Huijin Wastewater Treatment Ltd (hereinafter referred to as 'Changchun Huijin'), a CJV between Changchun Drainage Company (a local company) and the China Water Company Ltd (CWC, a Hong Kong based company in which the British Thames Water International holds nearly fifty per cent of shares).[81] Established in March 2000, Changchun Huijin was allegedly the first wastewater treatment project involving foreign investment in China.[82] The main purposes of this CJV were to build a wastewater treatment plant capable of treating 390,000 tonnes of municipal sewage per day.[83]

This CJV project initially received strong backing from the Changchun Government, so such so that the latter lay down a special local regulation in July 2000 to deal with its establishment and operation.[84] The local regulation granted Changchun Huijin the exclusive right to operate and manage this wastewater treatment project,[85] a public utility project that was normally only allowed to be run by a state-owned enterprise. The local regulation also stipulated the capital contribution and management structure of Changchun Huijin. According to the local regulation, in case the Changchun Drainage Company failed to pay the wastewater treatment charges to the Changchun Huijin, the Changchun Government undertook to make such a payment. The regulation stated that it would be effective for twenty one years, which was exactly the term of operation of this joint venture expired. However, the Changchun Government abolished the local regulation, in February 2002, only two years after the project was launched.[86] Accordingly,

[80] Yang, Mei, *A Hong Kong Investor is Suing the City Government of Changchun* (in Chinese), posted at http://rainbow.www46.cnidc.cn/cgi-bin/wz/ab3.cgi?menu=show&id=lyutao&slttitle=20040131195350&see=14 (03/10/2004). See also Wang, Ling, *The Rise and Fall of Water Market* (in Chinese), posted at http://www.hqcj.com/docs/2004_05/gb/content/fmgs2.htm (03/10/2004).

[81] *Ibid*. See also *The Changchun Wastewater Project*, at the website of the CWC: http://chinawater.com.hk/cwc-e_projects_changchun.html (04/10/2004).

[82] The Changchun Wastewater Project, at the website of the CWC: http://chinawater.com.hk/cwc-e_projects_changchun.html (04/10/2004).

[83] *Ibid*.

[84] See Administrative Rules on Changchun Huijin Wastewater Treatment Project, adopted by the People's Government of Changchun City on 14 July 2000.

[85] Art 4, Administrative Rules on Changchun Huijin Wastewater Treatment Project, adopted by the People's Government of Changchun City on 14 July 2000. Unless other wise specified, the following information in this paragraph is based on provisions in this local regulation.

[86] Yang, above, note 80.

the Changchun Government also suspended the promised payment of wastewater treatment charges.[87] The ground of these governmental actions were a Circular passed by the Chinese central government in 2002, which required all local governments abolishing all FIPs that promised to give foreign investors fixed return rates (the so-called 'fixed return projects') as they contravened to relevant national laws and regulations.[88]

Changchun Huijin considered that by abolishing the special local regulation, the Changchun Government breached the promises it made therein, which was the very foundation of the CJV project.[89] Changchun Huijin therefore brought an administrative lawsuit to the Intermediate People's Court of Changchun City challenging the legality of the Changchun Government's act to abolish the regulation. In late 2003, the intermediate court rendered its verdict rejecting Changchun Huijn's claims whilst upholding the legality of the Changchun Government's act to abandon the regulation. Changchun Huijn dissatisfied and submitted the case in February 2004 to the High People's Court of Jiling Province, the court of second instance for this case, whose decision would be final. Whilst it is yet to know of the final decision of the high court, it is undoubted that this case sounded the alarm bell to both foreign investors and Chinese local governments. Soon a similar case, *Fuzhou Xinyuan Case* occurred in Fuzhou, the capital city of Fujian Province in the southern China.

In July 2004, CIETAC accepted Fuzhou Xinyuan City Bridges Ltd (*Xinyuan*)'s arbitration application against the People's Government of Fuzhou City (Fuzhou Government), on the basis of a concession agreement concluded between the two sides in 1997.[90]This case ever since became another state-investor dispute that has surfaced and has drawn wide attention.

Xinyuan was a CJV established in May 1997, in which Hong Kong Xiuming International Corporation held seventy per cent of the shares. The purposes of Xinyuan were to build the fourth bridge across the Ming River that runs through the city of Fuzhou. In order to assure the Hong Kong investor, the Fuzhou Government entered into a concession agreement with

[87] *Ibid.*

[88] The State Council Circular on the Proper Handling of Issues relating to Existing Foreign Invested Fixed Return Project Guarantees, Guobanfa [2002] No.43.

[89] Yang, above, note 80. Unless otherwise specified, information in this paragraph is based on this source.

[90] Unless otherwise specified, the source information of this case is the special column on this case entitled 'The Case of Hong Kong China Travel Service BOT Project' published at *China's Legal Daily*, a newspaper of the Ministry of Justice of the Chinese Government, posted at http://www.legaldaily.com.cn/zb/2004–09/02/content_130048.htm (04/10/2004). Other reports of the case include *Who Should Pay for the Loss of this Hong Kong investment?*, posted at http://www.legaldaily.com.cn/bm/2004–07/13/content_116067.htm (04/10/2004); *A Foreign Investor is Suing Fuzhou City Government for Breach of Contract*, posted at http://www.sznews. com/n1/ca1044229.htm (03/10/2004); *Fuzhou Government Facing Dispute of 900 Million for Blindly Introducing Foreign Investment*, posted at http://info.news.hc360. com/html/001/002/003/013/61066.htm (03/10/2004).

Xinyuan, promising that Xinyuan would have the property rights and other affiliated right on the second, third and fourth bridges over Ming River and the Baihuting Toll Station for twenty eight years. Further, it promised that, in Xinyuan's first nine years of operation, all the vehicles going through the south gate of Fuzhou city would go via the Baihuting Toll Station, and in case the income from toll charges decrease significantly for some exceptional reasons, the Fuzhou Government should take back the concession and guarantee that Xiuming International would not only obtain refund of the initial investment, but also a fixed annual return of eighteen per cent.

The fourth bridge was built and the agreement carried out successfully until 16 May 2004, when the third phase of the second ring road of Fuzhou was completed. As the newly built road diverted vehicle flows dramatically from the Baihuting Toll, toll charge incomes dropped tremendously. It then became impossible for Xinyuan to carry out the concession agreement. After failed attempts of consultation, Xinyuan filed an application for arbitration to the CIETAC, requesting to terminate the concession agreement and to refund original investment and compensation of totally RMB 900 million. Fuzhou Government brought a law suit to the Intermediate People's Court of Fuzhou City challenging the jurisdiction of the CIETAC after CIETAC accepted the case on 6 July 2004. As it stands, it is unclear whether the case will be finally handled by the local court or the CIETAC. What is clear is, as with the Changchun Huijin Case, foreign investors and local authorities now have to wake up to be prepared for legal settlement of investment disputes. The no-dispute honey-moon between foreign investors and local governments is over.[91] The next stage would probably be a rise of investment cases submitted to the ICSID and other international tribunals, as a result China's open acceptance to international arbitration and in viewing of the general ineffectiveness of the Chinese dispute settlement system, as perceived by foreign investors.[92]

7.5 SUBROGATION AND INVESTMENT INSURANCE

Subrogation[93] provisions in BITs are closely linked to investment insurance schemes aiming at alleviating non-commercial risks of foreign investment. In

[91] It is estimated that there have been more than 200 'fixed return projects' similar to Fuzhou Xinyuan and Changchun Huijin, most of which are yet to be settled. Thus it can be reasonably predicted that more such cases will arise in near future. See *Fuzhou Government Facing Dispute of 900 Million for Blindly Introducing Foreign Investment*, posted at http://info.news.hc360.com/html/001/002/003/013/61066.htm (03/10/2004).

[92] The author's Questionnaire and Interviews suggest that, in practice, the Chinese system of dispute settlement lacks in effectiveness, as the laws are often inconsistently enforced by government officials and court and arbitration decisions are not always enforced. Details follow in Section 8.2.

[93] According to the Official Commentary on the MIGA Convention, 'subrogation is an accepted principle of insurance law. It provides for the assignment of an existing claim from the

order to promote outward investment, most OECD countries have established such national investment insurance programmes,[94] in addition to concluding BITs to provide general protection. However, one crucial condition for these foreign investment insurance schemes to be operated is that the host country of the insured investment agrees to recognise such subrogation, because the assignment of the investor's rights and claims to the insurer might not otherwise be valid under any applicable national law.[95] At the multilateral level, members of the MIGA Convention have agreed to recognise such assignment and subrogation of rights and claims from the guaranteed investor to the MIGA. At the bilateral level, such recognition is normally given by states as contracting parties to a BIT, in the form of a subrogation provision.

The following paragraphs, therefore, deal with the subrogation provisions in the EU-China BITs, the essentials of the MIGA regime and the investment insurance scheme of the People's Insurance Corporation of China (PICC).

7.5.1 Subrogation under EU-China BITs

All existing EU-China BITs have a subrogation provision, as shown in *Table 20: Subrogation under EU-China BITs* .[96] They provide that contracting parties should recognise such a transfer of rights and claims and the subrogation. For example, the Sino-Portugal BIT provides that,

> 'If a Contracting party or its Agency makes payment to an investor under a guarantee it has granted to an investment of such investor in the territory of the other Contracting Party, such other Contracting Party shall recognise the transfer of any right or claim of such investor to the former Contracting Party or its Agency to such right or claim.'[97]

Some BITs go further to give a more elaborate definition of the assignment and subrogation. Therefore, in the Sino-Denmark BIT, Article 7 reads,

> 'if a Contracting Party makes payment to its own nationals or companies under a guarantee it has accorded in respect of an investment in the territory of the other

guaranteed investor to a third party and the third party as subrogee acquires the same rights as the investor had.' See *Commentary on the Convention Establishing the Multilateral Investment Guarantee Agency* (hereinafter '*MIGA Commentary*'), Para 26, as reprinted in Shihata, Ibrahim F. I., *MIGA and Foreign Investment* (Martinus Nijhoff, 1988), at 400–01.

[94] Dolzer and Stevens, above, note 4, at 156.

[95] *Ibid.*

[96] See Art 5, Sino-Sweden BIT; Art 6, Sino-Germany BIT; Art 6, Sino-France BIT; Art 7, Sino-BLEU BIT; Art 8, Sino-Finland IT; Art 7, Sino-Italy BIT; Art 7, Sino-Denmark BIT; Art 8, Sino-Netherlands BIT; Art 6, Sino-Austria BIT; Art 9, Sino-Britain BIT; Art 6, Sino-Portugal BIT; Art 7, Sino-Spain BIT, and Art 7, Sino-Greece BIT.

[97] Art 6, Sino-Portugal BIT.

> Contracting Party, the latter shall recognise:
> (i) the assignment, whether under the law or pursuant to a legal transaction that country, of any right or claim by the national or company to the former Contracting Party, as well as,
> (ii) that the former Contracting Party is entitled by virtue of subrogation to excise the rights and enforce the claims of that national or company and shall assume the obligations related to the investment.'[98]

All but the Sino-Denmark BIT define the scope of the subrogated rights and claims. Eight BITs qualify the scope of rights and claims in that they should not exceed the original rights and claims of the guaranteed investor.[99] Eight BITs provide that counter claims to the subrogated rights can be made by the host government, or that subrogation should not affect the original rights of the host country to the investor concerned, or that obligation of the guaranteed investor should also be assumed by the subrogated (home) state or its agency.[100] The Sino-Britain BIT stresses that the home state or its agency should enjoy the same rights as those offered to the guaranteed investor.[101] The Sino-France BIT clarifies that litigation rights should be included in the rights subrogated.[102] Four BITs spell out that the subrogation of rights should not prejudice home state's right to invoke state-state dispute settlement procedure as prescribed in the BITs.[103]

Moreover, there are some other provisions related to subrogation in these BITs. Some are common clauses. For instance, many BITs reiterate that the investment-related transfer rules should cover transfer of proceeds by virtue of subrogation.[104] Others are specific to BITs. For example, the Sino-France BIT requires that investment insurance projects be approved by the host country,[105] the Sino-Netherlands BIT does not limit the insurer to a contracting party or its agent, but include any insurer or re-insurer of non-commercial risks 'under a system established by law',[106] while the Sino-Spain BIT provides that only economic rights, rather than property rights may be subrogated.[107]

[98] Art 7, Sino-Denmark BIT.
[99] See Art 6, Sino-Germany BIT; Art 6, Sino-France BIT; Art 8, Sino-Finland IT; Art 7, Sino-Italy BIT; Art 8, Sino-Netherlands BIT; Art 6, Sino-Austria BIT; Art 9, Sino-Britain BIT; Art 6, Sino-Portugal BIT; and Art 7, Sino-Greece BIT.
[100] See Art 5, See Sino-Sweden BIT; Art 6, Sino-Germany BIT; Art 6, Sino-France BIT; Art 7, Sino-BLEU BIT; Art 8, Sino-Netherlands BIT; Art 6, Sino-Austria BIT; Art 9, Sino-Britain BIT; and Art 7, Sino-Greece BIT.
[101] Art 9, Sino-Britain BIT.
[102] Art 6, Sino-France BIT.
[103] Art 5, See Sino-Sweden BIT; Art 6, Sino-Germany BIT Art 8, Sino-Finland IT; Art 6, Sino-Austria BIT.
[104] See Art 6, Sino-Germany BIT; Art 6, Sino-France BIT; Art 7, Sino-Italy BIT; and Art 6, Sino-Austria BIT.
[105] Art 6, Sino-France BIT.
[106] Art 8, Sino-Netherlands BIT.
[107] Art 7, Sino-Spain BIT.

Table 20 Subrogation under EU-China BITs

BIT	Recognise the transfer and subrogation of rights and claims	Scope of subrogated rights					Others
		Same treatment as the guaranteed investor	Including litigation rights	Without prejudice to home state's right to invoke state-state arbitration	Shall not exceed the original rights	Can make counter-claims to the subrogated rights	
Sino-Sweden BIT (Art 5)	1	0	0	1	0	1	0
Sino-German BIT (Art 6)	1	0	0	1	1	1	Transfer provisions apply
Sino-France BIT (Art 6) (prior approval)	1	0	1	0	1	1 (original rights of the host country)	Guarantee subject to host country's approval; Transfer provisions apply
Sino-BLEU BIT (Art 7)	1	0	0	0	0	1	0
Sino-Finland BIT (Art 8)	1	0	0	1	1	0	0
Sino-Italy BIT (Art 7)	1	0	0	0	1	0	Transfer rules apply
Sino-Denmark BIT (Art7)	1	0	0	0	0	0	0
Sino-Netherlands BIT (Art 8)	1	0	0	0	1	1	Any insurer or re-insurer 'under a system established by law'

Sino-Austria BIT (Art 6)	1	0	0	1	1	1	Transfer rules apply
Sino-Britain BIT (Art 9)	1	1	0	0	0	1	0
Sino-Portugal BIT (Art 6)	1	0	0	0	1	0	0
Sino-Spain BIT (Art 7)	1	0	0	0	0	0	Subrogation of economic rights, not property rights
Sino-Greece BIT (Art 7)	1	0	0	0	1	1	0
Total (13)	13	1	1	4	8	8	6

The preceding survey of subrogation provisions in EU-China BITs show that, whilst all of them assure that the transfer of rights and claims and the subsequent subrogation are recognised, they vary significantly in detail. Most provide that the assigned rights and claims shall not exceed the original rights and claims of the guaranteed investors. Nevertheless, the survey shows that these subrogation provisions, to a large extent, resemble general BIT practices in the world.[108]

7.5.2 Investment Insurance under MIGA Convention

MIGA is so far the only multilateral investment insurance scheme available in the world. As said in Chapter 3, MIGA plays an important, active role in promoting and protecting EU investment in China, since all EU member states and China are members of the MIGA Convention. Created in 1988 by the MIGA Convention,[109] its core activity is to provide insurance (including coinsurance and reinsurance) against political risks for investments made in a developing member country by another member country and therefore, to promote the flow of FDI to and among developing countries.[110]

Again, it is impossible to give a full scale analysis of the MIGA regime in the present book. Thus, the subsequent sections discuss only three of the central aspects of MIGA's operation, including covered risks, eligibility requirements and subrogation.

7.5.2.1 Scope of Covered Risks

MIGA insurance covers the risks of currency transfer, expropriation and similar measures, war and civil disturbance and breach of contract loss.[111]

Currency transfer insurance

Currency transfer insurance covers currency transfer restrictions imposed by a host government on the transfer of local currency into a freely transferable currency or another currency acceptable to investors. It also covers the failure of the host government to act within a reasonable period after the submission of a transfer application.[112] Upon receipt of the blocked local currency from

[108] Dolzer and Stevens, above, note 4, at 164.

[109] The MIGA Convention is reprinted in 24 ILM 1598. For detailed discussion of the Agency and the Convention, see Shihata, above, note 93, and Chen, An (ed) *MIGA and China: Comments on the Multilateral Investment Guarantee Agency* (Fujian People's Press, 1995).

[110] Art 2, MIGA Convention.

[111] *Ibid*, Art 11. A recent MIGA survey showed that, when evaluating foreign investment, investors were still generally 'very concerned' with all the key political risks including war and civil disturbance, currency inconvertibility, expropriation and compensation, and breach of contracts. See *Foreign Direct Investment Survey: A study conducted by the MIGA with the assistance of the Deloitte and Touche LLP.* January 2002, posted at http://www.ipanet.net/fdisurvey (visited on 16 July 2004), at 27.

[112] *Ibid*, Art 11 (a) (i).

the holder of the guarantee, MIGA pays in the currency of its guarantee. Nonetheless, risks relating to devaluation and depreciation of currency are excluded from the scope of this insurance coverage, as they are considered as 'normal business risks'.[113]

In China, the foreign exchange (forex) regime has undergone rapid change, particularly in recent years. Since December 1996, China has formally accepted the obligations of Article VIII of the IMF Articles of Agreement, removing exchange restrictions on current account transactions.[114] Although China still maintains some restrictions on capital account, they are compatible with WTO requirements, and will nevertheless eventually be phased out. Full convertibility of RMB is a set goal of the forex reform.[115] By the end of June 2004, China has accumulated a $470.6 billion foreign reserve.[116] Hence it can be said that it is very unlikely that FIEs in China will actually run into serious currency transfer risks.[117]

Expropriation and similar measures insurance

Expropriation and similar measures insurance covers any legislative or administrative action or omission attributable to a host government that deprives guarantee holders of their ownership, control of, or a substantial benefit from, their investment.[118] 'Expropriation and similar measures' generally encompass nationalisation, confiscation, sequestration, seizure, attachment and assets freezing.[119] However, this insurance coverage excludes 'non-discriminatory

113 Comeaux, Paul, and Kinsella, N Stephan, *Protecting Foreign Investment under International Law: Legal Aspects of Political Risks* (Oceana Publications Inc., 1997), at 170.

114 The World Trade Organisation Working Party on the Accession of China: *Report of the Working Party on the Accession of China* (hereinafter "*Working Party Report*"), WT/ACC/CHN/49 (1 October 2001), at 6–7.

115 Zhang, Weimin, 'Maintaining the Balance of International Payment, Proceeding to Full Convertibility of RMB', (2001) 15 Nov *People's Daily* (overseas edition), at 4.

116 Qin, Jingwu, China's GDP Growth in 2003 Achieved 9.1%, *People's Daily* (overseas edition) 21 January 2004, at 1.

117 It has been observed that under the previous forex regime, there could be two occasions where currency transfer risks might occur. The SAFE may unduly delay in handling a FIE's application for approval to transfer capital out of China, thus breaking Art 1.24 of the Operational Regulations of MIGA; Balance of payments (BOP) requirement on FIEs may also give rise to currency transfer risks. According to Art 75 of the previous Implementing Regulation of EJVL, if a Joint Venture fails to manage the balance of payments, due to reasons other than its failure to fulfil the Joint Venture contract, the 'Department in Charge' shall be held responsible. Hence, should the Department fail to act, foreign joint venturers may be unable to remit their profits out of China in lines with the contract terms, thus generating currency transfer risks. However, since 1996, China has realised the free convertibility of RMB under current transaction. This significantly mitigates the first kind of risk. Moreover, since the recent modification of FDI laws and regulations, China has abandoned the BOP requirement for FIEs and, therefore, eliminated the second potential risk. See Chen, An (ed), *MIGA and China: Comments on the Multilateral Investment Guarantee Agency* (Fujian People's Press, 1995), at 462–63. For a detailed discussion of the newly revised FDI laws and regulations, see Shan, Wenhua, 'Towards a Level Playing Field for Foreign Investment in China', (2002) 3 *Journal of World Investment* 2.

118 Art 11 (a) (ii), the MIGA Convention.

119 *MIGA Commentary,* above, note 93, at 391–416.

measures of general application which government normally take for the purposes of regulating economic activity within their territories'. According to the Commentary, such measures generally include taxation, environmental and labour legislation and normal measures for the maintenance of public safety.[120] This provision, nevertheless, is not to prejudice the rights of member countries or of investors under bilateral investment treaties.[121]

Upon assignment of the investor's interest in the expropriated investment, MIGA pays compensation. Compensation for total expropriation of equity investment includes the net book value of the insured investment. Where expropriation is partial, MIGA will compensate the insured portion of the expropriated fund or the net book value of the expropriated assets. As for loans and loan guaranties, MIGA insures the outstanding principal and any accrued and unpaid interest.[122]

Under the 'opening up' policy, it is very unlikely that China will expropriate foreign investment as it did in its earlier years. However, risks may still arise and should not be overlooked,[123] particularly given that China has not completed its transition from a central planned economy to a 'market economy' regulated by the rule of law. Also, inappropriate interventions from local authorities could cause serious problems on FIEs.[124] Moreover, unexpected changes of government policies and plans may also give rise to frustrations to foreign investors. For example, in 1994, McDonald's Corporation's land lease on its flagship restaurant near Tiananmen Square was reportedly cancelled by a decision made by Beijing municipal authorities.[125] Although it neither qualifies as a MIGA guaranteed investment, nor was it from the EU, this case had aroused widespread international concern and has been cited as one of the most recent examples of expropriation.[126]

[120] *Ibid.*

[121] *Ibid.*

[122] Comeaux and Kinsella, above, note 113, at 170.

[123] Chew, a US scholar, believes that despite the continuing increase of US investment in China, huge potential political risks persists and must not be overlooked. See Chew, Pat K, 'Political Risk and U.S. Investments in China: Chimera of Protection and Predictability?', (1994) *Virginia Journal of International Law.*

[124] This probably happened more commonly in the earlier years of 'opening-up', when local and central authorities were not so familiar with FDI. For instance, in 1986, a Sino-Japan joint venture fired two employees, which was an exercise of the JV's autonomy of management as provided by the EJVL. However, this action resulted in more than seven 'investigation groups' investigating the JV. Investigating groups include the Party Disciplinary Committee of the Tourist Bureau of Tianjian Municipality. The venture's operation was deeply and adversely affected by these investigations and the planned enlargement was stalled. See Chen, An, above, note 117, at 465.

[125] The Municipality authorities held that the location was needed as part of a larger redevelopment project funded by a Hong Kong investor. A settlement of the dispute, providing compensation to McDonald's, was reportedly reached between the parties in mid-1996. McDonald's was also allowed to open at least two more outlets along an adjacent street. See US and Foreign Commercial Service (US&FCS) (Telegraphic Report from the American Embassy in Beijing): *China: Investment Climate Statement for 1997*. See also Friedman, Thomas L, 'Fed Up', (1996) 12 Apr *New York Times*, at 29.

[126] Hill, Claire A, 'How Investors React to Political Risk', (1998) *Duke Journal of Comparative and International Law*, at 293–97.

War and civil disturbance insurance

War and civil disturbance insurance covers military action or civil disturbance occurring within the territory of a host country and includes revolutions, insurrections, *coups d'état* and similar political events, which are typically outside the control of the host government.[127] Acts of terrorism and similar activities specifically directed against an investor are not covered.[128]

If the investment is an equity investment, MIGA will compensate the investor's share of the least of the book value of the asset, replacement cost of the asset, or, for damaged assets, the cost of repair. In case of loans and loan guaranties, MIGA pays the insured portion of the principal and interest payments in default as a direct result of damage to the assets of the project caused by war or civil disturbance.[129]

From China's perspective, it is relatively unlikely that war or civil disturbance will break out in the near future. However, disputes over the South China Sea might give rise to future military action.[130] The Taiwan issue may also lead to civil disturbance. In the past 20 years, the 'June 4th' event of Tiananmen in 1989 might be the only possible example of 'civil disturbance'. As a result of that event, a few foreign investors temporarily withdrew from China. For example, all American staff in the Sino-American Shanghai Airplane Factory were repatriated, and the co-operation was halted for 20 days. The America-China Business Council (ACBC) also reported that at least three American companies pulled out their major engineers and announced *force majeure*.[131] While the Chinese Government admitted that it was a 'riot' or 'civil disturbance', they did not think it had constituted the 'risk of civil disturbance' as stipulated in the MIGA Convention, as its impact on foreign investors was more psychological than economically grounded.[132]

Breach of contract insurance

Breach of contract insurance covers breaches of contract by a host government with an investor where the investor have no recourse to other fora, where a decision of the other fora is not available within a reasonable period, or where such a decision cannot be enforced.[133]

The Chinese Government does not normally get involved in investment contracts and therefore does not acknowledge 'state contracts'. Even the joint exploitation contracts are signed between foreign investors and one of several

[127] *MIGA Commentary,* above, note 93, point 16.

[128] *Ibid.*

[129] Comeaux and Kinsella, above, note 113, at 171.

[130] In fact, in the 1980s, China had been involved in few small military conflicts with Vietnam and, international analysts considered the South China Sea as one of the places where war was most likely to break out. See Chen, An, above, note 117, at 467.

[131] Chen, An, *ibid*, at 469.

[132] See 'Unifying Thoughts, Stabilising Situation and Making up the Damages', in *Liao Wang Weekly* (Chinese), Nos 25 and 26, 1989. See also Chen, An, above, note 117, at 469 and 492.

[133] Art 11 (a) (iii), the MIGA Convention.

state-run companies, rather than by the government itself. However, this does not exclude the possibility that the Chinese Government may explicitly undertake certain specific investment issues with foreign investors, such as convertibility of currency.[134] Moreover, the acceptance of 'Build-Operate-Transfer' investment model might have shown China's willingness to accept 'state contract'.[135]

Except for the aforementioned insurances, MIGA insurance may also be written to cover certain other non-commercial risks, such as terrorism or investor-kidnapping or politically motivated strikes, upon a joint request of an investor and the host government and subject to approval by the Board of Directors of MIGA.[136]

7.5.2.2 Eligibility Requirements

Eligibility requirements define the scope of qualifying investors, investment projects and countries, as well the approvals required by the host country. Eligible investors of MIGA insurance must be nationals of a member county other than the host country, or juridical persons either incorporated in and having their principal places of business in a member country, or being majority-owned by nationals of member countries.[137] State-owned corporations are also eligible if they operate on a commercial basis.[138] Eligible investments are new investments that are 'economically sound' and comply with declared development objectives as well as the laws and regulations of the host country.[139] The host country in turn must provide 'fair and equitable treatment and legal protection for investment'.[140] Moreover, only investment made in the territory of a developing member country as listed under Schedule A to the MIGA Convention may be guaranteed by MIGA.[141] Finally, the host government must approve the investment project before MIGA issues insurance coverage.[142] Since all EU member states and China are MIGA contracting parties and China is a developing country, all EU investments in China are eligible for MIGA guarantees, provided that they are, as deemed by the MIGA, economically sound, consistent with China's development objectives and priorities, in compliance with Chinese law, and are approved by the Chinese authorities on the issuance of a MIGA guarantee.

[134] Chen, An, above, note 117, at 466.
[135] See Section 1.3.5.1.
[136] Art 11 (b), the MIGA Convention.
[137] Upon the joint application of both the investor and the host country, the Board may, by special majority, extend eligibility to a natural person who is a national of the host country, or a legal person who is either incorporated in and has its principal place of business in a member country, or is majority-owned by nationals of member countries, provided that the assets invested in are transferred outside the host country. *Ibid*, Art 13.
[138] *Ibid*, Art 13 (a) (iii).
[139] *Ibid*, Art12 (d).
[140] *Ibid*.
[141] *Ibid*, Art 14.
[142] *Ibid*, Art 15.

This raises an important question: Does China qualify itself as an eligible host country under the MIGA Convention, in providing 'fair and equitable treatment and legal protection for investment', particularly in relation to EU investment? The answer to this question lies in the Operational Regulations of the MIGA. Firstly, the Operational Regulations expressly state that investments can be regarded as being adequately protected if they come under the scope of a BIT between the host country and the home country of an investor.[143] That is to say, that with the exception of Ireland, investments from all EU Member States are adequately protected for the purposes of the MIGA Convention, as China has concluded BITs with these states. Secondly, as far as Irish investment is concerned, it is up to the Agency to clarify whether the current Chinese law and practices on the protection of foreign investment are consistent with international law.[144] If the Agency is not satisfied with the legal protection and treatment, it shall not issue coverage unless the Agency has concluded an agreement with the host country on the treatment of guaranteed investments.[145] It seems that the Agency was not satisfied by the general legal protection and treatment that China provided to foreign investors.[146] Thus, in 1991, China and MIGA entered into an agreement by way of exchanges of notes, on the legal protection of foreign investments guaranteed by MIGA. This agreement reads as follows,

> 'In view of the Agency's endeavours under Article 23 (b)(ii) of the Convention to conclude agreements relating to the treatment of the Agency with respect to investments guaranteed by it, the Government agrees to accord the Agency treatment no less favourable than treatment that the People's Republic of China has accorded, or will accord in the future, to any State or investment guarantee agency of such State in an investment protection agreement. This treatment applies only to the rights to which the Agency may subrogate as a subrogee of a compensated guarantee holder.'[147]

This 'most-favoured agency' provision actually enables MIGA to enjoy the best treatment available in China to any other country or its insurance agencies. Therefore, China fully qualifies as an 'eligible host country' for the purposes of MIGA guarantees.

[143] Art 3.16, *Operational Regulations of the MIGA.*

[144] It is provided that, 'When there is no such treaty, adequate legal protection should be ascertained by the agency in the light of the consistency of the law and practice of the host country with international law' *Ibid.* To substantiate this provision, Shihata proposed some criteria. See Shihata, above, note 93, at 245–46.

[145] Art 3.16, *Operational Regulations of the MIGA.*

[146] However, Chinese scholars believe that, in general, the legal conditions that China provides for FDI conform to the requirements of the MIGA Convention and its Regulations. See Chen, An, above, note 117, at 451–54.

[147] Art 2, the 1991 Agreement on the Legal Protection for Guaranteed Foreign Investment between the Multilateral Investment Guarantee Agency and the Government of the People's Republic of China, UN Treaty Series Vol. 1669 (1992), I-28715. Chinese version reprinted in Chen, An, above, note 117, at 691.

7.5.2.3 Subrogation

The most important provision in the MIGA Convention is arguably the subrogation clause, which provides the only multilateral recognition of the transfer and assignment of the rights and claims of the subrogation. According to the subrogation clause in the MIGA Convention, member countries agree that MIGA shall be subrogated to such rights or claims related to the guaranteed investment, as the holder of a guarantee may have against the host country and other obligors, so long as MIGA has paid or has agreed to pay compensation to the holder of a guarantee.[148] By subrogation, the MIGA Convention provides for the assignment of existing claims of the guaranteed investor to MIGA. As subrogee, MIGA acquires the same rights as the investor had. The terms and conditions of subrogation are defined in the contracts of guarantee, which are particularly important for the investor since MIGA will only compensate investors for part of their losses.[149] According to Article 18 (b), MIGA's right of subrogation is recognised by all members.

Besides, MIGA is entitled to be treated as favourably as the holder of the guarantee with respect to the use and transfer of local currency it received. Furthermore, it is authorised to use these currencies for the payment of its administrative expenditures or other costs and, where these currencies are not freely usable, to seek to enter into agreements with host countries on other currency uses.[150]

In order to facilitate MIGA's operation in China, MIGA and China signed three agreements in 1991, respectively on local approval procedures, the use of local currencies, and the legal protection of MIGA guaranteed foreign investments, the third of which was mentioned above. In the first agreement, the Chinese Government commits itself to respond to MIGA guarantee applications promptly and agrees that an approval will be inferred where no action has been taken by the Government within 45 days of the notification of the China Director in MIGA. According to the second agreement, MIGA is entitled to acquire compensation paid with freely usable currencies, as the subrogee of the compensated holder of a MIGA guarantee. Moreover, China agrees that MIGA can make arrangements on the disposal of local currencies it may attain, as long as they are not made with organisations or individuals whom the Chinese law prohibited from dealing with Renminbi (RMB).[151] Finally, three agreements provide that the Director-General of the Directorate-General of World Bank Affairs of the Ministry of Finance shall be responsible for MIGA issues.[152]

148 Art 18, the MIGA Convention.
149 *MIGA Commentary,* above, note 93, Point 26.
150 Art 18 (c), the MIGA Convention.
151 The Chinese Currency.
152 See the three agreements in Chen, An, above, note 117, 689–94.

7.5.2.4 Summary

MIGA is the only investment insurance institution in the world that can issue insurance for all EU investments in China against non-commercial risks. Since both China and all EU member states are contracting parties to the MIGA Convention and China is a developing country, all EU investments in China are, in principle, eligible for MIGA guarantees, provided that they satisfy MIGA that they are economically sound, compliant with China's declared development objectives and priorities, consistent with Chinese law and approved by the Chinese authority on the issuance of such a guarantee. On the other hand, China has qualified itself as an eligible host country for MIGA guaranteed EU investments, by the conclusion of BITs with most EU member states and a special agreement on the protection of MIGA guaranteed investments with the MIGA. MIGA insurance covers political risks, such as risks of currency transfer, expropriation and similar measures, war and civil disturbance and breach of contract loss. These risks all exist in China in different degrees, even though, in general, the likelihood that they will actually happen is low, as China now implements an 'open-door' policy.

Based on the MIGA Convention, MIGA's right of subrogation is multilaterally recognised by all contracting parties, including China. Further, MIGA has entered into another two agreements with China, on the use of local currency and the approval procedures by the Chinese authorities which undoubtedly facilitate MIGA's operations in China.

7.5.3 Investment Insurance Provided by the People's Insurance Company of China (PICC)

Except for the MIGA mechanism, EU investors in China may also take advantage of the Chinese investment insurance mechanism to protect their investment against political risks. The applicable regulations are the Regulations on Foreign Investment Insurance (Political Risks) by the People's Insurance Company of China (PICC), China's biggest state-run insurance company. The regulations apply only to foreign investments in China, rather than Chinese overseas investment and, therefore, are rather different from overseas investment guarantee systems of many capital exporting countries. The coverage of this insurance includes:[153]

- war, war-like actions, civil disturbance, strikes and riots;
- expropriation and confiscation by the government department concerned;
- foreign exchange restrictions by the government department concerned that make it impossible for the insured to send out of China the property

[153] Xu, Congli and Lin, Zhong, *Chinese Foreign Investment Law* (*Zhongguo Waizi Fa*) (Law Publishing House, 1998), at 187.

that belongs to the insured and that which is allowed to be sent out in line with the contract.

Moreover, the insurance excludes the following losses:[154]

- commercial losses of the insured resulting from damages to the investment project;
- losses resulting from expropriation or confiscation by the concerned government department due to breach or non-performance of investment contract, or wilful illegal acts, by the insured and his/her representatives;
- losses caused by the insured's non-remittance within the remittance period provided for by the government department concerned;
- losses caused by an atom bomb, hydrogen bomb or other nuclear weapons;
- losses resulting from expropriation, confiscation of properties other than that covered by the investment contract.

It can be argued that the PICC insurance against political risks is a mixed blessing for EU and foreign investors in China. On the one hand, it might be very reliable, given that its interest is tied to the state's interest, which means risks might be less likely to happen. On the other hand, the foreign investor may doubt whether the government will order the PICC not to compensate after it decides to expropriate or confiscate. If this is the case, the insurance will be meaningless.[155] In order to mitigate such worries, the PICC usually enters into arrangements with overseas insurance institutions so that the latter may guarantee the payment of compensation.[156] In other words, the insured foreign investor may claim compensation from the overseas insurance institution in case the PICC fails to compensate. With such extra arrangements, it can be said that, the PICC insurance serves, as an effective insurance scheme, to further strengthen the confidence of EU and foreign investors in China.

7.6 CONCLUSION

The EU-China BITs, the ICSID Convention, the MIGA Convention and Chinese law are the most important laws governing the settlement of investment disputes for EU investors in China. Now the EU-China BITs make it possible for most EU (except Irish) investors to automatically submit disputes about the amount of compensation to the ICSID, ie, without the need to seek specific consent of the Chinese government. However, other investment dis-

[154] *Ibid*, at 187–88.
[155] *Ibid*, at 188.
[156] *Ibid.*

putes are dealt with by Chinese courts and tribunals, unless both the Chinese government and the EU investors agree to submit them to an international forum such as the ICSID. Such an agreement (or, essentially, specific consent from the Chinese government) will no longer be required, once the new Sino-Germany BIT enters into force. The ICSID Convention further enhances the dispute settlement provisions in the BITs by providing detailed rules for arbitrations facilitated by the ICSID. Under Chinese law, EU investors can appeal to a higher administrative authority against an administrative decision. Also, they may bring a legal action before a court against 'specific administrative actions' by administrative authorities, many of which are regulatory activities. In case these specific administrative acts have caused damages, the injured investors may claim compensation for damages.

However, it can be argued that the current legal framework for the settlement of disputes for EU investors is inadequate. Firstly, without the consent of the Chinese government, most disputes still cannot be submitted to an international forum, including the ICSID. Instead, they have to be handled by Chinese courts and tribunals, which, as we will see in the following chapter, are considered ineffective in resolving disputes. Secondly, although recent Chinese BITs show that China has accepted general 'principles of international law' as applicable law to investment disputes, its exact meaning is still unclear. Finally, all EU-China BITs, particularly those signed before 1990, are outdated in their specific provisions on dispute settlement. Therefore, it is necessary for the EU and its member states to update and upgrade their BITs with China.

As far as the right of subrogation is concerned, it is recognised both in the EU-China BITs and the MIGA Convention. Thus the EU investors enhance their confidence in investing in China, by insuring their investments in China against political risks, with MIGA or their investment guarantee agencies of their home state. Additionally, they can also take advantage of the PICC insurance scheme, an investment insurance scheme sponsored by the state-run insurance company, the PICC.

7.7 CONCLUSION TO PART II

Part II examines the major substantive issues of the legal regime governing EU investment in China, such as the establishment and admission, post-establishment treatment, expropriation and compensation and settlement of disputes. It has come to two general conclusions.

On the one hand, the network of international and domestic law governing EU investment in China has provided substantial protections and has made significant improvements, in particular, since the early 1990s. The substantial protections can be seen from the guarantee of non-expropriation, the provision of appropriate compensation, the acceptance of international fora to adjudicate investment disputes, as well as the general provision of MFN and F&E treatments for EU and foreign investment. The significant improvements can be seen, at the domestic law level, from the greatly increased market access for FDI by the publication of investment directions, the broadening of investment areas and the elimination of certain PRs, from the decision to implement NT for FDI and from the promulgation of Administrative Procedures Law, which allows foreign investors to sue Chinese governmental authorities for administrative misconducts. At the international law level, this can also be seen from the signing and ratifying of MIGA and ICSID Conventions and from the upgrading of BIT provisions to broaden the scope of investment disputes to be submitted for international arbitration, to accept the automatic submission of certain investment disputes to the ICSID and to apply general international law.

On the other hand, it can be argued that there is room for further improvement on the substance of the legal framework. On investment admission, international law plays only a limited role and domestic law remains rather stringent: the one-by-one screening process is still in place and the approval process is still complicated and lacks transparency. On standards of treatment, the national treatment is still substantially qualified and a level playing field for EU and foreign investment is yet to be constructed. On expropriation, the interpretation of key concepts including 'indirect expropriation', 'appropriate compensation' and the scope of compensable 'values' is still controversial and needs to be clarified. On dispute settlement, only amount of compensation disputes may be automatically referred to an international forum while most investment disputes still, in principle, fall at the jurisdiction of the ineffective Chinese courts and tribunals. Moreover, it is observed that all EU-China BITs are outdated in some of the most important provisions. It can therefore be argued that a new international legal framework is needed to update and upgrade current rule on these substantive issues.

PART III

The Current Legal Framework of EU Investment in China: The Question of Effectiveness

8

The Current Legal Framework of EU Investment in China: The Question of Effectiveness

In the *Transition Report 1996*, the European Bank of Reconstruction and Development (EBRD) rightly pointed out, 'as important as what rules say ... is what they mean in practice. A pristine statute on investment that is unknown, unadministered and unenforced is ineffective'.[1] In the context of EU investment in China, indeed, what is equally, if not more, important than the question of the structure and substance of the legal framework is the question of the effectiveness of that legal framework. This chapter will, therefore, investigate the effectiveness of the current legal framework for EU investment in China, based on the author's Questionnaire. It will first analyse the general role that the law (including both domestic and international laws within the legal framework) has played in EU investors' investment decision-making, then proceed to the various specific aspects affecting the effectiveness of the Chinese legal system. The effectiveness of the legal system will be measured again the Ideal Institutional Paradigm developed by the World Bank and other development agencies.

8.1 THE ROLE OF LAW IN INVESTMENT DECISION-MAKING

There is now a broad consensus among academics, multilateral development agencies and bilateral aid donors that a state's legal system is an important factor affecting the location of FDI.[2] However, little empirical evidence has been produced to examine the impact of the operation of developing country's legal systems upon FDI.[3] Thus in the Questionnaire, three questions were included, with a view to determining to what extent the law, or the legal

1 European Bank of Reconstruction and Development (EBRD), *Transition Report* (London: EBRD, 1996), at 101.

2 However, Perry based her findings on her Sri Lanka case study and concluded that this is not always the case. Perry, Amanda J, *Legal System as a Determinant of Foreign Direct Investment: The Case of Sri Lanka*, London School of Economics PhD dissertation, 2000, and in particular, 94, 95.

3 Perry, *ibid*, at 47.

framework, has played a role in EU investors' decisions whether or not invest in China. The first is about the EU investors' perceptions on the general role of law when they made the investment decision, followed by a series of questions on whether and to what extent they had investigated the governing legal framework before the decisions were made. The last question is about the significance of investment incentives in making their investment decisions.

8.1.1 The Relative Importance of Law as a Determinant of Investment Decision

In the first question, investors were asked how (top, high, medium, low, none, do not know, do not understand) important was the nature of the legal system to them in their making the decision to invest in China, relative to other issues, such as market size, labour costs, environmental costs and raw material supply. The Questionnaire results (*Chart 11: Relative Importance of Law in Investment Decision Making*) show that when deciding to invest in China, most EU investors (83 per cent) considered law as an element of substantial importance (top, high or medium). Among them, five per cent of the respondents regarded law as the most important element in investment decision-making, while most of them considered it as of high (36 per cent) or medium (40 per cent) importance. However, there is a fourteen per cent of 'low' and five per cent of 'none' replies to this question.[4]

Admittedly, this result is rather high and may be higher than in reality, as those who answered this Questionnaire entitled 'Law and EU Investment in China' may be those who are more concerned about the legal aspects and have therefore paid more attention to the law whilst making the investment decisions. However, this may also be explained by the fact that the EU investors are unfamiliar with the legal environment of foreign investment in China and are therefore generally more concerned about it. Nevertheless, this result, in general, should be regarded as an affirmation of the mainstream view that law does play an important role in investment decision-making.

8.1.2 Investigation of Law before Investment

The second question consisted of a series of sub-questions designed to find out whether or not the EU investors actually carried out investigations of the legal environment before the investment decisions were made. The first question was to inquire whether they have investigated the legal elements of investment, including legal measures of investment promotion (eg, tax incentives) and protection (eg, expropriation and compensation and investment

[4] It is interesting to see that the one 'none' reply was accompanied with regretful remarks on the margin saying 'shall be top now'.

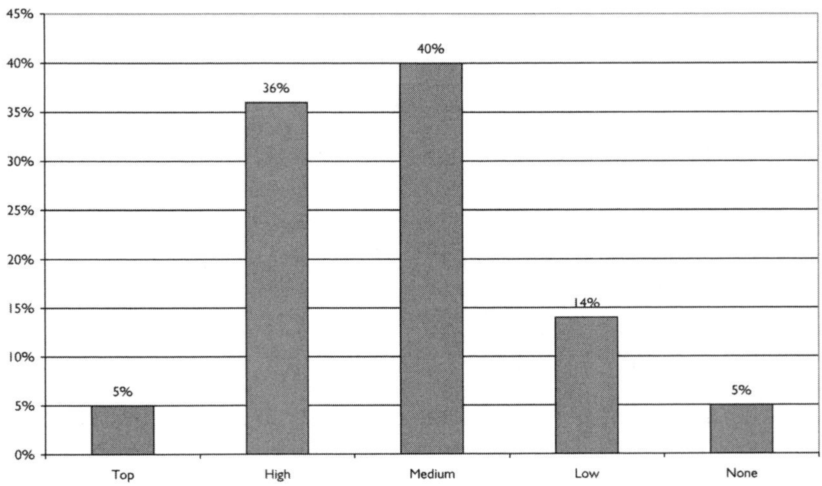

Chart 11: Relative Importance of Law in Investment Decision Making

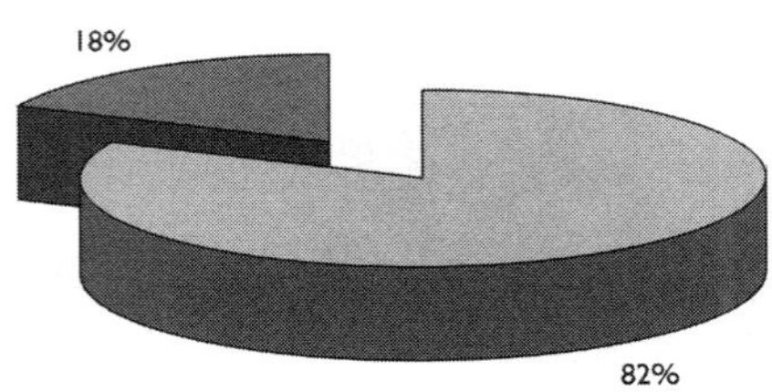

Chart 12: Investigation of Law before Making Investme*nt*

insurance). The answers (*Chart 12: Investigation of Law before Making Investment*) to this question correspond to answers to the previous one, ie, all those who considered law as of substantial importance, had investigated the legal environment, a very large proportion (83 per cent) of the respondent investors. The following sub-question was about the evidence used in investigating the legal environment, ie, whether they had investigated the written law ('law on paper') only or both the written law and the law in action (eg, levels of enforcement). As shown in *Chart 13: Evidence of Law Investigated*, in investigating the legal environment, more (55 per cent) EU investors relied on both the written law and the law in action than merely relied on the written law (39 per cent). This demonstrates EU investors' concern over the application of the law and law enforcement in China. A third sub-question on law investigation dealt with the scope of laws that were under investigation, ie, whether they had investigated both domestic (Chinese) law and applicable international investment treaties, or either or none of them. As *Chart 14*

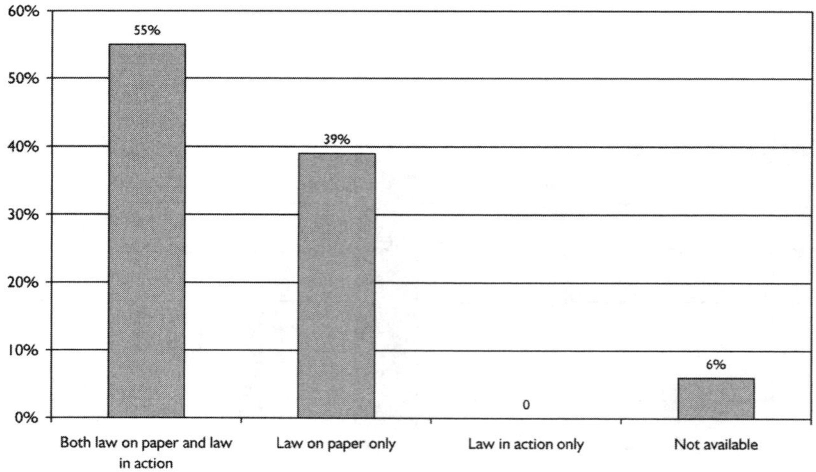

Chart 13: Evidence of Law Investigated

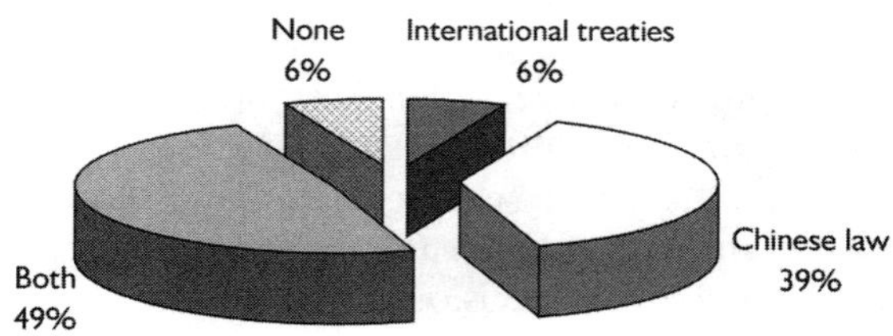

Chart 14: Chinese Law and International Treaties Considered

reveals, about a half (49 per cent) of those who investigated the legal environment studied both the Chinese law and the applicable international treaties. Six per cent of them investigated international treaties only. This shows that international treaties played a substantial role in facilitating investment flow to China. However, about forty per cent of these investors studied only Chinese law, which shows that, in the eyes of many EU private investors, domestic law nevertheless plays a much more important role than international treaties (*Chart 14: Chinese Law and International Treaties Considered*). The following sub-question is the last of this series, which aimed to unveil the specific international investment-related treaties that have affected EU investment in China. The Questionnaire results (*Chart 15: Awareness of International Treaties Aware of*) gave an unsurprising answer to this: most EU investors (68 per cent) were aware of bilateral treaties devoted to the avoidance of double taxation (DTTs), as cost of investment was obviously the primary concern for them. About half (45 per cent) of them knew that they

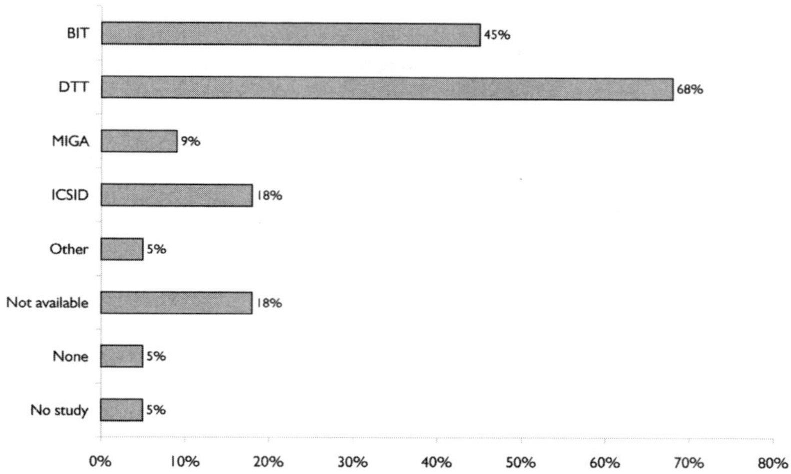

Chart 15: Awareness of International Treaties

could take advantage of bilateral investment treaties (BITs). ICSID Convention and MIGA Convention were only known to a few of these investors (18 per cent and 9 percent, respectively). Furthermore, the New York Convention on the Recognition and Enforcement of Foreign Arbitration Awards (New York Convention) had been specifically listed by some investors (about 5 per cent) as one of the relevant international treaties that they were aware of when making the investment decision (*Chart 15*).

8.1.3 Importance of Incentives on Investment Decision-Making

The third question aimed at determining whether the incentive measures that the Chinese Government used to attract FDI had worked. Thus it asked what importance the EU investors put on foreign investment incentives (such as tax exemptions for foreign investors generally, or specifically to those in particular industrial sectors or zones) offered by China, in making the decision to invest therein. This survey shows that the vast majority of EU investors (91 per cent) put investment incentives on medium or higher position when deciding to invest. Forty one per cent of them consider incentives as highly important factors in making their investment decision, while nine per cent of them considered it of the highest importance (*Chart 16: Importance of Incentives*). This is further confirmed by the concluding remarks by a respondent of the Questionnaire.[5] This result may be, to some extent, explained by the

[5] The respondent complained against the removal of the tax reductions for FIEs concerning imported materials and equipment, a policy China implemented from 1996 until 1997. See Section 5.3.2.2 for further details of the policy.

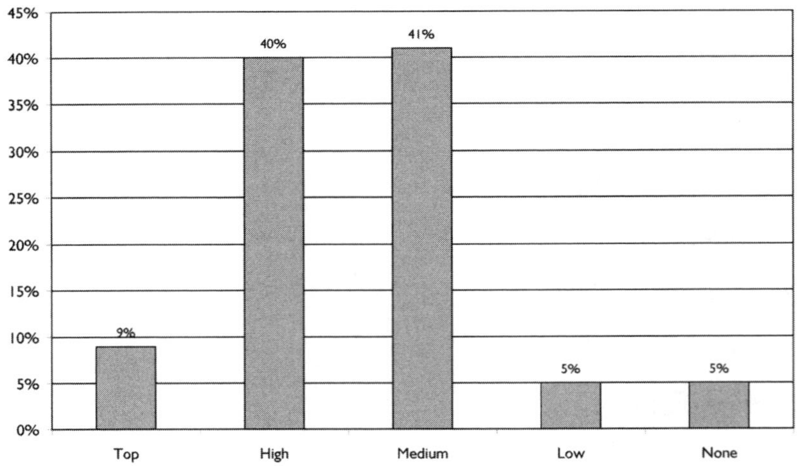

Chart 16: Importance of Incentives

fact that most of the respondents are not multinationals but small or medium sized enterprises (SMEs),[6] who are concerned more with the short term benefits deriving from incentives, rather than the long term benefits resulting from a stable and predictable legal regime. Nonetheless, it may be said that China's investment incentives have worked in attracting EU investors.

8.1.4 Summary

The preceding charts have demonstrated that law has played a very important role in investor's decision-making. The vast majority of EU investors had investigated the legal environment before they made their investment decisions. Among those investigating the legal environment, most looked at both the written law and the law in action while a substantial number of them had studied only the written law. About half of these EU investors did research on both Chinese law and applicable international treaties, but many of them just investigated the Chinese law, which they considered of vital importance. The most well-known category of applicable international treaties to these investors was DTTs, followed by BITs. ICSID Convention and MIGA Convention were known to less than twenty per cent of EU investors. The New York Convention was added by some respondents as one of the most important international agreements related to investment issues.

[6] Although a few large multinationals responded to this Questionnaire, the majority of the respondents were SMEs. However, at least one large multinational respondent had considered incentives of substantial (medium) importance.

An overwhelming majority of EU investors considered investment incentives to be a factor of substantial importance in the investment decision-making process. This result shows that China's investment incentives had been effective in attracting EU investment.

8.2 EFFECTIVENESS OF THE CHINESE LEGAL SYSTEM

According to the World Bank, an effective legal system for foreign investment normally has five features.[7] First, it provides a set of rules 'known' to foreign investors in advance. Thus the law should be published (accessible) and clear. Second, it relies upon rules which are actually implemented, and not just 'on the books'. Third, it ensures that rules are consistently applied. The discretionary power of state officials should, therefore, be limited to the narrowest possible field, in order to avoid abuse. Fourth, there must be an effective, independent mechanism for dispute resolution. The judiciary must be protected from intervention by other branches of the government, so that the government itself can be the subject of laws. Further, the judicial process must not be incapacitated by physical constraints due to poor facilities, unreasonable delays, prohibitive cost or uncertainty. Lastly, it has clear procedures for the amendments of rules, to prevent any arbitrary introduction or rejection of rules, and to clear out irrelevant rules.[8] Such a set of criteria constitute the core components of the Ideal Institutional Paradigm that the World Bank and other development agencies are offering to developing countries when giving law reform advices.[9]

Based on these criteria identified by the World Bank, 9 questions were included in the Questionnaire to examine the effectiveness of the Chinese legal system that governs EU investment in China. These questions focus on five aspects, including the accessibility and stability of the law, the enforcement of law by government departments, courts and arbitration tribunals, and the enforcement of court/arbitration decisions.

8.2.1 Accessibility of Law

In general, Chinese law has long been criticised for a lack of transparency.[10] Therefore, the Chinese Government has made a substantial effort to solve

[7] World Bank, *Governance and Development* (Washington DC: World Bank, 1992), at 4.

[8] World Bank, *ibid.*

[9] Perry has actually questioned whether there were alternatives to the Ideal Institutional Paradigm, on the ground that her Sri Lanka studies did not support such a paradigm. Perry, note 2 above, at 94, 195–99.

[10] Research published in the *Harvard Law Review* asserted that, '[T]he chief problem for students of modern Chinese law has often been one of finding it.' See Concepts of Law in the Chinese Anti-Crime Campaign (Note), 98 *Harvard Law Review* 1890, June 1985, at 1890. Also,

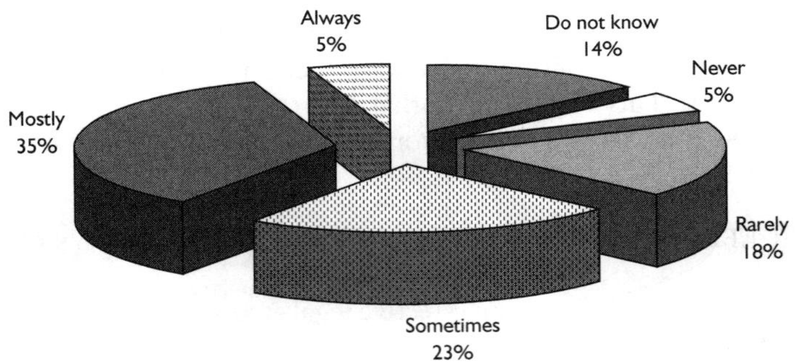

Chart 17: Accessibility of Law and Policy

this problem. For instance, the Investment Guidance and the Guiding Catalogue have been published to direct FDI admission and a Gazette of MOFTEC (now MOFCOM) is also available to publish new laws and regulations in a timely manner. However, there has been no empirical evidence as to how the foreign investors view the transparency and accessibility of law. Thus, in the Questionnaire, they were asked whether they thought FDI laws and policies were easily accessible. As *Chart 17: Accessibility of Law and Policy* demonstrates, forty per cent of the EU investors replied that laws and regulations are 'always' or 'mostly' accessible while twenty three per cent of them answered negatively ('rarely' or 'never' accessible). Another twenty three per cent among them gave a half positive half negative answer—law is 'sometimes' accessible, which might suggest that it was 'sometimes' inaccessible (*Chart 17*). In general, the Questionnaire reveals that further improvement on transparency and accessibility of the law is still needed, as a substantial portion of EU investors still regard access to the law as difficult.

8.2.2 Stability of Law

The stability of the law in China is another problem that is often raised.[11] Thus another question was included to determine, from the EU investors' experience, whether Chinese FDI laws and policies had been changed unex-

a number of studies on China's WTO accession have examined the problem of transparency in the Chinese legal system. See eg, Ostry, Sylvia, 'China and the WTO: The Transparency Issue', (1998) 3 *UCLA Journal of International Law and Foreign Affairs* 1, in particular 12–15; Hu, Patrick H, 'The China 301 on Market Access: A Prelude to GATT Membership?', (1994) 3 *Minnesota Journal of Global Trade* 131, at 143; Blumental, David, '"Reform" Or "Opening"? Reform of China's State-Owned Enterprises and WTO Accession—The Dilemma of Applying GATT to Marketizing Economies', (1998) 16 *UCLA Pacific Basin Law Journal* 198, at 234; Yuan, Anyuan, 'China's Entry into the WTO: Impact on China's Regulating Regime of Foreign Direct Investment', (2001) 35 *International Lawyer* 195, at 217.

[11] See eg, Zheng, Henry R, 'The Sino-U.S. Income Tax Treaty and Its Effect on Chinese Taxation of American Economic Interests', (1987) 40 *Tax Lawyer* 733, at 773.

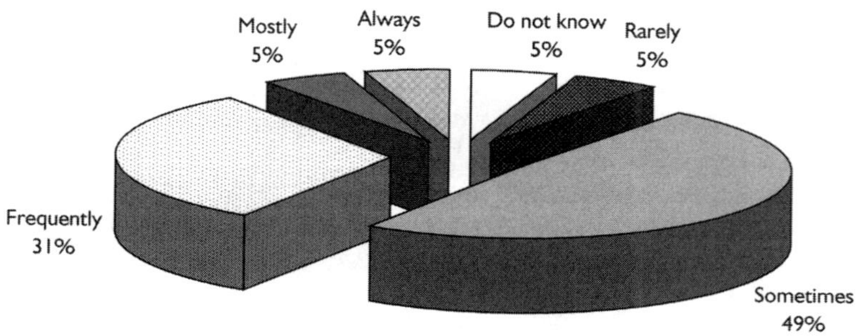

Chart 18: Unexpected Changes of Law and Policy

pectedly. The Questionnaire results confirm that stability of FDI law and policy is still perceived as a major problem in China. More than forty per cent of the surveyed investors replied that in China law and policies are 'always', 'mostly' or 'frequently' changed unexpectedly, while about half (49 per cent) reported that unexpected changes of law are 'sometimes' experienced. Only five per cent stated that they had 'rarely' encountered unexpected changes of law (*Chart 18: Unexpected Changes of Law and Policy*). Admittedly, as a country in transition, changes in law and policies may be inevitable and may not necessarily be unfavourable for investors. However, the high frequency of 'unexpected' changes of law, show that public participation in the law drafting and revision processes has been a continuous problem and needs to be improved.

8.2.3 Government Enforcement of Law

Two questions were devised to establish the experience with the enforcement of laws by government departments: one is on the consistency of enforcement and the other is the need to bribe government officials.

8.2.3.1 Consistency of Government Law Enforcement

It is said that in China laws are interpreted and implemented inconsistently by different departments and in different regions.[12] This perception is confirmed by this Questionnaire. As *Chart 19* shows, thirty five per cent of EU investors thought the law only 'sometimes' was enforced consistently, whilst fourteen per cent of them complained that such consistency had 'never' or 'rarely' been achieved. Only twenty three per cent of EU investors reported

[12] See Blumental, David, above, note 10, at 237. See also Kong, Kevin TS, 'Prospects for Asset Securitization within China's Legal Framework: The Two-Tiered Model', (1998) 32 *Cornell International Law Journal* 237, at 271.

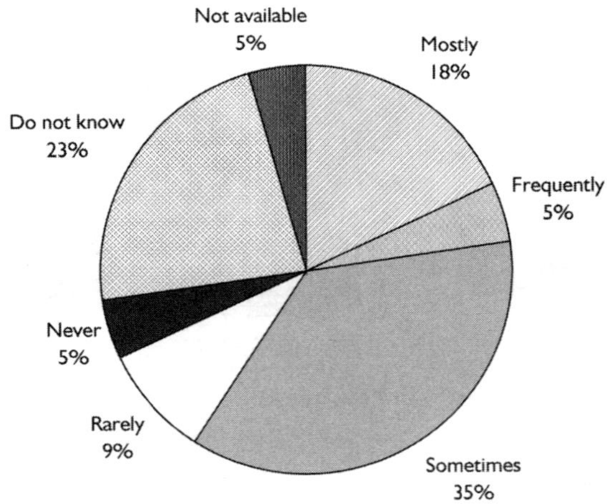

Chart 19: Consistency of Government Law Enforcement

that laws were 'mostly' and 'frequently' enforced in a consistent way (*Chart 19: Consistency of Government Law Enforcement*). The substantial percentage of distrust on the enforcement of law by the Chinese Government shows that improvement must be made.

8.2.3.2 Need for Bribery to Deal with Government Officials

In order to explore the role of bribery in relations between investors and government officials, it was asked whether it was 'necessary' to bribe government officials. The responses have shown that in dealing with government officials, bribery is normally unnecessary. Forty five per cent of surveyed EU investors reported that there had 'never' (40 per cent)[13] or 'rarely' (5 per cent) been a need to use bribery when dealing with government officials. Only five per cent answered that bribery was 'always' needed, while around nine per cent found it necessary 'sometimes' (*Chart 20: Need of Bribery for Officials*). Meanwhile, it must be noted that this question might have been too straightforward for some investors to answer honestly, probably due to certain regulations in their home countries and from the OECD with regard to bribery. Thus, there was a rather high percentage (31 per cent) of 'do not know' responses and a five per cent of 'unanswerable' reply.[14] Also, in an interview with the head of a Chamber of Commerce, doubt was expressed about the number of honest answers to this question.[15]

13 Among those who replied that bribery had 'never' been necessary, 2 (9%) suspected that others might have used it.

14 The actual answer was 'Do you really want an answer?'

15 The interviewee commented, 'this question is good and straightforward, but I do not know how many of them will answer honestly.' See Interview No. 1.

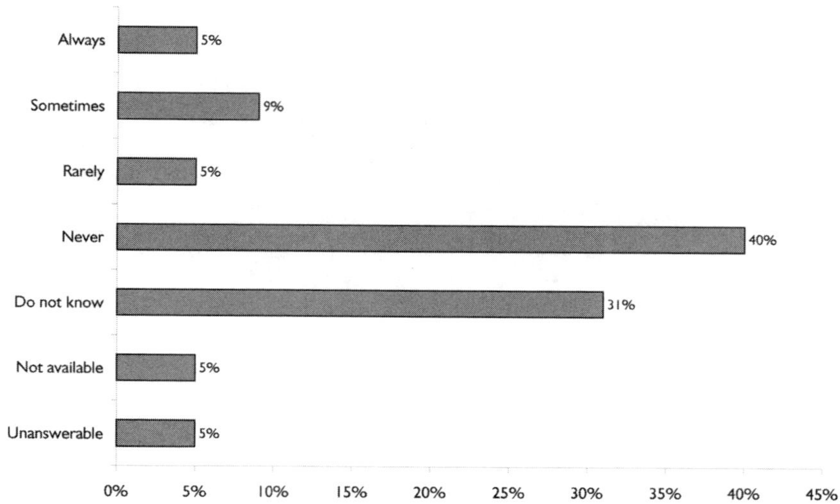

Chart 20: Need of Bribery for Officials

8.2.4 Court Enforcement of Law

The Courts are the centre of all law enforcement activities. Therefore, four questions were designed to examine the record of law enforcement by and around the Chinese courts: the objectivity of law enforcement by the courts,[16] the possibility of bribery impacting on court judgements, political interference on court decisions and unreasonable delays of court and arbitration procedures.

8.2.4.1 Objectivity of Courts Law Enforcement

On the question of the objectivity of court law enforcement, as *Chart 21* shows, the answers are about 50–50 per cent. About eighteen per cent of surveyed EU investors gave clearly positive replies ('mostly' and 'frequently'), while nineteen per cent of them replied clearly negatively ('Never' or 'rarely'). Twenty three per cent said that 'sometimes' such objectivity was achieved. However, the largest portion of respondents (40 per cent) 'did not know' (31 per cent) the question, which may suggest that they had neither experience nor knowledge of Chinese courts enforcement. The other nine

[16] It has been widely held that the Chinese court system cannot effectively resolve disputes and enforce its judgments. See Blumental, above, note 10, at 264. See also Clarke, Donald C, 'The Execution of Civil Judgments in China', in Lubman, Stanley (ed), *China's Legal Reforms* (1996), 65–81. Snyder, Kelley Brooke, 'Denial of Enforcement of Chinese Arbitral Awards on Public Policy Grounds: The View From Hong Kong', (2001) 42 *Virginia Journal of International Law* 339, at 340.

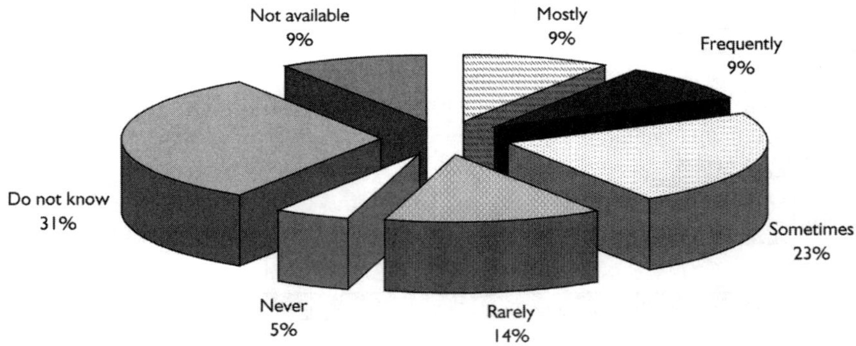

Chart 21: Objectivity of Court Law Enforcement

per cent did not answer the question (*Chart 21: Objectivity of Court Law Enforcement*). Therefore, two observations may be drawn. On the one hand, a substantial portion of EU investors have no experience or knowledge of Chinese courts. On the other hand, among those who answered, approximately half of them believed that the law was not objectively enforced. As courts are always expected to objectively enforce the law, this should generally be regarded as a negative answer.

8.2.4.2 Possibility of Bribing Judges

The question of the possibility of bribing judges has proved to be even more difficult to answer than that of bribing officials.[17] About ten per cent of respondents answered positively ('always' and 'frequently'), though they claimed that they based their answers on suspicion or belief of other companies' experiences. Another five per cent replied that bribery 'sometimes' could be used to influence judge's decisions. Thirteen per cent of the respondents stated that this had 'never' happened to them, but they suspected that other companies might have participated in bribery. Another nine per cent did not answer at all. Finally, there was also one response who directly challenged the propriety of the question, by asking 'do you really want an answer?' In short, like the question about bribery to officials, this question might have been too provocative to have solicited honest answers (*Chart 22: Possibility of Bribery Impacting on Court Decisions*).

8.2.4.3 Political Interference in Court Decisions

Similar to the previous question, most investors ticked 'do not know' (54 per cent) or simply did not answer (9 per cent) the question on whether politi-

[17] Snyder, *ibid.*

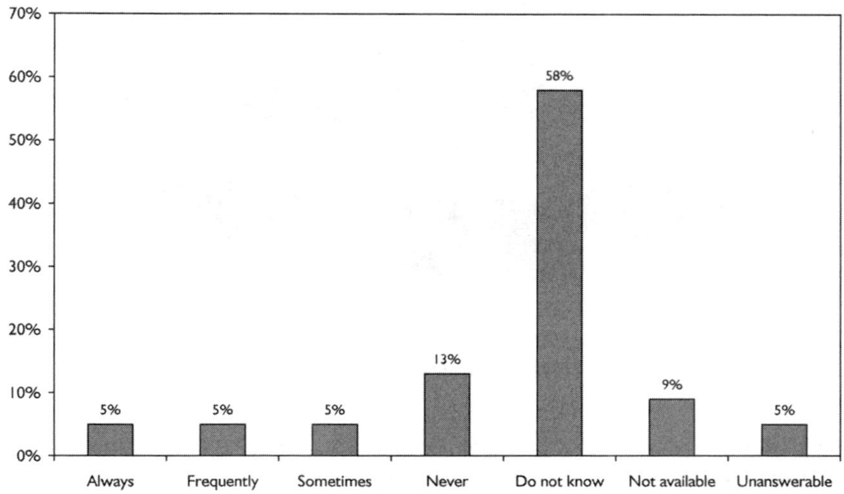

Chart 22: Possibility of Bribery Impacting on Court Decisions

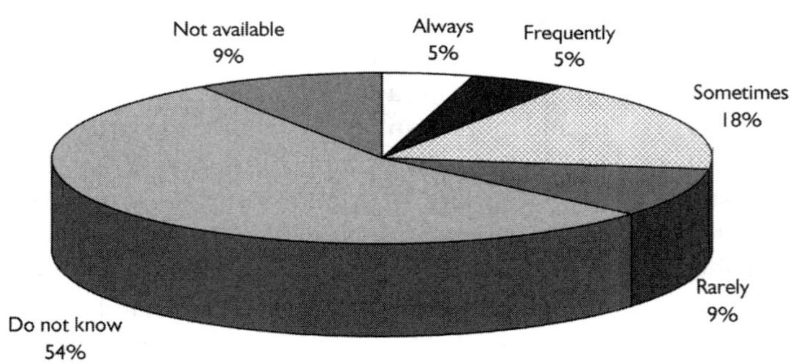

Chart 23: Political Interference in Court Decisions

cians interfere in court decisions. Among these who did give answers, ten per cent did positively ('always' or 'frequently'), nine per cent negatively ('rarely') and eighteen per cent vaguely ('sometimes') (*Chart 23: Political Interference in Court Decisions*). It may be concluded that political interference was experienced by about half of all those having direct or indirect court experience in China, indicating a rather severe problem.

8.2.4.4 Delays in Court and Arbitration Procedures

Answers to the question on the frequency of delays in court and arbitration procedures are clearer, although, similarly, more than a half (54 per cent) of

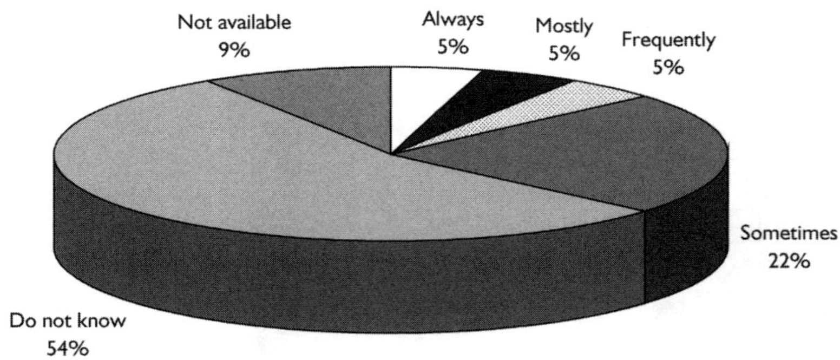

Chart 24: Unreasonable Delays in Court and Arbitration Procedures

respondents 'did not know' the answer and nine per cent did not answer it. In the thirty seven per cent that did answered the question, fifteen per cent clearly said yes ('always', 'mostly' or 'frequently') while twenty two per cent reported that it was 'sometimes' the case (*Chart 24: Unreasonable Delays in Court and Arbitration Procedures*). The fact that no one replied negatively has signalled the seriousness of this problem.

One interesting phenomenon in the responses to all those questions on court enforcement of law is that there was always nine per cent who did not answer any of them, whilst there was a substantial but varied percentage (31 per cent for the first one and more than 50 per cent for the latter three) of 'do not know' answers. The former may be simply explained as that they did not feel the questions were appropriate, or were not sure how to answer them. From the latter, we may draw two conclusions: on the one hand, that a substantial portion of EU investors 'did not know' the answer probably shows that they had no court experience at all; on the other hand, however, the differences in the exact percentages implies that some respondents might be unwilling, rather than unable, to answer some of the questions.

8.2.5 Enforcement of Court and Arbitration Decisions

In China, the problem over enforcement of court and arbitration decisions have been so prevalent[18] that a special terminology has been developed to describe it—'the Difficulty of Enforcement' (*Zhixin Nan*). As *Chart 25* shows, the experience of EU investors has confirmed that such a problem does exist. Although there are still more 'do not know' answers (45 per cent) than 'real' answers, among the real answers, there are more negative ones (19 per cent, 'never' and 'rarely') than positive ones (9 per cent, 'mostly', no one

[18] See note 16.

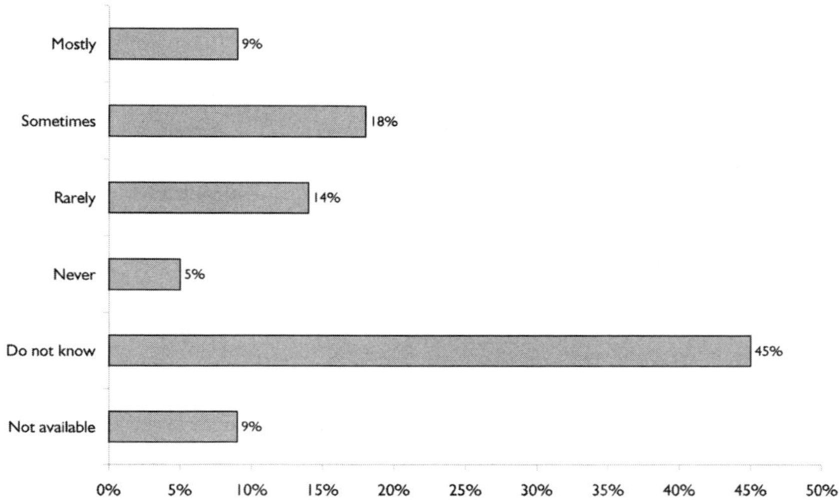

Chart 25: Enforcement of Court and Arbitration Decisions

answered 'always'). Besides, as with the previous questions, eighteen per cent of replies state that court and arbitration decisions are 'sometimes' enforced by the courts. Further, one of the interviewees had expressed desperation over the non-enforcement of the arbitration award he had won[19] (*Chart 25: Enforcement of Court and Arbitration Decisions*).

8.2.6 Measuring the FDI Legal System in China against the Ideal Institutional Paradigm

In order to compare the FDI legal system in China as experienced by the respondents with the Ideal Institutional Paradigm (IIP), responses to each of the nine questions on the effectiveness of the legal system were converted into a score based on a scale between 0 and 5, with 5 representing maximum conformity with the IIP.[20] Thus, for instance, on accessibility of law, the response 'always' obtains the maximum score (5) and 'never' receives the minimum (0). 'Mostly', 'frequently', 'sometimes', 'rarely' receive 4, 3, 2 and

[19] Interview No. 2.

[20] Perry has conducted a similar comparison in her case study on the effectiveness of the Sri Lankan legal system. Perry, PhD dissertation, note 2 above, at 195–99.

[21] 'Do not know' and 'do not understand' or blank responses are excluded in the conversion and calculation as they do not bear any quantitative meanings.

Table 21: FDI Legal System in China Measured against the Ideal Institutional Paradigm

Institution	Feature	Score	Descriptor
Laws (Average Score: 2.55)	Accessibility	2.65	Ineffective
	Predictability	2.45	Ineffective
Bureaucracy (Average Score: 3.03)	Consistency	2.29	Ineffective
	Corruption	3.77	Borderline
Courts (Average Score: 2.45)	Objectivity	1.85	Seriously Ineffective
	Corruption	3.33	Borderline
	Independency	2.75	Ineffective
	Efficiency	2.33	Ineffective
	Enforceability	2.0	Ineffective
Legal System as a Whole	–	2.68	Ineffective

1 respectively.[21] Details are included in Appendix II. Based on this conversion, the average score for each element (feature) was calculated. An average score for the legal system as a whole was generated on the basis of the average scores of the three major components, namely the laws, the bureaucracy and the courts. Elements scored 4 or above are described as 'effective', whilst others are described as 'borderline' (=3 & <4), 'ineffective' (=2 & <3), 'seriously ineffective' (<2). Details of the scores are presented in *Table 21* below.

As can be seen from *Table 21* and *Chart 26*, the FDI legal system in China as perceived by respondent does not conform to the IIP. None of the nine elements had achieved an '*effective*' mark. Only two features, namely corruptions by bureaucracy and courts, were on the *borderline*, the accuracy of which as explained above is doubtful. All the other seven factors were well below the *borderline* and were either *ineffective* or *seriously ineffective*. These included accessibility and predictability of laws, consistency in bureaucracy law enforcement, and objectivity, independency, efficiency and enforceability in courts' law enforcement. The worst situation was regarding objectivity in courts' enforcement of laws, which was *seriously ineffective*, followed by the poor enforcement of courts and arbitration decisions. Overall, the FDI legal system in China was perceived as *ineffective*, with a score of 2.68.

Such a finding was further confirmed by 'further comments' of respondents. Of the nine 'further comments' received, six were related to the weakness in the enforcement of laws, rather than in the laws *per se*. One respondent said that '[K]ey issue is not only 'regulations', but their

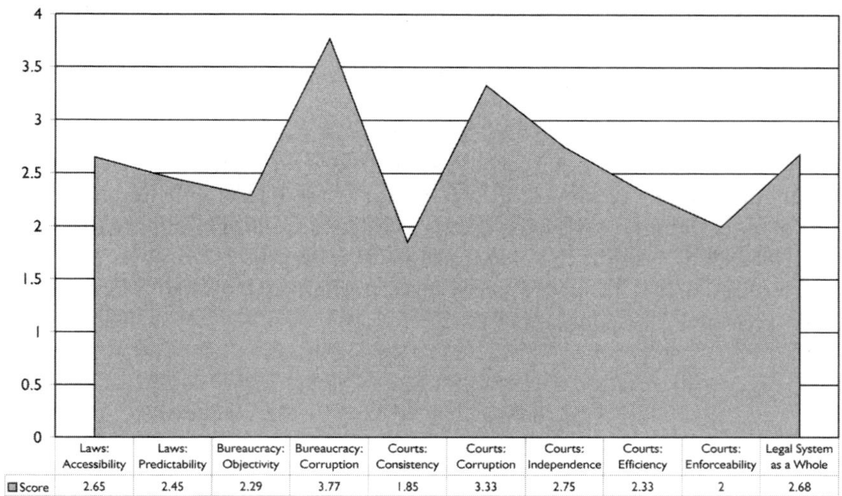

Chart 26: FDI Legal System in China Measured Against the Ideal Institutional Paradigm

IMPLEMENTATIONS.' Another commented that '[T]he legal environment is actually not that bad, the problematic part is the enforcement side.'[22] One respondent, nevertheless, acknowledged that 'there are significant improvements on the legal environment development and the enforcement development.'

On the whole, it can be concluded that, despite significant improvements, the FDI legal system in China remains ineffective, as it is sometimes inaccessible, often subject to unexpected changes, sometimes inconsistently and often subjectively enforced by government officials and courts, and that court and arbitration decisions are not well carried out.

8.3 CONCLUSIONS

The preceding investigations have resulted in two general conclusions: On the one hand law has played a very important role when EU investors decided to invest in China; on the other hand, the EU investors generally perceived

[22] Other comments included: 'It is utmost important that China evolves towards a real state of law…' '1. Elimination of corruption-Chinese and foreign investors-by clear law fully enforced; 2, Law separated from central politics—see US Constitution!!' 'The only frustrating part of doing business in China is that what you have been advised, initially, as being achievable by local authority representatives invariably ends up with several reasons why it is NO longer possible, usually at an advanced stage.' 'Arbitration processes are improving in China, but enforcement of court ruling often deficient.'

that the Chinese legal system was ineffective. The system is considered as sometimes inaccessible, subject to frequent and unexpected changes, inconsistently and subjectively enforced by government officials and even courts, and lacking effective enforcement of court and arbitration decisions. Considering that most EU investors tend to investigate the written law as well as the law in action, the perceived ineffectiveness of Chinese legal system is detrimental to the investment flow from the EU to China. Further, this results in a stronger demand on a wide access to international remedies, which is not readily available within the current legal framework.[23] A new international legal framework with wider access to international remedies is therefore needed to solve this problem.

[23] See Section 7.6.

PART IV

Towards a New International Legal Framework of EU-China Investment Relations

9

Towards a New International Legal Framework of EU-China Investment Relations

9.1 THE NEED FOR A NEW INTERNATIONAL LEGAL FRAMEWORK OF EU-CHINA INVESTMENT RELATIONS

The need for a new strengthened international legal framework (NILF) for EU-China investment relations can be justified by the fact that, as explored in previous Chapters, the current legal framework for EU investment in China is insufficient for the protection of the rapidly expanding EU investment in China.[1] For EU investment in China, the insufficiencies and deficiencies of the current legal framework can be seen from three perspectives as previously shown.

Part I demonstrates that the current legal system is incomplete, unsystematic and uncoordinated. This is because Chinese FDI law is unsystematic, the EU's role in international investment law making is limited, and because the applicable international treaties are neither complete nor consistent. Part II shows that although the current legal framework provides substantial protection for EU investment in China (except Irish investment), it still needs further improvement on substantive features like admission, treatment, expropriation, and dispute settlement. Finally, Part III demonstrates that whilst EU investors considered the governing laws a significant determinant when they made their decisions to invest in China, they viewed the Chinese legal system as ineffective, which suggests a strong demand for enhanced international legal framework.

The need for a new legal framework on investment between the EU and China has been clearly endorsed by the EU business community. The author's

[1] As mentioned in the Introduction, the expansion of EU investment in China in recent years has been unprecedented and in 2000 the EU became the biggest foreign investor in China. Further, more significant increase of EU investment in China can be anticipated in the 21st century, since China has become a formal member of the WTO in December 2001. See Section I.5.

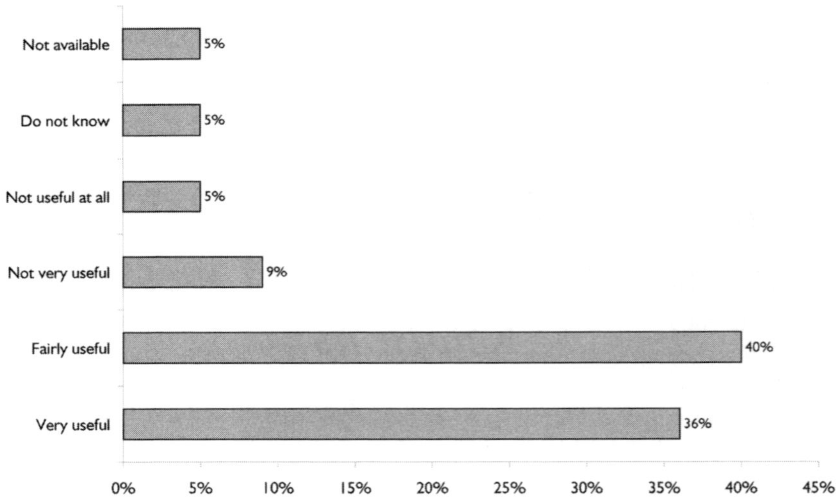

Chart 27: Significance of a New International Legal Framework between the EU and China

Questionnaire survey shows that an overwhelming majority (76 per cent) of EU investors considered an NILF will be of substantial use in promoting and protecting EU investment in China. (*Chart 27: Significance of a New International Legal Framework between the EU and China*). EU institutions have also been very keen on strengthening the legal institutions for the protection of EU investment in China. As early as 1984, for example, the European Parliament proposed to sign an individual investment and intellectual property treaty at the Community level with China.[2] In the 1998 Communication 'Building a Comprehensive Partnership with China', the Commission stated that

> 'The EU should aim at improving the investment environment for European companies in China. The construction of a sound and transparent regulatory framework for investment and a better enforcement of Chinese regulations on intellectual property rights are prime examples to achieve this objective.'[3]

A new and strengthened international legal regime for its investment in China is therefore necessary, at least from the EU's perspective. From the Chinese perspective, the expanding Chinese investment in the EU, particularly the 10 new member states, also makes it more and more desirable to have an improved investment regime. As EU-China investment relations intensify, the call for such an NILF will be stronger and stronger.

[2] See the *European Parliament's Resolution on Economic and Commercial Relations between China and the EEC*, OJ C 127/210, 1984.

[3] Communication from the Commission, '*Building a Comprehensive Partnership with China*', Section C. 1. 3, COM (1998) 181 (25.03.1998).

9.2 THE POSSIBILITY OF A NEW INTERNATIONAL LEGAL FRAMEWORK OF EU-CHINA INVESTMENT RELATIONS

The construction of a new international legal framework for EU investment in China is not only necessary and urgent but increasingly likely. If the time was not ripe for such a legal infrastructure in the 1980s,[4] it probably is now, for both the political and economical climates have changed significantly and favourably since then.

Firstly, EU's competence vis-à-vis its member states on international investment matters has been consistently confirmed and expanded within the EU by both the ECJ jurisprudence and the EU's extensive bilateral and multilateral treaty practices.[5] The 2004 Treaty Establishing a Constitution for Europe has finally confirmed that EU is to have exclusive competence on external FDI matters. FDI laws and policies have been further liberalised and harmonised within the EU with the launch of the Economic and Monetary Union (EMU) in general in the 1990s, and the Euro in particular in 2000. The EU has become the most active advocate of a multilateral investment agreement after the failure of the MAI within the framework of the WTO.[6]

Secondly, the establishment of a Market Economy is under way in China and the opening up to the outside world will be remarkably broadened and deepened by accession to the WTO. Externally China has been very positive in negotiating and concluding BITs, with 106 BITS having been signed by March 2003.[7] China has also been very active in participating in the multilateral negotiations on a global investment framework on occasions such as UNCTAD, the WTO, and the APEC.[8]

On a bilateral level, thirdly, the EU and China have emphasised their shared interest in furthering the bilateral investment relations. In the Joint

[4] According to interviews conducted by the author with a few officials of China or investment-related departments of the European Commission, it is believed that no further step might have been taken on the 1984 EP proposal and that it might have been overtaken by events. See eg, Interview No. 5, 6 and 10.

[5] See Section 2.1 for details.

[6] See *EC Approach to Trade and Investment*, at http://europa.eu.int/comm/dg01/1806ti.htm (11/11/99). See also Lord Brittan (Sir Leon Brittan as he then was), 'Investment Liberalisation: the Next Great Boost to the World Economy', (1995) 4 *Transnational Corporations*.

[7] See Xu, Chunlin, *Investment Protection on Fast Track of Development in China*, posted at http://fdi.gov.cn/common/frnreport.jsp?id=CENSOFT000000000.7375 (visited on 4 June 2003).

[8] In Chinese literature on a potential multilateral investment agreement, most scholars expressed a positive attitude. For example, Ma Yu, an investment expert in the MOFTEC (now MOFCOM), wrote that China should actively participate in investment negotiations within international organisations. See Ma, Yu, *Investment Liberalisation in the Context of Economic Globalisation in the World*, posted at http://www.etisu.com.cn/zgwmxh/tongxun/00126/02-0126-WTO1.htm (visited on 28 June 2003). Similar can also be seen in Ye, Xinping, 'Recent Trends of Foreign Investment and the Changing International Investment Norms: An Overview', (2002) 4 *Law Review (Faxue Pinglun)*, at 75. For China's activities within UNCTAD and APEC, see Zhao, Hong, 'Preliminary Comments on the "Multilateral Agreement on Investment"', (1999) 2 *Chinese Journal of International Economic Law*, at 264, notes 2 and 3.

Press Statement of the Fifth EU-China Summit for instance, leaders from both sides 'stressed the importance of foreign direct investment and the need for investment flows in both directions to increase further'.[9] On the negotiations of the Doha Development Agenda, which includes the issue of a multilateral investment framework, the two sides pledged to intensify their dialogue and to work together for 'an ambitious result' that fulfilled the expectations of all WTO members.[10] The EU's 2003 policy paper on China also stresses that EU will strengthen dialogue at all level with China on bilateral investment issues, among others.[11] From these developments it would be safe to conclude that a new legal framework for EU-China investment relations would not only be necessary but also possible.

9.3 THE FORMS OF A NEW INTERNATIONAL LEGAL FRAMEWORK OF EU-CHINA INVESTMENT RELATIONS

The NILF might be in either of the two forms: a multilateral investment agreement (MIA) to which both the EU and China are contracting parties; or a bilateral investment treaty (BIT) between the EU and China. Although they can serve the same purpose of facilitating EU-China FDI flows, they might be quite different simply because many more parties are involved in an MIA. The two possible solutions are explored below in turn.

9.3.1 Multilateral Approach: A MIA to which the EU and China are Parties

An MIA to which China and the EU are contracting parties is an inviting solution since it may provide uniform rules and therefore stability and predictability for FDI around the globe, not just between the EU and China. Both China and the EU are interested in the negotiations of an MIA. As noted above, the EU is one of the most active advocates of concluding an MIA within the WTO framework. At the same time all its Member States are OECD members and have participated in the three-year MAI negotiations. On the other hand, although not a member of either organisation, China, as the largest developing country and the second largest FDI recipient in the world, is closely watching these negotiations and is considering its own

[9] The fifth EU-China Summit took place in Copenhagen on 24 September 2002. The joint press statement was adopted by the summit. See http://www.europa-web.de/europa/03euinf/05CHINA/euchisum.htm (visited 17 December 2002).

[10] *Ibid.*

[11] See Commission Policy Paper for Transmission to the Council and the European Parliament: *A Maturing Partnership—Shared Inters and Challenges in EU-China Relations*, COM (2003), 533 fin, at 18.

position and counter-measures.[12] China is more and more willing to take part in a multilateral legal framework on investment as its overseas investment has been increasing rapidly particularly after the recent accession to the WTO.

It is likely that in future MIA negotiations both the EU and China will take a positive attitude in their respective roles of leaders of developed countries and developing countries.[13] According to the author's interviews with EC officials the multilateral approach might be the best choice to enhance the protection and promotion of EU investment in China.[14]

Three aspects are essential to the success of an MIA: the choice of forum, the full participation of interested countries, and the balance of interests.

9.3.1.1 The Choice of Forum

A prerequisite of concluding an MIA is to find an appropriate forum. The possibilities include mainly the OECD, the WTO, the United Nations Conference on Trade and Development (UNCTAD), and the World Bank (IBRD). Among them, the OECD is perhaps the most experienced organisation in terms of analysis discussions and negotiations on FDI issues, dating as it does back to the 1960s. Some negotiations have led to formal agreements, such as the Codes of Liberalisation of Capital Movements and Current Invisible Operations.[15] The WTO may be preferable because of its approach to negotiation issues, its size, and the nature of its memberships, which might guarantee a real global negotiation with wide participation.

The UNCTAD has long been involved in international investment issues too, and has planned to draft a multilateral framework on investment (MFI).[16] The advantage of UNCTAD as an MIA forum is that it is a UN insti-

[12] China participated in the both the negotiation on MAI and related discussions within the WTO, both as an observer. At the same time, many discussions on MAI have emerged recently in China, from both legal and economical perspectives. See eg, Ye, Xinping, 'Recent Trends of Foreign Investment and the Changing International Investment Norms: An Overview', (2002) 4 *Law Review* (*Faxue Pinglun*), at 68–75; Liu, Sun, 'The MAI as an Indicator of the Difficulty and the Prospect of a Comprehensive Multilateral Investment Agreement', (2001) 5 *Chinese Legal Science* (*Zhongguo Faxue*), at 137–44; Lu, Tong, 'Comments on the Negotiation on the "Multilateral Agreement on Investment", and Sheng, Boming, 'The Negotiation of Multilateral Agreement on Investment and the Countermeasures of Developing Countries', both in (1999) 7 *World Economy* (in Chinese). See also Zhao, Hong, 'Preliminary Comments on the "Multilateral Agreement on Investment"' and Chen, Huiping, 'The Progress and Prospects of the Negotiation of the "Multilateral Agreement on Investment"', both in (1999) 2 *Chinese Journal of International Economic Law*.

[13] The 2002 EU-China summit joint statement seems to have confirmed this. See the Joint Statement of the Fifth EU-China Summit, posted at http://www.europa-web.de/europa/03euinf/05CHINA/euchisum.htm (visited 17 December 2002).

[14] The EU officials believe, further, that, the second best would be bilateral agreements and the third unilateral legislation. Interviews Nos 6, 8 and 11.

[15] Brewer, Tomas L, and Young, Stephen, 'Towards a Multilateral Framework for Foreign Direct Investment: Issues and Scenarios', (1995) 4 *Transnational Corporations*, at 74–75.

[16] Chen, Huiping, above, note 12, at 308.

tution which is experienced in organising multilateral negotiations. It may be able to balance the interests between developed and developing countries.

The last option is the World Bank. It has successfully organised the negotiation of the ICSID Convention and the MIGA Convention and has drafted an influential Guidelines on the legal treatment of FDI. However, it has not so far initiated any proposal for making a formal MIA as such.

The EU and its Member States are keen on protecting their overseas investments, very prudent in the forum selection, and are generally in favour of an MIA either sponsored by the OECD or within the framework of the WTO.[17] Scholars have described the possible scenarios of MIA negotiations, including discussion at the OECD and implementation at the WTO, negotiation at OECD and preparation for negotiations at WTO, negotiation of new agreements in both WTO and OECD, and creation of an entirely new legal framework and organisation for FDI.[18] They also argue that it is necessary to establish an Inter-agency Working Group on International Direct Investment, composing of the OECD, WTO, UNCTAD, World Bank and International Monetary Fund (IMF), to link their positions and facilitate further movement.[19] Lord Brittan (Sir Leon Brittan as he then was) said that negotiations at OECD and WTO were not exclusive to each other and therefore could be undertaken simultaneously.[20]

As noted, China has been active in multilateral investment law-making in parallel to its efforts to build up a BIT network. As regards the forum China does not seem to oppose the MAI within OECD despite the fact that the OECD is a club of rich countries. China has sent government officials to participate in high level conferences on the MAI.[21] Many Chinese scholars, however, do not accept the MAI on the grounds that its standard of investment protection is too high for a developing country to afford; and its negotiating process virtually excludes any substantial participation by developing countries.[22] As for an MIA within the WTO regime, some Chinese commentators argue that the WTO might not be a proper forum for negotiating a global investment agreement since it is 'neither democratic nor transparent',[23] while many others do not object to it.[24] Some argue that UNCTAD, with its experiences and development orientation,[25] would be a better forum for such an MIA.

In short all the abovementioned four avenues, with their different merits, have the potential to become the forum of future MIAs. The two most likely

[17] Lord Brittan (Sir Leon Brittan as he then was), above, note 6, at 9.
[18] Brewer and Young, above, note 15, at 74–75.
[19] *Ibid.*
[20] Lord Brittan (Sir Leon Brittan as he then was), above, note 6, at 9.
[21] Zhao, Hong, above, note 12, at 266, note 6.
[22] See eg Zhao, Hong and Chen, Huiping, above, note 12, at 286–93 and at 302–06.
[23] See eg Chen, Huiping, *ibid*, at 307.
[24] See eg Zhao, Hong, above, note 12, at 289.
[25] Chen, Huiping, above, note 12, at 308.

are be OECD and WTO, as the World Bank has not yet developed an initiative thereon and the UNCTAD is not favoured by developed countries, the main driving force for such an MIA. The WTO may also stand a much better chance as compared with OECD, whose MAI proposal has failed to reach a consensus even among its member countries. The Doha Ministerial Declaration has confirmed that negotiations of a 'multilateral framework' for investment 'will take place after the Fifth Session of the Ministerial Conference on the basis of a decision to be taken, by explicit consensus, at that Session on modalities of negotiations'.[26] The Doha Work Programme adopted by the General Council on 1 August 2004 nevertheless decided that such a negotiation on investment would no longer be pursued during this Doha Round.[27] Another major effort to create an MIA was suspended.

No matter which venue the future MIA eventually uses, however, it is essential to guarantee that most interested countries, developed and developing countries alike, are substantially involved in the negotiations; and that the interests of all parties involving in international investment activities are fully reflected and balanced in the final act.

9.3.1.2 The Full Participation of Interested Parties

A truly global agreement must involve a sufficiently representative cross section of the international community.[28] This does not only mean offering all interested parties, particularly the developing countries, a chance to sign the agreement as the OECD's MAI negotiations did; but more importantly means allowing them fully to participate in the entire process of negotiation,[29] offering them the technical assistance necessary for such a participation.

The failure of the MAI in OECD is partially attributed to the lack of substantial participation by developing countries. Although it allowed some countries to participate as observers and tried to publicise the progress of the negotiations, non-OECD countries could only make comments and could not directly affect the final outcome. Obviously such limited participation is not sufficient for a global investment agreement. The participation of relevant international organisations is also valuable as the negotiation and

[26] The WTO: *Ministerial Declaration adopted by the Fourth Session of the Ministerial Conference at Doha* on 9–14 November 2001 (hereinafter "*Doha Ministerial Declaration*"), WT/MIN(01)/DEC/W/1 (14 November 2001), posted at http://www.wto.org/english/thewto_e/minist_e/min01_e/mindecl_e.htm (visited on 18 January 2002), at para 20.

[27] *Doha Work Programme*, Decision Adopted by the General Council on 1 August 2004, posted at http://www.wto.org/english/tratop_e/dda_e/ddadraft_31jul04_e.doc (visited on 29 August 2004).

[28] Ruggiero, Renato, 'Foreign Direct Investment and the Multilateral Trading System', (1996) 5 *Transnational Corporations*, at 7.

[29] Similar ideas have been expressed in Zhao, Hong, above, note 12, at 289–90. See also Ruggiero, above, note 28, at 7; and Brewer and Young, above, note 15, at 80.

implementation may therefore take full advantage of their legal and technical expertise on FDI-related matters.[30]

The Doha Ministerial Declaration affirmed the need for wide participation and the necessary technical support involved, and undertook to 'work in co-operation with other relevant intergovernmental organisations, including UNCTAD; and through appropriate regional and bilateral channels to provide strengthened and adequately resourced assistance to respond to these needs'.[31]

9.3.1.3 The Balance of Interests

The balance of interests is probably the most important element among the three mentioned because the other two elements are both about striking a good deal, a deal in which the interests of all participants in investment activities are considered reflected and balanced. There are two kinds of balance to be considered in particular.

One of these is the balance between the interests of the host country and foreign investors. It is evident that international investment agreements may establish sets of legal rights and obligations for Governments and firms.[32] The balance of rights and obligations between the two sides has been a central issue in the contents of international investment agreements. It is observed, however, that the discussion has changed from an emphasis on *firms' obligations and governments' rights* to an emphasis on *firms' rights and governments' obligations*.[33] The abandonment of the United Nations effort to develop a Code of Conduct on Transnational Corporations (TNC) and the dismantling of the United Nations Centre on Transnational Corporations (UNCTC) is clear evidence of this change.

The shift is due perhaps to two principal reasons. On the one hand, most developing countries' attitude towards FDI has changed: now FDI is widely regarded as a scarce resource that no country can afford to drive away, instead of being seen as a threat, as had been the case in the past.[34] A competition has been taking place globally to attract FDI, in both developing and developed countries. On the other hand most of these new international legal instruments are sponsored and drafted by industrial countries, without substantial participation by developing countries.

However future negotiations on a truly global MIA may refocus this discussion because developing countries have not given up their concerns about the conduct of transnational corporations (TNCs), especially the restrictive

[30] Brewer and Young, *ibid*.
[31] *Doha Ministerial Declaration*, above, note 26, para 21.
[32] Bergsten, F Fred, and Graham, Edward M, 'Needed: New International Rules for Foreign Direct Investment', (1992) 7 *The International Trade Journal*, at 15–44.
[33] Brewer and Young, above, note 15, at 70.
[34] Lord Brittan (Sir Leon Brittan as he then was), above, note 6, at 2.

business practices of TNCs, their transfer pricing, employment, environmental protection, and so on.[35] Whenever they can, developing countries try to maintain their rights to use domestic laws and regulations to manage and regulate activities of foreign investors.

For example, in the APEC statement of non-binding investment principles, developing countries insisted on the inclusion of a statement to the effect that 'acceptance of foreign investment is facilitated only when foreign investors abide by the host economy's laws, regulations, administrative guidelines and policies, just as domestic investors should'.[36] The early draft of the Code of Conduct of Transnational Corporations, the OECD Guidelines for Multilateral Enterprises of 1976, and the OECD Declaration on International investment and Multilateral Enterprises of 1994 may also be used as a basis for the provisions on firms' conduct in the possible MIA.

The other balance involves regulating the interests between developed countries and developing countries.[37] Although Renato Ruggiero has argued that the MIA issue should not be 'perceived as one of North-South relations, but as one of common interest',[38] it is inevitable that the developed countries and developing countries are standing in different positions and therefore have different interests in FDI matters. In the world FDI market, developed countries are major investors and investment recipients as well, whilst developing countries are attracting more and more FDI inflows. According to the *World Investment Report 1999* for instance, developed countries accounted for 91.6 per cent of FDI outflows and 71.5 per cent of inflows in 1998, while developing countries made up only 8.1 per cent of FDI outflows and 25.8 per cent of FDI inflows.[39] These figures show that on the one hand most investment activities were carried out between developed countries, and that on the other hand, in investment relations between developed countries and developing countries, the former are generally capital-exporters while the latter are capital-importers. Only a few developing countries invest abroad. Most of them are pure investment recipients.[40]

This situation is unlikely to change soon, and so in the course of future global investment law-making fora, developed countries, as representatives

35 Brewer and Young, above, note 15, at 70–71. See also Brewer, Tomas L, and Young, Stephen, 'Investment Policies in Multilateral and Regional Agreement: A Comparative Analysis', (1996) 5 *Transnational Corporations*, at 27–28.

36 APEC Non-binding Investment Principles, 'Investor behaviour' section. Reprinted as annex in Sornarajah, M, 'Protection of Foreign Investment in the Asian Pacific Economic Cooperation Region', (1995) *Journal of World Trade*, at 128–29.

37 It is worth noting that, however, those countries at similar development stage have conflicting interests which need to be balance as well. For instance, during the OECD MAI negotiations, various disagreements existed and it was mainly these sorts of 'internal conflict of interest' that lead the whole project to break down. See Engering, Frans, 'The Multilateral Investment Agreement', (1996) 5 *Transnational Corporations*, at 161.

38 Ruggiero, above, note 28, at 7.

39 UNCTAD, *World Investment Report 1999: Foreign Direct Investment and the Challenge of Development,* at 20, *Table* I.3.

40 UNCTAD, *World Investment Report 1999: Foreign Direct Investment and the Challenge of Development: Overview,* at 19.

of international investors, will go on seeking further liberalisation for FDI movement. Developing countries as host countries will struggle meanwhile to defend their rights of regulating and managing FDI activities. Such a conflict of interest will inevitably continue to be reflected in any future North-South negotiation of investment treaties, whether in the form of a BIT or an MIA.

Admittedly, however, there are common interests in FDI issues between developed and developing countries as well. There is surplus capital in the north looking for overseas markets; while in the south there is a widespread hunger for capital for economic development. This common interest is the basis of all the BITs between the two state groups and will be the grounds of all North-South negotiations on any future MIA. Nevertheless, an MIA will be a compromise of interests for all interested countries. Hence a fair balance of interests between the two groups of countries is crucial for an MIA's success.

To maintain such a balance, host countries must first be entitled to adopt laws and regulations to manage investment activities, to make sure they are in conformity with their national plans and development objectives in return for providing a higher standard of protection for foreign investors. Secondly the liberalisation of international investment should be done step-by-step, allowing countries at different developmental levels to have different transition periods and exemptions. Lastly, in some sensitive areas such as investment incentives and performance requirements where global consensus is unlikely to be attained at this stage, the 'voluntary acceptance' principle may be used. In this sense, the WTO 'plurilateral agreements' might be used as a reference.[41]

In conclusion, an MIA to which both the EU and China are members is a possible solution for more effective protection of mutual investment, provided that the agreement is negotiated with the full participation of all concerned countries and that their interests are fully reflected and balanced. A (global) investment agreement which is fair and equitable worldwide would be beneficial both for developed and developing countries and would contribute to the peace and prosperity of the future world. But the failures of MAI proposals in both the OECD and the WTO Seattle Conference have demonstrated that such an agreement cannot be achieved in a hurry. Although negotiations of this type of MIA have been included in the Doha agenda, the collapse of Cancún Ministerial Conference[42] and the 2004 Doha Work Programme demonstrate that there is still a long way to go create a real MIA.

[41] The Doha Ministerial Declaration seems to have adopted this approach for rules on admission. See *Doha Ministerial Declaration*, above, note 26, at para 22.

[42] The Fifth Ministerial Conference held in Cancún, Mexico ended without any outcome. On of the major sticky issue is the investment issue. See *Conference Ends Without Consensus*, posted at WTO official website: http://www.wto.org/english/thewto_e/minist_e/min03_e/min03_14sept_e.htm (visited on 20 September 2003)

9.3.2 Bilateral Approach: A BIT between the EU and China

A BIT between the EU and China may be easier to achieve than an MIA at this stage for the following reasons. Firstly, both sides are prepared to sign such a treaty as the bilateral political and economic links have been significantly improved and continue to do so. Secondly a bilateral treaty involves only two parties (the EU and its Member States as a whole) and therefore faces much less conflict of interest. It does not cost as much time and resources as an MIA. Furthermore, a BIT, unlike an MIA, is widely regarded as a pragmatic arrangement to attract and protect FDI. Hence some historically controversial issues, such as expropriation and compensation, are less likely to become serious problems. Also, the 13 BITs between China and EU Member States have laid a solid basis for the future negotiations of a BIT at Community level. Finally the Joint Committee mechanism established under the EC-China Co-operation Agreement may serve as the preliminary vehicle of negotiating such a BIT, with its competence to 'examine means and new opportunities of developing trade and economic cooperation'; and to 'make recommendations' in the areas of common interest.[43]

However, as the EU is now focusing on the multilateral agenda, bilateral talks on investment issues are very unlikely to take place unless they are given high political priority within the Union.[44] Now that the Fifth WTO Ministerial Conference has failed to launch the MIA negotiations, the EU probably will resort to the bilateral approach. According to EU officials China definitely will be a priority target for such bilateral talks.[45]

Under the general agreement between the EU and China (hereinafter the framework agreement), the EU-China BIT may take one of two forms: an individual, sectoral agreement under the framework agreement; or a substantial 'built-in section' within the framework agreement.

9.3.2.1 EU-China BIT as a Sectoral Agreement

An EU-China BIT might well fit in the current legal framework for the economic relationship between the EU and China. It could be a sub-agreement or a sectoral agreement under Article 12 of the EC-China Cooperation Agreement. While in Article 12 (2) the two sides undertake to extend the BITs by and to China and EU Member States, they also agree in Article 12 (1) that the two 'Contracting Parties' will 'promote and encourage greater and mutually beneficial investment' within the framework of their respective laws, rules and policies.

One may hesitate to say whether the EU has the right to join in the action of BIT-making with its Member States since this article has only mentioned

[43] Art 15, paras 2, 3 of the EC-China Cooperation Agreement.

[44] See Interview No. 11.

[45] See Interviews Nos 6, 8 and 11.

BITs between China and its Member States. However this provision will not prevent the EU from taking a joint action as such since the EU possesses such capacity of international investment treaty making, as confirmed by both the ECJ jurisprudence and practices of the EU institutions. Indeed it can be argued that since the bargaining power of any Member State could not be comparable with that of the Community as a whole[46] no Member State can expect a better BIT with China than that signed on the Community level.

9.3.2.2 EU-China BIT as a 'Built-in Section' within the Framework Agreement

The NILF may adopt the form of a 'built-in' chapter or section in the text of the framework agreement as an alternative to an individual BIT, following the NAFTA model.[47] In other words, the two sides may negotiate the revision of the agreement and then substantiate the section of investment with details of the potential BIT. This approach may be a bit more complicated as compared with the one described above, since it requires a review of the whole framework treaty. It may otherwise look an awkward fit in the current EC-China Co-operation Agreement because the current agreement is too slim to contain such a 'big' investment section.

It may be argued therefore that China could be 'upgraded' as an association country of the EU and substantial investment rules may be included in the future association agreement. This idea, despite its creativeness, may be too imaginative to be practical for the time being.[48] Nonetheless, it should be possible to adopt the form of a Free Trade Agreement[49] or a Partnership Agreement.[50]

[46] The results of the EU-China WTO accession talk may well serve as a good example. It would be incredible that any single state of the EU can attain a "big deal" as such. For details, see http://europa.eu.int/comm/trade/bilateral/china/hing.htm (22 05 2000)

[47] Chapter 11 of NAFTA contains everything that a normal BIT has, including a separate investment dispute settlement mechanism.

[48] In most cases, the conclusion of an association agreement implies a potential candidacy to the EU, which is something that no one might be able to foresee—because even the name 'European' Union would be called into question, if China were to be a member thereof. Moreover, China's human rights record, as seen by the Europeans, may prevent the two sides from the rosy prospect of 'association'.

[49] In negotiating a free trade agreement between the EU and the Mercosur (the EU-Mercosur FTA), the working group has elaborated the possible scenarios for the investment rules within the EU-Mercosur FTA. This exercise may be good guidance for the potential EU-China agreement on investment. See Working Group on European Union-Mercosur Negotiations, *Annual Report 2001–2002*, at 17–18, posted at http://chairemercosur.sciences-po.fr/negociations/rapport_anglais.pdf (visited on 31 July 2003). For further discussion, see Robert, Maryse, Sauvé, Pierre, and Steinfatt, Karsten, *Negotiating Investment Rules: Possible Scenarios for an EU-Mercosur Agreement*, posted at http://chairemercosur.sciences-po.fr/docs/livre/59696-265.pdf (visited on 31 July 2003).

[50] As observed by Peers, in choosing the title of a particular framework agreement, political discretion within the Community seems to triumph over legal rule. Therefore, it would be subject to the political wills of both the EU and China to determine the title of the potential new framework agreement. The 1998 Communication entitled 'Building a Comprehensive

An individual sub-agreement or sectoral agreement may be the most convenient choice of forms, while the model of a 'built-in' investment section in the existing EC-China Cooperation Agreement or a possible association agreement may face many more difficulties.

9.3.3 An EU-China BIT and then an MIA?

Although this section addresses the initiatives of a BIT and an MIA individually, they are not necessarily exclusive. On the contrary they are generally compatible with each other. The co-existence of bilateral treaties and multilateral treaties on the same subject is not rare. It is particularly common when the bilateral treaties are concluded before the conclusion of the multilateral instrument, as they normally are. The GATT/WTO has lived with numerous bilateral trade agreements for decades. [51]

The two agreements are nonetheless unlikely to be negotiated simultaneously for practical considerations. As interviews with EU officials show, whilst acknowledging the need and urgency of strengthening the protection for EU investment in China the EU prefers to achieve this by an MIA, particularly an MIA under the auspice of the WTO.[52] However if the proposed MIA fails the EU will double its efforts on the bilateral and regional fronts and will probably initiate such talks with China. In that case the BIT may well serve as a sound basis for any future negotiations of the MIA.

9.4 SUBSTANTIVE ISSUES OF THE NEW INTERNATIONAL LEGAL FRAMEWORK OF EU-CHINA INVESTMENT RELATIONS

Multilateral or bilateral, the new international legal framework will have to deal with the substantive issues such as admission, treatment, transfer, expropriation, subrogation, and dispute settlement. It is certain that the first step will be to consolidate the provisions of the existing EU-China BITs, which has been, by and large, discussed in Chapters 4–7. Each side will also probably seek further benefits or concessions from the other in negotiating the future NILF.

The EU may for instance wish to secure liberal investment admission conditions, unqualified post-establishment national treatment, complete

Partnership with China' suggests that the EU may prefer to use the title 'Partnership Agreement'. See Peers, Steve, *EC Framework of International Relations: Cooperation, Partnership and Association*, in Dashwood and Hillion, *The General Law of E.C. External Relations* (Sweet & Maxwell, 2000), at 160–76.

[51] However, an effective multilateral treaty may prevent the bilateral treaties of the same subject from further proliferation. For example, the old Friendship, Commerce and Navigation (FCN) agreement was no longer popular since the GATT was concluded.

[52] Interviews Nos 6, 8 and 11.

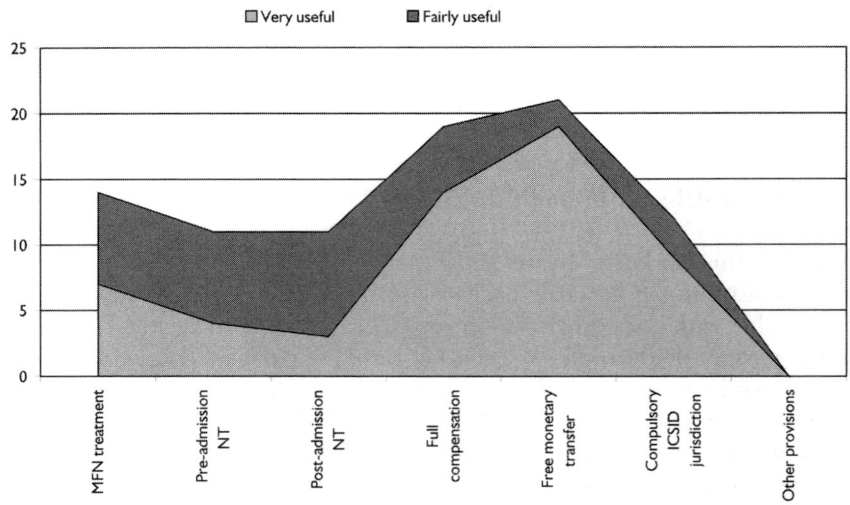

Chart 28: Useful Provisions in the Potential Investment Treaty

freedom in monetary transfer, 'adequate, prompt, and effective' compensation for expropriation and automatic submission to ICSID and other international fora for all investment disputes. It may wish to include 'social issues' such as human rights, labour and environmental standards, which have emerged during the recent MRIIs. The author's Questionnaire survey shows the provisions most desired by EU investors in the potential treaty are free monetary transfer, full compensation for expropriation, MFN treatment, NT for investment admission *and* post-admission stages, and compulsory jurisdiction of the ICSID in settling investment disputes (*Chart 28: Useful Provisions in the Potential Investment Treaty*). China may want to add rules of conduct for EU and foreign investors to the NILF whilst defending its right to guide, regulate and supervise EU and foreign investment within its territory. The following paragraphs, therefore, discuss some further controversies that may arise in the future EU-China NILF talks.[53]

[53] Since free monetary transfer is provided in existing EU-China BITs, it is less likely to have much difficulty. Therefore, it is not further discussed here. Also, it is possible to include rule on trade and investment in services sectors in the potential agreement. However, the following paragraphs focuses on the 'generic' issues rather than the 'product-specific' issues (services sector liberalisation). For a discussion of how services sector may be included in the agreement, see Working Group on European Union-Mercosur Negotiations, *Annual Report 2001–2002*, and Robert, Sauvé and Steinfatt, above, note 49.

9.4.1 A Liberal Admission Regime

As observed in Chapter 4, existing EU-China BITs have followed the traditional European approach on this issue, which basically leaves admission to the discretion of the host countries. But will the NILF follow the recent liberal trend on investment admission, eg by extending most-favoured-nation (MFN) and national treatment (NT) obligations on the pre-establishment stage of investment and prohibiting performance requirements (PRs) as conditions for admission?[54] To answer this question it is necessary to examine first the attitudes of both sides to the admission of foreign investment.

9.4.1.1 EU's Attitude towards Investment Admission

Although European BITs tend to leave the regulation of investment admission to the host countries, it seems that the EU and its member states have changed their attitude and have accepted the liberal approach in this matter. This change is shown by the EC's Statement on Investment Protection Principles which aims at elaborating upon principles set forth in the Lomé IV Convention, for the promotion of European investment in the ACP countries.[55] While acknowledging ACP countries' right to screen investments to ensure their inconsistency with appropriate legal requirements and development objectives, the Statement stresses that 'cumbersome admission procedures, disincentives and discriminatory performance requirements are inconsistent with the spirit of ACP-EEC development co-operation'. It suggests that a liberal approach should be adopted in the ACP countries where investments should be admitted 'unless particular circumstances indicate that they may be harmful to the host country'. The Statement also requires the ACP countries to admit European investments on the basis of NT and MFN treatment. Fair and equitable treatment should also be accorded to European investments, as an overriding principle that comprises principles such as transparency and stability of investment conditions, full protection and security, NT and MFN treatment and observation of undertakings.[56] Despite its non-binding nature the Statement indicates that the EU has accepted the liberal approach on the admission issue, even as regards investment relations with developing countries.

Other proofs of EU's acceptance of this liberal approach can be found in its participation in the making of investment-related treaties, notably in the ECT, the MAI, and the WTO. Both the EC and its member states have participated in the ECT and the drafting of the ECT Supplementary Treaty as well as in the MAI drafts. The inclusion of NT and MFN provisions on investment

[54] See *Table 11*.

[55] Shihata, 'Recent Trends Relating to Entry of Foreign Direct Investment', (1994) 9 *ICSID Review—FILJ*, at 47.

[56] *Ibid.*

admission in these treaties therefore suggests that the EC and its member states have agreed to these concepts. The EU's new liberal attitude to admission is more clearly demonstrated in its participation in the WTO's work on the relationship between trade and investment. In one of its Communications to the Working Group on Trade and Investment (WGTI) of the WTO, the EU surveyed the various existing international investment instruments from the perspective of the EU and its member states, and summarised its views as follows:

> 'The network of BITs concluded by the European Community's member states does not affect the right of the parties to regulate the admission of investors. However, the EC Treaty and some important instruments the Community and its member states have adhered to put obligations on the participants in these instruments which, taken together, amount to a very open regime for access of investors to the European Single Market, in recognition of the benefits that liberalisation brings. In all of these, however, horizontal or sectoral exceptions allow the participants to safeguard vital interests, such as national security or public order.'[57]

Later, in another Communication to WGTI, the EU elaborates in greater detail the 'key concepts' related to investment admission which appear in multilateral investment instruments to which the EU and its member states adhere. It concludes that

> 'The predominant instrument used to regulate the admission of investment in existing multilateral instruments is a combination of national treatment and most-favoured-nation treatment. Two conclusions are evident:
> – The scope of the non-discrimination clauses (MFN and national treatment) has been constantly enlarged and now covers the 'treatment' of investors as regards to the entire life of the investment, while initially pertaining only to limited measures such as authorisations.
> – One multilateral agreement has chosen a different concept than non-discrimination for the admission of investment: the GATS operates a market access criterion backed up by national treatment in sectors schedules, but MFN applies across the board. This shows that existing concepts allow for modulation according to the participants' needs.'[58]

These conclusions not only summarise existing practices but also demonstrate preferences. Clearly a liberal attitude to investment admission has been accepted and is preferred.

Last but not least, even in the field of BITs, some EU member states have

[57] Working Group on Trade and Investment (WGTI), *Identification of Common Features and Differences of Existing International Instruments from the Perspective of the European Community and Its Member States* (of 27 March 1998), at http://europa.eu.int/comm/dg01/invwgti1.htm (visited on November 1999).

[58] WGTI, *Checklist of Issues, Agenda IV: Identification of Common Features and Differences in International Investment Instruments* (of 2 September 1998), at http://europa.eu.int/comm/dg01/invwgti2.htm (visited on 11 November 1999).

started to sign BITs with NT and MFN extended to cover admission too. Some UK-foreign BITs, for instance, signed in the 1990s provide that NT and MFN treatment will apply to all the substantive provisions of the agreement.[59]

For these reasons it can safely be concluded that the EU and its member states have changed their attitude to investment admission and have adopted the liberal approach derived from the US BITs and NAFTA. While this is undisputedly reflected in their participation in multilateral investment instruments it is also shown in some recent European BITs.

Accordingly it is likely that in the potential talks on the NILF the EU will also demand a equally liberal approach on investment admission, requiring, for example, the extension of NT and MFN to cover 'establishment' an 'acquisition' of investment as well as the prohibition of performance requirements.[60]

9.4.1.2 Chinese Attitude towards Investment Admission

China as a developing country has traditionally rejected this liberal approach on investment admission. Firstly, the BITs between China and the EU member states show that China has not accepted any substantial limitation on its right to regulate the admission of foreign investment. On the contrary Chinese BITs stipulate that admission of investment is governed by its own laws and regulations. The US attempted to negotiate a BIT with China from 1983 to 1987, with NT covering investment admission. The negotiations broke down after six rounds because both China and the US would not make any concessions on admission and other sticky issues.[61]

Secondly, China, as the largest developing country, in multilateral scenarios voted in favour of the UN Charter of Economic Rights and Duties of States, which affirm host countries' sovereign rights 'to regulate and exercise authority over foreign investment within its national jurisdiction in accordance with its laws and regulations and in conformity with its national objectives and priorities'.[62] China had been very positive in the UN's effort to establish of a multilateral instrument regulating multinational enterprises, the UN Code of Conduct on Transnational Corporations.

Finally and most importantly, within its national jurisdiction China still

[59] See eg, UK BITs with Bahrain (1991), Barbados (1993), Lithuania and Uzbekistan (1994), all at Art 3. See Shihata, above, note 55, at 56, note 43.

[60] Indeed, this can be seen from its 1998 strategy document '*Building a Comprehensive Partnership with China*', which explicitly stated, 'Improve the conditions for foreign companies establishing in China. *This includes removing all restrictions on the legal form of establishment (whether as a joint venture or a wholly-owned company), lifting geographic restrictions and those on the scope of permitted activity, and removing pre-establishment conditions. It also includes the removal of export performance requirements and export subsidies.*' (emphasis added)

[61] Steinert, Timothy A, 'If the BIT Fits: The Proposed Bilateral Investment Treaty between the United States and the People's Republic of China', (1988) 2 *Journal of Chinese Law*, at 405.

[62] Art 2 (2) (a) of, UNGA Resolution 3281.

maintains a very rigid investment screening and scrutinising system. Under this system all investment projects must be approved by the central or local approval authority before they can be carried out. Certain investment projects in some areas are prohibited or restricted, while others are permitted or encouraged according to the Guiding Catalogue of Foreign Investment Directions. In addition China maintains some performance requirements on the entry of foreign investment, such as local equity requirements, investor qualification requirements, minimum registered capital requirements, and investment duration requirements.[63] Obviously this admission regime is far from the liberal admission approach that the EU has submitted to.

In recent years, however, China has shown its willingness to relax its investment admission regime. The first sign is its agreement to sign the APEC Non-Binding Principles on Investment of 1994, which require that

> 'with exceptions as provided for in domestic laws, regulations and policies, member economies will accord to foreign investors-in relation to *establishment, expansion*, operation and protection of their investment-treatment *no less favourable than that accorded in like situations to domestic investors*.'[64]

Although accompanied with substantial qualifications and included in a *non-binding* instrument, China's acceptances of this instrument probably has signalled a tendency to liberalise its policy towards investment admission.[65] Secondly, China has accepted the MFN obligation in respect of the admission of investment and the matters in connection therewith.[66] Also, as a result of China's accession to the WTO, China has submitted itself to the TRIMs Agreement and the GATS, both of which are closely related to investment admission. In light of the TRIMs Agreement, China has modified its FDI laws and regulations and abandoned all the trade-related investment measures, which are, in fact, pre-establishment performance requirements. Furthermore, in accordance with the GATS, China has undertaken the MFN obligation as a general principle in dealing with trade in services, including services through 'commercial presence', ie, investment. NT has also been accepted as a 'specific commitment' in committed sectors or sub-sectors as scheduled in the Annexes to the GATS. In other words, as a result of the

[63] Xu, Congli and Lin, Zhong, *Chinese Foreign Investment Law* (*Zhongguo Waizi Fa*) (Law Publishing House, 1998), at 58–62. Previously, China had local content and export performance requirements associated to investment admission. However, these requirements were eliminated in its recent modification of FDI laws and regulations. See Shan, Wenhua, 'Towards a Level Playing Field for Foreign Investment in China', 3 *Journal of World Investment* 2, at 331–37.

[64] As agreed by APEC Ministers, Jakarta, November 1994.

[65] Under Chinese political culture, it is likely that principles signed by the top leadership will be honoured. Indeed, an FDI expert at the think-tank of the MOFTEC (now MOFCOM) has argued that although the APEC investment principles are non-binding, they should be honoured and implemented, since they are endorsed by the top leader of the state. See Ma, Yu, *Investment Liberalisation in the Context of Economic Globalisation in the World*, posted at http://www.etisu.com.cn/zgwmxh/tongxun/00126/02–0126-WTO1.htm (visited on 28 June 2003).

[66] Art 2 (2), Sino-South Korea BIT.

WTO accession China has accepted a more liberal attitude towards investment admission, especially in the service sectors.

China's willingness to relax its admission regime is also evidenced by recent policies, statements of government officials and scholarly arguments. The State Council Decision on the Reform of the Investment Regime marked a big step towards a more liberal FDI market access policy. Chinese officials have indicated that in the future China's administration of foreign investment [a system featured as 'regulation, guidance, and supervision'.[67] Meanwhile some Chinese scholars have discussed the possibility of implementing a 'selective approval system' instead of the current 'one by one approval system'.[68]

9.4.1.3 Possible Compromise on Investment Admission in the NILF

The question is, how far can and will China go? Will China go as far as the EU would wish on this matter? In particular, will China agree to subject investment admission to NT and MFN obligation and to abolish performance requirements other than those listed in the TRIMs Agreement?

The author submits that China will probably accept MFN on investment admission just as China has accepted it in its BIT with South Korea[69] and in the GATS. As for the provision of NT on investment admission and the abandonment of performance requirements, these issues are bound to be problematic and will need compromise.

Pre-establishment NT

It is unrealistic at this stage for China to implement a 'full' NT including pre-establishment NT for foreign investment.[70] The delay of the conclusion of the Supplementary Treaty to ECT to extend NT to cover investment admission[71] shows that it has been more difficult than expected to reach agreement

[67] Liu, Dongkai, 'China Changes its Priorities on Utilising Foreign Investment', (2001) 25 Dec *People's Daily* (overseas edition), at 1.

[68] Xu and Lin, above, note 63, at 50. Cao, Jianming and He, Xiaoyun, 'WTO Accession and China's Foreign Economic Legislation', (2000) 1 *Chinese Legal Science* (*Zhongguo Faxue*), at 13.

[69] The Sino-South Korea BIT (concluded in 1992) grants MFN to investors from each other contracting party, in terms of investment authorisation and things relating to such authorisation. See Art 2 (2), Sino-South Korea BIT.

[70] In fact, on investment market access, what the Chinese government is trying to do is to accord 'NT' to Chinese private enterprises (Minying Qiye), eg, to allow them to enjoy the same rights and access investment areas and financial or fiscal privileges as that the foreign investors have after China's WTO admission. As a legacy of China's long practised socialist central planned economy, Chinese private capital has been disadvantaged and underdeveloped, even after China opened its door to foreign investors. In recent years, the government has constantly raised the profile of these private investors and allows them to play a more and more important role in China's economic life. This measure is the new development of this government policy. See 'China Opens its Door to (Domestic) Private Capitals—Domestic Private Investors Will Be Able To Do Whatever Foreign Investors Can Do', (2002) 2 Feb *People's Daily* (overseas edition), at 5.

[71] The ECT requires the Supplementary Treaty to be concluded by 1998 but it is still under negotiation. Art 10 (4), ECT.

between developed and developing countries on this matter. As a developing country in transition from a planned to a market economy China is still not strong enough to afford such a liberal approach on investment market access.

As noted in Section 5.3.2, the implementation of a full NT must meet two conditions: a real market economy and a competitive national economy. Thus although 'implementing NT for FIEs' has been an important established national policy in China, its implementation is bound to be progressive and take some time. The Chinese economy is still in transition from a planned economy towards a real market economy. There is still a quite long way to go to reform the State-Owned Enterprises (SOEs) and the state-owned banks into real economic entities running on a commercial basis.

On the other hand, although in absolute terms the Chinese economy has become one of the largest in the world, in relative terms it is still rather small. In 1998 for instance China ranked seventh in the world in terms of Gross National Product (GNP), reaching US$950 billion.[72] However the GNP *per capita* was still less than US$900, far lower than in developed countries.[73] In these circumstances one cannot expect an instant realisation of a full NT, but one can expect the Chinese government to create facilities and conditions to carry it out gradually and yet substantially.

It might be possible to adopt the GATS, 'bottom-up' approach on admission. In other words NT may be granted at the admission stage as a kind of 'specific commitment' rather than as a general principle. Both China and the EU have accepted this approach on investment in service sectors as reflected in the GATS. Moreover the EU has intended to take this approach in multilateral negotiations on investment.[74] This 'bottom-up' approach may prove to be the best realistic compromise available at this stage.

Performance requirements

There are similar problems so far as 'performance requirements' (PRs) are concerned. The Chinese consider these measures to be a part of economic sovereignty, which is essential to ensure that foreign investments conform to its objectives of development and are conducive to its economy and society. An outright ban of these measures will, therefore, be regarded not only as damaging to its economy but also as a threat to its sovereignty. Nonetheless it may be possible for China to agree to prohibit certain categories of PRs, given

[72] See Chinese Embassy UK: Economic and Social Development in the Past 50 Years, at http://www.chinese-embassy.org.uk/eng/13995.html (visited on 26 April 2002).

[73] US Embassy statistics shows that Chinese GNP per capita is $860, while in the US it is about $28000 and it is about $36000 in Japan. See GNP PER CAPITA, at http://www.usembassy-china.org.cn/econ/briefing1/sld005.htm (visited on 26 April 2002).

[74] According to the author's Interview with EC officials dealing with international investment negotiations, the EU intends to employ the GATS approach on 'market access' or investment admission, in the potential negotiations on a multilateral investment agreement within the WTO. See Interview No. 6.

that China has undertaken to abolish certain TRIMs under the TRIMs Agreement.

Again, a 'bottom-up' approach is essential. In fact, US BITs, ECT, NAFTA, and the MAI draft all adopt this approach although the measures covered are different. The US BITs only cover PRs as a condition for admission of the investment, ie, 'Direct PRs' like local content requirements and export performance requirements. Both NAFTA and the MAI draft cover not only 'Directs PRs' but also 'Indirect PRs', ie, investment measures as a condition for access to special privilege or benefits.[75]

ECT, following the TRIMS Agreement, only covers trade-related investment measures. Since China is keen on employing financial and fiscal privileges to attract foreign investment to certain areas and regions (eg, in infrastructure industries or in western China), it is more likely that China may agree to abolish 'Direct PRs' than 'Indirect PRs'. It will certainly be even easier for China to accept a 'best effort' commitment on the elimination of performance requirements, similar to that in the US-Tunisia BIT.[76]

9.4.2 Post-Establishment National Treatment

The EU and its member states have been active in promoting NT in their BITs with developing countries. According to the Commission's communication with the WGTI, 'European BITs provide strong rights for investors and strong obligations on host governments once the investment has been admitted (standards which have been accepted also by many other countries around the world)'.[77] NT obligation is 'typically' one of these obligations and standards.[78]

China has changed its attitude to NT for FIEs since 1992, as discussed at length in Chapter 5. However as a developing country in transition from a planned economy to a market economy China needs time to adjust its economic structure and to build up a competitive national economy. It is therefore anticipated that, for a considerable period, China will have difficulty in implementing a full or unqualified NT for foreign investment. A most recent manifestation of such difficulty is the new Sino-Germany BIT, in which a 'grandfather clause' was included particularly for China although a general NT obligation was committed.[79]

[75] Chen, Huiping, 'MAI and the International Investment Liberalisation', 3 *Chinese Journal of International Economic Law*, at 258–59.

[76] Art 2 (6), US-Tunisia BIT reads, 'Both Contracting Parties shall endeavour to avoid imposition of any performance requirements…'

[77] WGTI, *Identification of Common Features and Differences of Existing International Instruments from the Perspective of the European Community and Its Member States* (of 27 March 1998), at http://europa.eu.int/comm/dg01/invwgti1.htm (visited on November 1999).

[78] *Ibid.*

[79] See Section 5.2.3.1 for further details.

It may be expected that for post-establishment investment activities, NT may be in principle established in the NILF.[80] However exceptions may still have to be maintained to allow host countries to adopt measures necessary to regulate and supervise foreign investment, to ensure that they to conform to national development objectives, in addition to the general exceptions such as public order, international peace exceptions, and so on. Accordingly the elimination of performance requirements related to the operation of investment should be similar to that of PRs related to investment admission. In other words, the adoption of a 'bottom-up' approach is probably essential.

9.4.3 'Adequate, Prompt and Effective' Compensation for Expropriation

Will China accept an explicit reference to the Hull formula of 'adequate, prompt, and effective' compensation as the standard of compensation in the NILF? The answer is probably negative, and can be justified using evidence from both international and national (Chinese) perspectives.

The issue of the standard of compensation internationally is not simply a legal or technical one. It has aroused so much debate with such strong feelings between developed and developing countries that it has become a political issue. On a technical level it is not too difficult to adopt a high standard of compensation for expropriation, as can be seen from the EU-China BITs and other Chinese BITs. On a political level, as the largest developing country, China will find it very difficult to accept the 'Hull Formula' that it has fought against so long together with other developing countries.[81] Interestingly, in the NAFTA, the so-called 'state-of-the-art' investment agreement, the 'Hull Formula' is not included either, probably because of strong Mexican resistance.

Inside China, on the other hand, Chinese laws have adopted 'appropriate

[80] In fact, China has accepted post-establishment NT as a general obligation in the Sino-Japan BIT and the Sino-South Korea BIT, without the qualification 'in accordance with the stipulations of its laws and regulations' as appeared in the Sino-Britain and Sino-Spain BITs. However, both the Sino-Japan and the Sino-South Korea BIT have provided in their Protocols that such an NT should not prevent the host country from according discriminatory treatment, 'in accordance with its applicable laws and regulations, to nationals and companies of the other Contracting Party, in case it is really necessary for the reason of public order, national security or sound development of national economy.' Art 3 (2), Sino-South Korea BIT; Art 3 (3), Sino-Britain BIT; Art 3 (4), Sino-Spain BIT.

[81] For instance, China published an official declaration strongly supporting Egyptian Government in nationalising Suez Canal in 1956, stating that 'This action by the Egyptian Government is completely right from both legal and moral perspectives.' In 1974, DENG Xiaoping said that, as a Chinese Representative to the UNGA 6th Special Session, China support developing countries 'to control and regulate every kind of foreign capitals, particularly transnational corporations, including nationalising them.' See *People's Daily* (Chinese), August 15, 1956, at 1. See also the *Collection of Documents concerning the Chinese Delegation Attending UN Meetings (1973.7–1974.7)* (in Chinese), at 11.

compensation',[82] which may not be so easily changed. The difficulty in changing these rules is not merely because of complicated legal procedure, but again, of the 'strong feelings' against the Hull Formula, as witnessed by Official statements and scholarly writings.[83] A senior Chinese official once said that 'the terms "adequate, prompt, and effective" have long been used in capitalist countries for *extorting* compensations for liquidated assets'.[84] Judge Li Haopei, an eminent Chinese international lawyer states that 'to require the nationalizing state to make compensation to owners of foreign nationality may frustrate the exercise of the sovereign right of state to carry out economic and social reform, because it may be impossible or difficult for such state to assume an obligation to make compensation'.[85] In an article discussing 'international customs'[86] Professor CHEN An pointed out that the 'prompt, adequate, and effective' compensation formula

> '[i]s so demanding that it is equivalent to extorting. It substantially restricts or even fundamentally deprives the sovereignty rights of the poor developing countries to expropriate foreign investments within its territory. Because of its strong flavour of colonialism and imperialism, this so-called 'international customs' has long and constantly been resisted and criticised by developing countries.'

Against this background it is unlikely that China will swiftly change its long-standing policy and accept the Hull Formula in the potential NILF. On the contrary if the NILF is to have a 'principle' for the standard of compensation, it will probably be 'appropriate compensation' accompanied by high standard specific criteria such as 'fair market value' including interest, 'without delay', 'freely transferable', and 'fully realisable'.

[82] Most of the major Chinese laws and regulations on FDI have provision on expropriation and have provided that 'appropriate compensation' is the standard of compensation in the event of expropriation. See eg Art 2 (3) of EJVL, Art 5 of REON and Art 5 of WFEL. In a discussion on the Property Law that is under consideration, it is proposed that 'appropriate compensation' should be adopted as the general standard, rather than full or 'prompt, adequate and effective' compensation. Qu, Maohui and Zhang, Hong, 'Several Issues Concerning Expropriation', (2003) 2 *Law Review*, at 54. However, it is notable that Professor Jiang, Ping, a prominent Chinese lawyer, has proposed that 'full compensation' be adopted in the potential Property Law. See Jiang, Ping, 'Principle on the Protection of Private Property', (2003) 11 Feb *People's Daily*, at 9, reprinted in (2003) 5 *Xinhua Digest*, at 2.

[83] See Chen, An, 'The Marginal, Comprehensive and Independent Natures of the Science of International Economic Law', (1998) 1 *Chinese Journal of International Economic Law*, at 43–44. See also Yao, Meizhen, *International Investment Law* (in Chinese) (Wuhan University Press, 1987), at 380–98; Zeng, Huaqun, *International Investment Law* (*Guoji Touzi Faxue*) (Peking University Press, 1999), at 456; Yu, Jinsong, *International Investment Law* (in Chinese) (Law Press, 1997), at 318.

[84] See Gu, Ming (then Deputy Secretary-General of the State Council), 'Investment Environment Seen as Favorable', (1984) 16 Jul *Beijing Review*, at 16, as cited in Steinert, above, note 61, footnote 251.

[85] Judge Li Haopei, 'Nationalisation and International Law', (1958) 2 *Zhengfa Yanjiu*, at 10–15, translated and reprinted in Jerome Alan Cohen and Hungdah Chiu, *People's China and International Law: A Documentary Study* (Princeton University Press, 1974), at 721.

[86] Chen, An, above, note 83, at 43.

9.4.4 Automatic Submission of Investment Disputes to International Fora

A close comparison of Chinese BITs with recent MRIIs shows that two significant differences exist on the jurisdiction of state-investor disputes. On the one hand, although Chinese BITs have granted automatic consent to submit certain categories of state-investor disputes to ICSID arbitration, they have never committed to submit them to any other international arbitration institution. Hence automatic submission to ICC or the Arbitration Institute of the Stockholm Chamber of Commerce (AISCC) would be something totally new to China.

On the other hand unlike these MRIIs by which all state-investor disputes can be referred to ICSID arbitration without consent from the host country, current Chinese BITs (except recent BITs such as the new Sino-Germany BIT which has not been ratified) only allow disputes concerning the amount of compensation to be submitted automatically to the ICSID. This is further confirmed by China's reservation to the ICSID Convention, by which China agrees to submit disputes over the amount of compensation to the ICSID.[87] Submission of other state-investor disputes to international arbitration, within or without the ICSID, still requires mutual consent from the parties concerned.

Will China go further in the NILF submit 'automatically' other state-investor disputes to the ICSID as well? Will China agree to submit these disputes to other international arbitration institutions such as the ICC or AISCC?

9.4.4.1 Automatic Submission of Non-AOC Disputes

It would be possible now for China to give automatic consent to all state-investor disputes to the ICSID or other international arbitration, given that China has agreed to do so in some of the most recent BITs including the new Sino-Germany BIT.[88] Nevertheless, exhaustion of local administrative reconsideration procedure might still be required as a concidtion for such automatic submission to international arbitration. Also, local courts might still serve as an alternate to international arbitration.[89]

[87] Mu, Zili, *Chinese Government is to enact regulations to implement obligations under the ICSID Convention*, Arbitration and Law Communication (Published by the Chinese International Economic and Trade Arbitration Commission–CIETAC), No. 1 (1997), at 3–4.

[88] See Section 7.2.1.2 for details.

[89] Such exhaustion of local remedies requirements would be essential prerequisites for China to commit it to allow all investment disputes to be automatically submitted to international arbitration, which it traditional considered as contradicting with national sovereignty. As observed by a Steinert, an illustration of China's application of this principle can be seen in the belief that, any dispute relating to the treatment of a foreign individual or company on Chinese territory is inherently within the exclusive jurisdiction of Chinese courts and that third party adjudication of any dispute between a sovereign government and a foreign individual would place the individual on an equal footing with states, which contradicts the fundamentals of the international system and insults that state's sovereignty. Steinert, above, note 61, at 432.

9.4.4.2 Submission of Disputes to Other International Arbitration Institutions

Whether or not to accept the jurisdiction of other international arbitration institutions than the ICSID is not a matter of principle and it should not therefore be too difficult to reach agreement thereon. As the Chinese government has accepted *ad hoc* international arbitration of investment disputes and has often recommended that its companies settle international contractual disputes through international arbitration institutions like the ICC or the AISCC, it would not be very difficult for China to extend the jurisdiction of the ICSID to these well-received international institutions.

9.4.5 Social Issues

Traditionally, BITs address only traditional issues like those mentioned above. However, several other issues may also be discussed within the NILF context. These are mainly 'social clause' issues, including human rights, as well as labour and environment standards, which have been very actively advocated and promoted by the EU.[90]

9.4.5.1 Human Rights

Human rights issues are a far-reaching and sensitive issue between the EU and China, which are very likely to be discussed in the NILF negotiations. The EU, particularly the EP, has long criticised China's human rights records.[91] In a Resolution taken by the European Parliament adopted in 1994, it 'reiterates',

> 'its insistence on the need for the inclusion of a human rights clause in trade agreements with third countries and the at the same time consider that cooperation of any kind at Joint Committee, European Parliament or member states level must be accompanied by a specific assessment of the progress made towards democracy and of human rights situation in the PRC; undertakes not to approve any new cooperation agreements unless significant changes occur'.[92]

[90] It is noted that the concept of 'social clause' was first spelt out by former German Foreign Minister Kinker on behalf of the EU countries, in a summit meeting with ASEAN leaders, where he claimed that human rights, environment protection and labour conditions should be addressed by the world trading system and that the rights and health and safety conditions of workers should be linked with economic issues. See Chang, Kai, 'WTO, Labour Standards and the Protection of Rights of Workers' (in Chinese), (2002) 1 *Social Sciences in China*, at 128.

[91] Flinterman, Lees, 'The European Union and China', (1997) *Maastricht Journal of European and Comparative Law*, at 217.

[92] See European Parliament, *Resolution on Relations between the European Union and the Peoples' Republic of China*, A3–0011/94, OJ C61/71.

In May 1995 the European Commission adopted a new policy to include standard human rights clauses 'in all new draft negotiating directives for the Community agreements with third countries'.[93] It therefore looks inevitable that a human rights clause may have to be included in the future NILF. However, as observed by Ward, EU practices suggest that 'sectoral agreements' may be immunised from the inclusion of human rights clauses.[94] If so, the human rights issues may probably be immunised from the NILF, because, as argued above, the NILF can probably be treated as a sectoral agreement.

It is noted that, after the EU adopted a 'long term policy' towards China and upgraded this bilateral relations in 1995, the EU has shifted from the *persistent and robust criticism* approach to a *more delicate and protracted strategy of constructive dialogue* on the rights issue with China.[95] This policy seems to have worked in practice, as China has indeed made considerable progress in improving its human rights record.[96] Given that human rights issues are not normally included in BITs, it is arguable that it may be unnecessary to address the subject in the NILF.

9.4.5.2 Labour and Environmental Standards

Other controversial issues are the labour and environmental standards relating to foreign investment. It is noticeable that a shift of emphasis from investors' obligations to governments' obligations in international investment law makings can be clearly seen here. These issues had been discussed prior to the 1990s in international investment instruments such as the TNC Code, which requires the investors to respect these standards.[97] Now they are imposed as conditions or obligations of host country governments in some newly initiated investment instruments, such as the MAI draft.

In the MAI draft, provisions on labour and environmental standards appear in both the preamble and the text of the agreement. In the text, in particular, the MAI draft provides that a party should not lower health, safety, environmental or labour standards (measures) as an encouragement for the

[93] Ward, Angela, 'Framework for Cooperation between the European Union and Third World: a Viable Matrix for Uniform Human Rights Standards?', (1998) 3 *European Foreign Affairs Review*, at 511.

[94] Ward, *ibid*.

[95] Ward, *ibid*, at 514.

[96] For example, the EU has observed that China's economic reform has introduced greater freedom of choice in education, employment, housing, travel and other areas of social and economic activity. China has passed new civil and criminal laws to protect citizens' rights and has started signing some of the key instrument bringing the country closer to international norms. It has also taken steps to develop the electoral process at local level, allowing villagers to choose their local authorities. See *Human Rights: Dialogue Backed by Action* (October 1998), available at DG External Relations website of the EU: www.europa.eu.int/external_relations/china/introduction/index.html (visited on January 1999).

[97] For instance, the TNCs Code has very detailed rules, requiring investors to respect human rights of workers and local labour and environmental standards.

establishment, acquisition, expansion or retention in its territory of any investment of an investor.

If a party considers that another party has offered such an encouragement, it may request consultations with the other party and the two should consult with a view to avoiding any such encouragement. Although there are still a lot of debates on the substance of this provision and there have been several alternative versions of it, the fact that labour and environment standards have been included in the text of a draft OECD investment agreement shows the grave concerns of developed countries over the labour and environmental conditions in some developing countries. Developing countries, including China, have been very reluctant to accept them as they regard them as smokescreens which developed countries are using to protect their comparatively disadvantaged industries against developing countries.[98] Only 'soft' or highly flexible obligations around these issues might be expected in the NILF, if any.

9.5 CONCLUSION

Constructing a new international legal framework of EU-China investment relations is both desirable and viable. The NILF may take the form of either a MIA or a BIT. An MIA is preferable but may involve longer time of preparation; while a BIT between the two sides is relatively easy to reach and thus more practical, to satisfy the immediate need of investment protection and promotion. Now that WTO has failed to launch the negotiation of an MIA, it becomes more unlikely for the EU and China to engage into talks on the conclusion of an EU-China BIT.

Whilst the existing EU-China BITs have laid down good foundations for the future NILF, further controversies may arise over issues such as investment admission, treatment, expropriation, dispute settlement, as well as newly emerged 'social issues' including human rights, labour, and environmental standards. As far as admission and treatment of investment is concerned, although the EU may ask for the application of MFN and NT to the whole lifecycle of foreign investment and the elimination of performance requirements, it is expected that only MFN may be applied throughout the lifecycle of investment. In principle NT, however, can only be applied to post-establishment stage of an investment. It may also be possible that China and the EU agree to apply NT to investment admission and to eliminate performance requirements, provided that a 'bottom-up' approach is adopted.

[98] However, this does not mean that China will not make an effort to improve its labour and environment standards. Indeed, in the past twenty years, China has established a legal system dealing with labour issues and has ratified the UN International Covenant of Economic, Social and Cultural Rights. For details of China's laws and their conformity with international standards, see Chang, above, note 90, at 128–29.

Secondly, on the standard of compensation for expropriation, it is noted that China will not accept the Hull Formula of 'prompt, adequate, and effective' compensation, even though she may be ready to subscribe to high specific standards of compensation that are equivalent to this formula *in fact*. Moreover, as regards dispute settlement, submission of of non-AOC disputes to international arbitration would be possible, although it would be conditional on the exhaustion of local remedies. It would also be possible to submit investment disputes to other international arbitration institutions than the ICSID, such as the ICC or AISCC. Finally, although social issues such as human rights and labour and environmental standards are likely to be discussed in the context of the NILF, it may be unnecessary to address it in the NILF. Thus, only 'soft' or highly flexible obligations of these issues may be expected to be included in the NILF, if any.

PART V

The Legal Framework of Investment Relations Between China and the New EU Member States

10

The Legal Framework of Investment Relations between China and the New EU Member States

In May 2004, the European Union realized its fifth enlargement, the largest in its history.[1] Ten new Member States joined the Union, which made it a union of twenty-five States. The ten new Member States are Cyprus, the Czech Republic, Estonia, Hungary, Latvia, Lithuania, Malta, Poland, Slovakia and Slovenia (hereinafter collectively referred to as the EU 10; the EU Member States existing before May 2004 are collectively referred to as the EU 15).[2] Bulgaria and Romania are hoping to also join the Union in 2007, whilst another candidate country, Turkey, is not currently negotiating its membership. The 2004 EU enlargement successfully expanded the boundary of the EU to embrace eight former communist counties with which China has had and maintained good relationships.

Whilst this enlargement may not tremendously increase the general volume of EU investment in China, it probably will significantly promote Chinese investment in the EU. The legal framework of EU–China investment relations will likewise be modified by the enlargement.[3] This chapter thus deals with the legal framework governing the investment relations between China and the EU 10 States. It first explores the trade and investment relations between China and the EU 10 States and the applicable legal framework. Then it takes a closer look at the bilateral investment treaties concluded between the two sides.

[1] For further details of the enlargement, see *Enlarging Europe*, available at: news.bbc.co.uk/2/shared/spl/hi/europe/04/enlarging_europe/html/introduction.stm (last visited 16 September 2004). See also information about enlargement at the European Union's official Website, at: europa.eu.int/comm/enlargement/enlargement.htm (last visited 10 September 2004).

[2] Further details of these new Member States are available at the BBC and EU Websites, *ibid.*

[3] For a discussion of the legal framework governing Sino-EU 15 investment relations, see Shan, Wenhua, 'Towards a New Legal Framework for EU–China Investment Relations', (2000) 34 *Journal of World Trade* 5, at 137–79.

10.1 TRADE AND INVESTMENT RELATIONS BETWEEN CHINA AND THE EU 10 STATES

10.1.1 Trade and Investment Relations between China and the EU 10 States

China has a long trade and investment relationship with the EU 10 States, dating back to the 1950s soon after the People's Republic of China was established. China had, in particular, a close economic relationship with the eight former communist countries even before 1978, during the period when China was isolated from the Western world. For instance, the Chinese–Polish Joint Stock Shipping Company (CHIPOLBROK), established in 1951, was the very first joint-venture company that the People's Republic admitted.[4] This Section elaborates the investment relations between China and each of the EU 10 States in turn before giving an overview and comments on their implications.

10.1.1.1 Cyprus

China established diplomatic relations with Cyprus in December 1971.[5] The two sides have so far concluded a trade agreement (1981), a bilateral investment treaty (BIT) (2001)[6] and a bilateral double taxation treaty (DTT) (1990).[7] Whilst there are no specific statistics on bilateral investment, it is recorded that Sino-Cyprus trade nearly tripled between 1998 and 2002, from US$81.21 million in 1998 to US$225.94 in 2002.[8]

10.1.1.2 Czech Republic[9]

Sino-Czech trade relations date back to the 1950s.[10] Before 1991, bilateral trade was conducted in accordance with a clearing agreement and had

[4] For more about the company, see *Brief Introduction*, at its own Website, at: www.chipolbrok.online.sh.cn/e_gsjj.htm (last visited 10 September 2004).

[5] For details about Sino-Cyprus relations, visit China's Ministry of Foreign Affairs (MFA) official Website: www.mfa.gov.cn/chn/wjb/zzjg/xos/gjlb/1404/default.htm (last visited 10 September 2004).

[6] *Ibid.*

[7] Zhang, Xin, *The Law and Practice of International Taxation Treaties in China* (Wildy, Simmonds and Hill, London, 2003), in Appendix 1, 'China's Double Tax Treaties and Arrangements", at 683–85.

[8] *Ibid.* See also *General Information About Cyprus*, at the MFA Website, at: www.mfa.gov.cn/chn/wjb/zzjg/xos/gjlb/1404/1404x0/default.htm (last visited 10 September 2004).

[9] For further details, see *Sino-Czech Relations*, at the MFA Website, at: www.mfa.gov.cn/chn/wjb/zzjg/xos/gjlb/1726/default.htm (last visited 10 September 2004). See also *Sino-Czech Economic Relations*, at the Website of the Ministry of Commerce of China (MOFCOM), at: ozs.mofcom.gov.cn/article/200208/20020800037999_1.xml (last visited 24 August 2004).

[10] *Sino-Czech Economic Relations*, *ibid.*

reached an historic level of US$910 million in 1989.[11] Since 1991, when the clearing agreement was abolished, bilateral trade has decreased significantly.[12] Sino-Czech trade, however, has grown rapidly since 1999. In 2002, it reached US$62 million, a near three-fold increase since 1999.[13] By the end of 2002, the Czech Republic had made 248 investment projects in China, with a total investment of US$64.68 million.[14] There are also some Chinese investment projects in the territory of the Czech Republic.[15]

In 1991, China singed a BIT with the Czech Republic (then the Federal Republic of Czechoslovakia).[16] China also entered into a DTT and a general economic and trade agreement with Czech Republic in 1987 and 1993, respectively.[17]

10.1.1.3 Estonia[18]

Estonia established diplomatic links with China in 1991, and the two sides soon entered into three important economic agreements, namely an economic and trade agreement in 1992, a BIT in 1993 and a DTT in 1996.[19] Recent years have witnessed a dramatic surge in Sino-Estonia trade. It reached US$273 million in 2001, a near-twenty-fold increase in four years, from US$14.68 million in 1998.[20] There are by now fourteen Chinese-funded enterprises in Estonia, with a total investment of US$2 million. Most of them fall in the sectors of mobile phones, wholesale and retail trade, textile processing, and the entertainment and catering industries.[21]

10.1.1.4 Hungary[22]

Like the Czech Republic, Hungary started to trade with China in the 1950s and conducted trade in accordance with a bilateral clearing agreement until 1991.[23] As a result of the change of the trade arrangement, bilateral trade

11 *Ibid.*
12 *Ibid.*
13 *Ibid.*
14 *Sino-Czech Relations, above note* 9.
15 *Sino-Czech Economic Relations, above note* 9.
16 *Ibid.*
17 *Ibid.*
18 *Sino-Estonia Economic Relations*, at the MOFCOM official Website, at: ozs.mofcom.gov.cn/article/200208/20020800037919_1.xml (last visited 24 August 2004). For general Sino-Estonia relations (including trade relations), see *Sino-Estonia Relations*, at the MFA Website, at: www.mfa.gov.cn/chn/wjb/zzjg/xos/gjlb/1681/default.htm (last visited 10 September 2004).
19 *Sino-Estonia Economic Relations, ibid.*
20 *Sino-Estonia Relations*, above note 18.
21 *Sino-Estonia Economic Relations*, above note 18.
22 See *Sino-Hungary Economic Relations*, at the Mofcom official Website, at: ozs.mofcom.gov.cn/article/200208/20020800035951_1.xml (last visited 24 August 2004). See also *Sino-Hungary Relations*, at the MFA Website, at: www.mfa.gov.cn/chn/wjb/zzjg/xos/gjlb/1796/default.htm (last visited 10 September 2004).
23 *Sino-Hungary Economic Relations, ibid.*

dropped in the early 1990s but soon revitalized.[24] In 2002, Sino-Hungary trade reached US$1.6 billion, which made Hungary the largest trade partner of China among Central and East European countries.[25] Statistics show that there are about 100 Chinese State-funded enterprises or representative offices in Hungary and about 1,000 companies privately owned by Chinese residing in Hungary.[26] By 2002, China had invested in forty projects in Hungary, with a total investment of US$13 million.[27] Meanwhile, there were 424 Hungarian investment projects in China, contributing US$101 million of investment.[28] Hungary signed a BIT[29] and a DTT[30] with China in 1991 and 1992, respectively.

10.1.1.5 Latvia[31]

China established diplomatic relations with Latvia in 1991. Recent years have seen good progress in bilateral trade and investment relations.[32] According to the Chinese Customs, Sino-Latvia trade reached US$72.75 million in 2002, a two-fold increase since 2000.[33] At present, there are eight Chinese-invested enterprises in Latvia, with a total investment of US$1.50 million.[34] Most of these are private investments.[35] Important bilateral economic treaties include an economic and trade agreement of 1994, a DTT of 1996[36] and a BIT of 2004.[37]

10.1.1.6 Lithuania[38]

The Sino-Lithuania diplomatic relationship was established in September 1991. Soon after that, the two countries entered into an economic and trade

[24] *Ibid.*
[25] *Sino-Hungary Relations*, above note 22.
[26] *Sino-Hungary Economic Relations*, above note 22.
[27] *Sino-Hungary Relations*, above note 22.
[28] *Ibid.*
[29] Ministry of Foreign Trade and Economic Co-operation (now MOFCOM), *Collection of International Investment Treaties* (in Chinese and English) (Jingguan Jiaowu Press, Beijing), at 560–71.
[30] Zhang, above note 7.
[31] For more detail, see *Sino-Latvia Relations*, at the MFA Website, at: www.mfa.gov.cn/chn/wjb/zzjg/xos/gjlb/1736/default.htm (last visited 10 September 2004). See also *Sino-Latvia Economic Relations*, at the MOFCOM website: http://ozs.mofcom.gov.cn/article/200208/20020800035978_1.xml (in Chinese) (last visited on 24 August 2004).
[32] *Sino-Latvia Relations*, *ibid.*
[33] *Ibid.*
[34] *Ibid.*
[35] *Ibid.*
[36] *Ibid.*
[37] The text of this BIT is available at the MOFCOM Website, at: tfs.mofcom.gov.cn/article/200405/20040500218576_1.xml (last visited 10 September 2004).
[38] See *Sino-Lithuania Economic Relations*, at the MOFCOM Website, at: ozs.mofcom.gov.cn/article/200208/20020800035979_1.xml (last visited 24 August 2004). See also *Sino-Lithuania Relations*, at the MFA Website, at: www.mfa.gov.cn/chn/wjb/zzjg/xos/gjlb/1741/default.htm (10 September 2004).

agreement (1991), a BIT (1992) and a DTT (1993).[39] Recent years have seen a rapid increase in bilateral trade. According to the Chinese Customs, in 2002 bilateral trade reached US$110 million, a five-fold increase in five years' time.[40] Statistics of China's Ministry of Commerce (MOFCOM) show that there are now about 200 Chinese companies or joint ventures in Lithuania, the total investment of which is US$12.50 million.[41]

10.1.1.7 Malta[42]

Sino-Malta trade started in the 1950s.[43] With the establishment of diplomatic relations in the 1970s, bilateral trade gradually increased.[44] Rapid growth of bilateral trade, however, did not come until the 1990s.[45] In 2001, bilateral trade reached US$150 million.[46] Recent years have also seen considerable growth of Maltese investment in China.[47] By September 2000, there were twenty-five Maltese investment projects in China, with a total investment of US$8.17 million.[48] There are also a few Chinese investment projects in Malta, including the Mediterranean Traditional Chinese Medical Centre.[49] However, the Chinese government has provided, in four instalments, US$147.10 million in aid to Malta since 1972.[50] Malta has not yet signed a BIT with China, but the two sides have concluded a DTT (1993) and an economic and trade agreement (1997).[51]

10.1.1.8 Poland[52]

Like the Czech Republic and Hungary, Poland started to trade with China in the 1950s and conducted trade in accordance with a bilateral clearing agreement until 1991.[53] In 1989, bilateral trade reached US$910 million, a

[39] *Ibid.*
[40] *Sino-Lithuania Relations*, above note 38.
[41] *Sino-Lithuania Economic Relations*, above note 38.
[42] *Sino-Malta Economic Relations*, at the MOFCOM Website, at: ozs.mofcom.gov.cn/article/200208/20020800036006_1.xml (last visited 24 August 2004). See also *Sino-Malta Relations*, at the MFA Website, at: www.mfa.gov.cn/chn/wjb/zzjg/xos/gjlb/1867/default.htm (last visited 12 September 2004).
[43] *Sino-Malta Economic Relations, ibid.*
[44] *Ibid.*
[45] *Ibid.*
[46] *Sino-Malta Relations*, above note 42.
[47] *Sino-Malta Economic Relations*, above note 42.
[48] *Ibid.*
[49] *Ibid.*
[50] *Ibid.*
[51] *Ibid.*
[52] See *Sino-Poland Economic Relations*, at the MOFCOM Website, at: ozs.mofcom.gov.cn/article/200208/20020800035940_1.xml (last visited 24 August 2004). See also *Sino-Poland Relations*, at the MFA Website, at: www.mfa.gov.cn/chn/wjb/zzjg/xos/gjlb/1696/default.htm (last visited 15 September 2004).
[53] *Sino-Poland Economic Relations, ibid.*

161-fold increase since 1950.[54] The change of the trade arrangement in 1991 initially resulted in a sharp drop in bilateral trade,[55] which has gradually increased, however, since 1992. In 2002, Sino-Polish trade reached a new high of US$1.38 billion, making Poland one of the largest trade partners for China among Central and East European countries.[56]

As far as bilateral investment is concerned, the Chipolbrok, as aforementioned, was the first-ever Sino-foreign joint venture in the history of the People's Republic of China.[57] By 2002, Poland had invested US$43.35 million in China, which made it also one of the largest investors in China among Central and East European countries.[58] Meanwhile, there had been more than eighty Chinese-invested projects in Poland, with a total investment of US$45 million, which put China in the number 28th position in the Polish foreign investors' league table.[59] China signed a BIT and a DTT with Poland in 1988 and a general economic and trade agreement in 1993.[60]

10.1.1.9 Slovakia[61]

Slovakia and the Czech Republic share the same historical trade links with China before 1993, as they were then both part of the Federal Republic of Czechoslovakia. In 1994, Slovakia signed a general economic and trade agreement with China and formally accepted that the BIT (1991) and DTT (1987), *inter alia*, concluded between China and the Federal Republic of Czechoslovakia continued to be effective between China and Slovakia.[62] According to the Slovakian Customs, bilateral trade reached US$344 million in 2002.[63] Also, Slovakia had committed to eighteen investment projects in China by 2002, realizing a total investment of US$14.63 million.[64]

10.1.1.10 Slovenia

China established diplomatic relations with Slovenia in 1992 and a bilateral economic and trade agreement was concluded in the same year.[65] In the fol-

[54] *Ibid.*
[55] *Ibid.*
[56] *Ibid.*
[57] *Ibid.*; see also above note 4.
[58] *Ibid.*
[59] *Sino-Poland Relations*, above note 52.
[60] *Sino-Poland Economic Relations, above note* 52.
[61] See *Sino-Slovakia Economic Relations*, at the MOFCOM Website, at: ozs.mofcom.gov.cn/article/200208/20020800037924_1.xml (last visited 24 August 2004). See also *Sino-Slovakia Relations*, at the MFA Website, at: www.mfa.gov.cn/chn/wjb/zzjg/xos/gjlb/1766/default.htm (last visited 15 September 2004).
[62] *Sino-Slovakia Economic Relations, ibid.*
[63] *Ibid.*
[64] *Sino-Slovakia Relations*, above note 61.
[65] See *Sino-Slovenia Relations*, at the MFA Website, at: www.mfa.gov.cn/chn/wjb/zzjg/xos/gjlb/1771/default.htm (last visited 15 September 2004). See also *Sino-Slovenia Economic*

lowing years, the two governments entered into a BIT (1993) and a DTT (1995), among other agreements.[66]

China maintains good trade relations with Slovenia which date back to the former-Yugoslavia era.[67] According to Slovenian statistics, however, Sino-Slovenia trade remained rather low before Slovenia gained independence, and dropped in the first few years immediately after independence.[68] Since 1999, bilateral trade has grown rapidly, from US$36.10 million in 1998 to US$125 million in 2002.[69] In 1999, the *Market Access Strategy of Slovenia Economy in China* was formulated by the Slovenian government.[70] Under such governmental support, Slovenian investors have become more active in exploring the Chinese market.[71] On the other hand, there is also some Chinese investment in Slovenia, mostly specializing in the trading and catering industries.[72]

10.1.2 Overview and Implications on General EU-China Investment and Trade Relations

Trade and investment relations between China and the EU 10 States are summarized in *Table 22*. It shows that total trade between China and these new Member States reached US$523.869 billion in 2002, which comprised 6.13 per cent of the bilateral trade between China and the EU 15.[73] Considering that the combined gross domestic product of the 10 countries is less than 5 per cent of that of the EU 15,[74] this result demonstrates that the EU 10 States have a particularly close trade relationship with China. Among the EU 10 States, Hungary is China's largest trading partner, followed by Poland and the Czech Republic. The EU enlargement has a noticeable impact on general EU–China trade. Indeed, this enlargement has readily put the EU in the second place in China's foreign trade partners' league table, and it is predicted that the enlarged EU will soon become China's largest trading partner.[75]

Relations at the MOFCOM Website, at: ozs.mofcom.gov.cn/article/200208/20020800037923_1.xml (last visited 24 August 2004).

66 *Ibid.*

67 *Sino-Slovenia Economic Relations*, above note 65.

68 *Ibid.*

69 *Ibid.* See also *Sino-Slovenia Relations*, above note 65.

70 *Sino-Slovenia Economic Relations*, above note 65.

71 *Ibid.*

72 *Ibid.*

73 There are no direct statistics for EU–China bilateral trade for the whole year of 2002, but for the first eleven months the value of that trade was US$7,824.826 billion. The amount of bilateral trade in December was calculated according to the monthly average of the first eleven months' trade figures. For EU–China trade statistics in 2002 (January–November), see the MOFCOM Website, at: ozs.mofcom.gov.cn/article/200406/20040600237106_1.xml (last visited 15 September 2004).

74 See *Enlarging Europe*, above note 1.

75 See *EU Enlarged to be a Union of 25 Member States and the Largest Trade Partner of China*, available at: www.qingdaonews.com/content/2004-04/28/content_3066496.htm (in Chinese,

Table 22: Trade and Investment Relations with EU 10 States

New Member State	Bilateral Trade in 2002	Investment in China by 2002	Chinese Investment by 2002	Trade Agreement	DTT	BIT
Cyprus	225.94	n/a	n/a	1981	1990	2001
Czech Rep.	962.00	64.68	n/a	1993	1987	1991
Estonia	269.00	n/a	2.00	1992	1996	1993
Hungary	1600.00	101	13.00	n/a	1992	1991
Latvia	72.75	n/a	1.50	1994	1996	2004
Lithuania	110.00	n/a	12.50	1991	1993	1992
Malta	150.00[a]	8.17[b]	n/a	1997	1993	no
Poland	1380.00	43.35	45	1993	1988	1988
Slovakia	344.00	14.63	n/a	1994	1987	1991
Slovenia	125.00	n/a	n/a	1992	1995	1993
Total	5238.69	231.83	70	9	10	9

Units: US$ million.
[a]2001; [b]by 2000.

As far as foreign direct investment is concerned, whilst there is relatively small investment from the EU 10 States in China, there is a comparatively very large Chinese investment in the EU 10 countries. Table 22 shows that, on the one hand, a total amount of about US$231.83 million of direct investment was made in China by these countries by 2002, which amounted to only 0.68 per cent of the EU 15's investment in China for the same period. Hungary again led the league table as the top investor in China from these countries, followed by the Czech Republic and Poland. The relatively small amount of investment made by these countries in China suggests that the EU enlargement does not greatly affect the general position of EU investment in China. On the other hand, it does considerably change the picture of Chinese investment in the EU. China had invested at least US $74 million in these countries by 2002, which amounted to more than 19 per cent of China's total direct investment in Europe (including Russia).[76] The historical links between China and these countries must be the major reason underlying such a significant investment. It can be anticipated that even more Chinese investment will

last visited 16 September 2004). See also *Implication of EU Enlargement to Sino-EU Economic and Trade Relations*, available at: news.xinhuanet.com/newscenter/2004-05/03/content_1452167.htm (in Chinese, last visited 16 September 2004).

[76] Chinese statistics show that by 2003 China had invested US$530 million in Europe (Russia included). They also show that US$150 million of further investment was made in 2003. Thus, the total Chinese investment in Europe (including Russia) by 2002 should be US$380 million. For details of China's outward investment, see *2003 China Outward Direct Investment Statistical Report*, at the MOFCOM Website, at: www.mofcom.gov.cn/article/200409/20040900275569_1.xml (last visited 16 September 2004) .

be made in these countries following the enlargement in order to gain access to the huge, enlarged EU internal market.

It must be noted, however, that the EU enlargement might have a negative impact on the growth of bilateral trade and investment between China and the twenty-five EU Member States. In particular, 'internal" trade and investment activities between the EU 15 and the EU 10 States will be significantly intensified as a result of the enlargement, which may have a negative effect on China's trade and investment exchange with both the EU 15 and the EU 10 States.[77] However, it is believed that the positive effects of the enlargement should be able to offset the negative ones, particularly when viewing it from a long-term perspective.[78] One way for the Chinese business community to counter the trade-transfer effect of enlargement may be to increase its investment in these new Member States and make full use of the common commercial policy of the EU.

With regard to bilateral investment and trade arrangements, an extensive bilateral treaty network has been established between China and the EU 10 States, including 9 BITs, 10 DTTs and 9 trade (or economic and trade) agreements. This treaty network lays down a legal foundation for the development of bilateral trade and investment relations.

10.2 THE LEGAL FRAMEWORK OF INVESTMENT RELATIONS BETWEEN CHINA AND THE EU 10 STATES

Apart from the aforementioned bilateral treaties, particularly the BITs, the legal framework governing investment relations between China and the EU 10 States is composed of multilateral investment treaties to which both China and these States are contracting parties, as well as the domestic laws of China and the EU 10 States.

10.2.1 Multilateral Agreements to which China and the EU 10 States Are Parties

The multilateral agreements governing investment relations between China and the EU 10 States are the International Convention on the Settlement of Investment Disputes (the ICSID Convention), the Convention Establishing the Multilateral Investment Guarantee Agency (the MIGA Convention) and the World Trade Organization Agreements. As observed elsewhere, none of

[77] *EU Enlarged to be a Union of 25 Member States and the Largest Trade Partner of China*, above note 75. See also *Implication of EU Enlargement to Sino-EU Economic and Trade Relations*, above note 75.

[78] Luo, XiaoJun, 'How Will EU Enlargement Affect China': posted at *Nanfang Daily* website (in Chinese): http://www.nanfangdaily.com.cn/southnews/sjjj/200405030319.asp (last visited on 19 March 2005).

these agreements is a comprehensive treaty for investment protection, as each only touches upon certain specific aspects of international investment such as dispute settlement, investment insurance against political risks, and regulation of trade in goods and services.[79] The following elaborates some aspects of these agreements that are closely related to the investment relations between China and the EU 10 States.

10.2.1.1 The ICSID Convention

The ICSID Convention aims to set up a non-political international forum to settle investment disputes between host States and foreign investors by providing arbitration and conciliation facilities.[80] As *Table 23* shows, China, together with nine of the ten new EU Member States, is a Contracting Party to the ICSID Convention. Poland is the only exception in this regard. However, it would also be possible to bring a case between China and Poland before the ICSID by resorting to that body's Additional Facility.[81] As will be seen below, most BITs concluded between China and these countries have referred to ICSID arbitration, which puts the ICSID in a prominent position in settling State–investor disputes between the two sides.

10.2.1.2 The MIGA Convention

The aim of the MIGA Convention is to promote international investment flow, particularly to developing countries, by providing guarantees against non-commercial risks which might not normally be insured by commercial insurance providers.[82] All the EU 10 States and China are Contracting Parties to the MIGA Convention.[83] Given that all of them are developing countries for the purposes of the MIGA Convention, mutual investments between China and the ten countries can all be guaranteed by the MIGA.[84] This might provide a special incentive for Chinese companies to invest in the EU 10 States, as compared with the EU 15 States, as Chinese investment in the EU 15 could not be insured by the MIGA.[85]

[79] Shan, above note 3, at 142–53.

[80] For further details of the ICSID Convention and its interaction with Sino-EU 15 investment relations, see *ibid.*, at 142–45.

[81] The Additional Facility makes it possible for cases in which only one of the parties is a Contracting Party to the Convention to be heard by the ICSID, provided that both parties to the dispute consent to such a means of dispute resolution.

[82] For further details of the MIGA Convention and its interaction with Sino-EU 15 investment relations, see Shan, above note 3, at 146–49.

[83] *MIGA Member States*, at the MIGA Website, at: www.miga.org/screens/about/members/members.htm (last visited 14 March 2005).

[84] MIGA only provides guarantees for investments made in developing countries, not for those made in developed or industrialized countries. Therefore, MIGA has classified its Member States into two categories: 'Industrialized Countries" or 'Developing Countries"; see *ibid.*

[85] All the EU 15 States are 'Industrialized Countries" according to MIGA's classification, *ibid.*

Table 23: ICSID, China and the EU 10 States

State	Signature	Deposit of Ratification	Entry into Force of Convention
China	9 Feb 1990	7 Jan 1993	6 Feb 1993
Cyprus	9 Mar 1966	25 Nov 1966	25 Dec 1966
Czech Republic	23 Mar 1993	23 Mar 1993	22 Apr 1993
Estonia	23 June 1992	23 June 1992	23 Jul 1992
Hungary	1 Oct 1986	4 Feb 1987	6 Mar 1987
Latvia	8 Aug 1997	8 Aug 1997	7 Sep 1997
Lithuania	6 July 1992	6 July 1992	5 Aug 1992
Malta	24 Apr 2002	3 Nov 2003	3 Dec 2003
Slovakia	27 Sep 1993	27 May 1994	26 June 1994
Slovenia	7 Mar 1994	7 Mar 1994	6 Apr 1994

Source: *List of Contracting States and other Signatories of the Convention* (as of 3 November 2003) at the ICSID website: http://www.worldbankgroup.org/icsid/constate/c-states-en.htm (16 September 2004).

10.2.1.3 The WTO Agreements

The Agreement Establishing the World Trade Organisation (the WTO Agreement) is relevant to investment issues, not only because it has some sub-agreements that deal with investment issues (such as the Agreement on Trade-Related Investment Measures and the General Agreement on Trade in Services), but also because it has ongoing activities relevant to international investment law-making.[86] For example, the relationship between trade and investment has been one of Singapore issues of negotiations and was included in the Doha Agenda, although the Cancun Conference failed to formally launch the negotiation on a multilateral investment agreement.[87] All ten countries and China are Member States of the WTO,[88] which means that both sides can mutually benefit from the reduction of customs tax and other concessions, including commitments on investment liberalization.

[86] For further details of the WTO Agreement and its interaction with Sino-EU 15 investment relations, see Shan, above, note 3, at 149–53.

[87] For general work on the relationship between trade and investment within the WTO, see Trade and Investment, at http://www.wto.org/english/tratop_e/invest_e/invest_e.htm (last visited 18 March 2005). For the decision not to negotiate on investment issue, see Article 1(g) para 2 of the Decision Adopted by the General Council on 1 August 2004 (the Cancun Package), at http://www.wto.org/english/tratop_e/dda_e/draft_text_gc_dg_31july04_e.htm (last visited 18 March 2005).

[88] *Members and Observers*, available at the WTO official Website, at: www.wto.org/english/thewto_e/whatis_e/tif_e/org6_e.htm (last visited 16 September 2004).

10.2.2 Bilateral Agreements Between China and the EU 10 States

Among bilateral agreements and trade agreements, DTTs and BITs are the most important ones dealing with bilateral economic relations. As far as investment is concerned, BITs are the most important instruments, followed by the DTTs, which aim to avoid double taxation on foreign investors. *Tables 3* and *4*, respectively, give further details of the nine BITs and ten DTTs signed between China and the EU 10 States. Details of the nine BITs will be explored below. A close discussion of these DTTs is, however, beyond the scope of this book.[89]

10.2.3 Domestic Laws of China and the EU 10 States

Like China, the EU 10 States have extensive laws and regulations focused on international investment, particularly on inward direct investment. These laws and regulations, as well as the EU and Chinese laws on international investment,[90] constitute the domestic laws governing the investment relations between China and the EU 10 States. Whilst it would be interesting to investigate these domestic laws and regulations, it is beyond the scope of this chapter, where the focus is on the applicable international law. The MOFCOM Website has provided very good information for the legal environment of investment in these European countries, whilst the Chinese FDI Law system has been elaborated and examined throughout this book, particularly in Chapter 1.[91]

10.2.4 Summary

The major components of the legal framework governing Sino-EU 10 investment relations include multilateral agreements, bilateral agreements and domestic laws. On the multilateral level, the ICSID Convention, the MIGA Convention and the WTO Agreements are most relevant, as China and most of the EU 10 States have now become Members of these treaties and institutions. On a bilateral level, there are bilateral trade agreements, DTTs and BITs. Domestic laws and regulations of the EU 10 States, in addition to EU and Chinese laws in regard to international investment, also play a significant role in protecting and promoting mutual investment flows. Since this chapter

[89] DTTs deal with only one technical, albeit important, aspect of investment operations. For a good guide to China's DTT practice, see Zhang, above note 7.

[90] For further details of Chinese and EU FDI law in relation to Sino-EU 15 investment relations, see Shan, above note 3, at 158–65.

[91] *Sino-Europe Bilateral Economic and Trade Relations*, at the MOFCOM Website, at: http://ozs.mofcom.gov.cn/aarticle/cbw/200208/20020800036028.html (last visited 18 March 2005).

focuses on the applicable international law and most elements of the multilateral treaties have already been dealt in other chapters, the following Section of this chapter only further investigates the BITs concluded between China and the EU 10 States.

10.3 THE BILATERAL INVESTMENT TREATIES BETWEEN CHINA AND THE EU 10 STATES

BITs are the most important legal instruments to protect mutual investment between China and the EU 10 States. As can be seen from *Table 24*, these BITs were mostly signed after the BITs between China and EU 15 States were signed, some as late as 2004. It will therefore be interesting to see whether and how these BITs are different from the earlier BITs concluded between China and the EU 15 States.[92] This Section elaborates these newer BITs and compares them with the earlier ones by comparing the provisions on important issues such as investment admission, standards of treatment, expropriation and compensation, subrogation and dispute settlement. The following discussions will be based on the nine BITs existing between China and the EU 10 States.[93]

Table 24: BITs between China and the EU 10 States

Country	Date of Signature	Date of Entry into Force
Cyprus	15 January 2001	–
Czech Republic	04 December 1991	01 December 1992
Estonia	02 September 1993	01 June 1994
Hungary	29 May 1991	01 April 1993
Latvia	15 April 2004	–
Lithuania	08 November 1993	01 June 1994
Poland	07 June 1988	08 January 1989
Slovakia	04 December 1991	01 December 1992
Slovenia	13 September 1993	01 January 1995

Source: Compiled by the author in accordance with ICSID and UNCTAD data. See ICSID, Bilateral Investment Treaties, posted at http://www.worldbank.org/icsid/treaties/china.htm (18 September 2004); UNCTAD, Total Number of Bilateral Investment Treaties Concluded, 1 January 2003 (by China), posted at http://stats.unctad.org/fdi/treaties/bits/China.htm (18 March 2005).

92 For discussions on Sino-EU 15 BITs, see Shan, above note 3, at 155–57. For further details, see Shan, Wenhua, 'The International Law of EU Investment in China', (2002) 2 *Chinese Journal of International Law* 2, at 604–10.

93 In fact, it is only eight BITs, as the BITs with the Czech Republic and Slovakia are actually the same, ie, the BIT signed between China and the former Federal Republic of Czechoslovakia, which was later divided into the current two countries, the Czech Republic and the Slovakia.

Table 25: DTTs between China and the EU 10 States

Country	Date of Signature	Date of entry into force
Cyprus	25 October 1990	5 October 1991
Czech Republic	11 June 1987	23 December 1987
Estonia	12 May 1998	8 January 1999
Hungary	17 June 1992	31 December 1992
Latvia	7 September 1996	27 January 1997
Lithuania	3 June 1996	18 October 1996
Malta	2 February 1993	30 March 1994
Poland	07 June 1988	07 January 1989
Slovakia	11 June 1987	23 December 1987
Slovenia	13 February 1994	27 December 1995

Source: Zhang, Xin, *The Law and Practice of International Taxation Treaties in China* (Wildy, Simmonds and Hill Publishing Ltd 2003), in Appendix 1 China's Double Tax Treaties and Arrangements, at 683–85. See also UNCTAD, *Total Number of Double Taxation Treaties Concluded, 1 January 2003* (by China), posted at http://stats.unctad.org/fdi/treaties/dtts/China.htm (18 March 2005).

10.3.1 Admission

The provisions for admission of investments in the BITs between China and the EU 10 States are similar to those found in the BITs between China and the EU 15 States. In other words, they all follow the European tradition of leaving the right to regulate the admission of foreign investments to the discretion of the host government.[94] Thus, all eight BITs provide that the admission of foreign direct investment should be conducted 'in accordance with laws and regulations' of the host country. The recently signed Sino-Latvia BIT is not an exception in this regard (see *Table 26*). As with the Sino-Spain and Sino-Greece BITs,[95] eight of the nine BITs also require that the host country provide assistance and facilities when nationals from the other contracting party apply for visas or work permits in connection with the investment activities.

[94] For a detailed elaboration of these European BITs, see Dolzer, Rudolf and Stevens, Margrete, *Bilateral Investment Treaties* (Martinus Nijhoff, 1995), at 50–56. See also Shihata, Ibrahim FI, 'Recent Trends Relating to Entry of Foreign Direct Investment', (1994) 9 *ICSID Review–FILJ*, at 55–56.

[95] Sino-Spain BIT, Article 2.2; Sino-Greece BIT, Article 2.5.

Table 26: Admission under BITs between China and EU 10 States

BIT	In accordance with legislation/ laws and regulations	Assistance and facilities on visa and work permit applications
Sino-Cyprus	Art 2.1	Art 2.2
Sino-Czech BIT	Art 2.1	Art 2.2
Sino-Estonia BIT	Art 2.1	Art 2.2
Sino-Hungary BIT	Art 2.1	Art 2.2
Sino-Latvia BIT	Art 2.1	Art 2.4
Sino-Lithuania BIT	Art 2.1	Art 2.2
Sino-Poland BIT	Art 2	–
Sino-Slovakia BIT	Art 2.1	Art 2.2
Sino-Slovenia BIT	Art 2.1	Art 2.2
Total (9)	9	8

10.3.2 Standards of Treatment

10.3.2 1 General Standards of Treatment

The provisions on the general standards of treatment of foreign investors in the eight BITs are, in general, similar to those in the thirteen BITs between China and the EU 15 States, although there are also some differences. Most-favoured-nation (MFN) treatment and 'fair and equitable' treatment are established in almost all of the eight BITs, with MFN treatment being subject to normal exceptions such as customs union, border trade and taxation treaties. 'Preservation of rights' clauses are common in these BITs, enabling foreign investors to enjoy the best possible treatment provided by the host government.

National treatment (NT) is used in five BITs with the EU 10 States, and in all the five BITs its application is substantially qualified. In four of such BITs, the application of NT shall not prejudice domestic laws and regulations, which is a standard qualification China adopted in its BIT practice. The application of NT is further limited, among these BITs, by phrases such as 'to the extent possible'[96] and 'sound development of national economy'.[97] The Protocol to the Sino-Cyprus BIT, however, qualifies the NT application in China by attaching a 'grandfather clause'. Under this clause, the NT obligation does not apply to 'any existing non-conforming measures' and its continuation within the territory of China. Such a measure can also be amended

[96] Article 3.2, Sino-Slovenia BIT.

[97] Point 1, Protocol to the Sino-Czechoslovakia BIT (now the Sino-Czech BIT and Sino-Slovakia BIT).

provided that such amendment does not increase their non-conformity with the NT obligation. It is undertaken, nonetheless, 'it will be endeavoured to progressively remove the non-conforming measures'. Thus, it can be said that the Sino-Cyprus BIT has moved a step forward by 'freezing" the level of non-conformity to the NT principle in China to that on the date of entry into force of the BIT. It is unclear, however, whether Cyprus can maintain similar measures as the paragraph 4 of Article 3 of the Sino-Cyprus BIT which requires the application of MFN and NT obligations on a reciprocal basis.

Non-discriminatory (ND) treatment is granted under two recently signed BITs, namely the Sino-Cyprus BIT and the Sino-Latvia BIT (signed in 2001 and 2004 respectively, both yet to be ratified). However, whilst such non-discrimination treatment is subject to normal qualification in the Sino-Latvia BIT so that its application shall not prejudice domestic laws and regulations, it is not qualified in the Sino-Cyprus BIT. Given the limitation on the application of NT, such a failure to mention the normal qualification in the Sino-Cyprus BIT should not be regarded as a major advancement in this regard.

Unlike other BITs which only loosely refer to 'protection' of investment from the other contracting party, the Sino-Latvia BIT has also included a commitment to 'constant protection and security'. It can be argued, however, that such an addition does not add much more protection than that under the fair and equitable treatment, which is granted in most existing Chinese BITs.

It may be concluded that, on the one hand, the provisions on the standards of treatment provided for in the Sino-EU 10 BITs are generally similar to those in the Sino-EU 15 BITs, particularly in that MFN and fair and equitable treatments are provided and that the application of national treatment obligation in China is substantially qualified. On the other hand, Sino-EU 10 BITs do mark some progress in providing more favourable treatment to foreign investors. This is witnessed by, for example, the prohibition of further limitations on the application NT and the non-qualification on the application of non-discrimination in the Sino-Cyprus BIT and the inclusion of 'constant protection and security' treatment in the Sino-Latvia BIT. It can therefore be argued that the nine Sino-EU 10 BITs do add some more favourable treatment for EU 15 investors in China, by the operation of the MFN clause. Details of these provisions are shown in *Table 27*.

10.3.2.2 Monetary Transfers

As shown in *Table 28*, the BITs between China and the EU 10 States guarantee free transfer of investments and returns without delay. Under these BITs, monetary transfers should be made in convertible currency, at the official rate or prevailing market rate. However, in most of the nine BITs, such freedom is subject to the domestic laws and regulations of the host State. Even the Sino-Latvia BIT signed in 2004 follows this model. The Sino-Czech and Sino-Slovakia BITs (formerly the Sino-Czechoslovakia BIT) do not refer to

Table 27: Treatment under BITs between China and EU 10 States

BIT	Fair and Equitable treatment	National treatment	MFN treatment	More favorable treatment	Non-discriminatory treatment	Constant Protection and Security
Sino-Cyprus BIT	Art 3.1	Grandpa[a] Art 3.3 and Protocol	Art 3.3	Art 10	Art 3.2	–
Sino-Czech BIT	–	DL[b] Art 3.2 and Protocol Point 1	Art 3.1	Art 10	–	–
Sino-Estonia BIT	Art 3.1	–	Art 3.2	Art 9	–	–
Sino-Hungary BIT	Art 3.1	–	Art 3.2	Art 11	–	–
Sino-Latvia BIT	Art 3.1	DL[b] Art 3.1	Art 3.3	Art 11.1	DL[b] Art 2.3	Art 2.2
Sino-Lithuania BIT	Art 3.1	–	Art 3.2	Art 9	–	–
Sino-Poland BIT	Art 3.1	–	Art 3.2	–	–	–
Sino-Slovakia BIT	–	DL[b] Art 3.2 and Protocol point 1	Art 3.1	Art 10	–	–
Sino-Slovenia BIT	Art 3.1	DL[b]	Art 3.3	Art 9	–	–
Total (9)	7	5 (DL[b] + Grandpa[a])	9	8	2 (1 DLb)	1

[a]Grandpa means that national treatment is qualified by a 'grandfather clause', which allows China to maintain and continue the maintenance of non-conforming measures.
[b]DL means that national treatment is granted only when it is not prejudicial to domestic laws and regulations.

Table 28: Transfer under BITs between China and EU 10 States

Investment Instruments	(Free) transfer without delay	Subject to domestic laws and regulations	Rate of exchange		In convertible currency
			official/ prevailing	IMF	
Sino-Cyprus BIT	Art 6.1	Special China clause[a] Protocol, Point 2	Art 6.2	–	Art 6.2
Sino-Czech BIT	Art 6.1	China clause[a] Protocol, Point 3	Art 6.1	–	Art 6.1
Sino-Estonia BIT	Art 5.1	Art 5.1	Art 5.2	–	Art 5.2
Sino-Hungary BIT	Art 5.1	Art 5.1	Art 6	–	–
Sino-Latvia BIT	Art 6.1	Art 6.1	Art 6.3	–	Art 6.3
Sino-Lithuania BIT	Art 5.1	Art 5.1	Art 5.2	–	Art5.2
Sino-Poland BIT	Art 5.1	Art 5.1	Art 6	–	–
Sino-Slovakia BIT	Art 6.1	China clause[a] Protocol Point 3	Art 6.2	–	Art 6.1
Sino-Slovenia BIT	Art 5.1	Art 5.1	Art 5.2	–	–
Total (9)	9	7 (+3 China clauses)	9	0	6

[a]'China clause' normally refers to a special clause applicable to China which requires that all transfers be made from the foreign exchange accounts of the foreign-invested enterprise and that China guarantees the provision of foreign exchange in certain cases, as specifically prescribed, where the enterprise does not have sufficient foreign exchange in that account. See, for example, Point 3 of the Protocol to the Sino-Czech Bit. However, the Sino-Cyprus BIT has a 'China clause' that refers to only the 'formalities' of exchange control in China.

'domestic laws and regulations' in the text but include a 'China Clause' in the Protocol which effectively subjects monetary transfers to Chinese laws governing foreign exchange. However, the Sino-Cyprus BIT may again mark a step forward in this regard. Although it also includes a restrictive 'China clause', such a clause refers to only 'relevant formalities' stipulated by the present Chinese laws and regulations relating to exchange control. This seems to imply that China may only maintain or introduce 'procedural' restrictions (*formalities*), rather than substantive ones. If this understanding is correct, then it is a substantial liberalisation. It can be argued that, furthermore, the nine BITs do provide a further guarantee of the free transfer of investment and returns than the Sino-EU 15 BITs.

10.3.3 Expropriation and Compensation

The issues of expropriation are dealt with in BITs from three perspectives, namely its constitution, its conditions and compensation.

10.3.3.1 Constitution and Conditions

The nine BITs show striking uniformity in both the constitution and conditions of expropriation. All of them adopt a broad definition of expropriation which covers nationalization, expropriation and measures having equivalent effects (see *Table 29*). They all attach four conditions to expropriation—namely public interest, non-discrimination, due process of domestic law and

Table 29: Constitution of Expropriation under BITs between China and EU 10 States

BIT	Nationalisation	Expropriation	Measures having equivalent/similar effects
Sino-Cyprus BIT	Art 4.1	Art 4.1	Art 4.1
Sino-Czech BIT	Art 4.1	Art 4.1	Art 4.1
Sino-Estonia BIT	Art 4.1	Art 4.1	Art 4.1
Sino-Hungary BIT	Art 4.1	Art 4.1	Art 4.1
Sino-Latvia BIT	Art 4.1	Art 4.1	Art 4.1
Sino-Lithuania BIT	Art 4.1	Art 4.1	Art 4.1
Sino-Poland BIT	Art 4.1	Art 4.1	Art 4.1
Sino-Slovakia BIT	Art 4.1	Art 4.1	Art 4.1
Sino-Slovenia BIT	Art 4.1	Art 4.1	Art 4.1
Total (9)	9	9	9

Table 30: Conditions of Expropriation under BITs between China and the EU 10 States

BIT	Conditions			
	Public interest	Non-discrimination	Due process of law	Compensation
Sino-Cyprus BIT	Art 4.1	Art 4.1	Domestic Law Art 4.1	Art 4.1
Sino-Czech BIT	Art 4.1	Art 4.1	Domestic Law Art 4.1	Art 4.1
Sino-Estonia BIT	Art 4.1	Art 4.1	Domestic Law Art 4.1	Art 4.1
Sino-Hungary BIT	Art 4.1	Art 4.1	Domestic Law Art 4.1	Art 4.1
Sino-Latvia BIT	Art 4.1	Art 4.1	Domestic Law Art 4.1	Art 4.1
Sino-Lithuania BIT	Art 4.1	Art 4.1	Domestic Law Art 4.1	Art 4.1
Sino-Poland BIT	Art 4.1	Art 4.1	Domestic Law Art 4.1	Art 4.1
Sino-Slovakia BIT	Art 4.1	Art 4.1	Domestic Law Art 4.1	Art 4.1
Sino-Slovenia BIT	Art 4.1	Art 4.1	Domestic Law Art 4.1	Art 4.1
Total (9)	9	9	9	9

compensation (see *Table 30*).[98] These are even stipulated in the same provisions of the BITs, Article 4, which suggests that they have followed a model BIT, probably one provided by China. These BITs are slightly different from the thirteen China–EU 15 BITs in that they unanimously adopt due process of 'domestic law' rather than merely due process of 'law', which may include laws of other States and international law. This is probably another indication that the nine Sino-EU 10 BITs followed the same model treaty. Also, this suggests that the EU 10 States, as developing States, share the same view China has on applicable law of 'due process', that is, only the law of the host State.

[98] Most of these BITs state that contracting parties shall not expropriate foreign investments 'unless the following conditions are met'. However, the wording of the Sino-Czechoslovakia BIT (now the Sino-Czech BIT and the Sino-Slovakia BIT) suggests that 'public interest' is the only prerequisite/condition of expropriation and the other three 'conditions' are just what should be done after expropriation has taken place.

10.3.3.2 Compensation

The provisions on the amount of compensation in the nine Sino-EU 10 BITs are rather similar to those in the thirteen Sino-EU 15 BITs.[99] None of them refer to the 'Hull formula' of 'adequate, prompt and effective' compensation. None of the nine BITs even adopt an abstract standard of compensation, such as 'appropriate' or 'full' compensation. However, all of them guarantee that foreign investors will receive compensation, in case of expropriation, which shall be equivalent to the value of the expropriated investment (see *Table 31*). Seven BITs also expressly state that the amount of compensation must include interest. All nine BITs stipulate that the compensation should be paid without delay and be realizable and transferable.

Only two of the eight BITs have substantive rules on the evaluation of compensation. The 2004 Sino-Latvia BIT merely states that the determination of the value of the expropriated investment shall follow 'generally recognized principles of valuation'.[100] The Sino-Slovenia BIT goes a step further to adopt 'market value' as the basis of valuation.[101] In case such a 'market value' cannot be readily ascertained, the compensation shall be determined in accordance with 'generally recognized principles of valuation and equitable principles, taking into account, *inter alia*, the capital invested, depreciation, capital already repatriated, replacement value and other relevant factors'.[102] Whilst it is yet to be seen how it works in actual cases, this provision in the Sino-Slovenia BIT seems to have provided so far the most elaborate guidance on valuation of compensation in the twenty-one Sino-EU BITs. In addition, three BITs also provide for the possibility for the valuation of compensation to be reviewed by a judicial body or another independent body of the host country.[103]

10.3.4 Subrogation

The subrogation clauses in the Sino-EU 10 BITs are similar to each other and to those in the Sino-EU 15 BITs (see *Table 32*).[104] All these BITs require that a Contracting Party recognize the assignment of rights and claims from investors to the other Contracting Party if the latter Contracting Party has made any payment to its investor under a guarantee it has assumed in respect of an

[99] For a comparison of expropriation clauses in the Sino-EU 15 BITs, see Chapter 6, section 6.2.2.

[100] Article 4.2, Sino-Latvia BIT, above note 37.

[101] Article 4.3, Sino-Slovenia BIT.

[102] *Ibid.*

[103] Article 4.2, Sino-Czechoslovakia BIT (now the Sino-Czech BIT and the Sino-Slovakia BIT); and Article 4.3, Sino-Poland BIT.

[104] For a comparison of subrogation provisions in the Sino-EU 15 BITs, see Shan, above note 3, at 155–57. See also Shan, above note 92, at 604–10.

Table 31: Compensation for Expropriation under BITs between China and the EU 10 States

BIT	Value of the expropriated investment	Adequate, effective and prompt	Without delay, realisable and transferable	Valuation of expropriated investment
Sino-Cyprus BIT	Plus interest Art 4.2	–	Art 4.2	–
Sino-Czech BIT	Plus interest Art 4.2	–	Art 4.1	No method Subject to judicial review (Art 4.2)
Sino-Estonia BIT	Art 4.2	–	Art 4.2	–
Sino-Hungary BIT	Art 4.	–	Art 4.2	–
Sino-Latvia BIT	Plus interest Art 4.2	–	Art 4.2	Generally recognized principles (Art 4.2)
Sino-Lithuania BIT	Plus interest Art 4.2	–	Art 4.2	–
Sino-Poland BIT	Plus interest Art 4.2	–	Art 4.2	No method Subject to judicial review (Art 4.3)
Sino-Slovakia BIT	Plus interest Art 4.21	–	Art 4.1	No method Subject to judicial review (Art 4.3)
Sino-Slovenia BIT	Plus interest Art 4.2–3	–	Art 4.3	Market value, or generally recognised principles and equitable principles (Art 4.3)
Total (9)	9 (7 include interest)	0	9	

Table 32: Subrogation under BITs between China and the EU 10 States

BIT	Recognise the transfer and subrogation of rights and claims	Scope of subrogated rights				
		Same treatment as the guaranteed investor	Including litigation rights	Without prejudice to home State's right to invoke state-state arbitration	Shall not exceed the original rights	Can make counter-claims to the subrogated rights
Sino-Cyprus BIT	Art 7	–	–	–	–	–
Sino-Czech BIT	Art 7	–	–	–	Art 7	–
Sino-Estonia BIT	Art 6	–	–	–	Art 6	–
Sino-Hungary BIT	Art 7	–	–	–	Art 7	–
Sino-Latvia BIT	Art 7	Art 7	–	–	–	–
Sino-Lithuania BIT	Art 6	Art 6	–	–	–	–
Sino-Poland BIT	Art 7	Art 7	–	–	–	Art 7
Sino-Slovakia BIT	Art 7	–	–	–	Art 7	–
Sino-Slovenia BIT	Art 6	–	–	–	Art 6	–
Total (9)	9	3	0	0	5	1

investment in the territory of the former Contracting Party. Accordingly, the latter shall be entitled to assert such rights and claims to the same (or not to exceed the) extent as its predecessor (its investor) in title.[105] The Sino-Poland BIT further stipulates that any rights and counterclaims of the former shall also be taken into account.[106]

10.3.5 Dispute Settlement

Following general BIT practice, the nine Sino-EU 10 BITs deal with State–State disputes and State–investor disputes separately.

10.3.5.1 State–State Disputes

The State–State dispute settlement clauses are the same in all eight BITs. They all state that the parties shall endeavour to settle such disputes through diplomatic channels. However, if disputes cannot be resolved in six months, either of the two parties may submit the dispute to an *ad hoc* arbitration tribunal.[107] They also stipulate how the tribunal shall be set up and what procedural and substantive rules shall be followed (see *Table 33*).[108] In short, the State–State dispute settlement provisions are not different from these in the Sino-EU 15 BITs.[109]

10.3.5.2 State–Investor Disputes

Two important aspects of State–investor dispute settlement are commonly dealt with in BITs, namely the jurisdiction and the applicable law.

(a) *Jurisdiction*
The jurisdiction issue is essentially an issue of whether and to what extent the host country accepts international arbitration as a venue to settle its disputes with foreign investors. In this regard, the provisions in the nine Sino-EU 10 BITs vary from each other. Although all nine BITs accept international arbitration, the degrees of acceptance are different. In four BITs, only disputes concerning the amount of compensation for expropriation (AOC cases) can be submitted to international arbitration, and the arbitration has to be *ad hoc*

[105] Article 7, Sino-Czech BIT; Article 6, Sino-Estonia BIT; Article 7, Sino-Hungary BIT; Article 7, Sino-Latvia BIT, above note 37; Article 6, Sino-Lithuania BIT; Article 7, Sino-Poland BIT; Article 7, Sino-Slovakia BIT; Article 6, Sino-Slovenia BIT.

[106] Article 7, Sino-Poland BIT.

[107] Article 8, Sino-Czech BIT; Article 7, Sino-Estonia BIT; Article 9, Sino-Hungary BIT; Article 8, Sino-Latvia BIT, above note 37; Article 7, Sino-Lithuania BIT; Article 9, Sino-Poland BIT; Article 8, Sino-Slovakia BIT; and Article 7, Sino-Slovenia BIT.

[108] *Ibid.*

[109] For a comparison of provisions on State–State dispute settlement in the Sino-EU 15 BITs, see Shan, above note 3, at 155–57. See also Shan, above note 92, at 604–10.

Table 33: Dispute Settlement under BITs between China and EU 10 States

BIT	State–State disputes: Negotiation/ consultation + *ad hoc* int'l arbitration	State–Investor disputes							Future supple-mentary agreement on ICSID arbitration
		Jurisdiction				Applicable law			
		Exclusive domestic jurisdiction	International Arbitration			Domestic law (of the host country)	The present Agreement	Principles of international law adopted by both parties	
			Ad hoc		Submission to ICSID arbi-tration				
			No reference to ICSID procedures	Reference to ICSID procedures					
Sino-Cyprus BIT	Art 8	Shared with the ICSID and others (Art 9.2)	–	Art 9.5	Art 9.5 (any legal dis-putes)	Art 9.7	Art 9.7	Art 9.7 (mutual adoption not required)	–
Sino-Czech BIT	Art 8	Art 9.2 except AOC & Others[a]	Art 9.21 (except AOC & Others)	–	–	–	–	–	–
Sino-Estonia BIT	Art 7	Art 8.2–3 (except AOC	–	Art 8.5 (AOC)	–	Art 8.7	Art 8.7	Art 8.7	–
Sino-Hungary BIT	Art 9	Art 10.1 (except AOC)	–	Art 10.3 (AOC)	–	–	–	–	Protocol
Sino-Latvia BIT	Art 8	Shared with the ICSID (Art 9)	–	–	Art 9.2 (all legal dis-putes)	Art 9.3	Art 9.3	Art 9.3 (no mutual adop-tion required)	–
Sino-Lithuania BIT	Art 7	Art 8.2 (except AOC & Others)	–	Art 8.4 (AOC & Others)	Art 8.2 (AOC & Others)	Art 8.7	Art 8.7	Art 8.7	–

Sino-Poland BIT	Art 9	Art 10.1 (except AOC)	Art 10.2 (AOC)	–	–	–	–	–	–
Sino-Slovakia BIT	Art 8	Art 9.2 (except AOC & Others)	Art 9.2 (AOC & Others)	–	–	–	–	–	–
Sino-Slovenia BIT	Art 7	Art 8.2–3 (except AOC)	–	Art 8.2–5 (AOC)	–	Art 8.6	Art 8.6	Art 8.6	–
Total (9)	9	7	3	4	2	4	4	4	

[a]'AOC' refers to 'disputes concerning the amount of compensation'.
'AOC & Others' refers to both AOC disputes and other disputes as agreed by both parties to the disputes (to submit them for international arbitration).

arbitration.[110] All other investment disputes fall exclusively within the domestic jurisdiction of the host country. The Sino-Czech and the Sino-Slovakia BITs concluded in December 1991 went a step further to allow investment disputes other than Aoc cases to be submitted for *ad hoc* arbitration.[111] Another progress was achieved by the Sino-Lithuania BIT concluded in late 1993, under which Aoc cases can be automatically submitted to the ICSID for arbitration.[112] Other investment disputes may also be submitted to ICSID arbitration, provided that both parties to the disputes so agree.[113] Interestingly, the Sino-Lithuania BIT provides for *ad hoc* arbitration for the settlement of these investment disputes in case both countries were not contracting parties to the ICSID Convention.[114] Among the eight BITs providing for *ad hoc* arbitration, five expressly state that the arbitration tribunal may refer to the ICSID Arbitration Rules in establishing its arbitration procedures.[115]

A final breakthrough on jurisdiction came with the Sino-Cyprus BIT, which was followed and further strengthened by the Sino-Latvia BIT[116]. All the three BITs were signed after 2000 and are yet to be ratified. In accordance with the Sino-Cyprus BIT, any state-investor dispute, if it cannot be settled after six months of consultation, may be submitted to either a competent court of the Contracting Party involved, or the ICSID or an *ad hoc* arbitration tribunal, 'at the request of either party'. The two choices are mutually exclusive. In other words, if the investor chooses to submit the case to a domestic court, he/she loses the right to submit the case to international arbitration. Further, the Contracting Party involved 'may' require the investor concerned to exhaust the domestic administrative review procedure before submitting the dispute to international arbitration. The Sino-Latvia BIT maintains that all legal disputes concerning investment may be automatically (ie, without the need to seek the concerned Contracting Party's specific consent) submitted to the ICSID for arbitration.[117]. It further de-localised the jurisdiction by stipulating that even if the foreign investor had submitted it to a local court, the investor could withdraw the case from the court and then submit it to the ICSID.[118] The Sino-Latvia BIT nevertheless includes in its Protocol a special requirement by China to exhaust local administrative review procedures

110 Article 8.2-3, Sino-Estonia BIT; Article 10.1, Sino-Hungary BIT; Article 10.1, Sino-Poland BIT; Article 8.2-3, Sino-Slovenia BIT.

111 Article 9.2, Sino-Czechoslovakia BIT (now the Sino-Czech BIT and the Sino-Slovakia BIT).

112 Article 8.2, Sino-Lithuania BIT.

113 *Ibid.*

114 *Ibid.*, Article 8.3-7 .

115 Article 8.5, Sino-Estonia BIT; Article 10.3, Sino-Hungary BIT; Article 8.4, Sino-Lithuania BIT; and Article 8.2-5, Sino-Slovenia BIT.

116 The New Sino-Germany BIT signed in December 2003 (pending ratification) has similar provisions on the jurisdiction of state-investor disputes. See Article 9.1-3, the New Sino-Germany BIT.

117 It does not, however, provide the opportunity for *ad hoc* arbitration. See Article 9.1-2, Sino-Latvia BIT, above note 37

before resorting to the ICSID arbitration. Such a local administrative review shall take a maximum of three months.[119]

It can thus be anticipated that China will be exposed to a much greater extent to international arbitration, particularly ICSID arbitration, after these newly signed treaties enter into force. As it stands, only Aoc cases can currently be submitted automatically to the ICSID and no other investment cases may be submitted to international arbitration unless the Chinese government so approves.

(b) *Applicable law*

Five of the nine BITs explicitly stipulate the law applicable to State–investor disputes. Three of them follow the normal route and accept laws of the host country, 'the present BIT' and (generally recognized) principles of international law *adopted by both parties.*[120] Again, the Sino-Cyprus BIT and Sino-Latvia BIT, the two newest ones among them, mark another breakthrough in that they accept generally recognized principles of international law, without the need for such principles to be specifically adopted by the contracting parties.[121] This provision has obviously followed the pattern of the Sino-Morocco BIT concluded in 1995.[122] Whilst it is still unclear what precisely these agreements mean by 'principles of international law', they clearly demonstrate China's growing confidence in general international law.

10.3.6 Summary

The Sino-EU 10 BITs are, by and large, similar to the Sino-EU 15 BITs. They follow the general European BIT practice and leave the right to regulate investment admission in the hands of the host country. Under the Sino-EU 10 BITs, foreign investors enjoy fair and equitable treatment and most-favoured-nation treatment. To a limited extent, they also enjoy national treatment and non-discriminatory treatment. Monetary transfers in convertible currency at the official or prevailing market rate of exchange are guaranteed, but they are still subject to domestic laws and regulations, particularly in the case of foreign investment in China.

Expropriation is broadly defined and conditional on the fulfilment of four conditions: public interest; due process of domestic law; non-discrimination; and payment of compensation. As far as compensation is concerned, none of these BITs refer to a particular general standard of compensation such as 'full', 'appropriate' or 'adequate, prompt and effective' compensation. They

[118] *Ibid.*, Article 9.2 .

[119] Protocol to the Sino-Latvia BIT, above note 37.

[120] Article 8.7, Sino-Estonia BIT; Article 8.7, Sino-Lithuania BIT; and Article 8.6, Sino-Slovenia BIT.

[121] Art 9.7, Sino-Cyprus BIT; Art 9.3, Sino-Latvia BIT.

[122] Article 10(4), Sino-Morocco BIT.

nonetheless all guarantee that compensation will be equivalent to the value of the expropriated investment and, in most of the BITs, plus interest. Whilst most Sino-EU 10 BITs do not define the methods of the valuation of compensation, the Sino-Slovenia BIT stipulates that valuation shall follow 'generally recognized principles of valuation and equitable principles, taking into account, *inter alia*, the capital invested, depreciation, capital already repatriated, replacement value and other relevant factors'. With regard to investment guarantees, all of the Sino-EU 10 BITs recognize the subrogation of rights and claims from guaranteed investors to the contracting party providing such guarantees.

As it stands, only disputes between the host government and the foreign investor concerning the amount of compensation can be automatically submitted to the ICSID or an *ad hoc* international arbitration tribunal. Submission of other investment disputes still requires approval from the government concerned. However, once the Sino-Cyprus BIT and the Sino-Latvia BIT enter into force, all State–investor disputes may be automatically submitted to the ICSID for arbitration upon request of the foreign investor. In terms of the law applicable to State–investor disputes, a few BITs explicitly refer not only to the laws of the host country and 'the present BIT', but also to 'generally recognized principles of international law', which is sometimes qualified by 'adopted by both parties'.

On the whole, the nine Sino-EU 10 BITs have provided substantial protection for mutual investment between China and these nine new EU Member States. The eight BITs have also demonstrated the increased and increasing confidence of China in international arbitration and international law. However, the Sino-EU 10 BITs do not add much more protection for the EU 15 States, as they have already enjoyed an equivalent level of protection. The 2001 Sino-Cyprus BIT and the 2004 Sino-Latvia BIT will have the effect of significantly upgrading the protection level, notably by tightening up the restrictions on the application of national treatment and by granting foreign investors the right to bring all State–investor disputes to the ICSID for arbitration. However, it is yet to be known whether and when these BITs might enter into force.

10.4 CONCLUSION

China has a long and close investment and trade relationship with the EU 10 States, mainly due to their shared past communist experience. A significant growth in trade and investment has been seen in recent years between the two sides. A notable feature of the bilateral economic relationships is that there has been significant Chinese investment in these EU 10 States and it is set to further increase in the future.

The current legal framework governing Sino-EU 10 investment relationships is mainly composed of multilateral agreements, bilateral agreements and domestic laws. Most importantly, the multilateral agreements include the ICSID Convention, to which China and nine of the EU 10 states are Contracting Parties, as well as the MIGA Convention and the WTO Agreement, to both of which China and all the EU 10 States are Members. The most important bilateral agreements are BITs and DTTs. So far, nine of the EU 10 States have concluded BITs with China and all of them also have DTT arrangements with China. Finally, both China and the EU 10 States have extensive domestic laws and regulations on foreign investment.

A close examination of the Sino-EU 10 BITs shows that they do not differ significantly from the Sino-EU 15 BITs, as both sets of treaties follow the traditional European BIT practice. Under the Sino-EU 10 BITs, mutual investment is encouraged, but the right to regulate investment admission is still left in the hands of the host governments. Mutual investment is facilitated by the provision of equitable and fair treatment and most-favoured- nation treatment and, to a certain extent, national treatment and non-discriminatory treatment. Subject to domestic laws of foreign exchange control, the freedom of monetary transfers is also guaranteed.

Foreign investment is free from expropriation, unless such expropriation is conducted in the public interest, following due process of domestic law, in a non-discriminatory manner and accompanied by compensation. Such compensation will be equivalent to the value of the expropriated investment, plus necessary interest. Subrogation is recognized in all these BITs to facilitate the operation of government investment-guarantee schemes.

At the request of a foreign investor, it is now possible to directly submit State–investor disputes concerning the amount of compensation to the ICSID for international arbitration. Submission of other State–investor disputes is also possible, provided that such submission is approved by both parties to the dispute. After the Sino-Cyprus BIT and the Sino-Latvia BIT enter into force, it will be possible for all State–investor disputes to be automatically submitted to the ICSID for arbitration without the need to seek approval from the host country concerned. Some BITs make clear that the applicable law to such disputes is the domestic law of the host country, 'the present BIT" and general principles of international law.

Although the Sino-EU 10 BITs do not add much more protection for the existing EU 15 States, the enlargement of the EU does further enhance the bilateral investment and trade links between the two sides. Despite the trade- and investment-transfer effects the enlargement may have, the enlarged EU has become the second-largest trade partner of China and will likely soon lead China's trade partners' league table. EU–China investment relations will be likewise expanded, not only by increased EU investment in China but also by growing Chinese investment in the EU, particularly in the EU 10 States. Whilst the current legal framework does provide substantial protection for the development of mutual investment, and new BITs will foster such protection, it would still be better to have an investment arrangement with China at the EU level as envisaged in Chapter 9, since such a new international legal framework between China and the EU would provide sufficient protection for *all* EU Member States, including those that have no BIT arrangements with China.

Appendix I

Questionnaire on Law and European Investment in China

PLEASE answer all questions and return to the address below. MANY THANKS for your support.

Your Profile

Your designation:. . . . .
Nationality of your company . . . .
Location of investment . . . .
Industrial sector of investment . . . .
Date investment established: . . . .
Intended duration of investment (year): . . . .
Investment amount (£):. . . . .
Foreign equity participation (%):. . . . .
Foreign participation in management: . . . .

I. General Role of Law in Investment Decision Making

1. In making the decision to invest in China, how important was the nature of the legal system to your company, relative to other issues (eg market size, labor costs, environmental costs, raw materials etc.)?

_ Top
_ High
_ Medium
_ Low
_ None
_ Do not know
_ Do not understand

2. Did your company investigate the general legal environment for investment from the EU (eg tax incentives, protection from expropriation, investment insurance etc.) before deciding to invest?

_ Yes
_ No
_ Do not know
_ Do not understand

3. In making the decision to invest in China, what importance did your company put on foreign investment incentives (such as tax exemptions for foreign investors generally, or specifically to those in particular industrial sectors or zones) offered by China?

__ Top	__ None
__ High	__ Do not know
__ Medium	__ Do not understand
__ Low	

4. If your company did investigate the legal environment before investing, what evidence did it use? Please tick all that apply:

__ Law on the paper	__ Do not know
__ Law in action (eg levels of enforcement)	__ Do not understand

5. If your company did investigate the legal environment before investing, which laws were considered? Please tick all that apply:

__ Domestic (Chinese) law	__ Do not know
__ International investment treaties	__ Do not understand

6. Which of the following investment protection and promotion treaties between China and your company's home country was your company aware of when making the decision to invest? Please tick all that apply:

__ Bilateral Investment Treaty (BIT)[1]
__ Bilateral Double Taxation Treaty (DTT)[2]
__ Convention Establishing the Multilateral Investment Guarantee Agency (MIGA Convention)
__ Convention on the Settlement of Investment Disputes between States and Nationals of Other States (ICSID Convention)
__ Other International Investment Rules (Please specify)

II. Experience of Chinese FDI Legal System

7. Does your company feel safe to invest or re-invest in China?

__ Yes	__ Do not know
__ No	__ Do not understand

[1] Bilateral treaties that aim to promote and protect mutual investment, eg, the Sino-Britain BIT signed in 1986.
[2] Bilateral treaties that aim to avoid double taxation on trans-border business.

If 'Yes', which of the following instruments (if any) has contributed the most to your company's sense of safety? Please tick ONE:

__ Legal protection provided by domestic and international law
__ Investment insurance against political risks
__ Political promise and social stability
__ Others (please specify)

8. Has your company suffered from any sort of nationalization or expropriation in China **in the last 20 years**?

__ Yes	__ Do not know
__ No	__ Do not understand

Have you heard of any other company which has suffered from any sort of nationalization or expropriation in China **in the last 20 years**?

__ Yes	__ Do not know
__ No	__ Do not understand

Have those nationalizations or expropriations that your company or other companies have suffered been compensated 'adequately, promptly and effectively'?[3]

__ Never	__ Mostly
__ Rarely	__ Always
__ Sometimes	__ Do not know
__ Frequently	__ Do not understand

9. In recent years, the Chinese government has been trying to implement national treatment for foreign investors. To what extent would you think the new policy might improve the investment climate?

__ Significantly	__ Do not know
__ A little	__ Do not understand
__ Not at all	

10. Has your company encountered any difficulty in transferring its investment or profit out of China?

__ Never	__ Mostly
__ Rarely	__ Always
__ Sometimes	__ Do not know
__ Frequently	__ Do not understand

[3] This means that the compensation shall be able to put the expropriated enterprise in the same financial situation as if it had not been expropriated. The compensation shall also be paid in convertible currency and without undue delay.

11. Is your company satisfied with the Chinese system of intellectual property rights protection?

__ Yes
__ No
__ Not relevant
__ Do not know
__ Do not understand

12. Has your company insured your investment against political risks based on MIGA or a BIT?

__ Yes
__ No
__ Do not know
__ Do not understand

13. Has your company has had any legal disputes with the Chinese Government?

__ Yes
__ No
__ Do not know
__ Do not understand

If yes, has such a dispute been submitted to the ICSID for arbitration, according to the ICSID Convention and the applicable BIT (see Question 6)?

__ Yes
__ No
__ Do not know
__ Do not understand

14. Are you satisfied with the rule that Chinese law must govern all joint venture and joint exploitation contracts?

__ Yes
__ No
__ Do not care
__ Do not know
__ Do not understand

15. Has the Chinese government insisted on the inclusion of any of the following performance requirements in legal documents as a prerequisite for giving approval and/or preferential treatment to your company? Please tick all that apply:

__ Local content requirement[4]
__ Export performance requirement[5]
__ Foreign exchange balancing requirement[6]
__ Technology transfer requirement

[4] An obligation on foreign funded enterprises to obtain all or part of their supplies from local suppliers.

[5] An obligation of exporting a minimum level of products manufactured by foreign funded enterprises.

[6] A requirement by host government on foreign funded enterprises to maintain foreign exchange balance.

__ Local employment requirement
__ Compulsory joint venture requirement
__ Limitation on ownership of local subsidiaries
__ Other performance requirements, please specify:

16. Are Chinese FDI laws and policies easily accessible in China?

__ Never	__ Mostly
__ Rarely	__ Always

17. Are the laws and/or policies of China changed unexpectedly?

__ Never	__ Mostly
__ Rarely	__ Always
__ Sometimes	__ Do not know
__ Frequently	__ Do not understand

18. Do government officials enforce laws consistently?

__ Never	__ Mostly
__ Rarely	__ Always
__ Sometimes	__ Do not know
__ Frequently	__ Do not understand

19. Is it necessary to use bribery when dealing with government officials?

__ Never	__Mostly
__ Rarely	__Always
__ Sometimes	__Do not know
__ Frequently	__Do not understand

20. Do the Chinese courts enforce law objectively according to published rules?

__ Never	__ Mostly
__ Rarely	__ Always
__ Sometimes	__ Do not know
__ Frequently	__ Do not understand

21. Is it possible to use bribery to impact on judge's decisions?

__ Never	__ Mostly
__ Rarely	__ Always
__ Sometimes	__ Do not know
__ Frequently	__ Do not understand

22. Do politicians interfere in court decisions?

__ Never	__ Mostly
__ Rarely	__ Always
__ Sometimes	__ Do not know
__ Frequently	__ Do not understand

23. Are court/arbitration procedures subject to unreasonable delays?

__ Never	__ Mostly
__ Rarely	__ Always

24. Are the decisions of courts and arbitrators well enforced by Chinese authorities?

__ Never	__ Mostly
__ Rarely	__ Always
__ Sometimes	__ Do not know
__ Frequently	__ Do not understand

III. A Possible Investment Agreement to which the EU and China are Parties?

25. How useful would the Chinese joining into the World Trade Organisation (WTO) be to improve the legal environment for foreign investment?

__ Very useful	__ Not at all useful
__ Fairly useful	__ Do not understand
__ Not very useful	__ Do not know

26. How useful would a new bilateral or multilateral investment agreement to which China and the EU are parties be to improve the legal environment for foreign investment?

__ Very useful	__ Not at all useful
__ Fairly useful	__ Do not understand
__ Not very useful	__ Do not know

27. How useful do you think the inclusion of each of the following provisions in a new international agreement would be?

Provisions	Very useful	Fairly useful	Not very useful	Not useful at all	Do not know	Do not understand
Most Favoured Nation (MFN) Treatment[7]						
Pre-establishment National Treatment[8]						
Post-establishment National Treatment[9]						
Adequate, prompt, effective compensation[10] in the event of expropriation						
Free transfer of property and profit						
Compulsory jurisdiction of ICSID over state-investor investment disputes[11]						
Other provisions (please specify)						

Do you have any further comments to make on the legal environment of FDI in China?

[7] A treatment by a host country (China) granted to investment or investors from another country that is not less favourable than that accorded to investment and investors from any third country.

[8] A treatment by a host country applied to investors or investment of another country that is not less favourable than that accorded to its domestic investors and their investment. If this treatment only applies to the post-establishment stage of investment, eg, the operation, management, maintenance, use, possession and sale or any other form of disposal, it is called 'post-establishment national treatment'. On the other hand, if it applies to the pre-establishment stage of investment, eg, the establishment, acquisition, or expansion, it is called 'pre-establishment national treatment'.

[9] *Ibid.*

[10] See note 3 above.

[11] This means that in the event of a dispute between an investor and the host country (China), the investor can brings a claim before the ICSID against the country without its consent.

Appendix II

Scores Allocated to Questionnaire Responses on the Effectiveness of FDI Legal System in China

16. Are Chinese FDI laws and policies easily accessible in China?

0 ___	Never
1 ___	Rarely
2 ___	Sometimes
3 ___	Frequently
4 ___	Mostly
5 ___	Always

17. Are the laws and/or policies of China changed unexpectedly?

5 ___	Never
4 ___	Rarely
3 ___	Sometimes
2 ___	Frequently
1 ___	Mostly
0 ___	Always

18. Do government officials enforce laws consistently?

0 ___	Never
1 ___	Rarely
2 ___	Sometimes
3 ___	Frequently
4 ___	Mostly
5 ___	Always

19. Is it necessary to use bribery when dealing with government officials?

5 ___	Never
4 ___	Rarely
3 ___	Sometimes

2 ___	Frequently
1 ___	Mostly
0 ___	Always

20. Do the Chinese courts enforce laws objectively according to published rules?

0 ___	Never
1 ___	Rarely
2 ___	Sometimes
3 ___	Frequently
4 ___	Mostly
5 ___	Always

21. Is it possible to use bribery to impact on a judge's decisions?

5 ___	Never
4 ___	Rarely
3 ___	Sometimes
2 ___	Frequently
1 ___	Mostly
0 ___	Always

22. Do politicians interfere in court decisions?

5 ___	Never
4 ___	Rarely
3 ___	Sometimes
2 ___	Frequently
1 ___	Mostly
0 ___	Always

23. Are court/arbitration procedures subject to unreasonable delays?

5 ___	Never
4 ___	Rarely
3 ___	Sometimes
2 ___	Frequently
1 ___	Mostly
0 ___	Always

24. Are the decisions of courts and arbitrators well enforced by Chinese authorities?

0 ___	Never
1 ___	Rarely
1 ___	Sometimes
3 ___	Frequently
4 ___	Mostly
5 ___	Always

Bibliography

I. OFFICIAL DOCUMENTS

China: *The Decision on Some Issues Related to the Establishment of the Socialist Market Economy by the Central Committee of the Chinese Communist Party*, published on the People's Daily, Nov. 7, 1993, at 1.

China: China's EU Policy Paper (13 October 2003).

EU: *Asia-Invest: Unlocks Partnership Opportunities for European and Asian Companies*, Office for Official Publications of the European Community, May 2000.

EU: *Chronology of EU-China relations*, posted at http://www.delchn.cec.eu.int/en/eu_and_china/Milestones.htm (visited on 20 August 2003).

EU: Commission Policy Paper for Transmission to the Council and the European Parliament: *A maturing partnership-shared inters and challenges in EU-China relations*, COM (2003), 533 fin.

EU: Communication from the Commission on the '*EC-International Investment Partners' Facility for Latin America, Asia and the Mediterranean*', COM (90) 575 final.

EU: Communication from the Commission to the Council and the European Parliament, *EU Strategy towards China: Implementation of the 1998 Communication and future steps for a more effective policy*, COM (2001) 265 final.

EU: Communication from the Commission, '*A Long Term Policy for China-Europe Relations*', COM (95) 279 Final (5 July 1995).

EU: Communication from the Commission, '*Building a Comprehensive Partnership with China*', COM (1998) 181 Final (25 March1998).

EU: 'Towards a New Asia Strategy', COM (94) 314 final.

EU: 'Europe Asia—Co-operation Strategy in the Field of the Environment', COM (97) 490 final.

EU: 'The European Union and Hong Kong: Beyond 1997', COM (97) 171 final.

EU: Directorate-General of Trade (DG Trade)'s *Overview on its 'Bilateral Trade Relations'* with China (October 2002), posted at http://europa.eu.int/comm/trade/index_en.htm, (visited 1 June 2003).

EU: *EC Approach to Trade and Investment*, at http://europa.eu.int/comm/dg01/1806ti.htm (11/11/99).

EU: *European Parliament's Resolution on Economic and Commercial Relations between China and the EEC*, OJ C 127/210, 1984.

EU: *Report drawn up on behalf of the Committee on External Economic Relations on economic and commercial relations between the EEC and China, PE 87.3431Fin.*

EU: *Report on the Trade Agreement between the EEC and China, EP.53.846/Fin.*

EU: *Investment Promotion and Protection Clauses in Agreements between the Community and Various Categories of Developing Country: Achievements to Date and Guidelines for Joint Action*, COM(80) 204 Fin.

EU: Report EEC-ASEAN, PE 62. 7981 Fin.

EU: Eurostat Press Releases No.7096 (21–10–1996): *EU Direct Investment in the Rest-of-world*, posted at http://europa.eu.int/en/comm/eurostat/compres/en/7096/6207096a.htm

EU: Report from the Commissions to the Council and the European Parliament: *European Community Investment Partners (ECIP) Report 1999*, COM (2000) 439 final.

EU: Report from the Commissions to the Council and the European Parliament on the *Implementation of the Communication 'Building a Comprehensive Partnership with China'*, COM (2000) 552 final (8 September 2000).

EU: *Results of the bilateral EU-China talk*, see http://europa.eu.int/comm/trade/bilateral/china/res.pdf (visited on 22 November 2001).

EU: *Statement on EU-China Trade Agreement by Romano Prodi, President of the* European Commission, at http://europa.eu.int/comm/trade/bilateral/china/prodi.htm (22/05/2000).

EU: Working Group on European Union-Mercosur Negotiations, *Annual Report 2001–2002*, at 17–18, posted at http://chairemercosur.sciences-po.fr/negociations/rapport_anglais.pdf (visited on 31 July 2003).

EU: Working Group on Trade and Investment (WGTI), *Checklist of Issues, Agenda IV: Identification of Common Features and Differences in International Investment Instruments* (of 2 September 1998), at http://europa.eu.int/comm/dg01/invwgti2.htm (visited on 11 November 1999).

EU: Working Group on Trade and Investment (WGTI), *Identification of Common Features and Differences of Existing International Instruments from the Perspective of the European Community and Its Member States (of 27 March 1998)*, at http://europa.eu.int/comm/dg01/invwgti1.htm (visited on 11 November 1999).

ICSID Cases, at http://www.worldbank.org/icsid/cases/cases.htm (visited on 29 July 2003). See also ICSID, *About ICSID,* at http://www.worldbank.org/icsid/about/about.htm(visited on 29 July 2003).

ICSID, *List of Contracting States and other Signatories of the Convention* (as of March 26, 2003), posted at http://www.worldbank.org/icsid/constate/c-states-en.htm (visited on 29 July 2003).

ICSID, *Report of the Executive Directors on the Convention on the Settlement of Investment Disputes between States and Nationals of Other States* (*Executive Report*), ICSID Doc. 2, March 18, 1965.

IFC, Foreign Direct Investment, Lessons of Experience (No. 5) pp. 9–20 (1997).

MOFCOM Invest in China: *Laws and Regulations*, posted at http://www.fdi.gov.cn/ltlawpackage/index.jsp?app=1&language=en

MOFTEC (now MOFCOM), *China's Attracting Foreign Investment Policy*, posted at http://www.moftec.gov.cn/moftec_en/zcjs/wzgl/wzgl_01_en.html (visited on 22 February 2002).

MOFTEC, *The New Compilation of Laws, Regulations and Ministerial Rules on Foreign Trade and Economic Co-operation of the People's Republic of China*, in Chinese (Law Press, 2002).

MOFTEC (now MOFCOM), *Collection of International Investment Treaties* (in Chinese and English) (Jingjuang Jiaoyu Press, 1998).

OECD Directorate of Finance, Fiscal and Enterprise Affairs, *Code of Liberalisation of Capital Movements* and *Code of Current Invisible Operations*, May 2001, available at, respectively, http://www.oecd.org/pdf/M00007000/M00007320.pdf and http://www.oecd.org/pdf/M00007000/M00007322.pdf (visited on 1 August 2002).

OECD Directorate of Finance, Fiscal and Enterprise Affairs: *Overview to the OECD Codes of Liberalisation* June 2002, available at http://www.oecd.org/pdf/M00031000/M00031423.pdf (visited on 1 August 2002).

OECD Guidelines for Multinational Enterprises: Frequently Asked Questions, at: http://www.oecd.org/EN/document/0,,EN-document-93-nodirectorate-no-21-18096-9,00.html (1 August 2002).

OECD: EU Member State Policies on FDI in the 1980s, as reprinted in 29 *Journal of World Trade* 1.

OECD: *The OECD Declaration and Decisions on International Investment and Multinational Enterprises: Basic Texts*, DAFFE/IME(2000)20, available at: http://www.olis.oecd.org/olis/2000doc.nsf/c5ce8ffa41835d64c125685d005300b0/c125692700623b74c1256991003b5147/$FILE/00085743.DOC (08/08/2001)

OECD: *Trends and Recent Developments in Foreign Direct Investment*, June 2003, posted at http://www.oecd.org/pdf/M00042000/M00042212.pdf (visited on 1 July 2003).

State Council, *Handbook of Foreign Economic Law (Vols. 1 &2)*, (in Chinese and English) (Law Press, 1997).

TN SOFRES Consulting (on behalf of the European Commission DG Trade), *Survey of the Attitudes of the European Business Community to International Investment Rules: Final Report*, April 2000.

UN: *Opening Statement by President Thabo Mbeki at the World Summit on Sustainable Development*, available at: http://www.un.org/events/wssd/statements/openingsaE.htm (visited on 1 January 2003).

UNCTAD, *1995 World Investment Report*, Chinese translation (Foreign Economic and Trade University Press, 1996).

UNCTAD, *Admission and Establishment*, UNCTAD/ITE/IIT/10/VOL.11.

UNCTAD, *China: WTO Accession and Growing FDI Inflows*, 11 December 2002, at 5, posted at http://r0.unctad.org/en/subsites/dite/pdfs/PRChina.pdf (visited on 18 July 2003).

UNCTAD, *Fair and Equitable Treatment*, UNCTAD/ITE/IIT/11 (Vol. III).

UNCTAD, *National Treatment*, UNCTAD/ITE/IIT/11 (Vol. IV).

UNCTAD, World Investment Report 1994: Transnational Corporations, Employment and the Workplace, An Executive Summary (UNCTC, 1994).

UNCTAD, *World Investment Report 1999: Foreign Direct Investment and the Challenge of Development.*

UNCTAD, *World Investment Report 1999: Foreign Direct Investment and the Challenge of Development: Overview.*

UNCTAD/World Bank, *World Investment Report 1994: Transitional Corporations, Employment and Workplace*, 1994.

UNCTAD, *World Investment Report 1996—Investment, Trade and Investment Policy Arrangements: Overview*, UNCTAD/DTCI/32 (Overview).

UNCTAD, *World Investment Report 1997*, United Nations, 1997.

UNCTC, *Bilateral Investment Treaties*, Graham and Trotman, 1988.

UNESCO, 'Country and Regional Experiences In Attracting Foreign Direct Investment For Development: Foreign Direct Investment in Africa,' Report by the UNCTAD Secretariat, 23 March 1994 (E/C. 10/1994/5).

United Nations, *Growth in United Nations Membership (1945–2003)*, posted at http://www.un.org/Overview/growth.htm (visited on 12 June 2003).

US International Trade Commission (USITC), *Assessment of the Economic Effects on the United States of China's Accession to the WTO*, Investigation No. 332–403, publication 3229, September 1999.

US and Foreign Commercial Service (US&FCS) (Telegraphic Report from the American Embassy in Beijing): *China: Investment Climate Statement for 1997*.

World Bank, *Governance and Development* (Washington DC, World Bank, 1992).

World Bank, *Legal Framework for the Treatment of Foreign Investment* (1992).

WTO Secretariat, *World Trade Organisation: Trading into the future*, 1998, 2nd edition.

WTO Working Party on the Accession of China: *Report of the Working Party on the Accession of China,* WT/ACC/CHN/49 (1 October 2001).

WTO: *Ministerial Declaration adopted by the Fourth Session of the Ministerial Conference at Doha* on 9–14 November 2001. WT/MIN(01)/DEC/W/1 (14 November 2001).

II. BOOKS AND ARTICLES

Akehurst, M, *Akehurst's Modern Introduction to International Law*, Chinese translation (Chinese Social Sciences Press 1981).

Al-Nauimi, Najeeb and Meese, Richard eds., *International Legal Issues Arising under the United Nations Decade of International Law (*Martinus-Nijhoff Publishers 1995).

Amerasinghe, CF, Issues of Compensation for the Taking of Alien Property in the Light of Recent Cases and Practice, 41 *International and Comparative Law Quarterly* 22 (1992).

Anand, RP, Attitude of the Afro-Asian States towards Certain Problems of International Law, 15 *International and Comparative Law Quarterly* 55 (1966).

Aréchaga, Eduardo Jiménez de, State Responsibility for the Nationalisation of Foreign Owned Property, 11 *NYU Journal of International Law and Politics* 179 (Fall, 1978).

Aréchaga, Jiménez de, International Law in the Past Third of a Century, 159 *Recueil des Cours* 1, 302 (1978 I).

Balekjian, WH, *Legal Aspects of Foreign Investment in the European Economic Community* (Manchester University Press, 1967).

Bates, Lawrence W, Protecting Foreign Investments in China: the Sino-Japanese Bilateral Treaty: Comparison with Earlier BITs and U.S. Positions, 10 *East Asian Executive Report* 9 (1988).

Beauvais, Joel C, Regulatory Expropriations Under NAFTA: Emerging Principles & Lingering Doubts, 10 *New York University Environmental Law Journal* 245 (2002).

Beijing Engineering Consultancy, *Guidelines to BOT Projects* (Dizhen Press, 1995).
Bergman, Mark S., Bilateral Investment Protection Treaties: An Examination of the Evolution and Significance of the U.S. Prototype Treaty, *New York University Journal of International Law and Politics*, Fall (1983).
Bergsten, F Fred, and Graham, Edward M, Needed: New International Rules for Foreign Direct Investment, *The International Trade Journal*, 7, Fall 1992.
Bethlehem, Daniel L, International Economic Relations, in Dugard, John, *International law: A South African Perspective*, 2nd ed (Cape Town, Juta, 2000).
Bethlehem, Daniel L, International Law, European Community Law and National Law: Three Systems in Search of a Framework, in Koskenniemi, Martti (ed), *Legal Aspects of the European Union* (Kluwer Law International, 1997).
Bethlehem, Daniel L, Submissions on Points of Fact and Law: Written and Oral Pleadings Before the International Court of Justice, in Weiss, Friedl (ed), *Improving WTO Dispute Settlement Procedures: Issues & Lessons from the Practice of Other International Courts & Tribunals* (Cameron May, 2000).
Beveridge, Fiona, *The Treatment and Taxation of Foreign Investment under International Law* (Juris Publishing, 2000).
Blumental, David, Reform' Or 'Opening'? Reform of China's State-Owned Enterprises and WTO Accession–The Dilemma of Applying GATT to Marketizing Economies, 16 *UCLA Pacific Basin Law Journal* 198,(Spring, 1998).
Bowett, DW, State Contracts with Aliens, 59 *British Yearbook of International Law* 49 (1988).
Brewer, Tomas and Young, Stephen, European Union Policies and the Problems of Multinational Enterprises, 29 *Journal of World Trade* No. 1 (1995).
Brewer, Tomas and Young, Stephen, Investment Policies in Multilateral and Regional Agreement: a comparative analysis, *Transnational Corporations* vol. 5, no. 1 (April 1996).
Brewer, Tomas and Young, Stephen, Towards a Multilateral Framework for Foreign Direct Investment: issues and scenarios, *Transnational Corporations* vol. 4, no. 1 (April 1995).
Brewer, Tomas L. and Young, Stephen, *The Multilateral Investment System and Multinational Enterprises*, (Oxford University Press, 1998).
Brittan, Lord Leon, Investment Liberalisation: the next great boost to the world economy, *Transnational Corporations* vol. 4, no. 1 (April 1995).
Brittan, Lord Leon, *Opening Address at the EU-China Business Dialogue*, 1998, Beijing.
Broadbeut, KP, China and the EEC, the Politics of Trade Relationship, *World Today* 195 (1976).
Broches, Aron, *Selected Essays: World Bank, ICSID, and Other Subjects of Public and Private International Law* M(artinus Nijhoff Publishers, 1995).
Brok, Elmar, and Tsatsos, Dimitrios, Representatives of the European Parliament at the Intergovernmental Conference, *IGC 2000-Commercial Policy and International Agreements,* CONFER 4759/00, Brussels, 11 July 2000.
Brower, Charles N, and Tepe, John B, Jr, The Charter of Economic Rights and Duties of States: A Reflection or Rejection of International Law?, 9 *International Law* 295 (1975).
Brower, Charles N, Current Developments in the Law of Expropriation and Compen-

sation: a Preliminary Survey of Awards of the Iran-United States Claims Tribunal, 21 *International Law* 639 (1987).

Brownlie, Ian, *Basic Document in International Law*, 5th edition (Oxford University Press, 2003).

Brownlie, Ian, *Principles of Public International Law*, 4th edition (Oxford University Press, 1998).

Burnett, Robin, Negotiations of International Agreements in the Field of Commerce and Investment: Problems of Relevance to Newly—Independent States, 9 *Journal of World Trade Law* 231 (1975).

Burt, Eric M, Developing Countries and the Framework for Negotiations on Foreign Direct Investment in the World Trade Organization, 12 *American University Journal of International Law and Policy* 1015–1061 (1997).

Campbell, Colin, China to Pay Britons Compensation, *The Times* (26 February 1988).

Cao, Jianming and He, Xiaoyun, WTO Accession and China's Foreign Economic Legislation, *Chinese Legal Science (Zhongguo Faxue)* No.1 (2000).

Cassese, Antonio, *International Law* (Oxford University Press, 2000).

Chang, Kai, WTO, Labour Standards and the Protection of Rights of Workers (in Chinese), *Social Sciences in China* No. 1 (2002).

Chen, An, edited: *Comments on ICSID* (in Chinese) (Lujiang Press, 1990).

Chen, An, edited: *MIGA and China: Comments on the Multilateral Investment Guarantee Agency* (in Chinese) (Fujian People's Press, 1995).

Chen, An, *International Investment Disputes Arbitration—A Study on the ICSID Mechanism* (Fudan University Press, 2001).

Chen, An, *International Investment Law* (in Chinese) (Lujiang Press, 1987).

Chen, An, *OPIC Case Studies* (in Chinese) (Lujiang Press, 1986).

Chen, An, The Marginal, Comprehensive and Independent Features of the Science of International Economic Law, *Chinese Journal of International Economic Law Law* Vol. 1 (1998).

Chen, Hanfeng, Zhou, Weiguo and Jiang, Hao, The Relationship between International Treaties and Municipal Law and the Practices of China, *Tribune of Political Science and Law (Zhengfa Luntan)* No.2 (2000).

Chen, Huiping, MAI and the International Investment Liberalisation, *Chinese Journal of International Economic Law Law* Vol. 3.

Chen, Huiping, The Progress and Prospects of the Negotiation of the 'Multilateral Agreement on Investment', *Chinese Journal of International Economic Law Law* Vol. 2, 1999.

Chen, Weihua, *China is Becoming an Important Outward Investor*, People's Daily (overseas edition), 22 May 2003.

Cheng, Faguang, *Foreign related Tax Regime and Its Tendency of Development*, presented at Symposium on China's Foreign Investment Policies, Sept. 1998, Xiamen, China.

Chew, Pat K, Political Risk and U.S. Investments In China: Chimera of Protection and Predictability? *Virginia Journal of International Law* (Spring 1994).

Cheyne, Ilona, Investment Promotion and Protection Agreements, 36 *International and Comparative Law Quarterly* 92–9 (1987).

Chu Baotai and Dong Huiyuan, *Sino-Foreign Contractual Joint Venture Law* (in Chinese) (Zhongxin Press, 1992).

Chu, Baotai, *Legal Issues of Foreign Investments in China* (in Chinese) (Enterprise Management Press, Beijing, 1988).

Chu, Baotai, *Questions and Answers Relating to Foreign Investments in China* (in Chinese) (Foreign Languages Press, Beijing, 1986).

Clagett, Brice M, The Cuban Liberty and Democratic Solidarity (Libertad)Act, 90 *American Journal of International Law* 419–440 (1996).

Clarke, Donald C, The Execution of Civil Judgments in China, in Lubman, Stanley (ed), *China's Legal Reforms* 65–81 (Oxford University Press, 1996).

Clegg, Jerry, Explaining Foreign Direct Investment Flows, in Buckley & Casson (eds), *Multinational Enterprises in the World Economy: Essays in Honour of John Dunning* 54–74 (Edward Elgar, 1992).

Clifford Chance, *Planning a Foreign Investment Enterprise in China*, Memorandum to Clients and Professional Contacts of Clifford Chance, May 1997.

Cohen, Jerome Alan and Chiu, Hungdah, *People's China and International Law* (Princeton University Press, 1974).

Comeaux, Paul and Kinsella, N Stephan, *Protecting Foreign Investment under International Law: Legal Aspects of Political Risks* (Oceana Publications, 1997).

Concepts of Law in the Chinese Anti-Crime Campaign (Note), 98 *Harvard Law Review* 1890 (June 1985).

Corne, Peter Howard, *Foreign Investment in China: the Administrative Legal System* (Transnational Publishers, 1997).

Coughlin, Williarn E, The U.S. Bilateral Investment Treaty. An Answer to Performance Requirements?, in Fisher, B and Turner, J (eds), *Regulating the Multinational Enterprise, National and International Challenges* 129 (Praeger Pub Text, 1983).

Craig and de Burcá, *EU Law: Text, Cases and Materials*, 2nd ed (Oxford University Press, 1998).

Crawford, James, *The International Law Commission's articles on State Responsibility: Introduction, Text, and Commentaries* (Cambridge University Press, 2002).

Cremona, Marise, The External Dimension of the Single Market: Building (on) the Foundations, in Barnard, Catherine and Scott, Joanne (eds), *The Law of the Single European Market: Unpacking the Premises* (Hart, 2002).

Curtis, Christopher T, The Legal Security of Economic Development Agreements, 29 *Harvard International Law Journal* 317 (1988).

Dashwood, Alan, Implied External Competence of the EC, in Koskenniemi, Martti (ed), *International Law Aspects of the European Union* (Kluwer Law International, 1997).

Dashwood, Alan, States in the European Union, 23 *European Law Review* 201 (1998).

Dashwood, Alan, The Attribution of External Relations Competence, in Dashwood, Alan and Hillion, Christophe (eds), *The General Law of EC External Relations* (Sweet & Maxwell, 2000).

De Smedt, P, Legal Aspects of the Economic and Trade Relations of the PRC with the European Economic Community, *Common Law Review* 180 (1986).

Delaume, GR, The Proper Law of State Contracts Revisited, 12 *ICSID Review—Foreign Investment Law Journal* 1 (1997).

Denza, Eileen and Brooks, Shelagh, Investment Protection Treaties: United Kingdom Experience, 36 *International and Comparative Law Quarterly* 908 (1987).

Dolzer, Rudolf and Stevens, Margaret, *Bilateral Investment Treaties* (Martinus Nijhoff, 1995), at 50–56.

Dolzer, Rudolf, Indirect Expropriation of Foreign Property, *ICSID Review—Foreign Investment Law Journal* Vol. 1, No. 1 (1986).

Dolzer, Rudolf, New Foundations of the Law of Expropriation of Alien Property, 75 *American Journal of International Law* 553 (1981).

Don, RY, *Protection of Foreign Investment under International Law* (Modern Management Foundation, 1979).

Doz and Prahalad, How MNCs Cope with Host Government Intervention, *Harvard Business Review* 149–157 (March-April 1980).

Edwards, Robert H and Lester, Simon N, Towards A More Comprehensive World Trade Organization Agreement on Trade Related Investment Measures, *Stanford Journal of International Law* 169–214 (1997).

Elias, TO, Modern Sources of International Law, in *Transnational Law in a Changing Society—Essays in Honour of Philip C. Jessup* (Columbia University Press, 1972).

El-Kosheri, Ahmed S, The Particularity of the Conflict Avoidance methods Pertaining to Petroleum Agreements, 11 *ICSID Review—Foreign Investment Law Journal* 272 (1996).

Emilou, Nicholas and O'Keeffe, David, *The European Union and the World Trade Law: After the Uruguay Round* (John Wiley & Sons Ltd, 1996).

Encarnation and Vachani, Foreign Ownership: When Hosts Change the Rules, *Harvard Business Review* 152–160 (September-October 1985).

Engering, Frans, The Multilateral Investment Agreement, *Transnational Corporations* vol. 5, no. 3, Dec. 1996.

Escobar, A, Introductory Note on Bilateral Investment Treaties Recently Concluded by Latin American States, 11 *ICSID Review—Foreign Investment Law Journal* 86 (1996).

Fatouros, AA, Towards An International Agreement On Foreign Direct Investment?, *ICSID Review—Foreign Investment Law Journal* Vol. 12, No. 2, 1995.

Fryeweather, J, *International Business Strategy and Administration*, 2nd ed (Cambridge, Ballinger, 1982).

Feuerwerker, Albert, *The Foreign Establishment in China in the Early Twentieth Century*, (Ann Arbor, Centre for Chinese Studies, 1976)

Flinterman, Lees, The European Union and China, *Maastricht Journal of European and Comparative Law*, 1997.

Folsom, R, Gordon, M and Spanogle, J, *International Business Transactions* (1986).

Foreign Investment in China–I: Changing Trends and Policies, EAER, Vol. 20, No. 4, (April 15, 1998).

Fox, Hazel, International Economic Law and Developing States: An Introduction, The *British Institute of International and Comparative Law* 1992.

Francioni, Francesco, Compensation for Nationalisation of Foreign Property: The Borderland between Law and Equity, 24 *International and Comparative Law Quarterly* 255 (1975).

Friedman, S., *Expropriation in International Law* (London, Stevens, 1953).

Friedman, Thomas L, Fed up, *New York Times*, 04 12 1996.

Friedmann, Wolfgang, National Courts and the International Legal Order, 34 *George Washington Law Review* 443 at 454 (1966).

Frisbie, John, Balancing Foreign Exchange, *The Chinese Business Review* March-April, 1988.

Gagné, Gilbert, The Investment-State Provisions in the Aborted MAI and in NAFTA, 2 *Journal of World Investment* 481 (2001)

Gao, Yongfu, *International Economic Law* (in Chinese) (Lixin Accounting Publications, 1993).

Getting Foreign Investments through the Approval Process, EAER, April 15, 1997.

Goldsweig, David N, Hypothetical Joint Venture: Ruritanian Refrigerator Company, Ltd., *International Joint Ventures* 3–4 (1990).

Gordon, David, The Polish Foreign Investment Law of 1990, 24 *International Lawyer* 335–363 (1990).

Grieco, Joseph M, Foreign Investment and Development: Theories and Evidence, in Moran, Theodore H (ed), *Investing in Development: New Roles for Private Capital?* (New Brunswick, New Jersey, Transaction, 1986).

GU, Angran, *The amendments to the China-Foreign EJVL is to adapt to the development of circumstances*, People's Daily (overseas edition), 10 March 2001, at 2.

GU, Ming (then Deputy Secretary-General of the State Council), Investment Environment Seen as Favorable, *Beijing Review* July 16, 1984.

Gudgeon, Nancy, United States Bilateral Investment Treaties: Comments on their Origin, Purposes and General Treatment Standards, 4 *International Tax and Business Law*, 1986.

Gudofsky, Jason L, Shedding Light On Article 1110 Of The North American Free Trade Agreement (NAFTA) Concerning Expropriations: An Environmental Case Study, 21 *Northwestern Journal of International Law and Business* 243, Fall 2000.

Guislan, Pierre, *Divestiture of State Enterprises: An Overview of the Legal Framework* 1–32 (The World Bank, 1992).

Guzman, Andrew T, *Explaining the Popularity of Bilateral Investment Treaties: Why LDCs Sign Treaties that Hurt Them*? Harvard Jean Monnet Working Paper 12/97, 1997.

Han, Christopher and Qin, Sidney, FIE Status and the 25% Rule, *China Law & Practice*, 15 (10), December 2001/January 2002.

Han, Depei, *Private International Law* (Wuhan University Press, 1989).

Harris, David, *Cases and Materials of International Law* (Sweet and Maxwell, 1998).

He, Xiaoyong, On the Application of WTO Agreements in Chinese Courts, *Journal of International Trade* (*Guoji Maoyi Wenti*), 2001, No.3.

Higgins, Rosalyn, The Taking of Property by the State: Recent Developments in International Law, 176 *Recueil des Cours* 263 (1982).

Hill, Claire A, How Investors React to Political Risk, *Duke Journal of Comparative and International Law* Spring 1998.

Hou, Huaixia and Zhong, Ruidong, Studies on the law of Enterprise Merger and Acquisition, *Chinese Legal Science*, 1999, No.2.

Hu, Patrick H, *The China 301 on Market Access: A Prelude to GATT Membership?*, 3 *Minnesota Journal of Global Trade* 131 (Spring 1994).

Hu, Yuanxiang, *Legal and Policy Issues of the Trade and Economic Relations between the EU and China* (Kluwer, 1991).

Jackson, John, Davey, William and Sykes, Alan, *Legal Problems of International Economic Relations*, 4th edition (West Group, 2002).

Jacobs, Kenneth, Reinvigorating ICSID With a New Mission and With Renewed Respect for Party Autonomy, 33 *Virginia Journal of International Law* 1992.

Jennings, RY, State Contract in International Law, *British Yearbook of International Law* 1961, pp. 156–182.

Jennings, Robert and Watts, Arthur, *Oppenheim's International Law*, 9th edition (Longman, 1992).

Jiang, Guoqin, Some Problems on International Law and International Treaties, at http://www.peopledaily.com.cn/GB/shehui/212/3572/3575/20001229/365132.html (visited on 5 January 2001).

Jiang, Ping, Principle on the Protection of Private Property, *People's Daily*, 11 February 2003, at 9, reprinted in *Xinhua Digest* 2003, No.5, at 2.

Juillard, Patrick, Freedom of Establishment, Freedom of Capital Movements, and Freedom of Investment, *ICSID Review—Foreign Investment Law Journal* Vol. 15, No. 2, Fall, 2000.

Kapur, H, *China and the EEC, the New Connection* (Martinus Nijhoff Publishers, 1986).

Karl, J, On the Way to Multilateral Investment Rules, 17 *ICSID Review—Foreign Investment Law Journal* 293 (2002).

Khalil, Mohamed I, Treatment of Foreign Investment in Bilateral Investment Treaties, in Shihata, Ibrahim ed, *Legal treatment of Foreign Investment: The World Bank Guidelines* (Martinus Nijhoff , 1993).

Kishoiyian, Bernard, The Utility of Bilateral Investment Treaties in the Formulation of Customary International Law, 14 *Northwestern Journal of International Law and Business* 327, (1994).

Kohona, Palitha TB, Investment Protection Agreements: An Australian Perspective, *Journal of World Trade Law* vol. 21, No. 2, 1987.

Kong, Kevin TS, Prospects for Asset Securitization within China's Legal Framework: The Two-Tiered Model, 32 *Cornell International Law Journal* 237 (1998).

Krishna, Raj, Exchange Controls under West German Treaties for the Protection of Private Foreign Investment, 1965 *Australian Yearbook of International Law* 71.

Kronfol, Zouhair A, *Protection of Foreign Investment: A Study in International Law*, (Leiden: AW Sijthoff, 1972).

Lauterpacht, H, *Oppenheim's International Law*, 8th edition (Longmans, 1955).

Lauterpacht, Elihu, Issues of Compensation and Nationality in the Taking of Energy Investments, *Journal of Energy and Natural Resources Law* 241 (1990).

Lauterpacht, Elihu, and Rayfuse, R, Introduction, in *ICSID Reports*, Vol. 1 (Grotius. 1993).

Lauterpacht, Elihu, International Law and Private Foreign Investment, *Global Legal Studies Journal* Vol. 4:259, 1997.

Lauterpacht, Elihu, Nationalisation and International Law: Testimony of Elihu Lauterpacht, QC, *International Lawyer* Vol. 17, 1983, 97–151.

Lauterpacht, Elihu, The World Bank Convention on International Dispute Settlement, in *Recueil d'etudes de droit international en hommage a Paul Guggenheim*, at 642, 660–61

Leich, Marian Nash, International Economic Law: Bilateral Investment Treaties, 80 *American Journal of International Law* 948 (1986).

Leonard, Sean, *The Dragon Awakens: China's Long March to Geneva* (Cameron May, 1999).

Levy, Tali, NAFTA's Provision for Compensation in the Event of Expropriation: A Reassessment of the 'Prompt, Adequate and Affective' Standard, 31 *Stanford Journal of International Law* 423 (1995).

Lewis, Eleanor R, The United States-Poland Treaty Concerning Business and Economic Relations: New Themes and Variation in the U.S. Bilateral Investment Treaty Program, 22 *Law and Policy of International Business* 527 (1991).

Li, Judge Haopei, Nationalisation and International Law, *Zhengfa Yanjiu*, No. 2: 10–15 (1958), translated and reprinted in Jerome Alan Cohen and Hungdah Chiu, *People's China and International Law: A Documentary Study* (Princeton University Press, 1974), at 721.

Li, Shishi, Bilateral Investment Protection Agreements: Practice of the People's Republic of China (in Chinese), in *Yearbook of Chinese International Law*, 1990.

Li, Xueling, ed., *The Laws of Special Economic Areas* (in Chinese) (Law Press, 1996).

Lilich, R, *The Valuation of Nationalised Property in International Law* (University Press of Virginia, 1972).

Lillich, R, and Weston, BH, Lump Sum Agreements: Their Contribution to the Law of International Claims, 82 *American Journal of International Law* 69.

Lillich, R., *International Claims: Their Settlement by Lump-Sum Agreements* (Charlottesville: University Press of Virginia, 1975).

Liu, Fengming, etc, *Introduction to Sino-Foreign Contractual Joint Venture Law* (in Chinese) (Wuhan University Press, 1992).

Liu, Jiangfeng, Combining the Three FIE Laws, or Including Them into the Company Law? At http://finance.sina.com.cn/g/43903.html (15–13–2001).

Liu, Sun, The MAI as an Indicator of the Difficulty and the Prospect of a Comprehensive Multilateral Investment Agreement, *Chinese Legal Science* (*Zhongguo Faxue*) 2001 No. 5.

Lowenfeld, Andreas F, *International Private Investment* (Matthew Bender, 1976).

Lu, Tong, Comments on the Negotiation on the 'Multilateral Agreement on Investment', 7 *World Economy* (in Chinese) 1999.

Ma, Yu, Investment Liberalisation in the Context of Economic Globalisation in the World, posted at http://www.etisu.com.cn/zgwmxh/tongxun/00126/02-0126-WTO1.htm (visited on 28 June 2003).

Macleod, I, Hendry, ID, and Hyett, Stephen, *The External Relations of the European Community* (Clarendon Press, Oxford, 1996).

Maniruzzaman, AFM, State Contracts in Contemporary International Law: Monist Versus Dualist Controversies, 12 *European Journal of International Law* 309 (2001)

Mann, FA, British Treaties for the Promotion and Protection of Investments, 52 *British Yearbook of International Law* 241 (1981).

Mann, FA, *The Legal Aspects of Money*, 5th ed. (Clarendon Press, 1992).

Marsh, Peter, EEC Foreign Economic Policy and Political Management of East-West Economic Relations, *Journal Of International Studies* 1980, pp 41–54.

Mashayekho, Mina and Murray, Gibbs, Lessons from the Uruguay Round Negotiation on Investment, 33 *Journal of World Trade*, No. 6, 1–26.

McMahon, ASEAN and the Asia—Europe Meeting: Strengthening the European Union's Relationship with South—East Asia? 3 *European Foreign Affairs Review* (1998) 233.

Mendelson, MH, Compensation for Expropriation: The Case Law, 79 *American Journal of International Law* 415 (1985).

Menotti, R, European–Chinese Relations in the Nineties, *The International Spectator* vol. 30, no. 4, Oct–Dec 1995.

Meron, Theodor, *Investment Insurance in International Law* (Dobbs Ferry, NY: Oceana Publications, 1976).

Mo, John S, Some Aspects of the Australia-China Investment Protection Treaty, 25 *Journal of World Trade Law* 43 (1991).

Mo, John, China, the World Trade Organisation and the Agreement on Trade-Related Investment Measures, 30 *Journal of World Trade* 5.

Mo, Lingxia, The Legal Nature and Features of the Sino-Foreign CJVs, *Tribune of Political Science and Law* (*Zhengfa Luntan*) No. 3, 2000.

Moser, Michael J (ed.), *Foreign Trade, Investment and the Law in the People's Republic of China*, 2nd edition (Oxford University Press, 1987).

Mu, Zili, *Chinese Government is to enact regulations to implement obligations under the ICSID Convention* (in Chinese), Arbitration and Law Communication (Published by the Chinese International Economic and Trade Arbitration Commission-CIETAC), No. 1, 1997.

Muchlinski, Peter, *Multinational Enterprises and the Law* (Blackwell Publishers, 1995).

Murphy, Rhoads, *The Outsiders* (Ann Arbor: University of Michigan Press, 1977).

Naghapetyants, Rafael, Encouragement and Mutual Protection of Foreign Investments, 6 *Foreign Trade (USSR)* 8 (1991).

Norton, Patrick M, A Law of the Future or a Law of the Past? Modern Tribunals and the International Law of Expropriation, 85 *American Journal of International Law* 474 (1991).

Organization of American States, *Inter-American Juridicial Committee Opinion Examining the U.S. Helms-Burton Act*, August 27, 1996, 35 ILM1322 (1996).

Ostry, Sylvia, China and the WTO: The Transparency Issue, 3 *UCLA Journal of International Law and Foreign Affairs* 1 (Summer, 1998).

Palmer, Michael and Roberts, Simon, *Dispute Processes: ADR and the Primary Forms of Decision Making* (Butterworths, 1998).

Pappas, Athena J, References on Bilateral Investment Treaties, 4 *ICSID Review—Foreign Investment Law Journal* 189 (1989).

Parra, Antonio R, Principles Governing Foreign Investment, as Reflected in National Investment Codes, in Shihata, Ibrahim, *Legal Treatment of Foreign Investment: The World Bank Guidelines*, 1993.

Pausson, J, SID's Achievements and Prospects, 6 *ICSID Review—Foreign Investment Law Journal* 380 (1991).

Pearson, Margaret M, *Joint Ventures in the People's Republic of China: the Control of Foreign Direct Investment under Socialism* (Princeton University Press, 1991).

Peers, Steve, EC Framework of International Relations: Co-operation, Partnership and Association, in Dashwood and Hillion, *The General Law of E.C. External Relations* (Sweet & Maxwell, 2000).

Peers, Steve, Free Movement of Capital: Learning Lessons or Slipping on Spilt Milk? in Barnard, Catherine, and Scott, Joanne, *The Law of the Single European Market: Unpacking the Premises* (Hart, 2002).

Perry, Amanda J, *Legal Systems as a Determinant of Foreign Direct Investment: The Case of Sri Lanka*, London School of Economics PhD Dissertation (2000).

Perry-Kassaris, Amanda, *Legal Systems as a Determinant of FDI: Lessons from Sri Lanka* (Kluwer Law International, 2001).

Phelan, Anne, '. . . *But Tariff Exemptions Eliminated For FIEs*', *EAER* Vol. 18, No. 1 (January 15, 1996).

Pogany, Stephen I, Economic Development Agreements, 7 *ICSID Review—Foreign Investment Law Journal* 1.

Price, Daniel M, An Overview of the NAFTA Investment Chapter: Substantive Rules and Investor-State Dispute Settlemen*t*, 27 *International Lawyer* pp.727–36 (1993).

Pritchard, Robert, *Economic Development, Foreign Investment and the Law* (Kluwer Law International, 1996).

Qiu, Yuanlun, The EU's China Policy and Sino-EU Trade and Economic Relations, *World Economy* (*Shijie Jingji*) No. 8, 1999.

Qureshi, Asif H, *International Economic Law* (Sweet & Maxwell, 1999).

Reading, Michael, The Bilateral Investment Treaty in ASEAN: A Comparative Analysis, 42 *Duke Law Journal* 61–69 (1992).

Redmond, J and ZOU, Lan, The European Community and China: New Horizons, *Journal of Common Market Studies* 1986, pp. 133–55.

Report on Bilateral Investment Treaties, 21 *International Lawyer* 274 (1987).

Ricupero, Rubens (Secretary General of UNCTAD), *Recent Development In FDI Trends and Policies and Their Implications for Developing Counties*, a paper submitted on the Forum on Direct Investment Strategies of the Multinational Corporations, Sept 1998, Xiamen.

Robert, Maryse, Sauvé, Pierre, and Steinfatt, Karsten, Negotiating Investment Rules: Possible Scenarios for an EU-Mercosur Agreement, posted at http://chairemercosur.sciences-po.fr/docs/livre/59696–265.pdf (visited on 31 July 2003).

Robinson, Davis R, Expropriation in the Restatement (Revised), 78 *American Journal of International Law* 176 (1984).

Rowat, Malcolm D, Multilateral Approaches to Improving the Investment Climate of Developing Countries: The Cases of ICSID and MIGA, *Harvard International Law Journal* Vol. 33, No. 1 Winter 1992.

Roy, Delwin A, The Bilateral Investment Treaty: Business or Politics?, 6 *Middle East Executive Report* 11 (1983).

Rubin, S, and Nelson, R, *International Investment Disputes: Avoidance and Settlement* (West Publishing Co., 1985).

Ruggiero, Renato, Foreign Direct Investment and the Multilateral Trading System, *Transnational Corporations* vol. 5, no. 1 (April 1996).

Sacerdoti, Giorgio, *Bilateral Treaties and Multilateral Instruments on Investment Protection*, in Hague Academy, Collected Courses, Vol. 269 (1997, pp. 251–460).

Salacuse, Jeswald W, BIT by BIT: The Growth of Bilateral Investment Treaties and Their Impact on Foreign Investment in Developing Countries, 24 *International Lawyer* 655 (1990).

Salacuse, Jeswald W, Making Global Alliances: Pay Attention to the Process, *Strategic Alliance Alert* Vol. 2, (1995).

Salacuse, Jeswald W, Towards a New Treaty Framework for Direct Foreign Investment, 50 *Journal of Air Law and Commerce* 969 (1985).

Sampliner, GH, Arbitration of Expropriation Cases Under U.S. Investment treaties—A Threat to Democracy or the Dog that Did not Bark?, 18 *ICSID Review—Foreign Investment Law Journal* 1 (2003)

Santa Maria, Alberto, *EC commercial law* (Kluwer Law International, 1996).

Sauve, P, A First Look at Investment in the Final Act of the Uruguay Round, 28 Journal of World Trade No. 5.

Sauve, P, Assessing the General Agreement on Trade in Services: Half Full or Half Empty?, 29 *Journal of World Trade* No. 4.

Schachter, O, Compensation Cases—Leading or Misleading, 79 *American Journal of International Law* 420 (1985).

Schachter, Oscar, Compensation for Expropriation, Editorial Comment, 78 *American Journal of International Law* 121 (1984).

Schmidt, Patrick L, The Exon-Florio Statute: How It Affects Foreign Investors and Lenders in the United States, 27 *International Lawyer* pp. 795–809 (1993).

Schreuer, Christoph H, *The ICSID Convention: A Commentary* (Cambridge University Press, 2001).

Schwarzenberger, George, *Foreign Investment and International Law* (Stevens and Sons, 1969).

Schwarzenberger, George, The Most-Favoured-Nation Standard in British State Practice, 22 *British Yearbook of International Law* 1945.

Seidl-Hohenveldern, Iganz, Communist Theories on Confiscation and Expropriation: Critical Comments, in Seidl-Hohenveldern, Iganz, *Collected Essays on International Investment and International Organisations* (Kluwer 1998), at 281 onwards.

Seidl-Hohenveldern, Iganz, Hierarchy of the Norms Applicable to International Investment, in Seidl-Hohenveldern, Iganz, *Collected Essays on International Investment and International Organisations* (Kluwer 1998), at 201.

Seidl-Hohenveldern, Ignaz, *International Economic Law*, 3rd edition (Kluwer, 1999).

Serradell, The Asia—Europe Meeting (ASEM): A Historical Turning Point in Relations Between the Two Regions, 2 *European Foreign Affairs Review* (1996) 185.

Sforza, Michelle and Nova, Scott, Global Investment Pact Threatens Labor, Environmental Safeguards, *Network* 10–11 (Nov/Dec 1997).

Shan, Wenhua, National Treatment for Foreign-funded Enterprises and the Conditions of its Implementation (in Chinese), 5 *Social Sciences in China* 1998.

Shan, Wenhua, Comments on the International Investment Rules within the WTO Agreement, (in Chinese), *CASS Journal of Law* no. 2, 1996.

Shan, Wenhua, Market Economy and National Treatment for foreign Invested Enterprises, (in Chinese), 5 *Chinese Legal Science* 1995.

Shan, Wenhua, National Treatment and the Transformation of FDI Laws and Policies in China, 6 *International Trade Laws and Regulations* No. 1, 2000.

Shan, Wenhua, The Development of Theories and Practice on the Compensation for Expropriation and China, *Law Science* No. 4, 1995, at 73 onwards.

Shan, Wenhua, Towards a Common European Community Policy on Investment Issues, 2 *Journal of World Investment* 603, September 2001.

Shan, Wenhua, Towards a Level Playing Field for Foreign Investment in China, 3 *Journal of World Investment* 2, 2002.

Shan, Wenhua, Towards a New Legal Framework for EU-China Investment Relations, 35 *Journal of World Trade* 5, 2000.

Shan, Wenhua, The International Law of EU Investment in China, *Chinese Journal of International Law*, Vol. 1 No. 2 (2002).

Shan, Wenhua, EU Enlargement and Legal Framework of EU-China Investment Relations, *The Journal of World Investment and Trade*, Vol. 6 No. 2 (2005).

Sharma, Surya E, Interpretation of Bilateral Investment Treaties: The Case of Asian Agricultural Products Ltd, 1 *Asia Pacific Law Review* 123 (1992).

Shaw, Malcolm N, *International Law*, 4th edition (Cambridge University Press, 1998).

Shea, Donald R, *The Calvo Clause: A Problem of Intern-American and International Law and Diplomacy* (Minneapolis: University of Minnesota Press, 1955).

Sheng, Boming, The Negotiation of Multilateral Agreement on Investment and the Countermeasures of Developing Countries, (in Chinese), 7 *World Economy* 1999.

Shenkin, Todd S, Trade-related Investment Measures in Bilateral Investment Treaties and the GATT: Moving toward a Multilateral Investment Treaty, 55 *University of Pittsburgh Law Review* 541 (1994).

Shihata, IFI, and Parra, A, Applicable Substantive Law in Disputes between States and Private Foreign Parties: The Case of Arbitration under the ICSID Convention, 9 *ICSID Review—Foreign Investment Law Journal* at 189 (1994).

Shihata, I, Promotion of Foreign Direct Investment—A General Account, with Particular Reference to the Role of the World Bank Group, 6 *ICSID Review—Foreign Investment Law Journal* 484 (1991).

Shihata, Ibrahim FI, *MIGA and Foreign Investment* (Martinus Nijhoff Publishers, 1988).

Shihata, Ibrahim FI, Factors Influencing the Flow of Foreign Investment and the Relevance of a Multilateral Investment Guarantee Scheme, 21 *International Lawye*r 671 (1987).

Shihata, Ibrahim FI, Recent Trends Relating to Entry of Foreign Direct Investment, 9 *ICSID Review—Foreign Investment Law Journal* (1994).

Shihata, Ibrahim, FI and Parra, A, The Experience of the International Centre for the Settlement of Investment Disputes, 14 *ICSID Review—Foreign Investment Law Journal* 299.

Snyder, Kelley Brooke, Denial Of Enforcement of Chinese Arbitral Awards on Public Policy Grounds: The View From Hong Kong, 42 *Virginia Journal of International Law* 339, (Fall 2001)

Sornarajah, M, Protection of Foreign investment in the Asian Pacific Economic Cooperation Region, 29 *Journal of World Trade* 1995, No 2.

Sornarajah, M, State Responsibility and Bilateral Investment Treaties, 20 *Journal of World Trade Law* 79, (1986).

Sornarajah, M, *The International Law on Foreign Investment* (Cambridge University Press, 1994).

Sornarajah, M, The New International Economic Order, Investment Treaties and Foreign Investment Laws in ASEAN, 27 *Malaya Law Review* 440 (1985).

Sornarajah, M, *The International Law on Foreign Investment* (CambridgeUniversity Press, 2nd ed, 2004).

Starner, Gregory M, Taking A Constitutional Look: NAFTA Chapter 11 as an Extension of Member States' Constitutional Protection of Property, *Law and Policy in International Business* Winter 2002.

Steinberg, Marc I, Emerging Capital Markets: Proposals and Recommendations for Implementation, 30 *International Lawyer* pp. 715–38 (1996).

Steinert, Timothy A, If the BIT Fits: The Proposed Bilateral Investment Treaty between the United States and the People's Republic of China, 2 *Journal of Chinese Law* Fall 1988.

Strange, Roger, etc. edited, *Trade and Investment in China: The European Experience* (Routledge, 1998).

Streng, William P and Salacuse, Jeswald W, *International Business Planning: Law and Taxation* (Matthew Bender, 1997).

Sullivan, Roger W, Do We Really Need a BIT?, 15 *China Business Review* No. 6 at 9 (Nov–Dec 1988).

Sun, Chao and Shen, Wei, BOT Investment: the Legal Conflicts and Analysis, *Chinese Legal Science (Zhongguo Faxue)*, 1997, No. 1.

Sun, Zhangli, Several Legal Issues Concerning the Board of Directors of the Foreign Invested Enterprises (in Chinese), *Law Review* 2001, No. 5.

T'ao, Ying, Recognize the True Face of Bourgeois International Law from a Few Basic Concepts, in Jerome Alan Cohen and Hungdah Chiu, *People's China and International Law: A Documentary Study* (Princeton University Press, 1974), vol. 1.

The American Law Institute, *Restatement of the Foreign Relations Law of the United States*, 3rd revision, Vol. 2, 1986.

The Economist, Free Trade, Fettered Investment, *The Economist* (Sept 14, 1996) p. 80.

Thompson, Tomas N, *China's Nationalisation of Foreign Firms: The Politics of Hostage Capitalism, 1949–1957*, University of Maryland Law School Occasional Papers/Reprints Series in Contemporary Asian Studies, No. 6–1979 (27).

Tschofen, Franziska, *Multilateral Approaches to the Treatment of Foreign Investment*, in Shihata, Ibrahim, *Legal Treatment of Foreign Investment: The World Bank Guidelines* (Martinus Nijhoff, 1993).

Usher, JA, *The Law of Money and Financial Services in the EC*, 2nd edition (Oxford University Press, 2000).

Vandevelde, KJ, Investment Liberalisation and Economic Development: The Role of Bilateral Investment Treaties, 36 *Columbia Journal of Transnational Law* 501 (1998).

Vandevelde, KJ, Sustainable Liberalism and the International Investment Regime, 19 *Michigan Journal of International Law* 373 (1998).

Vandevelde, KJ, The Economics of Bilateral Investment Treaties, 41 *Harvard International Law Journal* 469, Spring 2000.

Vandevelde, KJ, U.S. Bilateral Investment Treaties: the Second Wave, 14 *Michigan Journal of International Law.*

Vandevelde, Kenneth J, The Political Economy of Bilateral Investment Treaty, *The American Journal of International Law* vol. 92: 621, 1998.

Vendevelde, K, *United States Investment Treaties: Policy and Practice* (Kluwer, 1992).

Verma, DP, Rethinking about New International Law-Making Process, *Indiana Journal of International Law* Vol. 29 (1 & 2), 1989.

Vishny, Paul H, *Guide to International Commercial Law*, §§ 13.13, 13.14 (Shepard's/McGraw-Hill, 1994).

Voss, J, 'Introductory Note' to World Bank: Convention Establishing the Multilateral Investment Guarantee Agency, 24 *ILM* (1985) pp. 1598–605.

Voss, Jurgen, The Protection and Promotion of European Private Investment in Developing Countries: An Approach towards a Concept for a European Policy on Foreign Investments; A German Contribution, 18 *Common Market Law Review* 363, 369–74 (1981).

Voss, Jurgen, The Protection and Promotion of Foreign Direct Investment in Developing Countries: Interests, Interdependencies, Intricacies, 31 *International and Comparative Law Quarterly* 686 (1982).

Wälde, TW, *Stabilising International Investment Commitments: International Law versus Contract Interpretation* (Centre for Petroleum and Mineral Law and Policy, 1994).

Wallace, Cynthia D, *The Multinational Enterprise and Legal Control: Host State Sovereignty in an Era of Globalization* (New York: Martinus Nijhoff, 1983).

Wallace, Don, and Shanks, Robert B, *Model Foreign Investment Law: with Annotations*, annotations by Levy, David A (Washington, DC, International Law Institute), 1996.

Wan, Timothy Haosen, A Comparative Study of Foreign Investment Laws in Taiwan and China, *California Western International Law Journal* Spring 1981, as cited in Zhang, Xiangyu, China's Foreign Investment Law System, *Social Sciences in China* 1985, No. 5.

Wang, Guiguo, *International Investment Law* (in Chinese) (Peking University Press, 2002).

Wang, Judge Tieya, *International Law* (in Chinese) (Law Press, 1995).

Wang, Kui Hua, *Chinese Commercial Law* (Oxford University Press, 2000).

Wang, Xuan, The Permanent Sovereignty over Natural Resources of States, in *Chinese Yearbook of International Law* 1982.

Wang, Yongjun, *Investment in China: A Question and Answer Guide on How to Do Business* (CITIC Publication House, 1997).

Ward, Angela, Framework for Co-operation between the European Union and Third World: A Viable Matrix for Uniform Human Rights Standards?, 3 *European Foreign Affairs Review* 1998.

Waren, William T, Paying To Regulate: A Guide To Methanex v. United States And NAFTA Investor Rights, 31 *Environmental Law Reporter* 10986, August, 2001.

Weisenfeld, Lorin S, The Co-operation between MIGA and China and its Potentials, in Chen, An edited, *MIGA and China: Comments on the Multilateral Investment Guarantee Agency* (Fujian People's Press, 1995).

Westberg, John A, Compensation in Cases of Expropriation and Nationalisation: Awards of the Iran-United States Claims Tribunal, 5 *ICSID Review—Foreign Investment Law Journal* 256 (1990).

Weston, Burns H, The Charter of Economic Rights and Duties of States and the Deprivation of Foreign Owned Wealth, 75 *American Journal of International Law* 437 (1981).

Witherell, William H, The OECD Multilateral Agreement on Investment, *Transnational Corporations*, vol. 4, no. 2, Aug 1995.

Wyatt & Dashwood's, *European Community Law*, 4th edn (Sweet & Maxwell, 2000).

Xiao, Bin, *Legal Issues of the Foreign Investment Approval System* (in Chinese), paper presented at the 1996 Annual Conference of the China Association of International Economic Law.

Xiao, Zhiyue, *The EC and China* (Butterworths, 1993).

Xie, Lan, Government Intervention and the Legislation on BOT Concession Agreements, *Law Review* (*Faxue Pinglun*), 1999, No.4.

Xu, Chunlin, *Investment Protection on Fast Track of Development in China*, posted at http://www.fdi.gov.cn/common/frnreport.jsp?id=CENSOFT0000000007375 (visited on 4 June 2003).

Xu, Congli and Lin, Zhong, *Chinese Foreign Investment Law (Zhongguo Waizi Fa)* (Law Publishing House, 1998).

Xu, Congli, From China-Foreign Joint Venture Enterprises to China-Foreign Joint Capital Companies: The Multiplication of the Internal Organization Structure System, *Tribune of Political Science and Law* (*Zhengfa Luntan*) No. 5, 2000.

Xu, Congli, The Controversial Issues in International Investment Law and China's Countermeasures, *Social Sciences in China* No.1, 1994, at 23 onwards.

Xu, X and Chew, C, Foreign Investment Enterprises in China: A Comprehensive Guide to Approval Process (Part I), *EAER* November 15, 1995.

Xu, X and Chew, C, Foreign Investment Enterprises in China: A Comprehensive Guide to Approval Process (Part II), *EAER* December 15, 1995.

Yang, Zhongxiao, Report of the Conference on 'How to Apply Company Law to Joint Ventures', *Legal Science* (*Faxue*) No. 8, 1998.

Yao, Meizhen, *Comparative Foreign Investment Law* (in Chinese) (Wuhan University Press, 1993).

Yao, Meizhen, *International Investment Law* (in Chinese) (Wuhan University Press, 1987).

Yao, Meizhen, Legal Protection of International Investment, *Chinese Yearbook of International Law* Vol. 1, 1982.

Yao, Meizhen, *Textbook on Foreign Invested Enterprises Law* (in Chinese) (Law Press, 1989).

Ye, Ariel L, and Valentine, Stuart, More Haste, Less Speed: The Secret to Investing in China, *International Financial Law Review* January 2000.

Ye, Xinping, Recent Trends of Foreign Investment and the Changing International Investment Norms: An Overview, *Law Review* (*Faxue Pinglun*) 2002, No.4.

Yim, Soo J, Government Intervention and Regulation in Emerging Stock Markets: A Case Study of the Korean Stock Exchange, 8 *ICSID Review* 53–91 (1993).

Young, Alasdair R, The Adaptation of European Foreign Economic Policy: From Rome to Seattle, 38 *Journal of Common Market Studies* No. 1, 2000.

Young, Stephen and Hood, Neil, Inward Investment Policy in the European Community in the 1990s, *Transnational Corporations* Vol. 2, No. 2, 1993.

Yu, An, *Foreign Invested BOT Projects and Administrative Contract Law* (Law Press, 1998).

Yu, Jinsong, *International Investment Law* (in Chinese) (Law Press, 1997).

Yu, Jinsong, The Grounds for Compensation in Case of Expropriation under International Investment Law, *Social Sciences in China* No. 2, 1986, at 56 onwards.

Yuan, Anyuan, China's Entry into the WTO: Impact on China's Regulating Regime of Foreign Direct Investment, 35 *International Law* 195, (Spring, 2001).

Zamora, S, Is There Customary International Law?, 32 *German Yearbook of International Law* No. 9, 1989.

Zeng, Huaqun, *International Investment Law* (in Chinese) (Peking University Press, 1999).

Zeng, Huaqun, *Introduction to International Economic Law* (in Chinese) (Law Press, 1997).

Zeng, Huaqun, *Law and Practice of Sino-Foreign Joint Ventures* (in Chinese) (Xiamen University Press, 1991).

Zeng, Lingliang, *Application of WTO Agreements in China and a Revolution of China's Legal Construction,* Chinese Legal Science (Zhongguo Faxue), 2000, No. 6.

Zeng, Yabo, Attracting FDI Should Be Cautious of 'Three Irrespective' Theory, *People's Daily* (overseas edition), 7 August 2002.

Zhang, Mei, The Unification of Foreign Invested Enterprises, in *Legal Aspects of Doing Business in China* (*zhongguo touzi falu zhinan*), Vol. 1 (Law Press, 1999).

Zhang, Mo, China's Move toward National Treatment of Foreign Investors: New Shenzhen Regulations, 18 *East Asia Executive Report* 9, 15 November 1996, No. 11.

Zhao, Hong, Preliminary Comments on the 'Multilateral Agreement on Investment', in Vol. 2, *Chinese Journal of International Economic Law Law* 1999.

Zhao, Jingping, *Analysis and Prediction on the Trends of Foreign-Invested Industries*, posted at http://www.fdi.gov.cn/common/frnreport.jsp?id=CENSOFT 0000000007250 (visited on 4 June 2003).

Zheng, Henry R, The Sino-U.S. Income Tax Treaty and Its Effect on Chinese Taxation of American Economic Interests, 40 *Tax Lawyer* 733 (Spring, 1987).

Zhong, Liguo, Codifying FDI Legislation to Improve Investment Environment, *International Economic Co-operation* (in Chinese), 1996.

Zhou, Jian, National Treatment in Foreign Investment Law: A Comparative Study from a Chinese Perspective, 10 *Touro International Law Review* 39, (Spring, 2000).

Zhu, Shuibing and Lin, Weiming, The Legal Nature of BOT Concession Agreements (in Chinese), *Chinese Legal Science* 1999, No. 4.

III. PRINCIPAL WEB-BASED SOURCES

China

Ministry of Commerce (formerly Ministry of Foreign Trade and Economic Co-operation, MOFTEC): http://english.mofcom.gov.cn/

Invest in China: http://www.fdi.gov.cn/main/index.jsp

China Association of Enterprise with Foreign Investment (CAEFI): http://www.etisu.com.cn/

People's Daily: http://english.peopledaily.com.cn/

Xinhua News Agency: http://www.xinhuanet.com/english/

China Central Television (CCTV): http://www.cctv.com

China Council for the Promotion of International Trade (CCPIT): http://www.ccpit.org/

European Union

The European Union: http://europa.eu.int/index_en.htm
DG Trade of the European Commission: http://europa.eu.int/comm/trade/index_en.htm
DG External Relations of the European Commission: http://europa.eu.int/comm/dgs/external_relations/index_en.htm
Asia Invest http://europa.eu.int/comm/europeaid/projects/asia-invest/.
EU Delegation in China: http://www.delchn.cec.eu.int/
European Chamber of Commerce in China (EUCCC): http://www.euccc.com.cn/
British Chamber of Commerce in China (BCCC): http://www.britaininchina.com/
China-Britain Business Council: http://www.cbbc.org/
UK Department of Trade and Industry (DTI): http://www.dti.gov.uk/
Financial Times (UK): http://news.ft.com/home/uk
British Broadcasting Corporation (BBC): http://www.bbc.co.uk/

International

World Trade Organisation (WTO): http://wto.org.
International Centre for the Settlement of Investment Disputes (ICSID): http://www.worldbank.org/icsid/
Multilateral Investment Guarantee Agency (MIGA): http://www.miga.org/
World Bank: http://www.worldbank.org/
United Nations Conference on Trade and Development (UNCTAD): http://www.unctad.org/Templates/StartPage.asp?intItemID=2068
Organisation of Economic Co-operation and Development (OECD): http://www.oecd.org/home/
International Court of Justice (ICJ): http://www.icj-cij.org/
IRAN-US Claims Tribunal: http://www.iusct.org/index-english.html
Energy Charter Treaty (ECT): http://www.encharter.org/index.jsp
Asian Pacific Economic Co-operation (APEC): http://www.apecsec.org.sg/
Asia-Europe Meeting (ASEM): http://asem.inter.net.th/

Index

Please note that any page references to non-textual material such as Tables are in *italic* print and any references to footnotes have an 'n' following the page number